Idol Talk

IDOL TALK

*Women Writers
on the Teenage Infatuations
That Changed Their Lives*

Edited by ELIZABETH SEARLE *and*
TAMRA WILSON

Foreword by Peter Noone

McFarland & Company, Inc., Publishers
Jefferson, North Carolina

ALSO OF INTEREST

Soap Opera Confidential: Writers and Soap Insiders on Why We'll Tune in Tomorrow as the World Turns Restlessly by the Guiding Light of Our Lives, edited by Elizabeth Searle and Suzanne Strempek Shea (McFarland, 2017)

LIBRARY OF CONGRESS CATALOGUING-IN-PUBLICATION DATA

Names: Searle, Elizabeth, 1962– | Wilson, Tamra.
Title: Idol talk : women writers on the teenage infatuations that changed their lives / edited by Elizabeth Searle and Tamra Wilson ; foreword by Peter Noone.
Description: Jefferson, North Carolina : McFarland & Company, 2018. | Includes index.
Identifiers: LCCN 2018013619 | ISBN 9781476669120 (softcover : acid free paper) ∞
Subjects: LCSH: Popular music—Social aspects. | Popular music fans. | Teenage girls. | Young women.
Classification: LCC ML3916 .I38 2018 | DDC 306.4/84—dc23
LC record available at https://lccn.loc.gov/2018013619

BRITISH LIBRARY CATALOGUING DATA ARE AVAILABLE

ISBN (print) 978-1-4766-6912-0
ISBN (ebook) 978-1-4766-3244-5

Front cover: Herman's Hermits in a 1966 publicity photograph. Back row, from left, Karl Green, Barry Whitwam and Derek Leckenby; front row, from left, Keith Hopwood and Peter Noone (Photofest)

Printed in the United States of America

McFarland & Company, Inc., Publishers
Box 611, Jefferson, North Carolina 28640
www.mcfarlandpub.com

For Our Mothers

Barbara Price Searle, who fell in love with Bill Searle while dancing to Elvis Presley's "Love Me Tender" in February of 1957; Mom married Dad four months later, playing "Love Me Tender" as their song through a long, happy marriage with three kids, even finding an anniversary card that played it when opened; so the sacred card was opened only once a year, to "save" their song— a romantic annual ritual which always reminded us kids that we owed our lives to Elvis.

Enid McKinley McElroy, who crushed on Buddy Rogers, "America's Boyfriend," the curly-haired actor who played a combat pilot in the silent film *Wings*, and inspired Mom to name her first car, a 1934 Pontiac, "Buddy." Fittingly, she later fell for a real-life pilot, Lynn McElroy, who encouraged my brother and me to aim high and fly right.

Acknowledgments

We thank all who took this voyage with us. What began as an email conversation is now this book, the first-ever collection of teen idol memories by women authors. We especially thank Ann Collette of Rees Literary Agency, who saw the magic in a teen idols revue, and Michele Barker, editor extraordinaire, for chasing away the bugs. To our spouses for their support while we swapped notes and edits between Massachusetts and North Carolina.

We are indebted to the wonderful contributors who were willing to board the ship. The project could not exist without the idols who captured our hearts—those famous first loves—role models and more, who helped each of us navigate the choppy water between childhood and young adulthood. We're glad that you were there to throw us a lifeline and pull us to shore.

And to our readers, thanks for coming along on the ride.

Table of Contents

Acknowledgments   vi

Foreword by Peter Noone   1

Introduction: The Truth Behind the Sighs
    TAMRA WILSON   2

Always on My Mind

Love Me Tender (JUDY GOLDMAN)   5

The Hands of Time: A Paul Newman Love Story (NANCY SWAN)   10

Twisting the Night Away: I'm Sorry, Sam Cooke (BREENA CLARKE)   16

Can't You Hear My Heartbeat

Back to Hermania (TAMRA WILSON)   24

P.S. I Love You (B.A. SHAPIRO)   32

Love Is the Ultimate Trip (MICHELLE SOUCY)   38

Meeting Mark Lindsay: A Story of Friends and Fandom (AMY ROGERS)   45

Here's Lookin' at You

Bogie and the Boys: Humphrey Bogart and Bobby Sherman
    (ELIZABETH SEARLE)   50

Beneath the Surface (ANN HARLEMAN)   56

My Horrible Celebrity Crush (LINDA K. SIENKIEWICZ)   60

This Crush Is My Crush (JANICE EIDUS)   65

Three Stars Will Shine Tonight

Parallel Secrets (KATHARINE DAVIS)   71

When I Stumbled Over Rob Petrie (JILL MCCORKLE)   77

Cowboy Jesus (MARIANNE LEONE)   82

She Loves You

Yeah Yeah Yeah: John, the Thinking Girl's Beatle (SUSAN LILLEY)   86

Now I Need a Place to Hide Away (ANN HOOD)   90

George (LISE HAINES)   93

Groovy's Hat (MARIANNE GINGHER)   97

Loves Me Like a Rock

The Stuff Daydreams Are Made Of (HANK PHILLIPPI RYAN)   102

When I Fell for Dylan (SUSAN SHAPIRO)   107

Dear Miss Joni Mitchell (MARJORIE HUDSON)   111

Followed by a Moonshadow: My Secret Life with Cat Stevens
    (MORGAN CALLAN ROGERS)   119

I Got You Babe

Cher Bliss (LESLÉA NEWMAN)   122

Piece of My Heart (LESLIE LAWRENCE)   126

Bobby Orr (SUZANNE STREMPEK SHEA)   133

What Would Chrissie Do? (KATIE HAFNER)   136

Endless Love

Pretty Brown Girl with Big Brown Eyes (DARLENE R. TAYLOR)   139

Good Guys (LISA WILLIAMS KLINE)   145

Julie on My Mind (MARY GRANFIELD)   150

Rescue Me (LESLIE PIETRZYK)   154

Rock with You

I Should Have Married Michael Jackson (SUSAN WOODRING)   160

Cry, Baby (KATE KASTELEIN)   166

Confessions of a Would-Be Duran Duran Groupie (CAITLIN MCCARTHY)   170

Can't Smile Without You

Songs That Make the Young Girls Cry: My Life with Manilow
    (STEPHANIE POWELL WATTS)   174

Oh, Misha (ANN ROSENQUIST FEE)   178

What a Feeling (LEE J. KAHRS)   183

Dear MJ: A Love Letter, Late (SHARA MCCALLUM)   186

I Will Always Love You

Sending My Representative: Whitney Houston and Black-Girl Perfectionism
(DOLEN PERKINS-VALDEZ) 192

"Digging for Fire": 1990s' Nostalgia and the Pixies
(HEATHER DUERRE HUMANN) 198

Distiple: An Obsession in Ten Albums (LISA BORDERS) 202

My Heart Will Go On

I'll Never Let You Go (MARY SULLIVAN) 208

"Bowie" (DIANA GOETSCH) 213

Mary Sue in Search of Lemons (EMLYN MEREDITH DORNEMANN) 214

We Were All in Love with Michael Jackson (SUSAN STRAIGHT) 219

About the Contributors 223

Index 229

Foreword

Peter Noone

I never expected to be a so-called teen idol. I was a sixteen-year-old boy, and at home I was the "spotty little brother," although some of my sister's eighteen-year-old friends thought I was "cute" and had nice hair.

The idea that I would ever be popular as a sort of heartthrob never entered my mind. I only wanted girls to like my recordings and my live concert persona. A look at my early days as a pop tart will show that I downplayed any sexuality and even chose a name that no girl would ever scream, "HERMAN!"

I hope all the other teen idols in this book had a good long and happy career, and that like me, they decided to take Paul McCartney's advice and get a life and share it with your career.

Overcoming teen idol status is hard on a lot of young men and women, and even harder on the older ones.

I overcame my stress by being grateful and humble and remembering that people bought the recordings before they saw the teen pop tartery. I also kept learning. I wanted to be a great entertainer.

Humility is having the willingness to learn, and I still yearn to learn.

I wish all my fellow teen stars a great life, and I hope you have never disappointed your following. I hope I haven't disappointed any of you and that you enjoy this book and the stories of idol worship of the nicest kind.

Peter Noone is an English singer-songwriter, guitarist, pianist and actor, best known as Herman of the 1960s pop group Herman's Hermits.

1

Introduction

The Truth Behind the Sighs

Tamra Wilson

When Elizabeth Searle and I proposed this book, we didn't have to twist many arms. Contributors were eager to get on board, for what woman doesn't like to wax nostalgic about her teen idol?

Each of our authors admitted to adolescent crushes. Many had cut photos out of fan magazines and pinned them to their bedroom walls, or more discreetly taped them to the back of a closet door. Learning how teen idols affected the lives of these accomplished women was a revelation.

Teen idols are celebrities—first loves, if you will—who are shared by millions of admirers. They're part of girl culture. Like a first date or a first kiss, their smiles are etched in our brains. Few of us want to talk about the baser side of growing up—acne, training bras, and braces. Teen idols hover in the middle of all that as semi-embarrassing footnotes. As adults we don't want to admit that we were once smitten by a famously handsome face with (or without) famously admirable talent.

Rolling Stone once described the teen idol as "a special kind of rock star—their popularity may fall as fast as it rises, but it tends to rise higher and inspire more ecstatic adoration than any other kind of artist."

Traditional teen idols are musicians or actors with an inherent boyish charm. You know the type: Paul McCartney, Peter Noone, Davy Jones, Bobby Sherman—baby faces who age slowly. Others are machos with a swaggering, bad-boy image—Elvis, Sam Cooke, John Lennon, Johnny Depp. But whoever they are, they capture our young hearts like no other. Decades later, we stop in our tracks when we hear their voice or see their image. As with a first kiss or a first dance, we can't forget the intense feelings we had for them. Years later, we gasp at the sight of "our" idol on a magazine cover or a movie marquee or on a fundraiser for public television.

Teen idols capture the imagination like a perpetual game of Mystery Date. We fangirls skip over disheveled schoolboys in favor of airbrushed dreamboats on movie posters or on the covers of fan magazines and record albums.

These Prince Charmings appear on that dreamy bridge of time between toys and dates, when the fan is no longer a child and not quite an adult. But teen idols are more than mere stars. They occupy our hearts. Once they step in, they never completely step out. Though we marry, pay mortgages, and do all of the things adults do, our teen crushes remain part of our personal history that never fully dissolves.

Whether he arrived in 1960 or 1990, Mr. Teen Idol comes from the Land of the Gods, endowed with good looks, charm, and talent. Love letters and marriage proposals fill his mailbox. Idol worship is as old as Moses, and, contrary to conventional wisdom, teen idols actually predate Elvis, Frank Sinatra and Rudolph Valentino. Social historians say the first teen idol crown was worn by Franz Liszt, the nineteenth-century Hungarian pianist. He is credited as the first performer to have "mania" associated with his name and the first to perform in concert as a piano soloist. Reportedly all eyes were upon him. During the 1840s, and when he played his top hit, "Liebesträum," swooning fans in sweeping skirts and corkscrew curls gathered at the footlights, thus setting the stage, quite literally, for generations to follow.

In compiling this collection, Elizabeth and I learned that teen idol worship doesn't necessarily refer to crushing on a *male* star. For many LGBT teens, a crush on a celebrity can trigger the first stirrings of understanding their own sexual orientation.

Adolescent girls look beyond themselves to tap the font of universal charisma and attraction to explore the kind of adults they want to become. Some of our contributors said they picked a female idol such as Peggy Lipton or Diana Ross to emulate fashion, beauty, talent and overall "coolness." These factors allowed us to broaden the notion of what a teen idol can be.

Psychologists say that preoccupation with celebrities helps a young girl transition to the teenage years and adulthood. Crushing on a teen idol means that she is "individualizing" herself apart from her parents. Too young to date, she can divert her eyes to her teen idol, a safe alternative. She can pin a celebrity's photograph on her wall, buy his or her records, and daydream a dress rehearsal for adult relationships.

But whether we're thirteen or thirty-three or sixty-three, we're all teens at heart. We thrill at the thought of meeting our idol, or of being in proximity to the special person, finally breathing the same oxygen in the same room or stadium, as the case may be. We want to feel the power of one who had the incredible good fortune to be struck by golden lightning. By meeting that person, maybe some of the magic will rub off.

Elizabeth and I relished the fun of learning who claimed which idol. Writers as artists are famous for breaking the rules. There are some odd socks in this laundry. Bob Dylan, Woody Guthrie and Bobby Orr never graced the cover of *Tiger Beat*, but they held special appeal for authors Susan Shapiro, Janice Eidus and Suzanne Strempek Shea. Just as Ann Harleman and Jill McCorkle crushed on popular TV stars Raymond Burr and Dick Van Dyke—neither are among the usual teen idol suspects.

Like the final reveal on *The Dating Game*, it was fun to learn who had crushed on whom. We read tales of dubious hairdos inspired by John Taylor of Duran Duran, singing "Daydream Believer" live with Davy Jones and what it was like to see Elvis perform on stage back in 1956. These entertaining, thoughtful essays provide some serious insights about the world of teen heartthrobs and how teen idol crushes can have a long afterlife.

If we are lucky enough to meet our crush later in life, we are forced to confront the bare-bones truth that youth is over, and our idol is struggling with that same reality. He or she has gained weight, acquired glasses, gray hair and a rounded posture. Time has taken its toll, though we want so desperately for that not to be the case. We want a solid memory to come to life: the same handsome face on the album cover, the retouched photo in the fan magazine, the dashing image on the screen. We want our idols to be constant. We pray, *Dear God, let them look like they used to*. Let that early version still exist. But, of course, the actual person, the real human being, must grow old with us or, sadly, die before his or her time.

I was forty-three before I crossed paths with my idol, Peter Noone. By then "Herman" of Herman's Hermits was performing an oldies concert in Charlotte. After the show, he greeted fans with Bobby Vee, another performer in the lineup. There they were, two idols dropped from heaven into the lobby of Independence Arena. I knew who Bobby Vee was, but he belonged to an earlier time. Peter was my idol, and there he was, holding court with a felt-tip pen as fans inched through the autograph line. He was an older version of the star I remembered. As he chattered away in his Mancunian accent, I felt my palms grow sweaty. This was *him*! This was *really Herman*! We shook hands over the autograph table, and for a split second I thought I saw a glint of recognition, that he somehow knew I had torn his photo from a 1967 issue of *Teen Datebook,* pinned it to my lavender bedroom wall back in seventh grade.

Peter Noone sent me on a trajectory. Without my schoolgirl crush on this British pop star, I might not have developed an interest in England and would never have spent the second half my sophomore year there, where I bought a Cambridge University T-shirt—the very one I wore the night I met my future husband, a young man from my hometown, who happened to have English relatives visiting for his sister's wedding, thus giving him an excuse to ask me to dine with them and talk about England.

What goes around often sparks what comes around.

Elizabeth and I are indebted to each of our contributors who agreed to confess their deep-seated memories of adolescence. And we are honored to include the reflections of Peter Noone himself, who has spent more than fifty years in the glow of the footlights.

Love Me Tender

JUDY GOLDMAN

Oh, Elvis! You future-changing, world-shaping thing! How I loved you! Beginning that Sunday night in 1956, when I was fourteen and all my friends were at the Methodist or Episcopal or Presbyterian or Baptist church for one of those youth-group gatherings. I usually went, too, even though I was Jewish. Rock Hill, South Carolina, was like that. You could be Jewish and best friends with a Methodist, Episcopal, Presbyterian, or Baptist. But that night, I was sniffly with a cold and could not join my friends, so I was moping on the leather sofa in our pine-paneled den, feeling sorry for myself, tuning in to our one television channel, trusty old WBTV, not imagining that the season premiere of *The Ed Sullivan Show* would introduce me to a roiling god who sang like a gate swinging off its rusted hinges, whose whole being was like something left bare.

Mattie and I were the only ones home. When the program began—probably with a commercial showing a woman in a cocktail dress driving a Mercury—Mattie joined me on the sofa, pulled the leather ottoman close so we could both rest our feet. I'm sure she needed to rest her feet more than I did. Sometimes, when she was especially tired, I massaged her soft, pillowy shoulders. She said I had magic in my hands.

My parents and my older sister were out; my older brother had just graduated college and was living away. If I was going to share a big, rare moment of musical clarity with anyone, I'd choose Mattie, the black woman who'd worked for my family since I was three, who lived with us and helped raise me. It was her gospel hymns Jesusing through our house all the years of my childhood that had comforted me, steered me to rhythm and blues, to the late-night radio disc jockey, Gene Nobles, who featured black groups singing rock 'n' roll on WLAC in Nashville. Rare back then—black groups on radio or TV. You had to search the dial. I resented the Crew-Cuts and their very white version of "Sh-Boom," which became more popular than the one by the Chords, a black group. Not unusual, though, for a black group to record a song first and a white group to then score a hit version. I was such a fan of Gene Nobles that, when I became a cheerleader, I used the music from his commercial for Royal Crown Hair Dressing as the melody for a pep song I wrote to cheer on our high school's football team.

But wait. Ed Sullivan is recuperating from a head-on car crash? Charles Laughton, the overweight, many-chinned character actor, is filling in for him? Laughton, his British accent sounding to this South Carolina girl like a mixture of knowledge and arrogance and honey, informs the audience that the next performer, Elvis Presley, is not actually in the New York studio, but in the CBS studio in Hollywood, where he has been filming his first movie.

"Away to Hollywood to meet Elvis Presley!" Laughton announces. A grand, dramatic flourish for this singer nobody around has ever heard of.

The camera settles on a fellow wearing a plaid jacket that looks a little like our breakfast-room tablecloth. He's saying that appearing on this show is "probably the greatest honor I have ever had in my life."

He starts in on "Don't Be Cruel." I'm taking in his face—the alertness, the joy there—and wondering why in the world anyone would ever be cruel to him. The camera hovers above his waist, teases us with glowing close-ups of his face, occasionally dips far enough down to show his fingers picking his guitar. Then the camera moves sideways for views of his backup singers, the Jordanaires. (Oh, to be a backup singer for this man! I can't sing a note, but that doesn't stop me. I've taken tap and ballet and piano for years, so I just assume that, because I can dance and play, I can sing. Millions of talent contests I enter, singing and dancing to "Ragtime Cowboy Joe," "Undecided," "America, the Beautiful," but I never win, never even come in second.)

Are those screams? The audience? I can't see who's screaming, and I don't know what the unnameable urgency is, but it's pretty obvious Elvis Presley is doing something to get the girls in the theater riled up. He finishes the song and says, with a Southern politeness his mama no doubt taught him, "Thank you, ladies."

He then says he's going to sing the title song from his movie, *Love Me Tender*. He adds that it's "completely different from anything we've ever done."

Mattie and I are side by side on the sofa, the brown, green, and orange afghan knitted by my diabetic grandmother covering my pajama legs and slippered feet, covering Mattie's shimmery nyloned legs and polished white work shoes. Every now and then, she pats my arm or knee. I sidle up to her. She smells like the peaches she peeled and sliced and served in cream for my family's dessert tonight. The only thing that would make me happier than the peaches: for her to sit at the table and eat those peaches with us. Nobody even thinks of this. When I was very young, my parents, brother, and sister would leave the table when they ran out of patience waiting for me to finish everything on my plate. The family joke for years: I ate my green peas one at a time. After everyone left, Mattie would come in, sit at the table beside me, keep me company. We would daydream together about the tiny house going up one street over, how we might buy that house and go live there together.

Elvis is definitely crossing a line. This white boy is singing black. I recognize this. I understand. When I was little, I talked like Mattie. (When New York friends of my parents visited on their way to Florida, they couldn't make out a word I said.) I wished we all were part white, part black.

Other acts by other performers follow. But they're a blur. I can't concentrate because Charles Laughton has told us that Elvis will return later in the program. Mattie and I take a break and go to the kitchen for Cokes and potato chips. We don't need to waste our time watching anybody but Elvis. I grab the Charles Chips can from the pantry; Mattie pours the drinks.

Now we're back on the sofa, twirling the ice in our tall glasses and munching noisily. Here comes Elvis, singing the raucous "Ready Teddy." Then, two verses of "Hound Dog," even more raucous. The camera is now allowing us to see his whole body, from the top of his pompadoured head to the toes of his boots. Has the stage completely let go of him? It cannot contain him and his wild jig. But each time his legs and hips convulse like a storm rolling in, the camera quickly switches to a close-up of his face.

Judy Goldman's crush on Elvis was something to cheer about in the fall of 1958 in Rock Hill, South Carolina. Two years earlier, she crossed paths with The King at the Charlotte Coliseum, three miles from where she lives and writes today.

The girls in the audience are screaming even louder than before. I can see the way he leers at something or someone off to the side, but then he turns back to Mattie and me with a quick flash of a smile. Sometimes he just halts everything for a few seconds, stands perfectly still. Time stops. The world stops. We don't move closer to tomorrow. Nobody anywhere gets any older. When he does that freeze thing, it drives the audience crazy. Their screams move decibels up the scale. I'm almost too afraid to look. *I could easily go crazy over that freeze thing.*

Mattie and I are the only people in my family who know what real music is. My sister watches *Your Hit Parade*, a lineup of white stars singing pastel songs. My parents watch *The Lawrence Welk Show*; I don't need to say any more about that.

When Elvis is done, when the storm has passed and the seams all over this country have been ripped open, Charles Laughton says, "Well, what did someone say? Music hath charms to soothe the savage breast?"

My friend's older sister and her boyfriend drive the two of us and another friend—five of us in his brand new '56 Chevy—to the Charlotte Coliseum. Charlotte is twenty-six miles from Rock Hill, but seeing Elvis—seeing him *in person!*—is constellations away from our ordinary, everyday lives. The car shakes and shivers with our excitement.

And then, we're inside the Coliseum, a great, domed structure that could have whirled in from a distant planet and plopped itself down on busy Independence Boulevard.

We find our seats. Amazing seats, close to the stage.

The lights come on. Glassy, flashing lights. Coming and going. Dark. Light. Dark. Light. Strobes roving all over us.

And then, Elvis! Onstage! Right there! Igniting the entire place! My two friends and I, my friend's older sister, even her boyfriend—all of us—scream and pump our arms, sway and weave as though we could all pass out any minute.

I wish Mattie were here. But, of course, that's out of the question. What's not out of the question is how devotedly she'll listen tomorrow morning, when I report every detail of this evening. I'll say how much I wanted her there with me. She won't say out loud how much she wishes she could have been there. That, too, would be out of the question. But I'll know. And it will make me sad.

At intermission, I flag down a guy who's selling Elvis souvenirs, ask if I can take a look at one of the paperback books of Elvis's music. I want to buy it so that I can teach myself to play his songs on the piano. But first, I need to see if the music is too difficult.

The Elvis Presley Album of Juke Box Favorites. Cover: pink with a black-and-white photo of Elvis wearing a white suit, dark shirt, two-toned black-and-white loafers. He's playing his big guitar, crooning, head thrown back, eyes half-closed, legs all a-swivel, loose-jointed. The book costs one dollar.

An ad inside the front cover:

Show Stopper: ... Elvis Presley
Important!
Join the Elvis Presley Fan Club.
Write today to:
Elvis Presley Fan Club
Madison, Tennessee

Black-and-white photos throughout the book. One of Elvis—in his driveway, I'm guessing—standing on tiptoes, waxing the top of his car. He's wearing white shoes, light-colored pants with a thin black belt, black shirt, sleeves rolled up above his elbows, the waist of his shirt tied in front, showing belly skin.

Elvis likes to keep his running equipment looking sharp and spends many a summer afternoon polishing and waxing his cars. Here he is shown working on his Cadillac Fleetwood, which he takes on every one of his many trips. Luggage carrier on top is used to transport the bass fiddle. His pink and black sedan is becoming a well-known sight throughout the country as he rolls up the mileage on his constant personal appearance schedules. Needless to add, Elvis also makes sure that everything is just as tuned up under the hood as it is shined up on the surface.

Another photo shows Elvis water-skiing, wearing a plaid bathing suit and a puffy life jacket. You can see his quivery shadow in the water.

... Cuttin' up a mighty fancy figure on Ol' Miss. He's wearing a life jacket snugged in as in case of an accident and being knocked out, he'll continue to float. Note his reflection.

I'm thumbing through the book, trying to decide whether to spend my dollar, when the guy selling the Elvis stuff disappears into the endless rows of people. Where'd he go? My eyes search the stands, but he's nowhere. I didn't pay, and the book is still in my hands. I feel guilty getting it for nothing, but not guilty enough to track him down. Too many people. And besides, I'm a little dizzy from the music.

August 16, 1977, my husband and I drive from our home in Charlotte to Blowing Rock, the radio playing James Taylor, his slow and gentle "Handy Man," the two of us humming along. Uncle Irwin has offered his mountain house for the weekend, with its great stone fireplace, wood rafters, balcony overlooking Grandfather Mountain; how lucky we are to celebrate my husband's thirty-eighth birthday here.

But when we open the front door, there are dead flies everywhere. Scattered over the carpet. Their green shimmer. In the cushions of the extra-long sofa, in all the chairs. Stuck in the corners of the rooms. Some still alive. Barely. Flying blindly into lamps and walls. Buzzing lazily in the rafters. I grab a magazine off the coffee table and swat a few. My husband takes off a sneaker and swats more. We'll later learn that flies laid eggs in the attic fans, and those eggs have hatched. All we know now is that there are dead and half-dead flies everywhere. Out the sliding glass doors, Grandfather Mountain does not appear the least bit disturbed.

I turn to the teak credenza, which houses the radio, TV, and stereo, and flick on the radio. We'll need music to tackle this job.

News flash! Elvis Presley dead! The whole world in shock!

Between stories of Elvis's rise to fame, stories of his flailing about, his decline, between reactions to his death by singers across the globe, the station plays every song he ever recorded.

I'm sweeping dead flies into little piles. My husband comes along behind me and vacuums them up. We have the radio turned high so that we can hear Elvis's voice over the roar of the Hoover.

It's been years since I was an Elvis fan. Grown-up Elvis, jeweled Elvis, jumpsuit Elvis, bloated Elvis does not appeal to me. But the songs I used to love are filling these rooms. My husband and I sweep and vacuum and sing along: "Love Me Tender." "Heartbreak Hotel." "Don't Be Cruel."

I feel as though, while I'm burying something, I'm excavating something.

Excavating the past.

My past.

When I sang "America, the Beautiful," unaccompanied, in a talent show on WRHI radio; when I tap-danced, solo, to "Sweet Georgia Brown" my dance recital in the Rock Hill High School auditorium, my pink fringed costume; when I played "I Was the One" on our piano in the living room, *The Elvis Presley Album of Juke Box Favorites* open before me, played it over and over until I got it right, until my older sister, hands clapped over her ears, yelled, "*For crying out loud, stop!*"

Now Elvis's gospel hymns: "Take My Hand, Precious Lord." In the notes, I hear Mattie at the kitchen sink, her pearly voice, her quick fingers flicking peach peels. I'm sitting beside the little table across from her, by the windows, singing along, toes tapping the linoleum.

Now I'm lying in the twin bed next to my sister, windows pitch dark. She's sound asleep, doesn't hear Gene Nobles hawking Royal Crown Hair Dressing, spinning the next record, somebody letting loose a piece of song. My head is sinking into the pillow; down and down I sink, my cheek cool against the cotton, and I'm dreaming of some boy in my grade, whom I'm waiting to kiss when I learn how to kiss; it won't be long now. The music is taking me deeper into the groove of adolescence; I'm beginning to understand what's at stake; I can almost taste it, can almost taste the kiss, can almost taste the words to this song, just working out the notes, following the strains.

My husband and I sweep and vacuum. The radio plays. We bury Elvis. I will bury Mattie, too, who'll be dead in a few years. Outside, Grandfather Mountain still doesn't move a muscle, but the sky narrows.

The Hands of Time

A Paul Newman Love Story

Nancy Swan

The Spring of My Seasons

Fresh from the shower, I close my bedroom door, stand before it, and let my robe fall from my shoulders. I give my small, thin frame a cursory inspection in the full-length mirror. My body continues to betray me. Next week I will be thirteen. Nothing is happening—no nubs on my chest, no waistline or the least curve of hips, no body hair but the slightest peach fuzz, no legs that need shaving, and not a period on the horizon. Not a single cramp, ever. Zip, zilch, nada. My grandma calls me her little pixie, which is not what I want to hear. My mother tells me I am just a late bloomer, easy for *her* to say. I have seen pictures of her when she was thirteen, and she had the makings of a figure going on. It is no help that I skipped a grade in school, and my girlfriends are all a year older and filling out A cups, and one even a B! My sweaters hang straight down from my scrawny shoulders, and the darts in my blouses are empty, pointy things.

But I have a plan. School just let out for the summer, and I am going to beg my mother to let me start wearing slightly padded bras. The other day, she asked me what I wanted for my birthday, and I told her I would think about it and let her know. A couple of these bras will be my answer: one to wear and one to switch out for laundry. My thinking is this: If I were to start wearing them now, it would be feasible that by next fall, when school starts up again, people will think I have grown my own breasts, or at least the beginnings of breasts, over the summer. I am going to hit her hard with my idea tonight and keep at it until she caves. Maybe even plea-bargain if I can offer some service that would especially please her, like extra babysitting for my little brother or doing the kitchen floors.

Turning from the mirror, I hurry to get dressed. Today is Saturday. I've finished my chores, and Mom has promised to drop me and a couple of my girlfriends at the movies. I love movies and am looking forward to this one, *The Long, Hot Summer*. I've read the book in my advanced reading class and am heavy into Faulkner right now, with his dark tales of tangled family relationships set in the Deep South. The movie stars Paul Newman, Joanne Woodward, Lee Remick, and Orson Welles. They are all new to me, so it should be interesting.

A rap on my door, and I find my older brother standing there with his soccer ball under his arm. He and his friends need one more player for the game they are going to start up on the street in front of our house. Tomboy that I am, I hardly ever pass on a game, but today I tell him I'm off to the movies. They'll have to play without me. To me, boys are still fun to be friends with and teammates for softball, soccer, and kick-the-can.

I check my clock. Time to go. My mother's purse and car keys are on the kitchen table, but she is busy with my younger brother, a three-year-old who requires a lot of attention.

"Mom, it's eleven thirty. We need to leave, okay?" I hate to miss the beginning of a movie, and we still have to pick up my girlfriends.

"I'll be right there. Go get in the car," she replies.

"I've got your purse and keys, Mom," and I'm out the door to the garage.

While waiting in line at the ticket booth, we take a quick glance at the poster advertising the movie. The background is a stately antebellum mansion. Superimposed on it are head shots of the stars that seem to fade into the house itself like it is swallowing them up. Their features are indistinct, but the lead, Paul Newman, looks like he might be cute. We buy our tickets. Balancing popcorn and sodas, my girlfriends and I enter the semidarkness of the theater. We're a little early—just the way I like it—and head for the best seats in the house, halfway down the aisle and centered on the screen. We pass the time with idle chatter, already digging into our buttered popcorn and sipping on Cokes.

The house lights slowly darken, and we settle in for the show. First is a newsreel, then cartoons, and finally the main feature begins with a swell of background music. A river barge is drifting landward, and there's a distant shot focused on a lean young man wearing a hat, a suitcase at his side, lounging on the deck. The camera pans closer, Paul Newman's face is centered on the screen, and my hand stops midway between my popcorn bag and my mouth. *Not "might be cute." Beautiful!* His eyes are riveting, aquamarine blue, alight with a glint of mischief and anticipation of things to come. His face has the look of a Greek god: high cheekbones, chiseled jaw, shallow dimple in his square chin, full sculpted lips, close-cropped wavy hair. His hat is cocked back on his head at a rakish angle. He saunters to the bow of the barge, with a boyish grin gives a wave to the captain, raises his suitcase over his shoulders, jumps off into knee-deep water, and wades ashore.

My eyes feel dry. I haven't blinked. I finally swallow. I need to do something with the buttery popcorn still clutched in my fingers, and I stuff it in my mouth. For the next two hours, I am perfectly still in my seat, hanging on every word, every expression, every action of Paul Newman as he moves through the story like a lion on the prowl. When he locks a penetrating, mischievous gaze on his counterpart in the film, Joanne Woodward, and gives her fair warning of what he has in store for her, the scene is as sensual as if they were naked in bed together. He throws down the gauntlet, challenging her to step out of her rigid, high-brow, virginal state. My breathing is shallow, my heart thudding in my chest. She rebuffs him. I find myself thinking, *No, no, no, how could you possibly?* And, for the first time in my life, lust nibbles at the edges of my brain. Of course, he wins in the end, and she succumbs to his charms, embracing the passion he has aroused in her, and she agrees to marry him.

When we leave the theater, I am unusually quiet. I may have entered it as an almost-thirteen girl in a childlike body, but my brain has taken a quantum leap. I am infatuated, utterly captivated with Paul Newman, and my nerve endings are dancing.

At the end of the year, I go to see *Cat on a Hot Tin Roof.* Paul Newman is like a white-hot flame burning up the screen as he plays the role of the tormented son of a domineering, cruel father. Somewhere between the beginning of the movie and the end, I go from infatuated to madly in love with my Paul. I make a pledge to myself as I leave the theater: I will never, ever miss a Paul Newman movie from that point on. And I don't. I see *The Young Philadelphians, From the Terrace, Exodus, The Hustler, Paris Blues, Sweet Bird of Youth, The Adventures of a Young Man, Hud,* and the list goes on. And as I immerse myself in my adoration of Paul, time goes by, my girl-body blooms, and young woman-hood is upon me.

At fifteen, I am dating often now and find myself measuring my dates by an almost impossible standard. I want a Paul Newman boyfriend, someone who lights my fire, full of the mischief he so often portrays on film, a rogue, but one who has the emotional depth and intelligence that is always a part of his characters. I want glorious blue eyes that rock my boat with every glance. So far, no one has made it to first base, not even close.

My brother is all geared up today. His best childhood friend, Bill, has moved back to our neighborhood and is coming over to the house. I was eleven and Bill fourteen when his family left. I'm curious to see him and am hanging out, waiting. There is a knock on the door, and Bill is standing there. He is now eighteen, my brother's age, three years older than I am. From the corner of the couch where I am sitting, I watch them envelop each other in a bear hug, pounding on one another's backs in their excitement. I try not to stare but am instantly walloped with Bill's grin, his chiseled features, dancing blue eyes, and lean frame. I feel like I am looking at a Paul Newman body double. He did not look like this when he left. Or if the beginnings were there, I didn't notice. I was a child. My heart starts a slow drumbeat that I can hear in my ears, and I am having trouble breathing.

Nancy Swan's idol Paul Newman resembled her first love, "Bill." A late bloomer as a writer, she has published in two anthologies and captured the Dana Award for Fiction in the Novel.

Over my brother's shoulder, Bill's eyes fasten on me, a brilliant blue gaze. His smile fades, replaced by a look of surprise. "Nancy?" he asks. I guess I have changed a lot, too, in four years.

A flush rushes up my neck and into my cheeks. "Hi" is my lame response.

For a brief moment, he studies my face, my hair, my petite frame tucked into the couch. Then he cups my brother by the back of the neck, jostling him, and says, "You never told me you had a beautiful sister!" His smile is back, full and infectious, and I find myself smiling, too, my heart tripping along faster.

"Thank you," I say shyly, as our eyes connect and hold fast.

My mother has been waiting for Bill's arrival, too. She always loved him best of all my brother's friends. Now she is looking back and forth at us, sizing up the flash of chemistry at once.

Bill shifts gears, moving toward her with open arms. "Mama Dorothy!" using the nickname he gave her years ago. He throws his arms around her slim waist and twirls her gently. She laughs like a girl, her face suddenly alight. I have never seen this side of her and am in awe. She seems as taken with him as I am, holding him at arm's length and saying, "Look at you!" But later she will say to me, "He's too old for you, Nancy Ann," and "He's not a Mormon, Nancy Ann," (which we were) and do her damndest to keep us apart. But nothing works. Bill and I become a couple, a force to be reckoned with. He is my Paul Newman, and my mother doesn't realize that is part of the equation, an integral part, a girl's dream come true.

We have long-range plans. After two years at the community college, Bill goes off to the University of Southern California at Santa Barbara to complete a degree in oceanography and marine engineering. At the same time, I graduate early from high school and begin my college education at Brigham Young University in Utah. My mother's tears and pleadings and repeated reminders that I had promised to attend BYU wear me down, and I give in and don't go to USC with Bill.

But we work around the logistics of our separation. Every eight weeks or so, one or the other of us flies student standby to spend a three-day weekend together. It is a very cheap way to travel, and we scrimp and save for these trips. Our schedules are arranged so that we cram all our classes into Mondays through Thursdays. We fly out on Thursday evenings (usually the red-eye express, when there are empty seats available for our student-standby status) and return the same way on Sunday evenings or in the wee hours of Monday mornings. Holidays at home, we are glued together. My mother continues her litany of "He's not a Mormon, Nancy Ann," but has had to drop the "He's too old for you," as I am now nineteen. When I graduate, we are planning to marry.

These are my glory days, the four years of my spring that are filled with joy, passion, laughter, and anticipation of the future ahead. Bill is even a Paul Newman fan, enjoying his movies as much as I do. Not intimidated in the least by my adoration of Paul, he buys me a life-size poster of him, which adorns the wall in my apartment at school. We agree he is a remarkable actor, go to his movies whenever one is playing, and watch as his star rises to iconic levels.

Suddenly, Winter

The phone rings in my off-campus apartment. My roommate calls out, "It's your mom, Nancy," and I leave my studies and pick up.

"Hey, Mom. How are you?" There is an unaccustomed moment of silence. "Mom?"

"Bill has had an accident," she says. "Roger just called." Roger is Bill's older brother. My heart begins to race. My throat feels tight. "An accident?"

"He's gone, Nancy. He went diving alone two days ago." She takes a breath and rushes on. The receiver is pressed to my ear so hard it hurts. "His friend was waiting for him on the boat, but he never came up. They found his body this morning."

I sink to my knees, unable to stand, unable to speak. The receiver dangles in midair on its coiled cord.

"Nancy? Nancy Ann?" My mother's voice is a receding echo. My roommate stares at me with a question in her eyes as I circle my arms tight around my waist and bend low toward the floor.

"Hang up," I say to her in a whisper, darkness enfolding me. There is a brief exchange of words between my mother and my roommate, then silence, and I am alone with my grief.

Stunned, mute, I move through my days like the walking dead. The pain is too deep even to cry. I want to scream, claw at my face, rip great handfuls of hair from my head in my agony, but that would take energy that has been sucked from me. Months later, when I force myself to go to a Paul Newman movie, *Cool Hand Luke,* the tears finally fall in great torrents. I go alone, not wanting any witness to the anguish I know will come, that I am *inviting* to come. The tears well up the moment the theater darkens, and they stream hot down my cheeks and neck into the collar of my blouse, making it damp against my skin. There is my Paul on the big screen, playing the role of a misfit trapped in a prison system that will ultimately take his life, and in his face and the way he moves I see so much of Bill. I don't fight the pain, just let it rip through me. I seek solace in my idol, release, and, for several years to come, his is the face that allows my heart to unburden and be with Bill again, if only for a brief moment in time.

The Summer of My Seasons

I am married now. Although I never found another Paul Newman, my husband is a fine man. We have three beautiful young daughters. Sitting in the window in our family room, I watch them at play in the backyard. My heart is full of them. They are everything to me, and I am content with my life. The doorbell rings. The babysitter is here to watch over my girls while I go to an afternoon movie with a friend. We cover all the usual instructions, I kiss my daughters good-bye, and I'm out the door, eager to see Paul in his latest film, *The Verdict.* During the movie, I study his face for every nuance in the drama. As always, he doesn't disappoint; his character, a washed-out attorney who is reborn, emerges with the depth and richness so typical of his acting. He is aging gracefully, his sculpted face a little softer around the edges, but his famous blue eyes as captivating as ever. I still find him beautiful, and he still elicits in me memories of days long ago and my years with Bill. But now these brief, unbidden thoughts that surface from my deepest heart are sweet, the pain gone, for they tell the story of my becoming a woman with a young man who cherished me.

My daughters are growing up fast, in their teens now, and I am still a devout Paul fan. Lately I find myself focused not only on his movies but also on the type of person he is in his private life. He does not seek out the limelight, never has, although his body of work is astounding in both quantity and quality. In love with life, he has taken up race-car driving. He is a generous philanthropist, sharing his vast wealth. By all accounts, he is a faithful and loving husband and attentive father, and has always remained aloof from the sordid side of Hollywood. I find myself admiring him more with every passing year, his work ethic amazing as he continues to make films, *The Color of Money* gaining him an Academy Award late in life.

The Autumn of My Years

Picking up a *People* magazine in the waiting room of my dentist's office, I am stunned to see Paul's face with the headline that he is terminally ill. I quickly turn to the page indicated on the cover and scan the article. My eyes sting with tears, and just as quickly I close the magazine and bring it up to my breast, holding it close. *No, not Paul.* After a moment, I open to the article again and read carefully, every word adding to the ache in my heart. I have long since come to grips with the fact that he is elderly now, that there will be no more movies, no more race-car driving. He is in the winter of his life. I think of his wife, Joanne Woodward, and my first introduction to them years ago in *The Long, Hot Summer*, when sparks flew and their chemistry burned hot on the screen. *She must be dying inside at the thought of losing him.*

My name is called, and I set the magazine aside and go into the inner sanctum of my dentist's office. I barely notice what he is doing, my thoughts spooling back on Paul's career and all it has meant to me: my first experience with infatuation, my first encounter with the niggling feelings of lust, the standard I set for prospective boyfriends, and Bill and the solace I found in Paul's films after his death. I think of him as a person, not only a movie star, one who has lived life to the fullest and helped others along the way.

In the fall of 2008, Paul dies at the age of eighty-three. I am watching television when the news is announced. His passing makes me feel my age, sixty-three. I watch as pictures of Paul from his beginnings through the end of his life stream across the television. *The hands of time.* Eyes blurred with tears, I experience again his extraordinary beauty, his talent, and his character. When the news commentators finally run dry, and the accolades for Paul come to an end, I make a mug of tea and go out to my orchard and sit in my favorite lawn chair under an aged apple tree. The boughs are bending low, heavy with ripe fruit, harvest time. Tilting my head back, I let the dappled late afternoon sun warm my face. Again, I think of my life and the riches Paul unknowingly added to it.

At sixty-nine, as a writer, I am invited to contribute an essay to a pop-culture anthology comprised solely of stories by women writers revealing their Teen Idols and how they affected their lives. Paul instantly comes to mind, and I take on the project with joy. When the manuscript is completed, I ask my daughter, who is visiting, to read it as we lounge on the back patio of my home.

When she is finished, she looks up at me, quiet for a moment. Then, "I remember, Mom. I remember even when I was very young how you would light up when you were going to a Paul Newman movie. All these memories…" Her voice trails off, eyes gentle upon me.

A smile plays at my lips, widens, and spreads to my eyes. "Yes, all," I say. "All good. Like it was yesterday, just yesterday."

Twisting the Night Away

I'm Sorry, Sam Cooke

BREENA CLARKE

The Twist is a dance inspired by rock 'n' roll music. From 1959 to the early '60s, it became the first worldwide dance craze, enjoying immense popularity. The movement is made by bending at the knees, moving the legs from side to side together while rotating the upper body in the opposite direction, like wringing out a mop. The Twist is said to have inspired the Sloop, the Funky Chicken, the Swim, the Monkey, the Watusi, the Jerk, the Pony, the Mashed Potato, the Slop, and the Slow Drag.

A Sam Cooke Chronology

- *January 22, 1931:* Sam Cooke was born in Clarksdale, Mississippi.
- *December 5, 1955:* Rosa Parks, an African American woman, was arrested in Montgomery, Alabama, for refusing to surrender her seat to a white person. This action began the Montgomery Bus Boycott. The boycott continued until December 20, 1956, when a federal ruling, *Browder v. Gayle*, took effect and led to a United States Supreme Court decision that declared the Alabama and Montgomery laws requiring segregated buses to be unconstitutional.
- *May 4, 1961:* The first Freedom Ride left Washington, D.C. Civil rights activists rode interstate buses into the segregated Southern United States in 1961 and subsequent years to challenge the non-enforcement of the United States Supreme Court decisions *Morgan v. Virginia* (1946) and *Boynton v. Virginia* (1960), which ruled that segregated public buses were unconstitutional. Freedom Riders were attacked, beaten, and jailed.
- *June 12, 1963:* Civil-rights activist Medgar Evers murdered.
- *August 28, 1963:* March on Washington for Jobs and Freedom.
- *September 15, 1963:* 16th Street Baptist Church bombing.[1]
- *November 22, 1963:* President John F. Kennedy assassinated.
- *February 1964:* The Beatles come to the U.S.
- *December 11, 1964:* Sam Cooke dies in Los Angeles, CA.
- *December 10, 1967:* Otis Redding, soul singer, dies in plane crash.
- *April 4, 1968:* Dr. Martin Luther King, Jr., assassinated.

Sam Cooke died at the end of 1964. I was thirteen, and the world was in an awful swirl. It was the era of the Civil Rights Movement, and the second time I felt a hole in my soul at the loss of somebody I didn't know. We had lost John F. Kennedy, our president, in 1963. That was a sore loss because we'd been delighted by his youthful good looks, his seemingly deep compassion, his modernity. I still tear up to remember my great-aunt kneeling before the TV, praying as though her prayers were going back through the TV screen that had announced this unfathomable horror. We felt like Sam Cooke was a family member, too, so it seemed like we'd lost another family member—sort of—as I recall.

"You Send Me"

We used to dream about Sam Cooke. We imagined we might be his girlfriend some-day. I always think "we" because of my childhood BFF, CeeCee. She was my partner in Sam Cooke worship. We imagined that all he'd have to do was get a chance to see us. He'd be smitten! We were far too young to be noticed as women then. We were black middle-school bobby-soxers. I went to Catholic school, and CeeCee went to public school. We were swooning before the record player, being "sent" by Sam Cooke's lovely, smooth, crooning, caramel voice long before we honestly knew what it meant to be thrilled.

He died—was killed. I still remember how painful that was, because CeeCee and I lost each other—our friendship, too—around that time. We went to different schools, and I took piano lessons, and CeeCee and I weren't friends in the same way after that. I don't fully understand why. The music remained, and that was all we had of Sam Cooke. I suppose it was inevitable. Our essential innocence was gone.

It was a specific moment in my life. If Sam Cooke had lived, the fascination would have faded but, in any event, I don't think I could ever forget the beauty of his voice. Dancing was a big part of it. The things I remember most about my Washington, D.C., childhood are social dancing and automobiles and all the trappings. All of that had to do with propriety and heteronormative behavior practice. Sam was one of the kings of teenage dance music, and teenage dancing was a handy surrogate for sex acts. All I know about dancing I learned from Sam, in the basement, practicing with CeeCee.

Many of Sam's tunes actually delineated the popular dance moves of the day. Listen, follow, succeed.

"Everybody Loves to Cha Cha Cha"

We believed we were doing the cha-cha. It was a lot of fun. Again and again, we played this hit and practiced. One two, one two, up now and back now, cross now, turn now. I included it in the first variety show we—i.e., CeeCee, me, and the two younger boys who lived next door, plus the two other younger boys who lived next to them, plus my younger sister—put on in the living room while piano playing and lip syncing. All of our parents were in the audience, sitting on the sofa and a few chairs brought in from the dining room. It was my older sister's idea to hang up a blanket between the dining room and the living room for our curtain. We were dorky and endearing. It was all in front of her then: college, mother's cancer, death, alcohol, death, her cancer, her death.

"Cupid"

"Cupid" was probably the A side of "Cha Cha Cha," so we would have played it again and again in the basement, too. I know we played it over and again. It has a stupidly even beat that's perfect for rehearsing a two-step, still required for social dancing in the '60s in DC. She was more gangly, less graceful than I was, but I was no dancer. It's embarrassing to remember how much we loved those Sam Cooke tunes and how I still remember each nuance of the melodies. But music is like that. It catches you in a thrall, and you are held. Don't fail me, 'cause I need you.

We developed a narrative of play with Sam Cooke and the other singers from the record player. That's what the device to play audio was called then. Ours was the chief feature of our basement, along with old typewriters, old library books, and old badminton shuttlecocks. We stacked the fat forty-five spindle, the thing that converted a thirty-three-rpm small-hole player to the delightful fat-holed forty-fives of teenage music. Decca, Capitol, Stax, Motown. All I remember was that we danced and cavorted. Learning to dance in DC was mandatory, and we practiced. The road to social success ran through the Twist, the Two-Step, the Mashed Potato, the Pony, the Sloop, the Funky Chicken, and the Slow Drag, a preliminary taste of sex.

When Sam Cooke sings, I recollect the smell of my pressed-straight hair. (Most of the laborious process of lacquering my hair into acceptable straightness was less than pleasant.) We were well-behaved girls. Our hair was well behaved, straight as possible under the circumstances of hot combs, pressing oil, quiet behavior, clean behavior. My aunt owned a beauty parlor.

"Only Sixteen"

When Sam Cooke sang "Only Sixteen," we were younger than that, so we loved the song as something we could be: the wonderful girl of this wonderful boy's dreams. Sam was the first singer I got the tingles for. I think her, too. It was largely built upon his embodiment of the nice, friendly, slightly funky, well-meaning Negro man with a beautiful voice, an angel's voice. We played at being the woman of his dreams. He was so good at saying exactly what his dream girl should be. With eyes that would glow.

"Having a Party"

Oh, how we longed to be the "baby" of the "me and my baby" line. Blue lights in the basement parties were a teenage staple of '60s teenagers in Washington. CeeCee and I were too young to party, but we knew the customs, were practicing the culture. All of our parents occasionally danced at lodge and church events and cabarets. Their photo albums were full of snapshots of parties and social functions.

I never really knew how much her parents drank. They would be considered alcoholics now. They were alcoholics. They drank more than the other neighbors and my parents. I came to know that later. They maintained a proper public façade, nothing inappropriate that a child would notice. I wonder if she knew then, when we were young, that her parents were heavy drinkers. Was she keeping their secrets back then? She seemed to idolize them. I thought highly of them. I might even have been envious because her parents seemed more solicitous of her than mine were of me. Solicitous is perhaps the wrong word entirely and, in thinking back, I think I was wrong about that then, too. Her parents, her mother, had more time. She didn't work. My mother did, in a municipal-government office. I admired my mother's clerical skills, but I occasionally wished she was a stay-at-home cookie-baker mother. Different lives. Different styles. A lot of different dances.

"Everybody Likes to Cha Cha Cha," "Shake," "That's Where It's At"

CeeCee's basement had the five gazillion toys her older, indulgent parents had given her, the overflow from her toy-packed bedroom. It was cool, too, and we played there on alternate summer days when we were still little kids, when Washington's summers were hot, and women put powder between their breasts, and kids took refuge in cool basements.

I think I was always safe in my family's basement. Lucky for me. I never really had my guard up in the rec room with the record player, the old typewriters, the flotsam and jetsam.

We lived on an island of safe space, my sisters and I. I see that now. I'm not sure CeeCee ever did. Did it only get bad later? Sam Cooke, despite dying in a violent, though public, domestic incident under questionable circumstances, gave us a gift of gentle musical innocence in a time of public turmoil. He was the sweet boy next door. He was our one true tweenager idol of the '50s and '60s.

If I'd ever seen Sam Cooke in the flesh, I'm sure I would have fainted, even though I'm pretty steady. My aunt (my mother's younger sister) is said to have fainted on the sidewalk in the presence of the beautiful Billy Eckstine some time during the 1940s.

My parents were considered a handsome couple. She had a beautiful face and a nice figure. He was tall and lightly muscled, with a kind face and mellow eyes. I imagine that my father's particular love of the ballad "Tennessee Waltz," as sung by Patti Page, must have to do with dancing close and letting my mother's lovely breasts brush his chest. He liked Sam Cooke's up-tempo version much less.

Sam Cooke brought gospel music to the mainstream by sneaking it in on a honeyed voice that clarified some of its rawness like what happens when heating butter melts all its impurities away. What remains is clear, throbbing, and bouncy. He was, on a crude, elemental marketing level, the Black Bobbysoxer, except that it would have been "colored" bobbysoxer or Negro Bobbysoxer.

"A Change Is Gonna Come"

Sam's recording of "A Change Is Gonna Come" begins with unbelievably schmaltzy strings, then explodes with Sam's beautiful, strong-gospel intonations. There have been times when I thought I couldn't last much longer. His recording has made it a perennial anthem of the Civil Rights Movement, a song that beautifully bespeaks sufferings caused by injustice, lack of opportunity, and social segregation. Nevertheless, it's a hopeful song.

In it, the oppressed eke out some optimism. Sam's voice says it better than any other voice could have, even Martin Luther King's. But change must surely come.

All these many years, I still thrill. I wonder how anyone could have heard MLK's words at the March on Washington for Jobs and Freedom that August day in 1963 and not resolve to have King's dream as their own. When Sam sings "A Change Is Gonna Come," I say, "How can you not want your shoulder with his?" That glimmer of hope. Things have to improve over time, don't they?

In remembering and in preparing, I've discovered many covers of other peoples' hit songs that Sam Cooke made his own. I'm surprised he wasn't shot by one of his contemporaries whose version of a song fell into the dust when he covered it. Elvis. Freddie Mercury. Nat King Cole. Sam Cooke's infinitely complex stylings of popular hits are stunning, and Sam was able to sing notes between notes that others could reach only by yodeling. Sam Cooke made a slew of recordings.

Did Sam Cooke appear on TV? Yes, definitely. He appeared on *The Ed Sullivan Show, American Bandstand, The Steve Allen Show, The Dick Clark Saturday Night Beechnut Show, The Jimmy Dean Show, The Arthur Murray Party,* and *General Electric Theater* in something called "The Patsy" that starred Sammy Davis, Jr., among a whole lot of other appearances. *The Merv Griffin Show, The Tonight Show, The Mike Douglas Show.*

The death of Sam Cooke occurred at a point in my life when everything was changing, and everything was on TV. Sandwiched between the assassinations of JFK and MLK, I recall combing my hair and watching TV reflected behind me in 1968 when they broke in to say that MLK was murdered.

When I look at Sam Cooke's face today in black-and-white photos and YouTube videos of early film clips, I see a lot less innocence, less gentleness than I remember. But then, of course, it is me, isn't it? It is all about my naïveté projected onto his creamy, dreamy voice. In 1964, I was barely pubescent. I was still trying to get used to accommodating sanitary napkins—locating them at the bottom of the sparsely filled double closet in my parents' room. My father's closet was a peculiar place for sanitary napkins, but the economy boxes were huge, we were three girls, and men had fewer clothes than women in those days.

I did not accept the official version of the death of Sam Cooke. I can no longer remember where I was when I learned. It was December. I would have been all caught up in Christmas. JFK was dead, assassinated, the year before. He was the only president I had a crush on. His family had their pictures on trading cards, just as baseball players did. One afternoon, his motorcade swirled around a downtown street corner at home in Washington as I was waiting to cross. I saw his face. It was quick. I felt a vibration of excitement in my toes hanging just over the lip of the curb.

So he was the first heartthrob lost. Sam Cooke was the next. The '60s were brutal for deaths: JFK, Sam, Otis Redding, Medgar Evers, MLK. And then there were the deaths of Addie Mae Collins, Cynthia Wesley, Carole Robertson, and little Carol Denise McNair. Carol was only eleven; the others were just fourteen. They died in the Sixteenth Street Baptist Church bombing. In Ava DuVernay's film *Selma*, they are depicted briefly talking about hairstyles, as any young girls might, carefree as we were. Not enough attention has ever been paid to these lives up in smoke. Their deaths have to be consequential, meaningful. For me, for my older sister and my younger one, and CeeCee, and for Viv, too.

Our Sam Cooke fantasy moment: Sam takes your hand and teaches you the cha-cha, and you get it immediately because when you touch his fingers your hips sway and

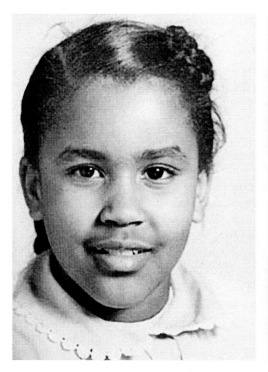

By age ten, Breena Clarke was living in Washington, D.C., and had discovered the immortal Sam Cooke. Today, Breena is an honored novelist who co-organizes the renowned Hobart Festival of Women Writers in the Catskills.

your feet move just right. He sings with a civilized exuberance that lifts you. Every note is available to him, so he doesn't push. He never has to ugly up a note to accomplish it. *Mellifluous.* We were bright, but we didn't know that word then. I've since learned it, and in my visual dictionary, it is beside a picture of Sam Cooke. That is how his voice was and still is. The meaning is small, simple, but the word is just right. Sweet and musical. It is almost untrustworthy because you wonder if it is truly a human voice. And it belies a certain way a man can be: not sweet, not nice, not musical.

In old black-and-white photos, girls try to grab him, him singing about God and them wanting to do deviltry.

"Touch the Hem of His Garment"

Can you believe it? Can you imagine being able to touch Sam's sleeve or his pants, not to mention his face and his naked body? *Wow.* And could you be such a hussy in heels that you'd take his clothes and steal his money and run off, and then have your ugly confederate shoot him when he ran out to stop you? But just listen to him singing; go back and listen to that raw, gutbucket sensuality. It is there, is always there. His style was to let a little bit out at a time, tease between sweet and sexy. And the sex is soft, adolescent.

I keep thinking that because I was a Negro teenager who attended a Catholic school in the 1960s, I am invested in an image of Sam Cooke as a sweet-voiced, sweet-hearted, only just slightly naughty-ish Negro man. Not a drunk turned suddenly nasty when crossed or a careless, overindulged, predatory celebrity like Bill Cosby. This picture informs the fictional characters I create. But I'm grown enough now to figure Sam Cooke probably was less nice than naughty, and the unfortunate shooting may have happened sort of the way they said. It is the most likely scenario. At the very least, I have to entertain the possibility that he was threatening the life of the woman who shot him in self-defense. It is so hard not to want to go back to the ice-cream-and-cake vocals, but, as the daughter of a woman courageous enough to kill a man to save her life, I have to consider that another woman did the same.

For a girl raised in the far less musically engaging Catholic Church, Sam's gospel-inflected rhythm and blues and his religious singing have been a visceral pleasure. Sam's musical Jesus, a character in his material with the legendary Soul Stirrers, is an exceptional friend who intercedes with his sterner Father on behalf of all of his struggling, sinning acquaintances. The feeling comes through especially in those songs with the Soul Stirrers when Sam addresses Jesus directly. So much the better way to pray. With that voice, Sam surely has Jesus's ear. Let Sam do the praying … er, singing.

Which explains Sam's early death? Jesus wanted him to come home to heaven? A lot of his fans thought that, said that. But this is just the sort of thing that disabuses me of belief in God, in Jesus. Why would Jesus want Sam to die that way? Why not call him in his sleep or right after a last, pretty, angelic note? Wasn't Sam beloved of Jesus? That voice! Weren't our beloveds JFK or MLK? Those four sacred children: Cynthia, Carole, Addie Mae, and the other Carol? Medgar Evers? What is this plan in the mind of God, of Jesus?

My father, who worked at night was known to be at home most all the time. He was our daytime, at-home parent. My mother worked in an office, he worked at night, and he slept a slice in the evening. Still, he never did anything to harm anyone that I know. And, correcting for my intense idolization of him, I still have never heard a word said against him. He and my mother seem to have created a bubble of protection for my sisters and me. They gave us three girls a safe space. They had a staunchness to them that later I learned was composed of complex stuff. And still, a girl to the right of us if you face the alley between streets that is a Washington, D.C., feature, was fondled and bothered by a male relative in her basement, and the girl to the left of us was abused by her father. My best, best friend. CeeCee. Maybe not when I knew her? Still, I marvel that, at the time, I knew so little, that there was so little protection for a girl, a good daughter in this nice, Negro people's neighborhood. Why was it that a girl had nowhere to go to be believed about her brother-in-law's or her father's transgressions?

I just know that when I hear Sam Cooke's voice, which is distinctive above all others, a shiver comes over me, and I probably will always instantly smile, feel the warmth. Often I make a remark. I always recollect with pleasure. I have no doubt added things to his beautiful singing that cause it to trigger these pleasant endorphins of innocence. I can go blissfully back to my parents' basement, where I enjoyed prepubescent virginity in the cool recreation room, the storage-and-general-whatever room that everybody's house had, with my first best friend, CeeCee.

She's dead, and I'm feeling a bit of survivor's guilt. Our bond was deep one while. After Sam Cooke, we were Beatles fans together. In fact, when the Beatles landed in the U.S. in February 1964, CeeCee and I were two of that seventy-three million who watched them on Ed Sullivan's variety show. We were hooked. We gave up dancing to Sam in the basement and got Beatles dolls and imagined ourselves to be Patti Boyd or Twiggy.

I think traumatic stuff weakens the immune system. I believe the body is affected by harm in numerous, incomprehensible ways. I've outlived both my childhood neighbor-girls. My sisters are still strong and thriving. Our folks bequeathed us some fortitude, some good health, some common sense. I keep trying to make something out of the fact that Sam Cooke was thirty-three when he died and, this year, I'm twice that. I don't understand anything about death at all except that it is, it happens.

My teen angel was no teenager and certainly no angel. He was twice married, had three children in his second marriage and two outside of it. By all accounts, he was grounded in a Christian tradition of faith and music. How'd he come to be running near naked from a motel room and shot dead? Who knows? I also remember all kinds of bright, plastic things, especially radios, portable radios in delicious, flavorful colors: lemon, mint green, party-cake pink and creamy vanilla.

Sam Cooke's Music

"Unchained Melody":
https://youtu.be/n-RWYn8Octk?list=PLOSNsaNaWuNDbh7rLkvV2MzShI-WnkYDFX
"Send Me Some Loving":
https://youtu.be/NXR5tuqLGOc?list=PLOSNsaNaWuNDbh7rLkvV2MzShI-WnkYDFX
"Nobody Knows the Trouble I've Seen":
https://youtu.be/rQzlzH5wymc
"A Change Is Gonna Come" (Official Lyric Version):
https://youtu.be/wEBlaMOmKV4
"What a Wonderful World":
https://youtu.be/R4GLAKEjU4w
"The Great Pretender":
https://youtu.be/PyIo1M-Sp1g
"Movin' and Groovin'":
https://youtu.be/YHCKL2II5GM

Note

1. The bombing resulted in the deaths of fourteen-year-old Addie Mae Collins, fourteen-year-old Cynthia Wesley, fourteen-year-old Carole Robertson, and eleven-year-old Carol Denis McNair. Often treated as a footnote to the bigger events of the Civil Rights Movement, the death of these ordinary innocents is a stark reminder of the horrors of the Southern resistance to civil rights and equal opportunity.

Back to Hermania

TAMRA WILSON

It's November 1997, and Magic 96.1 radio in Charlotte is sponsoring an oldies concert: the Jingle Bell Hop featuring Peter Noone.

"Who's he?" my husband Tym asks.

I explain that Peter was Herman of Herman's Hermits. He sang "I'm Henry the Eighth, I Am" and "Mrs. Brown, You've Got a Lovely Daughter." I wonder how it is that we've never talked about my Teen Idol. Peter is a taboo topic. Up until now, he has never entered married conversation, not that he should. Discussing a Teen Idol is like talking about an old boyfriend from the days before reality set in.

"Is he still around?" Tym says.

I wince. Surely Peter Noone hasn't faded into nothingness, though I admit that I haven't heard anything solid about him since he appeared in *Pirates of Penzance* on Broadway. That was fifteen years ago. For all I know, he owns a Roto-Rooter franchise in Keokuk.

"Yes, he's still out there," I say, adding, "He was my Teen Idol."

I don't dare explain how I was going to marry this entertainer. Tym has no idea such a ridiculous, parallel universe ever existed. Besides, as the mother of Lantz, our twelve-year-old son, I should project a mature, sensible image. I should never admit that I was once a swooning seventh grader.

The Jingle Bell Hop may be my last chance to see Peter Noone in person. I shouldn't put it off as I did with Elvis. By the time I called for tickets back in 1977, they were sold out. Two months later, he was dead.

I do the math. Peter is already eight years older than Elvis was back then.

Over dinner, I explain to Lantz why we're spending a Friday night at an oldies show.

"Herman's Hermits were bigger than the Backstreet Boys," I say.

Lantz's eyes roll. He's the age I was when Peter Noone burst into my life. My friend Suzanne bought the "There's a Kind of Hush All Over the World" single, and we walked back to her house and slipped the 45 onto the turntable. She showed me her fan magazines and when I saw Herman's boyish JFK smile, I was smitten.

That Friday at the Jingle Bell Hop in Charlotte, Tym, Lantz, and I sit in the top tier of Independence Arena. After the Drifters, Bobby Vee, and Johnny Rivers perform, the audience roars for the main attraction. Peter Noone strides onto the stage, and I gasp and cheer. At last, there's my Teen Idol in an argyle pullover and slacks. He looks like somebody's dad. The years have rounded his face, but he has the same bouncy humor, the same boyish hair, same voice garnering the same pep-rally chants for "I'm Henry the Eighth, I Am."

"He's like a big kid," Tym says.

Peter rocks the house, and after the last strains of "There's a Kind of Hush All Over the World," we follow the crowd to the lobby. And when I catch a glimpse of him signing autographs, the adolescent inside me quakes. "I've got to do this," I tell my boys. I'll do anything to see my old heartthrob up close.

Lantz and I inch forward. Yes, that's really Peter Noone, as animated as the entertainer I remember from TV and movies—laughing, joking. I stuff a ten-dollar bill into Lantz's hand to buy Peter's *On the Road* CD. I can't help but notice the cover photograph showing the same blue eyes that stared back at me from fan magazines and LPs. I'll have the CD autographed, an extra excuse to meet the star.

I grip the camera in my hand, which is sweaty at the thought of actually speaking to the one and only Herman. I must play it cool. This isn't junior high.

Peter's felt-tip pen is in constant motion, signing one autograph after another. He isn't posing for photographs, and I don't have the nerve to ask for one. He might say "no" like a jerk, and I'll be sorry that I'd ever followed him in the first place.

"I want Herman to sign it to me," Lantz says.

Peter Noone was *my* idol, but I concede to this small sacrifice.

I hear the English accent, the one that made my seventh-grade heart melt. Lantz's curly blond haircut is facing Herman's blond shock of Hermit hair. I point my lens as Peter signs the CD.

Then Peter looks up through his wire-rimmed glasses. And there we are, face to face, his eyes bluer than I remember on his albums. My heart pounds. I can feel my face flush. "It's so nice to meet you," I say.

"Nice to meet *you*," he says. We shake hands, and I think I see a glint of recognition, as if he somehow remembers his photo on my lavender bedroom wall in junior high, that he knows I was always there, listening on my transistor radio.

I step from the line and ask Tym to take my photo with Peter in the background. Lantz stands off to the side, unsure what his mom sees in this chubby, middle-aged man with Hollywood hair. And then, when Peter looks up to greet another fan, the flash goes off. At last Herman and I occupy the same frame. Though I'm forty-three years old, I feel thirteen.

I'm no different from any other woman meeting her Teen Idol. We want to make a good impression, not appear star struck or anxious, though we are all of those things. The adult exterior acts nonchalant while the adolescent inside screams to be set free. And, like any momentous occasion, I remember what I wore: a red cardigan with pearl buttons, black slacks, and ballet-slipper flats. I remember the echoey roar of the Coliseum, the even grip of Peter's handshake, and the fleeting notion that I might never wash my right hand again.

Facing my adolescent crush, I confronted an uncomfortable truth: my youth was in the past, and Peter was struggling with the same reality. He was still handsome, but no longer nineteen. Over the decades, he had acquired glasses, hints of gray hair, and a rounded posture. I, like other fans, wanted so desperately for that not to be the case.

Fans of Teen Idols want a solid memory to remain: the striking face on the album cover, the retouched photo in the magazine. We want our idol to be forever young. We pray, dear God, let him look like he did in *16* and *Tiger Beat*. We beg for that early version to exist, but the real person cannot oblige. He must age like the bittersweet memory of "Mrs. Brown" before it became a Magic 96.1 oldie.

There was something about Peter's happy-go-lucky image that appealed to my schoolgirl sensibilities. He was cute. He looked wholesome and safe.

Thanks to Suzanne's fan magazines, I became engulfed, consumed, devoured by a twenty-four-hour-a-day-and-night preoccupation with the cute blond-haired singer with the toothy grin. Maybe that was what being in love was supposed to feel like.

It was hard to keep up with Peter—what he was doing, what he was singing, and—horrors—who he was dating. If we'd had a mutual friend or a number to call for updates, it would've been easy. He couldn't go anywhere without being noticed. It must have be awful to be imprisoned in a hotel or a backstage dressing room, hiding from mobs of screaming girls, and oh, how I longed to be one of them!

It's 1967 and there I am, hopelessly trapped in junior high, a hundred miles from Kiel Auditorium in St. Louis. A lot of acts play there—the Rolling Stones, the Monkees, Paul Revere and the Raiders, and Herman's Hermits. Seating capacity is over nine thousand—twice the population of Shelbyville, Illinois. I have never been in a building that large. Getting my hands on a pair of tickets will take extreme good luck or convincing my mother to write a check. It isn't safe to send cash in the mail. But there's no way she will write a check for three dollars, the cheap seats, much less four dollars for the medium-good ones. Of course some fans will get front-row seats. I will want to choke these people.

There is less chance that Mom will drive Suzanne and me to St. Louis, assuming that Suzanne's parents lose their minds and allow her to go. Kiel is a two-hundred-mile round trip that would involve city traffic and the Chain of Rocks Bridge, a spindly, palm-sweating segment of Route 66 that stretches high over the Mississippi River. The bridge gives my mother the shakes just thinking about it. Only dire necessity will make her drive me to St. Louis, and a Herman's Hermits concert won't be it.

A week before my thirteenth birthday, I write a letter to the Keith Morris All Request Show on KXOK in St. Louis. *Dear Mr. Morris, Please play "Mrs. Brown, You've Got a Lovely Daughter" for my birthday*, I write in my neat, rounded script, so it will be easy to read. This is my present to myself: hearing my favorite Herman's Hermits song from Radio Park in St. Louis.

On August 14, 1967, I sit in front of the stereo console, my reel-to-reel tape recorder at the ready. At last I hear the plunky guitar intro of the requested song. Keith Morris doesn't mention my name, but I am sure he has seen my letter. "Mrs. Brown" couldn't have been requested by anyone else. I record the song on my reel-to-reel tape player, preserving the audio moment like a souvenir.

I hear something even more breathtaking on KXOK that day: the Hermits are coming to Kiel on August 25. The warm-up band is somebody called The Who.

August 25 is a Friday. The school year will be under way, which makes the chances of going to the show plunge into negative numbers. I know about negative integers from math class. I create my own word problem. "If the chance of Tammy seeing a Herman's Hermits concert is zero, according to her mother, and the chance of seeing them is negative fifty, according to her dad, what are the actual chances?"

Answer: Zero times anything is zero.

It must be weird to be Peter Noone. One day, you're a regular person, and then you wake up as an Idol, drafted into the company of Elvis and the Beatles. The whole world wants to be your friend. Your photo is everywhere. You're invited to appear on *The Ed Sullivan Show* and *Hullaballoo* and *Dean Martin*.

Being a Teen Idol means you rise early to catch a flight. You have to answer fan mail, pose for pictures, and give interviews even when you have a cold or a headache. You're sick of answering the same questions. Why are you called "Herman"? Where do you come from in England? What is your favorite song?

You get up at four a.m., in time for the makeup call for a movie that you can't go see without being mobbed. It must be awful to be a Teen Idol, but it would be fun to see how awful.

I use part of my birthday money to buy my first album, the dreamy turquoise one, *There's a Kind of Hush All Over the World*, with Herman's image in profile, wearing a navy-blue blazer with brass buttons that would put anyone on the Best-Dressed List. The album costs $3.19 plus tax. Over weeks and months, a badly worn stylus takes its toll. After so many plays, I will never hear "Jezebel" without hearing Peter's voice stick in mid-verse. "Jezzeh … zzezzeh … zzezzeh…"

"Will you make that stop?" Mom calls.

I touch the tone arm, but I fumble, and the needle makes the sound of a loud zipper. Peter will never finish "Jezebel" again without my help.

I study the album cover. Peter is gazing off in deep thought, trying to decide if he's Herman or Peter. I wonder what he's doing this very instant. Maybe he's rehearsing his next hit song. Or maybe he's on some lonesome northern railroad, like the one he sang about in "Rattler," trading cities like an old goat. Or is it coat?

Peter is one of those cheerful sorts who lives and breathes cool. He never has greasy hair or athlete's foot or blemishes, thanks to the airbrush. He's the boy you *wish* would move next door. If that happened, I'm sure I would be speechless. Worse yet, I doubt if I could understand what he was saying. He curls the ends of sentences as if he's asking a question. Sometimes he swallows entire syllables. R become "uh." That's what being from England will do for you.

Suppose Peter takes a road trip for fun. When he and his driver reach Shelbyville, they spot the Dog 'n' Suds and circle the gravel parking lot. The blue Jaguar makes heads turn, and so does the long-haired blond guy in the passenger seat. No Future Farmers of America member has long hair. A wide-eyed carhop approaches the sports car to take the order. A few minutes later, she hooks a tray onto the driver's window.

When the passenger tells the carhop to keep the change, in his Mancunian accent, she shrieks, "It's Herman!"

Onlookers pile out of their vehicles to rush the Jag. In a panic, the driver starts the engine, slips the car into reverse, and spins away with the food tray still attached to the window.

When I tell this story to Suzanne, she laughs. "How do you dream up such crazy stuff?"

I can't imagine Herman's Hermits playing in a dinky place like Shelbyville. Herman and his band are on top of the world, or at least on top of the charts. They're the only group I've ever liked—I mean *really* liked—but the chance of seeing them in concert is nil. I'm absolutely, positively sure of it. If I ask my parents to take me, they'll come up with more excuses: I'm too young to be in a stadium full of screaming teenagers. I'll get trampled. Somebody will snatch my purse. The noise will make me deaf. But I have to go. If I'm going to marry Peter, I should meet him first.

I have it all figured out. I will win a backstage pass from KXOK. Never mind that the odds of winning are one in nine thousand. I'll slip through the dressing-room door, and there he'll be—the star in a classic Chesterfield jacket, his thick blond hair brushing the collar.

I stand frozen in my pink calico shirtdress and bangle bracelets. I'm glad I dabbed on an extra splash of Heaven Sent. I steady myself against the Formica countertop. Bare light bulbs surround the mirrors like a white-hot picture frame. I feel sweaty. Herman, or Peter, rather, cracks jokes I pretend to understand. The four Hermits offer the backdrop for the real star. Herman smiles his famous eyetooth grin and thrusts his right hand toward me.

"Hello. I'm Peter Noone. And you are…"

"Tammy McElroy," I mumble.

We shake hands. No, he gives me a hug, and oh God, I'm inches from Peter's heart. I've worn flats because I'm the tallest girl in my class, and I don't want to make him look like a shrimp. I've read that he's five foot nine. I'm five foot eight and a half. I toss my chestnut-brown hair behind my shoulders.

"Where are you from?" he says.

Tamra McElroy (Wilson) during her first round of Hermania at age 14. Forty-five years later, she was finally photographed with Peter Noone after a concert in Lenoir, North Carolina. Her blog about that evening sparked the idea for *Idol Talk*.

This is my cue to explain how far I live from St. Louis. "Shelbyville, a hundred miles away."

"That's rather far."

"You're farther," I say, and I realize that this sounds silly. In England, it's tomorrow already.

The Hermits chuckle. I know their names: Keith Hopwood, the rhythm guitarist; Karl Green, the bass player; Barry Whitwam, the drummer; and Derek Leckenby, lead guitarist. Derek, the tallest, is the most distinctive Hermit, with horn-rimmed glasses. His hair is shorter than the other Hermits.' He doesn't look like he belongs in a rock band at all, not that his bandmates look scruffy. They're wearing suits and ties as if they're going to church.

Peter smiles. "Where are you in school?"

It's his backdoor way of asking how old I am. I bite my lip. "I'm going into eighth grade." My throat is dry. I cough.

He shifts back a step. I'm way too young to date, much less marry. He will have to check into a rock-star monastery and wait until I'm old enough, say eighteen. That won't happen until 1972. Maybe Peter will take me in as Elvis did with Priscilla when she turned seventeen. I will attend recording sessions. I will watch quietly and patiently with the other girlfriends of rock stars. Peter will hire a tutor to help me finish high school. No, this is a dumb idea. Even if I were eighteen this instant, my parents would forbid me to run off with a rock singer. People in show business are shiftless, no better than gypsies.

Mom will squint through her cat-eye glasses. "Run off with that Hermit? That's what *you* think, Missy."

Peter will have to bide his time in the monastery. There must be one in London. I'll go to college there. Of course! By then it will be 1972. Peter will be desperate to find me after enduring throngs of girls clawing at his door for five years. One day the monks will let him out on good behavior. He'll be strolling along the Thames like an overdressed Prince Charming and spot me near Tower Bridge, the one pictured in Yardley of London commercials.

Overwhelmed at such good fortune, he'll call, "Tammy from Shelbyville! I knew I'd find you again!"

Then we'll rush into each other's arms. Violins will play the glassy intro to "There's a Kind of Hush," and we will live happily ever after in a stone cottage in Shropshire, because it has such a cool name.

"Dream and make it true," Mom says. "Be careful what you wish for, because it might happen."

Could I ever be this lucky? I'm breathless when I hear Herman's Hermits on the radio. Their music is what I hope to hear when I listen to the radio, which is almost every waking minute. When one of their songs is played, it's like opening a love note on perfumed stationery and smiling at the familiar script.

I cannot say if my infatuation with Peter Noone caused things to happen as they did. I do know that my curiosity about England prompted me to set goals. Thanks to incredible good fortune, I visited England at age sixteen and again at nineteen, where I spent a semester in college. The following year, 1975, I crossed paths with a Shelbyville guy who, realizing I had studied in England, asked me to dinner with relatives who were visiting from County Kent.

My date was Tym Wilson, whom I married four years later. We spent our honeymoon in the British Isles; though I don't remember hearing "There's a Kind of Hush," we did stroll past Tower Bridge.

Peter remained off my radar until 2013, when he gave a concert in Lenoir, North Carolina, and I discovered that his fan club of "Noonatics" was still alive and well. Fans in their '50s and '60s were as devoted as ever, thanks to social media and Peter's constant communication with them.

As a new "lifetime" Peter Noone Fan Club member, I was eligible for a backstage pass. A year later, as I was preparing to fly to Las Vegas as a retirement treat to myself. I retired from the library system one day and flew out the next. I wasn't the Vegas type, but I was going because Peter was performing at the Golden Nugget Resort Casino, and a Noonatic friend I'll call "Serena" would be there to show me around.

And then, lucky me, I received an e-mail from the fan club president. "Congratulations, Tammy! You are the lucky lifer. Please stop by the souvenir table when the doors open to be escorted backstage."

It's Friday night, January 30, 2015, and Peter Noone is expecting me. The theater door opens. Serena and I are led past a warren of dressing rooms. Billy and Vance, the current guitarists, watch us make our way to the room at the end of the corridor. We step inside the golden-lit room. There is Peter, wearing a dove-gray shirt and tie, jeans, and Beatle boots. I keep reminding myself: *You are really here, in Herman's dressing room. Don't make him look like a shrimp.* The fan magazines didn't lie. He's five foot ten at most, and I'm wearing flats, just like I imagined forty-eight years ago.

"Please excuse the mess," he says.

My eyes cut around the room. A laptop computer sits in a tangle of cords on the counter, a blue-plaid shirt drapes over one of the chairs, a black garment bag hangs over a closet door.

He points at Serena, puzzled.

"She's my chaperone," I explain.

We laugh and skip the introductions. We know who he is, he and I know who Serena is. Serena knows who I am. And since he's expecting me, he knows who I am too. In all likelihood, he has already found me on Facebook. He isn't called the King of Social Media for nothing.

The first order of business is a photo. Billy snaps two pictures, and hands the iPhone back to Peter, who taps the images for me to view.

"Which do you like?" he says.

"The second one is better of you," I say.

That works for him. I knew it would.

He asks me who he shall say is in the photo. I tell him Tammy Wilson, spelling Tammy with a Y. I sense that he already knows this before I tell him. "Tammy Wilson and Herman backstage passers," the caption reads.

"When will it post?"

He taps the *send* button. "Right now."

Then I say, "Now everyone will know where I am. I retired on Wednesday, and I ran away from home on Thursday."

"We're all retired. We just don't know it yet," he says.

The room can't be more than nine by twelve feet. Upholstered chairs occupy opposite sides of the room, which is carpeted with beige Berber. The writer in me takes mental notes to remember what's being said, who's doing what.

Peter straightens his tie. "How does this look? It's supposed to be a half inch below the belt buckle." Serena and I stare at his midsection, nod our approval. Then he throws on his jacket, a perfect match to the tie and shirt. "Does my tie hang right? Do I look all right?"

This is surreal. Peter Noone is asking *us* how to dress? I'm grateful that Serena is along to help carry the day. It feels warm in here.

Then I blurt out, "Now I'm one degree of separation from Dennis Miller." I've done my homework. Comedian Dennis Miller is his neighbor and good friend.

Peter looks at me as if I've lost my mind.

"No really. I *love* Dennis Miller. I think he's hilarious," I say.

The conversation makes a ninety-degree turn as Peter banters about how hard it is to keep up with Miller when they have lunch together, which is most every week. "You need a dictionary," he says. When they book a reservation, they say they're "Miss Anthrope." "It's a word Americans don't use much."

I knew my flats would help us see eye to eye. After a few more laughs, it's almost show time.

As we pass the refreshment table—bottles of water, cookies—Peter urges us to help ourselves to a large chocolate chip cookie. I wrap mine in a napkin and tuck it into my handbag.

This evening, I'm in the front row, and when Peter sings "Mrs. Brown," he's not eight feet in front of me.

I manage to bring the prized cookie home, intact. Two months later, when The Cookie is fully dried and shellacked, I gather it along with my Golden Nugget napkin, show ticket, and backstage photographs and head to a local frame shop.

The young clerk there asks about the items to fit into a shadow box. "Why do you want to keep this stuff?" she says.

"I met Peter Noone. He gave me the cookie," I say sheepishly. "He was my Teen Idol."

"That's awesome," she says, though she has no idea who Herman's Hermits were, much less Peter Noone. "Was he sort of like the Backstreet Boys?"

The Backstreet Boys never outsold the Beatles. They were never in feature films, or hosted a VH-1 program, or were disc jockeys for a satellite radio show, or played a starring role in a Broadway musical. They've never matched wits with Dennis Miller. I know that Peter Noone is head and shoulders above the Backstreet Boys, but I don't want to sound smug. After all, I'm trusting this young woman with my precious souvenirs, including The Cookie.

"Sort of," I say.

She gives me a knowing smile, and for an instant we're both thirteen again.

P.S. I Love You

B.A. Shapiro

We're waiting for the bus on the corner of Wiltshire Lane and Albany Avenue—my best friend Maggie and me, heading into Hartford. We're each going to buy a copy of *Introducing.... The Beatles*, the Beatles' very first album, which is being released today at the record store on Asylum Street.

Maggie's father has a friend who works for someone called Vee-Jay, who got her the single "Please Please Me" (A side) and "Ask Me Why" (B side), which we listened to so many times that it's all scratchy. But now we'll have a brand-new record: an LP with twelve whole songs on it. We're going to be in heaven in just an hour, listening to the album at my house. We're very excited.

Until we see her father's car coming up Wiltshire Lane, nosing up to the stop sign. We scramble into the bushes. If he sees us, he'll want to give us a ride. We want to go on the bus by ourselves. We're practically grown-up, both just turned twelve, and if anyone from school saw us getting a ride into the city in some parent's car, it would be humiliating.

I love Paul and she loves George, but we both love the Beatles. I don't tell her that I love Paul more than the Beatles. More than anything in the world, including Scarlett, my cocker spaniel, who I've always loved more than anything in the world. Until now.

Paul McCartney, what can I say? He's everything to me. I have posters of his face covering the walls of my purple bedroom. My parents were mad when they discovered I'd mounted them with Scotch tape, but once the damage was done, they let the photos stay. So Paul's the last thing I see every night, the first thing every morning. I visit him in my dreams whenever I can make that happen. I try every night, picturing him in my mind and my thoughts right before I fall asleep, but it doesn't usually work. So I pretend.

Paul looks at me with those beautiful, rich eyes, full of pride that he's with a girl like me. He loves me so deeply, so fully, that he can barely breathe. And I feel just the same about him. We don't need to talk; just staring into each other's eyes is enough for us. He writes song after song attesting to his devotion. One's even in French. He calls me *Michelle* because it rhymes with *belle*, which I think is so cute.

Yesterday in science class—which is boring, boring, boring—Mr. Thayer was lecturing us about covalent bonds or some such gobbledygook that I'll never ever have any use for, when he finally said something interesting. It seems that the air we breathe is made up of molecules that get rearranged and then reused by other people when we

32

exhale. This happens over and over all over the world throughout history. He said we might even be breathing in air that was once breathed by Napoleon or even Moses.

I raised my hand, and Mr. Thayer looked surprised, as I hardly ever, maybe never, raise my hand.

"So this would happen a lot between people living at the same time, right?" I asked. "Breathing each other's molecules?"

"Yes," he said, clearly pleased. "That's right."

"Even if they were way across the ocean from each other?"

A wide grin split his pudgy face. "Right again. Good thinking. Although it's not as likely as breathing the same molecules as one of your classmates, because of photosynthesis and wind currents and travel and other phenomena, it's quite possible."

"So I might be breathing in the exact same molecules Paul McCartney breathed yesterday!" I cried, thrilled to my core.

Mr. Thayer didn't look pleased anymore. He rolled his eyes. "Let's get back to the bonds between nitrogen, oxygen, and other gases, shall we?"

So, last night before I went to sleep, I stared at my favorite picture of Paul, both his hands raised at ear level, palms facing out, fingers dancing in a playful way. His eyes were focused on something off to the side, and I knew they were looking right at me. Usually I kiss this picture, but instead I pressed my nose to his adorable one and breathed him in. Then I exhaled so that he'd have a chance to share my molecules, too.

The bus finally comes, and we clamber onboard, giggling about how we fooled her father and saved our reputation. We talk about nothing but Paul and George on the ride into the city. Well, maybe a little bit about John—who Maggie thinks is very intellectual, but whom we both dismiss because he's old and married—and Ringo, who's so ugly he's almost cute.

Maggie takes piano lessons, and her mother plays the cello, so she thinks she knows more about music than me. She's always talking about George's phrasing on the guitar, what a true genius he is at the instrument. I counter that Paul plays guitar, but she makes a face and tells me I don't know what I'm talking about, that Paul plays the bass guitar, which isn't even a guitar.

I don't get why it's called a guitar if it's not one, so I tell her that Paul's much cuter than George, which she can't deny. Our differences are forgotten as soon as the bus stops on Main Street, right across from G. Fox & Co., the biggest department store in the whole city. Probably the whole state.

We climb down to the sidewalk and link our arms. People bustle around us: men in suits, and women dressed up for a day of shopping, most wearing short white gloves and high heels. We don't even glance in the windows at G. Fox or those at Sage-Allen or Kresge's.

We march down Main Street and take a left on Asylum. The record store is on the next corner. We grin at each other. We're going to have the new Beatles album in our hands in mere minutes. My heart's pounding as if I just ran the six-hundred-yard dash the stupid gym teacher makes us do in the fall. I can't run the whole way and always come in with the last handful of stragglers. Running's hard.

But loving Paul McCartney isn't hard at all. As we approach the record store, we see a poster of the Beatles in the front window. It's the album cover. We stop in our tracks, clutch each other, take in quick breaths. Against a beige background, there they are, almost life-size in brown suits with pink shirts. *Introducing…. The Beatles, England's No 1 Vocal Group*, right on the other side of the glass. We rush into the store.

There's a stack of albums on the counter, and we each grab one. Then we rush back to the bus stop to get to my house as soon as possible. I don't have my own record player, but there's one in the den. Maggie carefully slips the album from the cover. She reverently hands me the record, holding it with her palms on either side of it so as not to touch the grooves. I just as reverently place it on the turntable, lift the arm, and gently drop the needle down.

We listen to the whole thing three times. Then my mother says that's enough, that we have to stop because she's getting a headache. Then and there, I decide I'll babysit that brat Pamela after school five days a week like Mrs. Dunn wants me to, instead of the two I already hate to do. I calculate quickly. In two months, I should have enough for my own record player.

Maggie, of course, likes "Do You Want to Know a Secret" the best because George sings it. And I'm a little jealous, because the lyrics are about whispering in her ear that he's in love with her. But then I listen more closely to my Paul's "P.S. I Love You" and don't care what George says to Maggie anymore. Paul is writing me a letter to send all his love and to remind me that he'll always be in love with me. The whole time we're listening, we're crying, which feels right, but I couldn't tell you exactly why.

Even with all the photos of my Paul in my room, from that moment on I always picture him writing at his desk, sending me love letter after love letter, pining for me as, from the other side of the wide ocean, I pine for him. We plan to marry when he comes to America, although my parents will probably make us wait a few years.

I wake up every morning to my clock radio tuned to WDCR, which plays "A Block of Beatles"—four songs in a row—every hour. Of course, you don't know when in the hour it will be, so I keep it on till the last minute before I have to go to school. When I get home, I turn it right back on and leave it that way until my mother makes me turn it off when I go to sleep.

One day last week, the block was only half over when it was time to go to the bus stop, but I had to hear the whole thing. My mother was yelling at me to put my coat on, and I tried to explain that they might play "P.S. I Love You," our song. My mother got really mad and yelled even louder and told me she was going to take the clock radio away if I didn't turn it off this very minute. The tendons in her neck were sticking out, so I did what she said. I know they played "P.S. I Love You" right after I left, because I didn't hear it for the rest of the week.

Then it's the big night: the Beatles are on *The Ed Sullivan Show*. My father wants to watch one of his dumb shows, so my mother tells me I have to watch Ed Sullivan on the little television in their bedroom. I don't understand why he gets his way all the time, and I never do. The TV in the bedroom is so tiny you can barely see the people, so how am I going to be able to let my Paul know I'm watching him? I tell them I'm going over Maggie's, that her dad said he'd pick me up, but they won't let me because it's a school night. I hate my parents.

"Ladies and gentlemen, the Beatles," Ed Sullivan says with a sweep of his hand. "Let's bring them on."

And then there he is, in the flesh, my Paul, moving and smiling and—*oh, my God!*—singing. With the first words out of his mouth, he tells me to close my eyes and he'll kiss me.

Barbara Shapiro has loved Paul McCartney since the days of Beatlemania she shared with her cousin Becky Berger (left). Barbara narrowly missed seeing the Fab Four live at Shea Stadium in 1965, but made up for it 51 years later in Fenway Park.

I grip the edge of the tall bureau the television sits atop, close my eyes as he requested, press my lips to the screen, and kiss him. "I miss you, too," I tell him. "And I send all my loving to you."

Even if the TV's small, I know he feels my love, that he knows I'm here, waiting for him, loving him. He also knows I cry all the way through the performance, then go to my room to stare at his picture and cry some more.

Maggie cries through the whole show, too, and over the next year we celebrate as their next album, *Meet the Beatles!*, hits number one on the charts, five of their singles hold the top five positions on *Billboard* simultaneously, and the world suddenly understands what we've known all along. We see their movie, *A Hard Day's Night*, seven times. On the day the movie opens, we get up at six o'clock in the morning and take the bus into Hartford to make sure we get into the first show.

But we're not early enough—some girls have been sitting on the sidewalk since midnight—and the line for tickets snakes all the way down Main Street for what looks like miles. It takes three hours to get a ticket for the four o'clock show. We're disappointed but don't really care. A girl behind us has a transistor radio, and WDCR is playing Beatles all day in honor of the movie's release.

And then the worst thing happens. Maggie's father's friend from Vee-Jay—now that I finally have *Introducing.... The Beatles*, I know how it's spelled—gets two tickets to the Beatles concert at Shea Stadium in New York City, and her father says she has to take her cousin Allyn—who ever heard of such a stupid name for a girl?—instead of me.

Maggie begs and begs, but in the end she goes to the concert with Allyn. I stay in my room the whole weekend, listening to Beatles albums, staring at Paul, and moping. My mother comes in and yells at me, tells me it's a beautiful day, and I need to go to the pool with everyone else. But I refuse. She yells some more but finally, disgusted, leaves me at home.

And then the very, very, very worst thing happens, way worse than Shea Stadium. I come home from school and, as I always do, go straight to my room and turn on the radio. I wonder how long it will be before DCR plays a Paul song. Sometimes they play a lot of the Dave Clark Five, who some stupid people think are as good as the Beatles. There's a girl in my Spanish class who says that, and even though we were friends in elementary school, I'm not inviting her to my birthday party. It's going to have a Beatles theme.

But the disc jockey is talking instead of playing. I hate it when they do that. Like, who wants to hear them when you could be hearing Paul? I tune out until I hear the word *Beatles*, and then I'm completely tuned in.

"The two were seen shopping for houses in London!" The DJ's voice is wild with enthusiasm. "The ritzy Saint John's Wood! And we've just got word that they're engaged to be married!"

My first thought is that it must be George or Ringo, because John's already married, and Paul's going to marry me. Ringo's pretty homely, so it probably isn't him. It's George. Poor Maggie's going to be so upset. I rush into the kitchen, unplug the phone, bring it into my room, and shut the door. For my last birthday, my parents gave me a phone jack, which was just what I wanted, but now all they do is threaten to take it out whenever I get less than a B.

I hope Maggie hasn't heard it from the radio. It will be much better for her to hear it from me. Then I'll be able to console her. Maybe my mother will drive me to her house, so I can be there for her in her heartache. But before I can dial her number, the DJ starts talking again.

"Although there has been no official statement, a number of people have confirmed seeing a large diamond ring on Jane's finger! Lucky Jane! So it—"

Jane. My finger freezes above the phone. *Jane Asher.* That girl some people say is dating Paul. Which isn't true; he's only interested in me. His lyrics send me this message every day.

"—looks like hearts are going to be broken all over the world today! Girls, it seems that Paul is taken!"

I feel like someone punched me in the stomach, and I fall forward with a moan, curl myself around the telephone in my lap. *No. No.* This isn't possible. It can't be true.

"We know that Asher was the inspiration for McCartney's 'All My Loving,' as well as 'We Can Work It Out' and 'I'm Looking Through You'! But given this latest news, I'm betting she's the woman behind many more of his love songs!"

I clutch my stomach as the DJ spouts more excited nonsense about how in love the "young couple" is. Then I remember the lyrics to "I'm Looking Through You." The song's about how Jane didn't treat him right and how his love's disappeared because of it. I sit up. The disc jockey is wrong.

The phone rings. It's Maggie, calling to console me. I tell her that it isn't true and explain my reasoning. She's silent for a long time.

"What?" I demand. "What?"

"I'm, I'm just thinking…," she says hesitantly. "What about the words to 'All My Loving'? That he's pretending to kiss her, that he misses her, sending all his love?"

"That was before!" I cry triumphantly. "That came out in '63, and 'I'm Looking Through You' was this year!"

"Ah, Barb, ah, you, you don't think they could have made up since he wrote the song?"

"No."

"There's been confirmation," the disc jockey chortles from my radio and in my ear from Maggie's. "The owner of one of the homes Paul and Jane visited yesterday confirmed they're interested in buying his house. A done deal!"

I burst into tears. Maggie murmurs consoling words, but my heart is broken. Paul isn't going to marry me. He's going to marry someone else. How could this have happened? Now I'm going to be an old maid for the rest of my life. Just like fat Aunt Molly. I wail.

My mother comes running into the room, crouches down next to me, puts her arms around me. "What is it, Barbara? What's wrong, honey?"

I can't speak, so she takes the phone from me. "What happened?" she demands.

When she hears the answer, she thanks Maggie and hangs up. She's nicer to me than I expect, bringing me a glass of water and patting my shoulder while I lie in bed crying. After a few minutes, she gets up and goes to make dinner.

But I don't want any dinner. I don't want to live. I refuse to leave my room, and I hear my parents and brother eating in the kitchen. I cry and cry and cry. My life is ruined. It's over. After they finish eating, my father and brother come to see me. They stand at the foot of the bed, watching me cry.

"Really, Bobsie," my father says. "Don't you want to come and have some dinner?"

"I can't! I'll never eat again. My life is ruined…" I sob with renewed strength. "My Paul's going to marry someone else!"

Then my brother starts to snicker. My father tries not to, but I can see his lips squirming.

"Get out!" I scream at them. "You have no idea of my pain!"

This turns their snickers into full guffaws. I throw a pillow at them, but it misses by a mile. "Get out and shut the door!"

They do, but I hear them laughing even louder on the other side of the door, and I sob even harder than before. No one understands. No one knows. My Paul, my love, my life, is gone from me forever. I will never recover from the loss.

Almost exactly fifty years later, I stand in front of a huge stage in the outfield of Fenway Park. I'm with my husband of thirty-five years. He stands behind me, arms wrapped around my shoulders, chin resting on my head. I kiss his knuckles, press my cheek into his shoulder, still the romantic I became at twelve, forever shaped by my first love.

Paul's singing "P.S. I Love You." I close my eyes, and he sings right to me, just as he did so long ago. When he finishes, he bows, scans the audience, and his eyes catch mine. I gasp when he doesn't look away, that mischievous-little-boy smile on his aging but still handsome face.

Then he points to the full moon hanging above the first-base line, notes how magical it is. I follow his finger, think about how I might be breathing in his molecules this very minute. And if I'm not, at least I know that my Paul and I are watching the very same moon at the very same time.

Love Is the Ultimate Trip

Michelle Soucy

The 1980s were dark times for hair. And for fashion. And for music. I'm not sure what happened to initiate the cultural collapse in judgment; maybe it was a kind of styling-product-fueled rebellion against our hippie-parents' love of all things "natural." But the whole world looked and sounded like it had been aerosol-hair-sprayed into a stiff and angry gloss. Subtlety was dead, or at least in an induced coma. We wore panic-button-red sunglasses that zigzagged off the sides of our heads like lightning bolts. And speaking of lightning bolts, those were also shaved into the buzz-cut hair of the boys in my school.

The clothing we chose to wear was as big as we could possibly get it and still be able to walk, but bunched up and held onto our bodies with fluorescent pink and green belts—many, many belts. Our fingernails, too, were painted in bright neon and sometimes enhanced with polka dots or, again, lightning bolts, giving the appearance of poisonous insects living on the ends of our fingertips.

And our hair, dear God, our hair. Perms like the summit of K2. Mohawks, spray-painted blue and purple. Rattails. Ducktails. Bangs that we burned into layers with our curling irons and bent upside down to hair-spray into what looked like a wild turkey's fanned tail feathers. When I look through old photo albums at my parents' house now, I feverishly flip past the photos of the '80s, pretending that couldn't really be me … no, no, ha-ha, no. But when no one else is looking, I flip back and sneak a peek, because my early-teen face really was quite sweet and doll-like. But you could barely notice it under that maniacally hair-sprayed mane. So, yeah, the '80s were a dark time, so dark that I was desperately compelled to dig for some light. And so I dug, and I unearthed for myself love … in the form of the Monkees.

It was the Monkees who saved me from the '80s.

While my friends and I drove to the beaches on weekends—Fort Myers, Cape Coral, Sanibel—whisper-crooning our blame of the rain and shouting about being hot for a teacher, or whining that we wanted to feel like a virgin, even though at the time most of us still were, I knew deep within that there had to be something better and more deserving of my ears and my soul. Luckily, my friends and I also kept our televisions constantly tuned to MTV when we were at home. One early-fall night, MTV aired a "Monkees Marathon."

Since it looked like a prime opportunity to make fun of something old—as young '80s teens so enjoyed doing—my good friend Dawn and I, both age fourteen at the time, decided to stay up and watch it. But almost from the first "Hey, hey!" I was totally hooked. Here was true carefree zaniness but with heart and soul like I'd never seen. These four young men stood up for one another, loved one another, and loved the world in which they lived. They sang about being the young generation, about having something to say. Yeah, right on! The happy, carnival-like colors, the playful clothing, the music full of life and meaning. The exaggerated—but totally full of wit—burlesque-tradition jokes ("You're standing on my foot!" "She's/He's/It's/They're gone!") ("You serve crabs?" "We serve anybody!") and "I'm working on my doctor's thesis." "Why can't your doctor work on his own thesis?") were brand new to us. And the Monkees spread sweetly absurd slogans like "Save the Texas Prairie Chicken," "Who Turned on the Dark?," "Age Only Matters If You're Cheese," and other messages of love that really meant something monumental to my teenage self.

The bottom line for me was that the Monkees didn't protest life, they celebrated it. By the morning after the Monkees Marathon, I emerged from Dawn's family's TV room a new young woman. I straightened my hair and wore it long, flowing, and natural. I went straight out and bought fawn-colored leather moccasin-boots that laced all the way up my legs (and wore them until I began to have problems with my ankles). I wore paisley, and denim, and a colorful guitar strap as a headband, and I handed out daisies to people in the hallways at school. I flashed the peace sign, spreading the message that "Love is the Ultimate Trip!" I pinned "Sock it to me!" and "Can you dig it?" buttons to my grungy denim jackets and wore beaded peace-symbol jewelry that I handcrafted myself (because such items weren't as available then as they are now). The Monkees opened up life for me—and layers of living.

From The Monkees, I went on to explore the Beatles (who inevitably blew the Monkees out of the water for me, but that's a story for another time), the Who, Pink Floyd, the Kinks, the Doors, Donovan, Led Zeppelin, Jimi Hendrix, Frank Zappa, and on and on and onto Joni Mitchell and James Taylor and Simon & Garfunkel. Who knew there was this whole vast, immense world out there of great music and philosophy for living? My friends, still stuck in the glossy, angry, hair-sprayed '80s, made fun of me. Some called me "Micky" (for Dolenz), which actually pleased me greatly, and my new "hippie" hair was the laughingstock of my school, but I didn't give up; I could never go back to the way I was prior to the Monkees. Life, for me, was groovy. I was digging it. I had the Monkees and their whole freedom-loving generation behind me. It was as if the world was demanding, "Will the real Michelle Soucy please stand up?" and I could answer, "I *am* standing up."

After I graduated from high school, though, the world and its brutal realities began to infiltrate. I moved out, moved four hours away from home to college in Orlando. My first years of college saw the Gulf War, the 1993 World Trade Center bombing, and OJ fleeing in his white Ford Bronco. I struggled with rent to pay and food to buy and car insurance, health insurance (or lack thereof), tuition, medical bills, taxes.

Dark holes, somehow, were everywhere. My Dodge Omni had a hole in the floor into which frogs would climb and travel slimily up my legs while I was driving. I had cavities in my teeth that I could not afford to have filled. Loved ones passed away, and I was unable to fund my airfare to their funerals. Life suddenly was not so groovy. Life was harsh and scary, and I was all on my own. I waited tables to put myself through college—attending school during the days and working every night, with never a vacation day.

To handle the stress of the days, my server friends and I would take a good deal of the money we made waiting tables every night and spend it at the lightless, seedy bars that were open all night in downtown Orlando. I was dating too many, too-much-older-than-me, too not-good-for-me men. I wore too-short, too-tight skirts and shirts. My skin grew paler, my hair darker from lack of daylight. I rarely slept; I drank more than I ate. In school, I was reading Milton and siding with the devil, reading *Native Son* and rooting for Bigger, and reading Hobbes and agreeing that life was nasty, brutish, and short.

When my friend Dawn, still living in Fort Myers, called me one night to insist that I drive down the very next day for the chance to meet Davy Jones, I scoffed, drinking a Michelob Light and turning up my R.E.M. cassette tape. I was too busy, too tired, too broke for such childish nonsense. She insisted. She begged. It was Davy. Davy Jones! Hardly any tickets had been sold yet; we had the chance to get right up close to the stage and maybe meet him. I sighed and looked through the piles of dollar bills scattered around my room from waiting tables. I supposed I had enough money for gas and a concert ticket. But could I really afford to waste it on seeing a washed-up old lounge-act hippie? It wasn't like it was going to be *Davy* Davy—the cute, dreamy, angel-faced boy from the TV show. I'd seen photos of him recently … he had a perm and … a mullet. His leathery-tan face was wrinkly and worn. No, the concert would be pathetic and sad … the stage was a place for young men, young musicians. Davy should leave it to them. These were the dark, plaid, grungy '90s, and we didn't have room for happy, smiling people. But Dawn begged me. She promised me the best day ever. I hadn't seen my friend for at least a year, so, okay, I decided I'd just go and get it over with.

I wore heavy platform sandals, short denim shorts, and an equally short halter top, and drove from the Orlando sunshine down into the even hotter, brighter south Florida sunshine. It was the end of September, so the heat had not broken yet. Dawn and her sister Misty were waiting for me, jumping up and down inside the grassy arena, wearing their Monkees T-shirts. I approached them, slow and cool in my black Wayfarer sun-

Michelle Soucy (right) and her friend Misty Gehly meet Davy Jones in Ft. Myers, Florida, in 1994. As a teenager in the 1980s, Michelle Soucy discovered The Monkees on TV re-runs. She now lives and writes in Bolton, Massachusetts.

glasses, smelling of clove cigarettes. Clearly, I was the coolest, deepest person there. The crowd was made up of middle-aged women (the teens of Davy's generation) and families and random groups of '80s MTV Monkees fans like us. Or like what I used to be. I let Dawn and Misty hug and pet me, their cool friend who'd gone off to the big city and who'd returned dark, bitter, and so very deep. I leaned on the handrail set up in front of the stage, without removing my sunglasses, and sighed. I wanted to get this silly thing over and done so we could go somewhere and drink.

People, I realized, were already screaming for Davy. I looked around. Yeah, they were screaming hard for Davy. They were jumping up and down, totally jubilant. Mouths open, hands in hair, pulling. They waved signs: "We LOVE you, Davy!" "Marry me, Davy!" *Wow.* Just like the signs they used to wave when Davy was a young pop idol. Dawn and Misty still bounced up and down next to me. But I realized they were jumping around for Davy, not because they were excited I had arrived. *Huh.* I stood up straighter, feeling a tingle. *Huh.* Davy actually really was here somewhere. Behind stage somewhere. Ready to come out and be here, in front of us. I held my hand against my tingling belly, listening to the screams. Davy would be right in front of us. Feet away from us. In person. Davy. Davy Jones.

I thought about the countless hours I'd spent watching the Monkees on VHS, listening to their records, reading about them in books and magazines. I remembered my room in high school, completely wallpapered with posters and magazine pullouts of Davy. I thought about the Monkees, how their records had outsold the Beatles and the Rolling Stones combined, how they had changed pop culture forever. My belly fluttered and flipped. My heart jumped and throbbed. I stared at the stage, where he'd be in a mere moment. Davy Jones. My Davy Jones.

And then, a large bearded man came out on the stage, waving his arms and talking about the day, the event, the venue. I couldn't even pay attention to him. I wanted Davy. I wanted the large man gone, and I wanted Davy there in front of me. The crowd heaved, jumping, screaming. I jumped, I screamed. The crowd chanted. I chanted. "Da-vy, Da-vy!"

And then—there he was. Oh, my God, there he was. Walking out onto the stage, smiling. No mullet, but a nice, clean, short haircut. Black T-shirt and casual jeans. Waving, smiling. Davy. With that infamous glint of almost impossible excitement for life in his eyes and his wide, beautiful smile. Davy! Looking just like he always did. Sure, okay, if someone had taken a photo of him at that moment they'd think, maybe, that he looked something more like an aging Michael Douglas—but not for us, in that moment, watching him walk, smiling, onto the center of the stage. For us, he was the twenty-two-year-old Davy Jones of the Monkees. Here, it was 1967, and we were all happy and loving. Here was Davy and we loved him. And he was smiling and waving: He loved us back.

And when Davy opened his mouth to sing, it was even more. It was more than time travel … it was maybe the first and only time I'd ever seen a purely talented showman. Davy was the consummate performer, a true entertainer. He appeared endlessly surprised and thrilled by the lyrics he sang, even though I knew he'd sung them thousands of times, after forty years in show business. But he never tired, never hesitated. Between songs, he'd joke though; he knew this was pop music, not rocket science. He didn't take himself seriously; he only told us, and showed us, that this was a time for us to let our hair down and have fun. He was like a light, and all of the crowd pushed toward him, attracted, as if by a physical pull, to that light. Davy's voice was as perfect and clear as ever, and his eyes genuinely sparkled. And all of us in the crowd, our eyes sparkled, too, like Davy's love interests from the old Monkees TV episodes, with white and silver cartoon stars popping from their eyes. Like magic. Davy was like magic.

Toward the end of the show, Davy announced that in the crowd there was a birthday girl who shared the name of one of his most famous Monkees songs, "Valleri." A woman pointed maniacally at the head of her young, perhaps ten-year-old daughter, nodding and laughing. Davy hopped right off the stage into the crowd and swooped the little girl in his arms, like a real-life Prince Charming. He sang "Valleri" to the birthday girl, dancing with her while he sang. He was a charmer, a ham, a true and wonderful ham.

Davy kissed the little girl's cheek and set her down as the opening piano chords of "Daydream Believer" began to twinkle from the stage. We screamed even louder than we had throughout the rest of the show. Davy walked in front of the crowd, singing the opening lines, and we all sang along loudly and happily. Then I heard Davy saying, cheekily, "Who knows the words? Who knows the words?" pointing at us. Davy walked along the edge of the crowd, closer and closer, and stopped in front of me, then moved next to me, still singing. And I was also singing. He pushed up next to me while the crowd yelled and pawed at him. He was just my height, maybe a little shorter. His face was smooth and tan, his singing teeth were white. He tipped the microphone near my lips, and I heard him say to me, "Do you know the words to this song?" I leaned to sing into the microphone about Sleepy Jean and a homecoming queen, while Davy grinned and nodded along, snapping the fingers of his free hand. Up close, his coffee-brown eyes glittered just as brilliantly as they did from a distance. He leaned his head close to mine, sharing the microphone, singing with me. And I lifted my hand, put my hand beneath his on the microphone. Davy slid his hand down so it covered mine. Davy's hand was covering mine, tightly. I knew I was singing; we were singing together. We sounded I realized, good together. I looked at Davy's youthful, tanned arms, his wrists, his pulsing triceps. There were cameras everywhere, people taking photos, videos, and also camera crews from the local news stations. I knew I was singing. I was with Davy Jones and we were singing. Smiling at each other and singing. I didn't know, or need to know, anything else. But I was with Davy, and we were singing.

I don't remember getting from that moment to the line in which we waited for Davy to sign our books, albums, and photos. I know it happened, because I do remember meeting him again in line and spluttering a feeble, "Thank you! I love you!" as he signed a photo and T-shirt for me. But what I remember clearly from that day is the purity, the joy. Dawn and Misty jumped on me, hugged me, pointed at me. "We told you it would be the best day ever!" And the sun was shining on us, the grass was green, the sky was blue and white with clouds. I wasn't thinking about money problems, health problems, work, or school. I'd just taken part in true and pure joy. I realized the Monkees had again helped me move out of darkness, if maybe only for a day. But I knew it was a day that would last. I felt awake again that day. I felt love, I felt light.

Nothing, as they say, is like the first time. The first loss, that is. And for me, that loss took place when I was sitting at work on a dark and bleak New England afternoon in February, and my phone lit up with a text from a friend that read only: "Davy Jones? Noooooooo!" It's hard to explain to those who haven't experienced it the surreal sensation of discovering your first big celebrity crush has died. It's like a little earthquake in your mind, in your heart. And suddenly, everything is different. Everyone is different, every place is different. You are changed. The world is changed. Life and death are changed. And there's no going back to the way things were before.

In those moments after knowing of Davy's death, I remembered my mother, a massive Elvis fan, rushing past me in my grandmother's kitchen when I was a child, covering her face with her palm, crying. *Crying.* My parents never wept in front of their children. But Elvis, the television had just announced, had died—and my mother had "discovered" Elvis before he'd made it big, you see. I remember thinking, as a kid, "Why is she crying? She didn't even know him." But we do know them, don't we? Or at least, we know what we want to know of them. We take of and from these celebrities what we want, what helps us, fills us, lifts us. We ignore and forgive and disbelieve the negative. We take and keep and hold on to the positive and what we want to plug into the holes of our own lives. Other artistic heroes of mine had been gone before I'd gotten into them—John Lennon, namely. But for my lifetime up to that point, Davy Jones had always been alive, walking the earth. The height of his popularity occurred years before I was born, but Davy Jones had been a constant in my life, and now he was gone. It wasn't like losing a person, really, it was more like finding out *pi* is no longer infinite, or Saturn's rings are gone. A constant, a part of the fabric of the earth, had vanished. All of my life, there was this wonderful person, Davy Jones, so full of life and light, who was always out there and always would be. But ... wrong. Davy died. As we will all die.

That February afternoon, I had texted and e-mailed a few friends, including my friends from the Davy Jones concert in Fort Myers twenty years earlier. We lamented via text, shared our disbelief. I told my friend Dawn I would call her on my way home from work. But every time I grabbed my cell phone to call her, I couldn't do it. I wasn't ready. I couldn't believe or accept that Davy was gone. It was as if discussing his death would make it real. When I got home, I talked to my husband, asked him about deaths of celebrities we loved. For him, the biggie was Joey Ramone, whom he had met and hung out with in person.

"There's something different about losing a celebrity when you've met in person," my husband said, recalling.

"Because we feel like we're closer to them? We feel like we have more of a right to them?"

"Mmm, I don't know. It's more ... because we like them as a person, too. As a real person. We like their music, but now we like who they are in real life, too."

Certainly that was how I felt about Davy Jones, too. I'd always hoped, imagined, that he was a cool, funny, genuine guy, along with being a monumentally talented entertainer. And when we sang together that day under the sweet Florida sunshine, Davy had been cool, funny, genuine, and monumentally talented. I realized upon his passing how apt is the expression "star" when referring to celebrities. Rock star, movie star, pop star. Davy Jones was most definitely a star. He was a light in the universe. Those twinkly cartoon sparkles that the makers of *The Monkees* series animated in front of Davy's eyes when he would fall hopelessly in love with yet another groovy damsel in distress were not so jokey as they seemed. There was a perpetual spark in Davy's eyes; you can see it from the very earliest photos and videos of pre-teen Davy as the Artful Dodger on Broadway all the way to his last concerts and interviews. It was a light of joy for living, and, as a fan, you want in on that light. And you feel it, a physical thing, when that kind of light goes out. The loss of Davy brought to my mind what Gene Wilder says as Willy Wonka: "So shines a good deed in a weary world." But with the loss of Davy Jones, his light was gone, and the cold, dark, weary world was left behind.

That week of Davy's passing, I watched interviews of the other Monkees' reactions to Davy's passing and was underwhelmed by the restraint of their comments: Micky Dolenz's "I remember him playing soccer," and "He was a jokester"; and Peter Tork's "I have a lot of affection and respect for all of those guys, in different ratios." Mike Nesmith's cryptic public statement at once irritated and calmed me: "I will miss him, but I won't abandon him to mortality. I will think of him as existing within the animating life that insures existence."

Okay…? I guessed maybe I agreed. Although I will admit I had to read the sentence several times to try to decide. Some online advice I read regarding coping with loss of a hero said to "Replace that hero." Replace Davy? Replace the irreplaceable? Well, that, too, didn't seem quite fitting advice. So I turned to other celebrities' comments on loss to help find some acceptance of Davy's.

There was an interview I saw of Yoko Ono from the year that would have been John Lennon's seventieth, when the interviewer asked her if she still felt a connection with John, and she replied adamantly, "Yes, we're together still." Together still. Okay, that was more like it for me. I could still and always revisit Davy on DVD, reruns, video, CD, iPod, and always in my heart.

When the remaining Monkees toured, just a few months after Davy died, instead of anyone in the band singing Davy's "Daydream Believer," they simply played the music and let the audience sing the lyrics. Micky Dolenz told the audience, "We can't sing this song anymore—" meaning himself, Peter Tork, and Mike Nesmith. "It doesn't belong to us anymore, it belongs to you."

Davy's music does belong to all of his fans now, and we're eternally thankful to him for sharing his talent, love, and life with us. We have to keep holding on to the comfort of knowing we've managed to be alive on the planet the same time as all the celebrities we love. Entertainers, artists, powerful spirits like Davy Jones lived full, incredible lives, and we truly loved them. And we still and will always have their music, love, and light.

We live; we learn that in life, change is the only constant. We may not be able to replace our heroes exactly, but we can honor what they left behind, for us and within us, of themselves. We have to remember their humanity, their adventures, their pain, their joy, their stories. We have to read their books, live by their philosophies, sing their songs, dance to their music. We have to be daydream believers. And we have to believe that we are, all of us, together still.

Editors' Note: Michelle dedicates this essay to her mother Rosemary, who passed away during production of this anthology, and who "discovered" Elvis, and to whom Michelle gave her word that she would, finally, start submitting her fiction, of which there is much, waiting to be read.

Meeting Mark Lindsay

A Story of Friends and Fandom

AMY ROGERS

We tore out the portrait pages from *Tiger Beat* magazine and pieced them together, seven across and seven down, into a quilt of pop-star faces we taped to my bedroom wall. Mark Lindsay, lead singer from Paul Revere and the Raiders, always occupied the prime position at eye level in the center of the right-hand row, closest to my pillow.

His thick, brown bangs covered his forehead, allowing his dark brows to peek out just a little. His chocolate eyes made me melt inside, and his juicy lower lip glistened tantalizingly. But all of that was secondary to the fact he had a *ponytail*. No one else had one, not even the mop-top Beatles.

The wall was a lot of upkeep for two junior-high girls in 1968. My best friend, Robin, and I would pedal our bikes to the newsstand in our town on Long Island, buy the magazines each month, devour the stories, and carefully cut out the full-page photos. A fresh portrait of Mark would mean we had to rearrange everything. I'd slide over Davy Jones of the Monkees and bump down TV star Bobby Sherman, making sure not to disturb the rest of Mark's band on the bottom row. Not that we didn't love band namesake Paul Revere, but with his blond hair and toothy grin, he was as goofy and familiar as a kid brother. There was nothing mysterious or romantic about Paul. Still, I didn't want to hurt his feelings.

We loved the silly Revolutionary War costumes the band sported. Of course, we weren't so shallow that we didn't genuinely appreciate the music. We adored it. Several songs made it into *Billboard*'s Top Ten, so we weren't alone. We swooned when Mark growled his way through "Hungry," promising his woman he'd break the rules if that was what it would take to give her a sweet life. We sang along with the plaintive "Him or Me—What's It Gonna Be?" as we tried to imagine what kind of idiot girl would even think of throwing over Mark for another guy. The band could get topical, too. They never mentioned drugs in the song "Kicks," but we understood the secret language when Mark warned his girl she'd better get straight before it was too late.

"Hi, it's Robin," my best friend would greet me as I answered the phone for our nightly call. I'd sit on the worn, vinyl floor and twirl the coiled cord from the kitchen wall-phone while we obsessed over boys—real ones and celebrities.

Robin was worldly, curvy, stylish, and sexy. She had a boyfriend. She knew all the words to the show tunes on Broadway, and she loved to belt out "Cabaret." She was gregarious and fearless. I was her opposite in almost every way: scrawny, shy, with stick-straight hair. Her glamorous mom stayed home while Robin's dad worked. My dad was a thousand miles away in Florida while my mom worked in New York City in the office of a fashion designer on Seventh Avenue.

Robin taught me how to wear lipstick and part my hair in the middle so I'd look more like the cool girls. We sewed patches on our jeans, painted our bikes with glow-in-the-dark paint, and made hippie jewelry with beads. We plundered thrift shops for vintage clothes. She could draw a silhouette of Mark from behind, with tight jeans and his iconic ponytail. We started using it as code to sign the notes we'd pass at school.

We tuned in every Saturday to watch *Happening*, a rock 'n' roll TV variety show Mark and Paul co-hosted. *Tiger Beat* and our other favorite, *16* magazine, cunningly ran stories about fans who met their favorite stars, either by accident or by winning contests.

Mark's birthday was March 9, which made him a Pisces and a perfect match for me, a Scorpio. We were both water signs. Robin was an Aries, which was fire. Everyone knew that love could never blossom when water puts out fire. That was my only advantage with Mark. Robin decided we'd make the world's biggest birthday card for Mark and send it to him. That would guarantee he'd mention us on his show. We taped nine sheets of poster board together into a huge, floppy square and began to embellish it. It was going to take some time.

We both stumbled along, learning to play a couple of cheap guitars our mothers bought us. I took some lessons from an older neighborhood girl and could easily manage "This Land Is Your Land" and "Michael, Row the Boat Ashore." Robin stunned everyone when she learned "The Impossible Dream," the complicated showstopper full of minor

Robin Feinberg (left) came from New York to visit her friend Amy Rogers in Florida in the early 1970s. Both idolized Mark Lindsay. Today Amy writes for WFAE, the NPR affiliate in Charlotte.

chords and sevenths from *Man of La Mancha*. She talked me into performing it with her once or twice. I've forgotten most of the embarrassing details that made me willing to march into that particular hell with her.

As new bands arrived on the scene in the 1970s, Paul Revere and the Raiders got less and less airplay on the mainstream AM radio stations, and none on FM, where underground and hard-rock bands like the raw and raucous Led Zeppelin were exploding into popularity with kids who protested the Vietnam War and experimented with drugs. Clean-cut bands like ours weren't cool. It was so unfair. Mark had already sung about drugs in 1967.

Robin decided we'd call the radio stations and demand they play the Raiders. We tried disguising our voices to make ourselves sound older. "If they just heard the music and didn't know, they'd play it," she explained to me. She was right. Using the pseudonym "Pink Puzz," the band sent an album to an L.A. station where unwitting DJs did play it.

By then, I was discovering James Taylor and Joni Mitchell, folk singers who pushed past the three-chord song structure into sophisticated compositions. Deceptively happy lyrics about fire and rain and big yellow taxis hinted at deeper yearnings a fifteen-year-old couldn't articulate. This music opened a window into what I was beginning to feel, so I climbed in and abandoned my childish worship of a ponytailed pop singer. I bought a music book with tablature charts of *Sweet Baby James* and immersed myself in trying to learn Taylor's elegant finger-picking. Robin gravitated to Barry Manilow, Bette Midler, and other heavily produced mainstream acts.

In 1971, I had to dismantle the photo wall when my family moved to Miami. I was a tenth-grade loner thrown into a sea of beach-going, sun-loving kids who drove Camaros and Firebirds. Back on Long Island, Robin panhandled quarters in the high-school cafeteria. When she got enough to buy a plane ticket, she sent for me. Several times after that, her parents allowed her to visit me, and our friendship continued as best it could.

The next part of the story is typical. We drifted apart, mostly because we no longer had anything in common. She went to college in New York; I went to work in Florida. In the early 1980s, a concert promoter hired me as a caterer's assistant. I cooked for Frank Zappa, Jeff Beck, Art Garfunkel, Little Feat, and other touring acts. I made it through several years of college, married, and after landing in North Carolina, eventually became a journalist.

Robin earned a master's degree, married, and raised three remarkable children, and spent decades working in education, where she taught and inspired countless kids in New York. In 2000, she sent me a New Year's card with a photo of her family all dressed in matching denim overalls. In 2004, I published a cookbook and sent her a copy.

When my marriage ended, having produced no children of my own, I sometimes wondered aloud if I'd contributed much to the betterment of the world. A kind friend replied that she saw in me a great capacity and gift for friendship. If that was true, I knew where I'd learned it.

One day in 2013, the phone rang and there she was. "Hi, it's Robin," she said, in the same voice I'd heard hundreds of times back when we were girls. She was passing through Charlotte on her way to Chapel Hill, where her youngest child was enrolled.

"Where are you?" I asked. "Stay right there. I'm coming over."

Within ten minutes, we were rummaging in a funky boutique and digging for beads, just as if more than thirty years hadn't gone by.

I insisted on driving her over to see the little house I was fixing up, and noticed she was wearing a truly giant diamond solitaire. "That's for surviving breast cancer," she explained matter-of-factly. I gasped, ashamed that I hadn't known. She had endured months of grueling treatments and their miserable side effects, and I'd never even bothered to send a perfunctory holiday card to my oldest friend in the world.

We promised we would reconnect in real life, and we did. In the next year and a half, I visited Robin three times. We careened our bikes around the beach like kids again and scoured the thrift shops of Cape Cod for vintage trinkets on the Fourth of July. She threw a sixtieth birthday bash for her husband, Barry, at the famed Rock 'n' Bowl in New Orleans, and the couple got up on stage to dance while wearing the burgundy team bowling shirts Robin had bought for us all (plus matching lipsticks for the ladies). That summer, she and I and spent a lazy Labor Day at her pool after the entire family helped one of her daughters move into a Brooklyn walk-up apartment. We were listening to "Under Pressure," the catchy Queen-David Bowie collaboration from 1981. I'd heard it countless times in clubs and on the radio, but had somehow never quite recognized its elegant demand for justice and love in world that "puts people on streets."

"I think this is the most important song of our generation," Robin said. At fifty-nine, she was still proclaiming her faith in humanity and her devotion to the power of popular music.

It was all such glorious, good fun. But Robin's cancer had come back, and it was relentless. She continued treatment despite the odds against it helping much, even as she grew more and more debilitated. At Christmas, the family went on a Florida vacation that had to be cut short. By February, she was gone.

Near the end, I told Robin what my friend in North Carolina had said about my capacity for friendship. "I want you to know that I learned everything I know about it from you," I said. "And I can never repay you for that."

Without missing a beat, she replied, "Did it ever occur to you that I learned it from *you?*"

Somewhere along the way, Robin did finish making the world's biggest birthday card, and she sent it to her Teen Idol, I think. And she did finally meet Mark Lindsay in person; of this I am certain. I want to say that I remember her showing me a photo of their meeting, but it's possible I only imagine it exists.

A couple of nights ago, I googled "Paul Revere and the Raiders" to fact-check my teenage memories. It was all there: thumbnails of the magazine covers, publicity photos of the band in their kitschy Colonial garb, the deep discography and long list of member changes. Ironically, the squeaky-clean band that wasn't cool enough for FM radio drew interest from punk artists in the 1980s. The Sex Pistols covered "(I'm Not Your) Steppin' Stone," and Joan Jett recorded a version of "Just Like Me."

Mark Lindsay had gone out on his own in the 1970s and had several hits. He worked as a producer and was making appearances as of 2017. His hair is still dark, but he no longer wears a ponytail. He is married. He turned seventy-six years old on March 9, 2018.

Paul Revere, founder of the band that survived more than forty years, died in 2014. Davy Jones of the Monkees is gone, too; he died back in 2012. As of this writing, Bobby Sherman is still with us.

Sometimes I wonder how many other faces from my photo wall we've lost, but I don't actually want to know the number. Eventually it will be all of them. All of *us*: musicians and fans, mothers and daughters, and once-young girls who became friends for life. Until then, let's promise each other we'll never stop riding bikes, wearing lipstick, and singing the songs that bring us joy, whether it's from Broadway, *Billboard*, or any place else we discover the true music in our hearts.

Editors' Note: A version of this essay appeared previously on sheknows.com. Reprinted by permission of the author.

Bogie and the Boys

Humphrey Bogart and Bobby Sherman

Elizabeth Searle

Bobby

Before Bogie, there were only boys. Before I discovered long-dead Humphrey Bogart on late-night TV, brooding into his cigarette smoke with his darkly glinting eyes; before I read nine Bogart biographies in one year and penned my own Bogie-inspired first "novel" titled *Blood and Lipstick*; before my sister and I stood in round-mouthed, lip-glossed awe inside the bedroom in Ohio where Bogart and Bacall had honeymooned, I hung back from those real-life beings known as boys.

The pimply boys at school with their blow-dried '70s hair and lazy gazes scared me. A group of them had followed me down the school hall in South Carolina, where I was a shunned new girl from up North. Those boys couldn't see my own pimples and stop-sign-shaped glasses, only my blue jeans with the colorful patches sewn on the back pockets.

"Hey girl, hey girl," they mumbled, but I was scared to turn around, scared I'd find they were making fun of me, like the girls who trailed me in the halls calling, "Hey, Elizabeth, hey—" in fake-friendly Southern voices until I'd say, "Hey," shyly back in my stiff Yankee accent and they'd dissolve in derisive giggles.

No wonder the only boy I dared to gaze at was the one on my cereal box. Sunny Bobby Sherman with his honeyed brown hair, his tan, blandly handsome face and sly, let's-go-surfing grin. He was kind of cute. He had a cleft in his chin like one that ran in my family. Jaggedly, I cut Bobby's round "record" off the candy-colored Raisin Bran cardboard. Why, I wondered, with the pang of pity I often felt for puppies in pounds, was poor Bobby Sherman stuck on a cereal box?

His clunky cardboard records barely fit the stylus on the turntable and spun lopsidedly, yet they played. sunshine melodies, including "Hey, Mister Sun." Plus a song that could have been an anthem for me, with my family's multiple moves: "The New Girl at School." And the song whose main title was "La La La." On TV, crooning "Easy Come, Easy Go," Bobby swayed his hips hypnotically. My sister and I rocked to Bobby's boyish voice, his soothingly repetitive beats: Julie, Julie, Julie, did she love him?

Nobody loved me. Well, my family did, but they didn't count. I loved them too, but I hated how they'd uprooted us from our friendly neighborhood in Pennsylvania to the wilds of Greenville, South Carolina, where our cat Cleopatra was shot dead on our front lawn. I slumped my daydreamy way into middle school: skinny and bucktoothed and hiding behind long brown hair, so oily I shampooed it daily. Whiffs of my Herbal Essence shampoo comforted me in the stale school halls.

Boys back then had their own fanatically shampooed hair—like Bobby, his lush, neatly layered hairdo tousled in a sculpted way. Decades later, he was hailed on *The Simpsons* as the epitome of "nonthreatening" handsomeness. Bobby's eyes had a daydreamy glaze, too, whenever he shook back his long, but not shaggy bangs. Sun-kissed Bobby: Mr. Sun himself.

"I think I love you," Bobby rival David Cassidy warbled. I *did* think maybe I loved Bobby S. He reminded me of our family's tail-wagging golden-retriever blend, Nick "the Wonder Dog." And yet. Somewhere—I'd sense as carefree Bobby bopped his glossy-haired head to his catchy guitar beat—there was something more.

In my lonesome teenage nights, I'd read grown-up books on the sly. Books discovered in our dim basement: my mom's Philip Roth paperbacks. I found within those provocative covers something dark and erotic, something beyond guileless, smiling Bobby Sherman. Something to do with men, not boys.

Bogie

Enter Humphrey Bogart. One fateful midnight, my existential junior-brooder gaze snagged another's, an older man's. Staying up late for a babysitting gig, I happened upon *Casablanca*. My sister was dozing on our babysitter family's couch, so that first night it was just us. Me and this sad, striking dude with the noble, craggy face, the thick, manly brows, and those shiny-dark eyes. Were there tears, real tears, in this Tough Guy's gaze as he squinted into his own past—flashback to Paris!—and drew a long, soulful drag on his cigarette? Smoke plus memory-mist blurred his rugged, ugly-handsome features. *Don't go*, I wanted to call out to that compelling, seen-it-all face, as it dissolved into a sexier, happier, younger Bogie-face.

Paris, 1941. A man in love. Emphasis on *man*.

"Here's looking at you, kid," Bogart toasted the radiant Ingrid Bergman with his wolfish grin, his gaze devouring her.

"Who the hell would want to kiss Bogart?" Warner Brothers exec Jack Warner allegedly asked after smarmy Ronald Reagan dropped out as *Casablanca*'s original lead. Ingrid Bergman was said to have replied quietly, "I would."

Bogart, I'd later read, became with *Casablanca* a new kind of antihero hero: a battered guy who actually seemed, unlike the pretty-boy leading men of the '30s, tough enough to face down Nazis. Bogie was no boy. He had—though I didn't yet know this word—gravitas.

Farewell, featherweight '70s crooners with their fluffy, feathered-back hair. Across the decades, I felt an utterly unaccustomed jolt inside me at the animal urgency with which Humphrey Bogart pulled weeping Ingrid Bergman toward him at last for their hungry long-lost-love kiss.

Bogie, oh Bogie! Of all the TV screens in all the world, he walked onto mine. Yes, the man was a dead 1940s movie star, and I was a 1970s teen. But that made my secret flame for him burn more intensely. Only I knew about Humphrey B., with his clunky first name and infamous lisp. The seductive black-and-white noir world of 1940s films was unknown territory to the blonde girls who ruled the pop-rock '70s terrain, where I, with my dark thoughts, felt like an alien being.

It was springtime in South Carolina. Suddenly, I walked the green, buzzing world with a new spring in my own step. I lived for the weekends. Grocery shopping on Saturdays at Winn-Dixie with our mom, I'd seize the new *TV Guide*. I'd slip into an aisle. With trembling fingers, I'd flip to the weekend late-night listings. A Bogart retrospective happened to be running on a Saturday Night Cinema Classics show that spring. Each weekend featured a new Bogart flick that my sister and I stayed up late to watch, savoring even the younger Bogie in his snarling gangster roles, his stepping-stones to *High Sierra*. In that classic, the bony older-Bogart face emerged as if carved in the granite of the boulders Bogie died upon, for once nobly. Falling from his rocky peak, he called out to Ida Lupino and their little dog, making the animal-loving teen me weep.

Bogart himself reminded me—but in a good way!—of a sad-eyed basset hound, mistreated by this world and awaiting my love. In *The Maltese Falcon*, Bogart, as seemingly sleazy detective Sam Spade, thrilled my geeky heart by quoting Shakespeare with his lisp as he hefted the black falcon statuette, muttering to the clueless cops that the bird was "the shtuff dreams are made of…"

My own dreams, both day and night, filled with Bogart. I even practiced kissing my favorite blown-up Bogie photo from one of the oversized old-movie books my sister and I collected—along with a Bogart beach towel and a canvas pillowcase showing Bogie in a black beret. I was photographed holding this pillow up beside my face on Christmas, an identical beret mysteriously perched on my own head. I gave Bogie the kind of sidelong gaze I'd never dared give any real boy at school. Beside this photo in our album, my librarian mother penned: "Bogart love affair."

One problem with loving a long-dead 1940s screen idol: you can't go see him onstage, live, can't screamingly cheer him on in a packed stadium. But, my ever-resourceful sister and I discovered, you can experience your beloved commanding a twenty-foot screen, holding a live audience in thrall.

Bogie and Bacall

What was your first erotic experience? Not first kiss—which sometimes, certainly in my case, isn't all that erotic!—but first bodily experience of sex as a physical force?

For me, it came when viewing with an art-house audience the film that launched the Humphrey Bogart/Lauren Bacall romance and real-life marriage: *To Have and Have Not*. Decades before reality TV, Bogart and Bacall's incendiary "just whistle" scene thrilled audiences (including mine, decades after the fact) by stirring genuine sexual sparks that flared on-screen along with the cigarettes the luminous duo kept lighting.

To Have and Have Not is not only a scintillating romance; it has lots of laughs, too: clever lines delivered with crack comic timing by young yet knowing Bacall. "It's even better when you help," she slurs to Bogart after a breathtakingly long screen kiss. The words electrified my curious teen mind. What exactly felt "even better"? What in the hidden lip-to-lip kiss had Bogie done to "help"? And was the impossibly sultry, husky-voiced Bacall really a teenager like me? Nineteen, anyhow, back in 1945. In the tense, almost reverent silences that accompanied Bogart and Bacall's lingering kisses, the audience and I "got off" together on two real-life lovers heating up our screen.

At the end, we applauded, even hooted and whistled. I'd never enjoyed school pep rallies, but in this musty, buttery-scented cinema, I felt for once at one with a crowd. A rowdy, yet sophisticated college-student-type crowd. Maybe in some foggy, post-high-school future, these could be *my* people, my tribe. I wanted to tell them all how I'd read that young Lauren Bacall had such tremulous hands in her first takes, she kept fumbling the cigarette pack Bogart tossed her. In the take that lives on, Bacall catches the pack perfectly, with a snap. Just as she'd captivated her man, right in front of us. Comfortably crushed together with my newly discovered fellow fans, I exited the theater on weakened knees.

My crush on Bogart morphed that night into a crush on Bogart and Bacall. Lucky for impressionable me, my first role-model romance was one characterized on-screen—and offscreen—by playful banter between equal wits, and ultimately by mutual respect. My first teenage stab at novel-writing, *Blood and Lipstick*, attempted to portray such a romance with an older Bogie-style private detective meeting his young Bacall-esque love match. Both the teen fan and future writer in me researched "B & B" obsessively.

On a car trip through Ohio, my sister and I even convinced our parents to make a detour at Malabar Farm, the unlikely site of Bogart and Bacall's small private 1945 wedding. Our tour of the historic farmhouse included a glimpse of a framed wedding photo of beaming Bogart and "Betty," plus a stop in the old-fashioned guest bedroom that had served as their honeymoon suite. A snapshot captures my shiny-faced amazement as I stood in bell-bottom jeans between the twin beds(!) that must have been pushed together on that night of nights. The prim bedroom itself betrayed no hint of what its flower-wallpapered walls had seen. Our pilgrimage into Bogie and Bacall's bedroom left me hungry to get even closer to the object(s) of my affection.

Though Bogie was dead, Lauren Bacall lived on. Then in her fabulous fifties, Broadway diva Bacall happened to be doing a star-turn tour in 1977 in the musical comedy

Elizabeth Searle during her "Bogart love affair," as her mother called it. Still a fan of Bogie, Elizabeth has authored five books of fiction and scripts for everything from film to rock opera.

classic *Wonderful Town,* playing in St. Louis—near enough to our new home in Louisville, Kentucky, that my sister and I persuaded our indulgent, theater-loving mom to drive us there so we could all see Lauren Bacall onstage, live.

Before the outdoor show, my sister Kate and I spotted a man walking a Cavalier King Charles spaniel we recognized as Bacall's own dog Blenheim (who obligingly posed for Kate's camera). That evening, entranced, we watched Bacall command the stage with her brusquely graceful strides, her giant lipsticked smile, her throaty laugh, and her deep, even more throaty voice. My sister and I cheered like teenyboppers.

Then we waited with a small but determined crowd outside the stage door, stunned when Ms. Bacall finally strode out. Clad in a casually elegant caftan, she moved with her same impatient stage grace. She shook back her ashy-blonde hair, her famous face more lined close-up, but her lipsticked smile—showing slightly crooked teeth!—wide and warm. Bantering with her fans, she signed a program for an eager young man who leaned close to her, Bacall sing-songing, "Just gimme someone to lea-ean on—"

Too stunned to take photos, I stood back as my brash younger sister Kate pushed forward.

> KATE: We drove here all the way from Louisville, Kentucky!
> LAUREN BACALL (bemused): Whatever for?
> KATE AND ME: To see YOU!
> LAUREN BACALL (with a laugh): Well I hope it was worth it…
> KATE AND ME: It WAS!
> (More chatter among the fans, then as Lauren Bacall bade us all farewell and turned to leave, she looked at my awestruck sister and playfully touched Kate's chin).
> LAUREN BACALL (to Kate): And YOU, calm down, child. It's going to be all right.

Post-Bogie: My Man

"Calm down, child," became a famous line in our family, often repeated by our gruff Dad in particular—not that Kate or I ever did learn to calm down. But our encounter with the real, down-to-earth Lauren Bacall did serve as a climax to our Bogie craze, and also as an overdue pushing-off point for my sister and me to—as Bacall wryly hinted—get a life.

Bobby Sherman, I was glad to read as I grew older, found a life beyond teen-idoldom. In his middle years, after suffering actual hearing loss from teenage girls' screams at his concerts, he stepped back from performing. In vintage Sherman clips on YouTube, Bobby informs the audience he is not married. The teen screams are indeed deafening. The older, wiser Bobby Sherman became an Emergency Medical Technician, an expert in CPR, and an advocate for police and health issues. So there had been, under all that hair, something serious, after all. But back in the day, I had sensed no hidden depths to adorable Bobby—even his name was so boyish.

In my actual romances, once they finally commenced, I skipped over "boys" altogether and fell for a guy nearly ten years my senior. Was the love of my life influenced by my primal, years-long crush on Humphrey Bogart? Certainly various brooding, dark-haired, dark-eyed dudes lured me in my early college crushes and practice dates. But I didn't really fall in love till I (at about the same age as young "Betty" Bacall) met at a crowded poetry-reading reception my older man with a noble, bony face, eyes that had seen pain, and a wry, knowing smile.

My future husband—then age twenty-eight, an Oberlin grad working in the Oberlin College library and dancing wildly at the Oberlin disco every night—noticed slim, nineteen-year-old me in my strapless sundress. Right away, I felt something deeply familiar in John's intent yet bemused grown-up gaze. His eyes locked mine, blocking out the college boys chattering around us. "Are you a dancer?" John asked me as his opening line.

Though I wasn't really, at all, he made me into one. Together we danced, talked, and laughed our way through my college years, marrying when I was twenty-two and he thirty-one. Like the Bogie of my dreams, John had weathered many adventures before I met him. Like Bogie, he hid a true and tender heart under a sometimes sardonic cool-dude persona. Unlike Bogie, John had plenty of hair (a mane of hair, longer than Bobby Sherman's). Plus, besting Bogie, John was tall, towering over me at six foot three. I literally looked up to him.

As with Bogie and Bacall, or any longtime couple, John and I grew stronger as a duo. He gave me confidence and guided me into the real world; I helped him stabilize his chaotic life and get his career on track. A forever marriage like my mom and dad's (Bill and Barbara, another "B & B") had always been my dream, even in my teen fantasies of love. My new husband taught me to appreciate '80s rock music, and I showed him the joys of '40s films. Together we grooved to Bogart and Bergman's haunting love song, "As Time Goes By," cuddling up in our crummy newlywed apartment, watching *Casablanca*.

From the night I first met Bogie's eyes in his *Casablanca* bar, I had always wanted someone not only older but wiser. The oldest, wisest man I ever met—my Irish "cousin" Dan, who visited us in the States in his '80s—enjoyed meeting my wise and witty husband. Later, Cousin Dan told me in his Irish brogue with its rolling Rs: "John is a serious man. His type is rare."

Rare, indeed. I'd had to time-travel back to World War II to find that type in the hippie dippie 1970s. I was lucky, indeed, to find myself a real-live serious man amidst the glitzy 1980s. Despite all the unglamorous bumps on our real road, despite all my worries as my older-man husband leads our way into our new shared adventure of old age, I've been luckier even than Betty Bacall Bogart to be married to my serious guy for thirty-three years and counting. His type is still my type, "As Time Goes By."

Beneath the Surface

Ann Harleman

Nights in my room, taking refuge from my mother's rages, I drew Raymond Burr's face over and over, a kind of gestural mantra. Raymond got me through high school. I am grateful to him still.

My family didn't acquire a television set until I was ten—time enough for me to become a rabid reader. Still, I was also a sporadically spellbound viewer, once I had the chance. My father (broad forehead, soulful eyes, jowls that framed a mouth womanly in its fullness) loved *Perry Mason*, so I did, too. And somewhere during the series' nine-year run, I fell in love with its star. Any distinction between the actor and the character he played blurred and eventually vanished. Raymond Burr (broad forehead, soulful eyes, jowls that framed a mouth womanly in its fullness) was everything I wanted in a man.

I wasn't interested in *boys*—possibly because they weren't interested in me. I wanted a sturdy, self-assured champion, a knight who rode full-tilt at dragons, crying, "Incompetent, irrelevant, and immaterial!"

Raymond was strong. He took the side of the underdog every time. A Los Angeles lawyer, he defended people everyone was sure were guilty: a man whose fingerprints were on the gun, a woman found with the victim's body in the trunk of her car. He presented their side of the story, and the world believed him. I still remember "The Case of the Ugly Duckling," in which he defended a young woman who was convinced of her homeliness. At the end of the episode, he held up a sketch of his client, and when she said, "What's that?" he answered, "It's a picture of a swan." I would have loved him for that alone! His strength helped others to find theirs, to solve their own problems. In my teenage years I had plenty of those, ranging from an alcoholic mother to the teachings of the Catholic Church regarding sex. Raymond's broad shoulders were shoulders I could lean on; the slope of belly not quite hidden by his suit jacket spoke of an unabashed appetite for the pleasures of life. He had what I thought of as a burning gaze, which couldn't fail to snare any woman it fell upon.

By the time I left teenagehood, *Perry Mason* had disappeared from the airwaves. But Raymond hadn't. To my delight (because teenagehood hadn't quite left *me*), he became the equally eponymous hero of a new detective series, *Ironside*. Robert T. Ironside, who solved mysteries as a consultant for the San Francisco Police Department, differed from Perry Mason in one central aspect. He was paralyzed from the waist down. His wheelchair—prominent in every episode—did nothing to diminish my crush. On the contrary, Raymond now held the galvanizing appeal that the damaged Mr. Rochester held for Jane Eyre. Raymond, like Mr. Rochester, bore his affliction—he'd taken a sniper's bullet in the spine—with quiet heroism. By now I was old enough to see my father, with his unremarked, unceasing care of my mother, as a quiet hero. I'd watched him washing vomit out of her hair, settle the down comforter over her unconscious body, sweep up the fragments of a glass she'd flung at us. All this made me want more in a man than strength and the validation of sensual pleasure. In *Ironside*, Raymond gave me that *more*. But as life at home—real life—got harder, my idol began to seem theoretical. He was a rescuer I could no longer afford to wait for.

At twenty, I fled into marriage. I married the first person who asked me: an ordinary mortal, a decent man—well, a boy-man—with none of Raymond's qualities. Impossible, then, to give up my crush. I'm ashamed to say that Raymond could have been cited for alienation of affection in my eventual divorce. Still, once I was on my own again, I found that somewhere in my decade of marriage, I had outgrown theoretical. I had, finally outgrown teenagehood. Now a single mother, I wanted the real thing, not only for my own sake, but for my small daughter's. While I searched in vain (the fiction I wrote during those years, justly unpublished, contained many manly, dark-eyed saviors), I learned to find satisfaction in my work as a teacher and in raising my child. And that was when…

Reader, I met him.

Across a crowded garden in the California landscape where both *Perry Mason* and *Ironside* were set, a man moving on the party's periphery caught my eye. He had, I swear to you, a burning gaze. We began oh-so-casually working our way through the crowd toward each other. When finally he stood opposite me (broad forehead, soulful eyes, jowls that framed a mouth womanly in its fullness)…

"Dance with me."

"But—I don't know you."

We introduced ourselves. His hand was large; his handshake, generous. The orchestra swung into "String of Pearls."

"You have lucky eyes and a high heart." He was still holding my hand. "Dance with me."

"But—I'm waiting for someone. One of the librarians is supposed to meet me here." The garden belonged to the Huntington Library; the party was a reception for the Library's summer Fellows.

"Dance with me."

Bruce's roomy, plush-upholstered car, blue like his tweed jacket, smelled pleasingly of pipe tobacco. After dinner at a Turkish restaurant, we drove up into the hills to see the moonrise. I loved Bruce's fierceness when he turned to me, and the warmth of his hands as he held my face. His lips with their lazy, sweet taste of apples; the whiskery feel of his jacket; the smell of eucalyptus, like Vicks VapoRub, when we rolled down the windows. The moon rose low and huge and orange; by the time we drove back, it had hardened into a small, bright button, intense as a searchlight.

"High noon moon," Bruce said. He drove looking straight ahead, both hands meticulously on the steering wheel, but I could feel his body listing toward me. "Pigs could hunt truffles by it, under these trees. My soul could be rooting through the universe for you, my truffle."

Then he hummed, *No-bod-y knows … the truffles I've seen.*

We both started laughing, and my nervousness about what we seemed to be getting into dissolved. How had he known that I'd hear *truffles* for *troubles*?

That moon followed us all the way back to the Huntington Library, right down to the shimmering stripes it laid across my bed, painting our bodies with light. Just before I fell asleep, I realized I'd stood up the librarian. She never forgave me—I think she had designs on Bruce herself—not even when, wickedly, we sent her an invitation to the wedding.

In the next year or so, Raymond Burr grew a beard, as if trying to catch up to my new husband. But my crush, having done its work, had ended. Bruce wasn't Raymond Burr—he was better. He was the man I'd imagined Raymond to be: not only strong and sensual, but warm, generous, devoted. Also, at times, arbitrary, irascible, and pigheaded—but these aren't the qualities that stick with me now that he's gone. We'd been married for four years when he was diagnosed with chronic progressive multiple sclerosis. MS, the most unpredictable of illnesses, careened into the future, dragging us with it. Dishes broke; fingers got cut; bruises bloomed. Then falls, blackouts, a couple of fender-benders. Then all the downward notches: cane, forearm crutches, walker, and, yes, wheelchair. Along the way there were many trips to the emergency room, always, it seemed, at midnight; I would sit by Bruce's gurney, sketching or reading, until, sometime near dawn, he was admitted.

It was during one of these all-night vigils, leafing through a news magazine someone had left on a table next to where Bruce lay dozing, that I found out Raymond Burr had died. My heart jerked, the way it did whenever Bruce fell. I caught my breath and read

Ann Harleman's self-portrait depicts her at 15, in the prime of her love for TV's Raymond Burr. Ann is a noted Bay Area author who still admires Perry Mason.

on. The article praised Raymond's ability to show what lay beneath the surface. Even when he played minor parts, even when he played villains, he gave his characters a depth and complexity that made viewers feel sympathy for them. His gift had always seemed to have its roots in tragedy. He'd claimed to be twice widowed and to have suffered the death of a young son. In reality, I read, Raymond Burr had enjoyed a long and happy relationship with another man. During his lifetime Burr maintained that the two were never more than friends; and the world believed him.

What's in a crush? We fall for the surface, for what we can see; but really we love something we imagine—something underneath. Maybe that something turns out to be real; maybe not. It doesn't matter. My crush, in its roundabout way, brought me Bruce. And Bruce was the real thing.

My Horrible Celebrity Crush

Linda K. Sienkiewicz

It was 1968. I was an awkward fourteen-year-old on a high-school field trip to see the musical *Oliver!* I slid down in my seat and yawned, expecting a musical about a street urchin in Victorian England to be as exciting as watching Liberace with my grandmother every Sunday evening. That bored attitude snapped to attention when Bill Sikes, played by the late British actor Oliver Reed, skulked onto the screen in his battered top hat. My heart ratcheted and my hands wrapped around the wooden arms of the theater chair. Who was this man? Why did I feel this way? Such a strange feeling was new to me, but I knew I liked it. I didn't know what significance Reed's potent machismo would have on me, or how sexual desire and fantasies would eventually lead to my success as a writer.

Charles Dickens describes Bill Sikes as "a stoutly-built fellow of about five-and-thirty, in a black velveteen coat, very soiled drab breeches, lace-up half-boots, and grey cotton stockings, which enclosed a very bulky pair of legs, with large swelling calves—the kind of legs which in such costume, always look in an unfinished and incomplete state without a set of fetters to garnish them. He had a brown hat on his head, and a dirty belcher handkerchief round his neck, with the long frayed ends of which he smeared the beer from his face as he spoke: disclosing, when he had done so, a broad heavy countenance with a beard of three days' growth, and two scowling eyes..."

Oliver Reed physically and emotionally embodied the villainous Sikes. His command of each scene was riveting, even when he was hissing endearments to Nancy, with his hand grasping her throat. In his first scene, he emerged from the darkness of the dank streets into a warmly lit bar, where she waited for him. He acknowledged her with a sly smile (as an adult, I'd call it carnal) as he booted someone out of a seat to take a table all to himself. She sang about what a fine life it is if you've got someone to love, as she brought him a mug, bottle of gin, and bowl of stew. He forwent the mug to drink straight from the bottle, slurped his stew, and fed his mangy dog from his spoon. Before he left, he gave Nancy a meaningful look, one that might have said, "See you later or maybe not, but you're still my girl," and then he walked back out into the night. She mooned after him, singing that she never wanted to be someone's happy wife in a happy home anyway.

In another scene, she was heating sausages in their flat while Sikes slept in. She teasingly asked if he loved her. He bolted upright, wild-eyed and incredulous, and shouted, "Of course I do. I lives with you, don't I?" and flopped back onto the pillows.

I later learned Reed had originally conceived the line as "I fucks you, don't I?" Such a fine life they had.

Every time he appeared, the hair on my neck rose. I fidgeted in my theater seat, hoping none of my classmates noticed I was practically panting. It was all well until Nancy betrayed him. I cried when Sikes clubbed her to death. At least he redeemed himself when he choked up about it afterwards; I reasoned only a true psychopath feels no remorse. Bill Sikes was simply misunderstood, a good man at heart, his silver lining tarnished by a bad childhood, poor education, and lack of marketable job skills. All he knew was thievery. And sex.

You know the bad-boy trope: how women are attracted to charismatic, dominating risk-takers. Research shows women are drawn to ruthless cads because of hormones. Near ovulation, they delude themselves into thinking the sexy scoundrel will be a better provider, devoted partner, and better father. They believe a macho man is someone who'll fight to the death for them; Nancy even sang how Sikes would fight for her. Forget the nice, clean-shaven hero who plays by the rules. When women are ovulating, Mr. Bad News looks like good news.

At fourteen, however, I was not familiar with this trope, and the hormonal attraction I felt toward Oliver Reed confused me. In the late '60s, boys with smooth faces and teddy-bear eyes, like Bobby Sherman and Davy Jones, filled the teenybopper fan magazines. I had never seen anyone as intensely masculine as Reed before. That chiseled jaw! That menacing scowl! Those bushy muttonchops! That scarred face and five o'clock shadow! I longed to run my hand down his rough cheek and across his broad, sweaty chest.

He prowled through my dreams, snarling and cursing, piercing me with his cruel blue eyes. A side note about Reed's gaze is the fact that he has *sanpaku*, which occurs when the white part of the eye is visible beneath the iris. According to Chinese face reading, sanpaku indicates a physical, physiological, and spiritual imbalance. It was sanpaku that made Reed's intense gaze both unnerving and seductive. It made me twist in my bedsheets at night.

I never spoke of my horrible celebrity crush, certain my classmates would think I was deranged to be swooning over a brutish thug twice as old as me. My sensibilities were at odds with the other girls.' Added to that, I had trouble separating Reed from his villainous role in the movie. Was it wrong to lust after him? My only defense for crushing on a baddie was telling myself Sikes was a fictional character, and, in my fantasy world, I mended him. He was dangerous, yes, but in my dreams he never clubbed me.

Sike's lace-up half-boots firmly stamped the lure of the bad boy in my brain.

When I reached high school, my nights were set on fire by hell-raiser Jim Morrison, who had the same wide jaw, heavy brow, and lidded gaze as Reed. Morrison was sullen, erudite, and monstrously sexy in tight black leathers, evoking a soulful yet brutish masculinity. His voice was a conduit to the pulse between my legs; listening to him scream and croon was nothing short of an orgasmic experience. His song lyrics blew me away. Who else on the planet wrote about a killer's brain squirming like a toad? For an angst-filled, artsy teen dealing with a bad breakup, Jim's darkness was like a beacon of light. I didn't feel so alone. As with Reed, I imagined I was the only one who could soothe the savage. Nancy believed that "as long as [Sikes] needs me," everything would work out— she alone would allay the beast's emotional anguish and, in turn, he would spend the rest of his days fucking her delirious.

That's the real attraction of the bad boy.

What happens to those lusty dreams when the girl grows up? She moves on, maybe falls in love with a decent guy and gets married. She's happy.

But sometimes not. As a wife and busy mother of three, I set my creative ambitions aside. When my children were adolescents, I stumbled to depression. During this time, my interest in Morrison's life and work became an obsession. All I can say is thank goodness, because it sparked my creative energy.

The release of *The Doors* movie in 1991 created a surge of renewed interest in Mr. Mojo Risin.' Every week, I'd browse the magazine sections and bookstores and find yet another article or publication on Morrison, penned by former bandmates, women who'd loved him, or editors who believed they had insight into what had made this mythical demon tick. My fixation gave me something to look forward to. I also started seeing a counselor who suggested I write in a journal about Morrison or anything else that interested me. My journaling led to writing poetry.

The Lizard King frenzy eventually calmed down, and my depression lifted, but I continued to write and study poetry. It became a serious passion that ultimately brought me publishing success.

Then I found a new bad boy to lust after: the Australian actor Russell Crowe. Like Reed and Morrison, Crowe was another headstrong, hotheaded, snarling alpha male, a larger-than-life risk taker who tended to get himself in trouble.

In my online search for all things Russell Crowe, I discovered fan fiction: a vast community of women who wrote and posted stories based on his different film roles. These short pieces ranged from amateurish to amazingly well-conceived romances. I couldn't resist creating a few of my own. After churning out half a dozen stories based on Crowe's characters from *The Quick and the Dead*, *Gladiator*, and *L.A. Confidential*, I wrote a story inspired by a ruthless, charismatic skinhead named Hando from the Australian film *Romper Stomper*. I felt the story had potential beyond fanfic, but I needed to make Hando more palatable, so I recreated him as an outlaw biker. The revamped story was published in two magazines and nominated for a Best-of-Erotica award.

By 1972, Jim Morrison and Oliver Reed had captured Linda Sienkiewicz's attention. She writes fiction and poetry from Michigan where she has mused on her "horrible celebrity crushes."

My poetry editor, the late Rob Bixby from March Street Press, suggested I write a novel based on the characters. When I told him I had no clue how to write a novel, he said, "Sure you do. Make fourteen chapters, introduce a different character in each chapter, and *bam*, you got a novel." I laughed, but once he'd put the idea in my head, I couldn't let it go, which proves being obsessive is not all bad. I wrote my first novel, a freewheeling story about a biker and stripper that publishers didn't quite know how to place. I realized I had a lot to learn about story building if I wanted to continue writing novels. After years of hemming and hawing about getting a master's degree in poetry, I decided to pursue a degree in fiction, which eventually led to the publication of my first novel, *In the Context of Love*, in 2015.

As a writer, I was nagged by my inability to write anything about Jim Morrison, however, especially after so many years of devoted idolization. My solution was a Dear-John breakup letter to him that explained my crush on Russell Crowe. "Dear Jim" was published in *The Main Street Rag* and became the title poem of a poetry chapbook.

DEAR JIM

Thirty years is a long time, Morrison—
my mantra, my shaman, my sweet
erotic nihilist. It's too weird to think
you'd show up panting
at my back door, and I'm no longer
the lone, braless freak in a high
school full of fresh-faced cornhuskers,
no more the sweet sixteen leather-whip
whose kohl-lined, bloodshot eyes saw your face
in every Rorschach blot, who believed
she alone could light your fire.

Admit it, Jimbo, the closest I'd get
to you now is a zipless fuck with some
look-alike on your grave in Père Lachaise.
I've found a new bad boy—
dingo-barking-mad with your apocalyptic
intensity—ten thousand watts of it burning
night and day in my brain.

You think he likes older women? Okay,
so maybe he doesn't, but look, Mojo, I'm sick
of microwaving Lean Cuisine, washing
my pantyhose in the bathroom sink
every night, waking up in the same bed.
He'll be the gladiator to defend my dreams,
someone to squeeze when my day stumbles
down the stairs into the basement.

Yes, you're beautiful, you'll always
be beautiful—isn't that the tragedy
of The End? And maybe asking the Antichrist
to be an angel is a lot, but, I could use your help.
What I'm saying is: please look after him.
Don't let him die in a bathtub in Paris or
anything. I got a big load of laundry to do.

The poem expresses how I felt out of step with my peers when I was young, and how my crush on Morrison provided an escape valve. By the poem's end, I understand escapism is what I'm really looking for. Women shouldn't be ashamed to indulge an imaginary tryst with a domineering brute. We aren't being disloyal to our spouses or feminist sensibilities. Far from it. After all, a woman's brain is the most underutilized sex organ.

For nostalgia's sake, I recently rented *Oliver!* and watched Reed with quaint amusement, remembering how badly I once hungered for him. I can't say I feel the same attraction, but I believe a good measure of my success can be attributed to a man with a "broad heavy countenance with a beard of three days' growth, and two scowling eyes." He set the standard. Unlike the gawky fourteen-year-old who yearned for Reed, however, I'm no longer embarrassed to admit my celebrity crushes, horrible or not. Fantasies can be empowering, and you never know where your obsessions may lead you.

This Crush Is My Crush

Janice Eidus

My father and I sat side by side on worn-out armchairs in our cramped apartment in a housing project in the northeast Bronx. Loudly and off-key, we sang along to Woody Guthrie's *Dust Bowl Ballads* as it played on our turntable. I was eleven. My father was in his forties. Both of us idealized Woody for his music and left-wing politics.

My father had once been a card-carrying member of the U.S. Communist Party. He left the party upon learning the truth about Stalin's inhumane, totalitarian regime. In his heart, he remained a communist, fervently believing in the Marxist principle, "From each according to his ability, to each according to his needs." In its pure state, he felt that communism would lead to a "humane, classless, stateless society." He often proclaimed that "the proletariat needed to rise up against the bosses in a violent revolution" to achieve this.

My mother was a socialist. She was certain the same equality for all could be achieved through a socialist government that took power by peaceable means. She and my father argued frequently about whether this end justified violent means. I wavered between the two.

Woody, a "fellow traveler" of the party and a committed social activist, was a bond among the three of us, even though my mother was so depressed most of the time that she rarely listened to music. Still, Woody's name always brought a smile to her lips.

We were proud cultural Jews. Radical politics was our family religion. Woody was our god. When my father and I listened to Woody together, we were happy. Happiness was a rare commodity in our home, in large part because my handsome, blue-eyed father ruled over our family like a despot. ("A fascist leader," my current therapist calls him; my previous therapist described my childhood as "like living in a concentration camp." Both women are Jewish, in their '70s, and neither uses such words lightly.)

I could never predict what would set off my father's bouts of rage: leaving a dirty sponge in the bathtub; accidentally knocking over his glass of ginger ale; asking, "Daddy, can you lower the TV while I do my homework?"

When enraged, he punched, kicked, and threw things at me and my older brother and sister. He called us stupid and ungrateful. Although he never laid a hand on my mother, he found other ways to wound her. He made fun of her for not having gone to college, rather than sympathizing that she'd had to get a job immediately after high school to help support her family. He mocked her curvy hips as "steatopygian," the medical term, according to Merriam-Webster, for "an excessive development of fat on the buttocks." When she softly protested, he called her oversensitive.

Inside the walls of his "castle," he was the self-proclaimed king, the kind of person Woody Guthrie—a man who declared his guitar a "machine" that "kills fascists"—fiercely opposed. Yet my father's political views mirrored Woody's, despite the way he behaved at home, and despite their very different upbringings.

My father was born in Brooklyn to poor, Jewish, immigrant, left-wing parents from a long line of left-wingers. They cursed in Yiddish and smacked each other and their four children on an almost-daily basis with rolled-up newspapers, frying pans, and whatever else was available. My father's father, a struggling violinist, barely earned a living as a house painter.

Despite being from a musical family and loving Woody's music, my father possessed no musical gifts. Instead, he became a pharmacist who, after years of working for others, opened his own pharmacy in the West Bronx near Yankee Stadium. He ended up bankrupt, thanks to a combination of poor business acumen and a ferocious temper. He had a habit of throwing out of his store customers who were politically conservative or very religious (of any persuasion), and he would slam the door and yell, "Never come back!"

Woody was born in a small town in Oklahoma to Christian parents. According to Woody, his father, later in life, became a member of the Ku Klux Klan. During the Great Depression, Woody left home and traveled throughout the Dust Bowl alongside the Oklahoma and Texas farmers who'd lost their land and livelihood to the raging dust storms. Woody was angry toward the "bourgeoisie," especially the greedy bankers and landlords who evicted the farmers from their homes.

Beside his music and politics, I had another reason for adoring Woody: Sharing a "crush" with my father made me feel closer to him, something I yearned for, despite his temper and cutting tongue. I lived for those moments when my father said to me, "Your blue eyes are like a perfect sky. Like Helen of Troy, your face will one day launch a thousand ships."

Woody was one of my "Two Big Crushes," although I wasn't attracted to him in the way I was to Beatle George Harrison. That crush I didn't share with my father, who had zero interest in songs about wanting to hold your hand, songs that weren't meant to organize the workers of the world. In my fantasies about George, I didn't give a damn about The Revolution. Instead, he and I made frequent love. But since I didn't have a clue what lovemaking actually looked like, the details were sketchy and often anatomically impossible.

With Woody, I was chaste. Our only passion was for the land, the people, peace, and justice. Together, we rose up against the evil capitalist bosses. I did love Woody's rangy good looks: narrow face, squinting eyes that appeared to witness something profound in the distance, sexy cigarette dangling from his lips, jaunty cap tipped back on his head, strong hands caressing his guitar.

I imagined the two of us standing arm in arm and calling each other "Comrade," a word Woody sometimes used in his lyrics. We faced down the blinding dust storms raging around us. We fearlessly forced racist store and restaurant owners to allow black people the use of their bathrooms.

The Dust Bowl of Oklahoma, Texas, and other prairie states during the Great Depression was far removed from my life years later in a Bronx housing project. But I'd read *The Grapes of Wrath* numerous times. I'd listened over and over to Woody singing "Dusty Old Dust," "Tom Joad," and "This Land Is Your Land." I loved the image of the two of us driving along the open road in a beat-up jalopy. Woody's guitar wasn't the only one that killed fascists. My imaginary one did, too.

Growing up in Brooklyn, Janice Eidus shared a devotion to Woody Guthrie with her father. Guthrie's cry for social justice has seasoned Janice's career as a fiction writer, memoirist and writing coach.

Seated next to each other at our kitchen table, my father and I pored over articles in the party's newspaper, *The Daily Worker*. As a young man, Woody had sometimes written for it in a hillbilly dialect, the voice of the common man—another thing we loved about Woody.

I was acutely aware that my siblings, Eric and Alice, didn't listen to Woody (or any music) with my father or discuss political theory. Left out and adrift, Eric rebelled via drugs (which he eventually quit, after a long battle). Although he never rebelled against progressive politics, he and my father were distant, never sharing private, joyous moments.

My sister, too, felt left out. My father never compared Alice to Helen of Troy or praised her hazel eyes. At three years old, she'd had surgery to correct a wandering eye. But when she was tired, it still drifted. I felt guilty that he doted on her so much less than he doted on me. But I never spoke up for her. I was too hungry for his adoration and love.

In rebellion, Alice grew up to be very religious, attending synagogue and dating Orthodox men. She was right-wing, homophobic, and a supporter of overtly racist politicians. Woody and his brethren disgusted her. When Teddy Kennedy, Jr., was diagnosed with chondrosarcoma (a rare cancer in which tumors form in cartilage) and had to have his leg amputated from the knee down, she shook her head and said, "The sins of liberal fathers are visited upon their children…"

Some years later, the same rare cancer found her. Her tumor, already very large when discovered, was in her sinus cartilage. After two surgeries, her face was severely disfigured. I didn't remind her of her words about Teddy Kennedy and his son. I did wonder if she felt she was being punished for my father's beliefs. Right up until her death, despite the fact that I helped take care of her, she told me she hated me "for being Daddy's favorite." Once, she shocked me by saying, "I'm aware that my feelings are irrational, and that it wasn't your fault. But I can't help the way I feel."

At eleven, I didn't know much about Woody's current life. I was vaguely aware that he had Huntington's Chorea, but I didn't realize it was an incurable, inherited disease that results in the death of brain cells. As it progresses, sufferers develop dementia, uncoordinated movements, and unsteady gait, and lose the ability to speak. That Woody—middle-aged, ill, and dying—wasn't real to me. My father must have known about Woody's tragic situation, but never spoke of it to me. We both needed Woody to be forever young and healthy, singing "This Land Is Your Land" in his folksy, irresistible drawl.

Unlike the Woody of my fantasies, however, I couldn't stay one age forever. I left pre-pubescence behind and entered headlong into a rebellious adolescence. I dated bad boys, smoked weed, and tried acid. (My parents were staunch teetotalers, quite conservative in areas other than the political.) But I never rebelled against my parents' politics. I remained a passionate lefty, and my father and I continued to share moments of closeness, listening to Woody in our living room, attending concerts by Pete Seeger (a close friend of Woody's) and political rallies.

When I was sixteen, my father flew into a rage and threw a hairbrush at me. I had accidentally broken one of the drawers of a wooden dresser he'd built for me when I was in elementary school, and which I still used. The hairbrush barely missed hitting me in my eye—that same blue eye which, in his better moods, he compared to a perfect sky.

That night, while he and my mother slept, I packed a suitcase and fled to the apartment of my much older boyfriend. His father was a big shot in the Communist Party, which was much of his appeal to me. Other than one phone call to let them know I was safe, I didn't call my parents or tell them where I was. Knowing they were worried sick, I felt guilty but also very glad.

After a month, the guilt won out. I called again. My mother said, "Daddy swears he will never again raise a hand to you." She pleaded, "Please come home."

Mostly because I didn't feel safe with my boyfriend, I did so. He was addicted to heroin and dealt drugs to make money. Usually, he was too stoned to pay attention to me, and I sat by myself on his ratty sofa, frightened by the people who came over at all hours to cop drugs and get high.

When I returned home, my father kept his promise. He was never again violent toward me, although he still screamed and yelled. He and I were no longer close. We no longer spent afternoons sitting side by side, listening to Woody.

Not long after I came home, my mother made a serious suicide attempt. None of us knew that she'd been hoarding tranquilizers and barbiturates prescribed to her over the years by various doctors, waiting for the day when she'd feel ready to use them all at once. "The time had come," she told me afterward from her hospital bed. "You, Alice, Eric … none of you needed me anymore."

She downed the many pills with a huge bottle of Scotch (her first, since she'd been a lifelong teetotaler). She tightly tied a plastic bag over her head and got into the bathtub. But Eric returned home earlier than expected that afternoon. He found her in the bathtub and called for an ambulance.

After her stomach was pumped and many tests run, she was made to spend two weeks at a psychiatric hospital for evaluation. At the end of her stay, the doctors told us not to worry. "Just menopause," they assured us, although we all knew better.

Privately, right before she was released, she whispered to me, as if bestowing a gift, "Don't blame yourself. Blame Daddy. He made me so unhappy for so many years." She added, "My punishment is that I'm still alive."

I hated my father. I hated her. Sometimes I hated myself. All I wanted to do was leave home. First came college, and then I did part-time secretarial work to put myself through a graduate-school program in creative writing. Writing was my ticket out, I'd decided, away from the Bronx and my family. I'd written stories, poems, and plays since I was a little girl. Writing had long been an emotional escape for me. But I'd never before had the courage to envision myself as a professional writer.

As a child, I'd rarely shared my writing with my family. Once, I proudly handed my father my four-page play about a loving family who affectionately argued with one another about whether to have pizza (the children's vote) or steak (the parents') for dinner. At the end, they happily compromised on burgers. Waving the play in my face, my father said, "This is completely facile."

So it shouldn't have come as a complete surprise that years later, in graduate school, I willingly fell under the sway of some literary experimentalists whose writing was fiercely cerebral. Language was more important to them than character and theme. "My writing is free of all political text and subtext," I proudly declared. It was also extremely sexual, another form of rebellion against my puritanical parents (no "free love" in their lives). My father didn't hesitate to let me know he was disappointed in my "apolitical work."

No one was more surprised than I when my writing began getting published in magazines and anthologies. Master's degree in hand, I moved around the country for a while, picking up college teaching jobs. Finally, I settled back in New York, this time in the Bohemian West Village. Instantly, I felt more at home there than I ever had in the Bronx.

The more I wrote and published, however (including, by then, my first novel), the more I recognized that I wasn't really an avant-gardist in my heart. My eyes glazed over when my new friends spoke about the latest literary theory and why realism no longer mattered.

The writing I genuinely loved explored social issues like discrimination against minorities and women across the globe. And so my own work (as well as the friendships I made) changed once more. Perhaps my novels and stories wouldn't lead to global revolution, but perhaps they would inspire someone, somewhere, to want to change the world for the better. That was enough for me. I became the writer I was meant to be.

Also, now an adult with a satisfying career and a loving husband, I came to understand how damaged my father had been by his own childhood. With age, he'd calmed down and grown mellower, making it a lot easier to be around him. He and I met regularly for lunch at our favorite Indian restaurant. We shared curried shrimp and chicken, laughed, and discussed politics.

When his kidneys abruptly failed and he lay in a coma for two weeks, I sat by his hospital bed for hours each day. "I love you, Daddy," I said, loudly. "I forgive you." I hoped he could hear me. After his death, I lit candles, lay in bed, and spent an entire day listening to Woody. My crush on Woody had never gone away; his songs still helped me feel connected to my father.

And now I'm the mother of a teenage girl born in Guatemala and adopted as a baby by my husband and me. Sometimes during those precious moments when she's not busy with schoolwork and friends, and I'm not rushing to meet a writing deadline, she and I listen together to Woody. We sing "Talking Dust Bowl Blues" and "Goin' Down the Road Feeling Bad." Her voice, not inherited from me, is beautiful.

Our very existence as a transracial mother and daughter reminds me that I continue to believe the same thing that Woody believed (and which I refuse to find naïve): that no matter our religion, color, or gender, all of us, by working (and singing) together, can create a world filled with respect, love, peace, and justice.

Parallel Secrets

KATHARINE DAVIS

"Richard Chamberlain is way more handsome." I studied his photograph, gazing at his gentle blue eyes, his warm, slightly secretive smile. I was in love for the first time. I never missed an episode of *Dr. Kildare*, the caring young intern, always noble and good.

"Nuh-uh. Vince is more handsome. Check out the hair." Kathy grabbed her magazine and shoved it toward me. "See. Gorgeous." Vince Edwards's hair was dark and wavy, a few strands mussed, as if someone had recently run her hands through it.

We bent over the glossy movie magazines. "So?" I said, my voice a tad shrill as I defended my own Dr. Kildare. His blond hair was slicked back smooth and untouched. He smiled at me with neat, perfect teeth. I ran my tongue over my braces, unsettled and annoyed at Kathy's observation. I was about to have my first argument about boys—actually, men.

It was a hot, sticky afternoon in July 1962, the summer I turned fourteen. We were escaping the heat in Kathy Mahoney's basement rec room paneled in faux knotty pine. A pair of corduroy-covered daybeds at right angles created a seating area in the corner. Opposite this was an actual bar with red leatherette stools. The green wall-to-wall shag carpet smelled musty, with a hint of stale potato chips.

Up until recently we played career girl here, pretending this was the living room of our city apartment, where we would hang out after a long day at the office in Manhattan. The bar was our kitchenette. We imagined we were the secretaries for important bosses of large corporations. At that time, almost all the bosses were men.

My father was one of those bosses who worked in Rockefeller Center. Every morning he rode the train to the city from New Jersey. He wore a brimmed felt hat and carried a briefcase. He probably made life difficult for his secretary, just as the bosses in our games did.

In these rec-room scenarios, Kathy and I would pretend to make dinner and compare notes on our adventures at the office. Our bosses were handsome but demanding, and we did all we could to please them. That included making numerous cups of coffee, fetching dry-cleaning from the corner shop, and taking endless dictation on spiral-topped pads.

Kathy pretended to perch on the edge of her boss's desk, legs crossed, steno pad in hand. Her boss would lean closer and closer, leering at her slim ankles, forgetting what sentence he was on. "Miss Mahoney," he would say, "you look particularly fetching today." At this phrase, we would lean back on the throw pillows in our pretend apartment and howl with laughter. I loved the idea of looking alluring to these imaginary men.

I had no idea to what end.

In 1962, most girls didn't consider becoming business leaders with secretaries of their own. If we didn't marry or become a secretary, the only professions we imagined were nurse or librarian. I hated getting shots, and I didn't aspire to giving them. The librarians in our town were cranky old maids who wore cardigan sweaters held together by taut chains across drooping bosoms.

The other occupation I considered was teacher, but only if I couldn't find a husband. After seeing a movie at the Tuesday afternoon catechism classes at St. Mary's, I had a brief flirtation with becoming a nun. The possibility of a religious vocation didn't last long.

On that hot afternoon, Kathy and I had our first argument. Who was the more handsome? The TV star Vince Edwards, of *Ben Casey*, or Richard Chamberlain, of *Dr. Kildare*?

Until then Kathy and I never disagreed. Though I was a year older, we were best friends, even blood sisters, having pricked our fingers with sewing needles and rubbed them together. Kathy had two older brothers, which gave her not only an insider's knowledge of the teen years ahead, and also a familiarity and ease around boys. I, a shy oldest child, was the quintessential late bloomer.

We were both Roman Catholics, which pleased Kathy's mother, Rita, enormously, (my mother, a Presbyterian, couldn't have cared less), but we didn't attend parochial school. We both had pixie haircuts, flattering to Kathy's heart-shaped, freckled face, but a disaster on me. I was still years from growing into my nose.

We both had blue bikes with three-speed gears. We wore saddle shoes with white socks, and round-collared blouses tucked into full skirts. We took piano lessons from Dorothy Slifer on the east side of town. Our favorite game was Clue. We loved going to Jarvis's Drug Store and ordering cherry Cokes, which neither of us stirred, sipping slowly, anticipating the rush of sweetness at the bottom of the glass.

Our favorite color was pink. Our favorite singer was Gene Pitney. We both had piggy banks and were saving for a trip to Europe. We agreed that Paris would be our favorite city.

It was the summer before my ninth-grade year. We attended Roosevelt Junior High. I would never get to go across town to Westfield High, because my corporate father moved our family to Switzerland the following year. Instead of getting flip hairdos, circle skirts, and maybe a boyfriend with a letter sweater, I would attend a girls' boarding school, become fluent in French, learn almost nothing, and get a great education.

But that long-ago afternoon, all I cared about was Richard Chamberlain. Our conversation grew heated. "So he has wavy hair. Blond hair is better," I said, fingering my own listless, dirty-blonde locks.

"But it's not thick. Check out Vince's smile."

I had to admit Vince Edwards's smile was broader in one of the photos. In another, he rested his chin on his hand, his eyes staring moodily into the distance. Okay. Richard's mouth was smaller, but he had these captivating dimples on his smooth cheeks. Vince looked as if he needed a shave.

"Richard looks gentle and kind," I said, proclaiming that character was just as important as looks.

"Yeah," Kathy said, "just like the goody-goody he plays. Dr. Kildare is always sucking up to Dr. Gillespie."

"That's not true," I said. "He's really smart, and he cares for people."

"So? Dr. Ben Casey does way more than that."

I looked again at the pictures. Vince's gaze was intense, as though he knew something about you that you didn't want him to know.

In his role as Dr. Ben Casey, he often got angry. He argued with his superiors, and he didn't like it if he didn't get his way. Dr. Kildare cared about his patients' lives. He made the old and the sick feel better. What was wrong with wanting to please his boss, Dr. Leonard Gillespie?

"I don't see why you think he's more handsome," I said, pushing the magazine away. "You can have him. I love Richard Chamberlain."

Kathy picked up the picture and pressed her lips to Vince Edwards's face. She made kissing noises. "I love Vince," she said. "And he's the handsomest by far."

"You're gross," I said. It never occurred to me to press a paper picture against my face. I studied Richard Chamberlain, his soft mouth, those faraway eyes. I pictured him taking me in his arms. He would feel warm, strong, and smell of clean cotton shirts. His gentle hands would smooth the hair away from my face. And then? It was easy to love someone from afar.

Kathy shook her head. "You don't get it," she said.

"What?" I felt my face grow hot.

"Richard Chamberlain is more pretty than handsome. And he's not sexy."

"Sexy?" The word smacked me in the head with a rude thud, like a blow during one of our pillow fights.

"Sexy." She said it again more slowly. She cocked her head and smiled with satisfaction. "You don't even know what it means."

"What *what* means?"

Kathy jumped up, clutching the magazine to her chest. "Sexy, sexy, sexy," she called out in a singsong voice.

I grabbed my magazine. "I do so," I said, furious, heading toward the stairs. "Richard Chamberlain is more handsome," I yelled back at her. "And, he *is*—" I couldn't say the word.

While I coasted down the hill on my bike toward home, the word *sexy* clattered in my head. I knew it had something to do with men and women and what went on between them, that thing that happened in bed. We had had the reproduction talk in gym class, followed by the movie, which the girls viewed separately from the boys. This gross thing that men did to women to make a baby was all I got out of that. Still, it seemed there was something the gym teachers weren't telling us, some other story beyond the mechanics of swimming sperm and fallopian tubes.

The next Thursday, I tuned in to watch *Dr. Kildare*. As the drama unfolded at Blair General Hospital, I observed my heartthrob with renewed interest. I considered the actor himself. Richard Chamberlain still appeared handsome, his face registering all the good qualities in his role of the earnest young doctor. But sexy? I pushed the thought aside, content that the glossy photo I'd ordered from his fan club would be arriving soon. So what if Kathy thought that tempestuous Dr. Casey was more handsome? Richard Chamberlain was mine. All mine.

Once school started in the fall, Kathy and I still got together most afternoons. As if by tacit agreement, we no longer discussed our TV heartthrobs. we talked about teachers, homework, and who was cool. We both loved the lady art teacher who drove to school in a red MG. We hated the smell of the cafeteria. We were both afraid of the scary kids we called "hoods"—the girls with their teased hair and huge black handbags, the boys with ankle boots and tight pants. We walked over to St. Mary's for catechism classes on Tuesday afternoons. We practiced for Dorothy Slifer's recitals.

When Thanksgiving came, Kathy and I had our irreparable falling out. We were both excited about the impending arrival of our grandparents. She claimed that her grandparents were rich because her grandfather had invented the diner. I bragged that my grandmother had a farm in the country, and she must be rich, too, because she drove a Jaguar sports coupe.

Indeed, Kathy and I were on our bikes, cruising the neighborhood, when the gray Jaguar pulled into the drive. My grandmother, whom we called Gom, and my Aunt Kitty, with whom she lived, got out of the car. The timing couldn't have been better. Kathy could see for herself the red leather interior, the low-slung chassis—a sports car, and not some family station wagon.

Their two poodle dogs, Musette and Suzette, jumped out of the back. Gom wore her usual gray flannel pants and a sport coat like the one my father wore at weekend parties. Aunt Kitty, smoothing the skirt of her silk dress, bent to give me a kiss. She always smelled of Joy, her favorite perfume. She had a tan leather handbag and wore high-heeled pumps. Rows of gold bracelets jangled on her wrist.

Thirteen-year-old Katharine Pietsch of Westfield, New Jersey, was trying to outgrow her pixie haircut, but not her love for *Dr. Kildare*. Now a novelist, she remembers fondly the TV doctor played by Richard Chamberlain.

I no longer recall making introductions or what happened next. For the next few days, our relaxed suburban life was thrown into a tizzy. My father made extra trips to the liquor store, loading up on "hooch." My mother had been ironing napkins and making up the beds in my sisters' room, using the best sheets with scalloped borders. My lucky sisters got to move to the Hide-A-Bed in the den. Gom and Aunt Kitty always had breakfast in bed. Every morning I carried the tray to their room.

Except for Thanksgiving dinner, when the entire family ate together, we four children had our meals in the kitchen. The grown-ups ate in the dining room, candles lit, silver gleaming, and crisp linen napkins at each place. Earlier, we had been banished from the cocktail hour, which we didn't mind, as it meant more TV time in the den.

I was still in love with Richard Chamberlain. I scribbled his initials in the margins of my notebooks: *RC and KP*, surrounded by hearts and flowers. I had no interest in the pimply boys my own age, inches shorter than I, immature boys who pushed in the hallways and threw spitballs in study hall.

The Friday after Thanksgiving, I went over to Kathy's house. She introduced me to her grandmother, who was in the kitchen making snickerdoodle cookies with Kathy's little sister. Her grandmother pulled the first batch from the oven, buttery and golden at the edges. We sat at the Formica table and washed them down with cold glasses of milk.

Kathy's grandmother looked like the kind of grandmother you saw in books. She wore metal-rimmed glasses and had pearly gray hair in a bun. She wore lace-up old-lady shoes and an apron over a shirtwaist dress.

After we had one of those grandmother conversations where she asked us about school, we went up to Kathy's room to listen to the new Gene Pitney album.

"So, when did you get this?" I asked, studying the slick record jacket.

"Grandma gave me money, and we went downtown this morning."

I tried not to act jealous. My grandmother, Gom, gave me only books. That was for Christmas. We never got presents for Thanksgiving.

"Your grandmother is really nice," I said, a lump forming in my throat.

"Don't you think yours is a little weird?"

"What do you mean?"

"Well. No grandfather for starters."

"I told you he was dead. He died when my dad was only eight." The thought of growing up without a father was too terrible to imagine.

"Yeah, but she lives with that fancy woman."

The lump in my throat grew larger. "So? She's my godmother."

"I've never seen a grandmother who wears pants. Loafers, too. I think it's weird."

"She's not weird." Now I was mad. Okay. So my grandmother rarely brought presents, but that didn't make her weird.

Gene Pitney's voice crooned on.

"She's not like any grandmother I've ever seen," Kathy said.

I thought of the gray-haired lady baking cookies downstairs, playing games with her grandchildren. My grandmother wasn't like that. She raised sheep. She grew her own asparagus. She took photographs, not snapshots, which she developed and printed in her darkroom. She went hunting in the backwoods in Maine. She liked her hooch. She was always talking about the expense of running "the place," meaning her farm on a stream with a covered bridge.

Maybe she wasn't like most grandmothers. Still, I was furious at Kathy for pointing this out. She had insulted my family. How could she be my best friend?

That fall, our friendship fizzled. We no longer hung out together in the afternoons. I no longer cruised the neighborhood on my bike, but spent time on homework. I wanted to make the honor roll. I attended Barkley's Dancing School and wore pink lipstick. I slept in hair curlers, desperately trying to make my straight hair flip. I still loved Richard Chamberlain.

That next summer, we moved away. I had my first French kiss on the deck of a ship. I understood the word *sexy*. I got to Paris, but it was with my grandmother and Aunt Kitty, and I wished I were traveling by myself. I no longer watched American TV. I forgot Richard Chamberlain.

Years later, when I was back in the U.S. teaching French, married with two children, Richard Chamberlain came back into my life. This time he played Father Ralph in *The Thorn Birds*, a TV miniseries. I remembered my argument with Kathy. Here was my first crush, his hair a little darker, still handsome, and undeniably sexy. I loved the story of Father Ralph, a man torn between his duty, the priesthood, or succumbing to the love of his life. Here was a man with a secret.

Even then, I had no idea that Chamberlain was a gay man hiding his sexuality to succeed in his career as an actor. It wasn't until 2003 in his memoir, *Shattered Love*, that Richard Chamberlain came out publicly as a gay man. There was the story behind the story.

Long after the deaths of my grandmother and then Aunt Kitty, my sisters and I began to talk about our grandmother's sexuality. I met a cousin for the first time at my father's funeral. We shared stories about our grandmother. Our families had never discussed this. Our grandmother had married young. Her much older husband, a renowned architect, had taken his life in 1929. Did he suffer from depression? Had he been ill? Was it because he lost all his money in the crash? Or was it because my grandmother loved someone else? A woman? What was the story behind the story?

As I began my career as a writer, I learned that I needed to dig underneath the surface story, and to seek the deeper truth. Who was that girl with a crush on Richard Chamberlain? A crush merely touches the surface. A crush is remote, love from afar. Real love, like the truth, is something much deeper.

Who was that grandmother who wore loafers, drove a sports car, and lived with a woman? The real stories are buried in the secrets. I think of Richard Chamberlain still, especially when I search for my characters' stories, the truth beneath the surface. Those are the stories I want to find, the truths that make us human. Those are the stories I want to tell.

When I Stumbled Over Rob Petrie

Jill McCorkle

It might be safe to say that my *true* first crush was on that prehistoric-looking electrical box in the corner of our tiny den, because it was there, in that gray glass face, that I first glimpsed so many people and places. Every morning, Captain Kangaroo was there to read a book and wish me a good day, and at the end of each afternoon, I raced to see Huckleberry Hound and Yogi Bear. I loved television and spent hours seated on that brown braided rug that left indentations on the back of my legs. I was a devoted disciple, so it makes sense that this would be the place where I would find my first romantic crush: Dick Van Dyke as Rob Petrie.

I'm not sure what first attracted me. Maybe it was that I wanted to grow up to *be* Laura Petrie and wear those cute capri pants and ballet flats, or maybe I wanted to spend my days hanging out with Buddy and Sally, making up skits that would make people laugh. I loved Rob Petrie because he was smart and he was funny and he was not someone you would have ever *not* trusted. He was honest and nice and was a great dancer; he was a great husband and dad and son and friend and just klutzy enough that you knew he was a *real* person.

The Dick Van Dyke Show ran from 1961 to 1966, which means I was three years old in the first season—too young to have watched then—and even in later seasons, it aired past my bedtime. And yet, I have vivid early memories of watching that show. My older sister and I got to pick one night a week when we could sit up thirty minutes later than normal, and I often chose Wednesday so that I could watch *The Beverly Hillbillies*, and then, if I stalled, I could at least see the very beginning of *The Dick Van Dyke Show*: the memorable jingle that led Rob to enter his living room at 148 Bonnie Meadow Road. Would he trip over the ottoman or not? It happened both ways.

We also had a little footstool in the den where we watched television, a tiny knotty pine paneled room; the big boxy RCA filled one corner, and the chair my dad sat in (footstool in front of it) the other. The television dominated the room, and for many years it dominated my life, first with its tinfoil-sheathed rabbit ears and then with the clunky channel changer that would click around methodically to get the antenna on our roof to turn and pick up one of the three channels we got. My sister and I often took turns running outside to make sure the antenna was making its slow turn and search for a signal while inside it made a *chung-chung, chung-chung* sound as we waited for something to emerge from the gray static.

The television was my friend—one of my best, in fact—and it was like a little private university, though I wouldn't have thought of it that way at the time. It was also my escape from school—both Sunday school and regular school—and all that was mandatory in life. I was someone who went through a long period of terrible separation anxiety, one of the pediatricians in the practice where my mother worked as a secretary diagnosing me as someone with *schoolitis*. If you had this particular illness, or could convince someone that you were about to vomit, or couldn't stand up straight because your stomach hurt so bad, you might end up at home curled up in that big chair, watching reruns of many of those shows that came on too late for you to see in regular life.

There was a time when television could cure anything, and these channels were the medicine, the paths to my favorite places—the Ricardos and Mertzes far, far away in New York City, Rob and Laura out in New Rochelle, the Cartwrights on the Ponderosa, the Jetsons in outer space, and Andy and Opie safely tucked away in Mayberry. I spent hours striding into the den to the tune of *The Dick Van Dyke Show*, and then flipping over our little ottoman, sometimes changing over to the little side-step hop of later seasons. I loved the Petries' living room and that sectional sofa. I liked the pass-through from the kitchen, and the way Laura could pop in with a question or hide, like the time she accidentally dropped the huge, hideous Petrie family heirloom brooch in the garbage disposal. (The Ricardos' kitchen also had this pass-through, something I coveted.)

I liked that Rob Petrie's life was so simply contained between that comfortable home he shared with Laura and son Richie, and his office in the city that he shared with Buddy and Sally. I liked the routine of his life. I liked how Buddy constantly made fun of Mel's baldness, and that Rob by the end would find a way to make it up to Mel, or to at least smooth everything over. Rob was the great diplomat who allowed you to laugh at another human's expense, but within the realm of decency. I couldn't have articulated any of this at the time, but I think what I loved most about Rob Petrie was how balanced he was. He was smart and funny and decent. He made you laugh AND he was loyal and ethical.

Dick Van Dyke appeared on the McCorkles' TV set every Tuesday night, and young Jill took notice. Jill remains a Rob Petrie fan as she enjoys the writing life in Hillsborough, North Carolina.

I didn't tell anyone I loved Rob Petrie, and that I was going to grow up to be Laura Petrie and also do ballet exercises before bed. I feared, of course, being laughed at, but worse, I feared if I said I loved Rob Petrie that someone would try to take him away from me. I have a sister three years older, and all of our cousins were older, and so were most of the children in our neighborhood, and so NOT getting your first choice was just the way it was. When we played (and when they let me join in), we all fought over who was married to Dr. Kildare or Dr. Ben Casey. That's how it worked: someone would say "I have Dr. Kildare!" and everyone honored that. They also claimed Napoleon

Solo and Illya Kuryakin from *The Man from U.N.C.L.E.*, and Dr. Richard Kimble, *The Fugitive*, who was out there running for his life—a hard boyfriend for whoever had him (or so I was told), because he was always about to get caught or killed. Their crushes were serious men caught up in dangerous and dramatic life-threatening situations.

Had Rob ever performed surgery? Had Rob had to outsmart the Russians or hide from the One-Armed Man?

By the time they got to me, the dramatic heroes were all taken, and rather than risk exposing my real true love and the life I was going to grow up to have, I usually just accepted a boyfriend among the more obvious choices. There was always Timmy Martin, and, of course, what was good about being him was that it automatically included Lassie, who could save you from anything. There was also the older brother on *Flipper*, Sandy; I liked his sun-bleached beach-boy look, but what I liked most was that he knew and communicated with Flipper daily. I wanted Flipper to belong to ME, and I wanted Lassie to come home to ME. I might have considered Robbie or Chip Douglas of *My Three Sons*, or Wally Cleaver, but those guys usually got snapped up, too. I was offered Ernie Douglas (no) or Lumpy Rutherford (no) or Gomer Pyle or his cousin, Goober (okay, then I wasn't playing).

And when the neighborhood turned to Westerns, there were all kinds of choices. People fought over who got Little Joe Cartwright, and they fought over who got Heath Barkley on *The Big Valley*. The most dominant members of the play circle got to go steady with Little Joe and Heath Barkley; second-tier people weren't doing so badly with Nick and Jarrod Barkley or Adam Cartwright. But nobody rushed in to claim Hoss *ever*, and though this made me sad for him, I didn't want to go with him, either.

Did Rob ride horses and shoot guns?

Not that I had ever seen, or perhaps only safely on the set of *The Alan Brady Show*, and that was just fine with me.

And sure, I liked the Beatles and Elvis and Frankie Avalon, and I liked Kurt Russell, and I liked Herman (Peter Noone) of Herman's Hermits, and Davy Jones—all legitimate and worthy crushes of the day, especially as older members of the neighborhood moved on to real boyfriends and stopped playing with us, and the more popular choices were available for claiming. I knew girls whose whole rooms were papered with pictures of Bobby Sherman or David Cassidy or Greg on *The Brady Bunch*. They were all on television as well, and yet I remained faithful (still) to those black-and-white reruns and the familiarity and comfort found there.

I have figured out that the first episode I saw of *The Dick Van Dyke Show* is one called "I'd Rather Be Bald Than Have No Head at All." It aired in 1964. Rob, fearing that he is going bald, undergoes treatments from a barber who basically prescribes a headwrap of oil and vinegar. What I recall is having gotten up to go to the bathroom, tiptoeing and then standing where my parents couldn't see me, behind the doorway into the den. I did this often, lured by the canned laughter and sometimes that of my parents mixed in. My dad was in his chair—the one we always referred to as *Daddy's chair*—which was in the corner opposite the television, and my mother in another chair beside him. Trying to sneak and kneel there in the doorway to watch was an ongoing thing, and so they would call out things like *I'd better not find someone out there in the hall.* On the screen, Rob Petrie's hair was being messed with in a way I found attractive. Laura, dressed in her robe with marabou trim, gave him a sweet and gentle kiss, her hands rubbing the hair he thought he was losing. It was a sexy kiss (maybe because of that robe), but it was also loving, unconditionally so, as she promised that she would always love him no matter what, hair or no hair. The other parts of the show were spotty: Rob was doing Richie's homework after Richie had gone to bed (really?!), and then there was a weird dream where the oil and vinegar turned his hair into a head of lettuce.

I'd better not find somebody out in the hall!

I have to use the bathroom! (This was not something denied a person who had been known to have some accidents.)

Okay, but then straight to bed.

In the bathroom, I could still hear the laughter. I loved that bathroom, dusty-pink tiles and tub. The scale there in front of the toilet (we said commode) with a perfect little hole from one of my mother's stilettos, the wicker clothes hamper in which my sister had placed me on numerous occasions in a game called "Prince in the Dungeon." I loved that I could be in there and still hear the television on the other side of the wall.

I think it's bedtime.

And back I went into the room I shared with my sister, that loving, unconditional kiss firmly in my mind forever more, as was a great desire to someday own a flouncy, sheer robe with marabou trim.

I was six, and around that same time, I went to the Carolina Theatre—a regular Saturday outing of my childhood—and saw *Mary Poppins* for the first time. We often showed up around one o'clock for the first show and then stayed the whole day, watching the movie a second time and sometimes a third. There was no clearing of the theater, and the reels never stopped, cartoons filling in the space before the next show. *Mary Poppins* was magical and memorable for many reasons. The Bird Lady made me cry. Ed Wynn made me laugh. I wanted to BE Mary Poppins and float up into the sky, magic black bag in hand. But more than any of those things, I wanted to be best friends with Bert—none other than Dick Van Dyke, who until that moment I had never seen in color. I had no idea that Rob Petrie had such piercing, beautiful blue eyes. I didn't know he could speak with such an impressive Cockney accent. I did know he could sing and dance and make some really great silly faces, and in *Mary Poppins* those talents were all front and center.

Just like Rob Petrie, Bert was completely well rounded, a man with a foot firmly planted in both the realms of comedy and drama. He could pull his pants down low and walk like a penguin, and he could also philosophize about the importance of life and how you spend your time. Those blue eyes against that sooty face on the backdrop of the night sky of London when he paused to take it all in—*Coo, what a sight!*—moved me to tears in a way I didn't understand; it was just pure, raw emotion. Bert was spiritual and kind, wiser than all the others (Mary's equal, really), even though very few people saw him that way. He was a comical one-man band, a chimney sweep, a sidewalk artist being tossed coins by those who walked past. It was Bert, after all, who helped Mary lead the inattentive Mr. Banks to realize all that he was missing out on with his children.

Bert was a prophet, really, a poet, an artist. He could create a picture in chalk and then jump right into it. And I remember wishing that Mary Poppins would stay right there and never leave his side. That's what I would have done.

When I look back on when Dick Van Dyke first got my attention, now over fifty years ago, I understand even more why I was drawn to him and how he might have very well informed my own decisions in life about what I wanted to do. If you will recall, Rob Petrie was a comedy writer by day, but he was also always working on a novel he kept tucked away. His career as Rob Petrie was about making people laugh; and in the role of Bert he made people laugh; and most memorable of all, he also played the old-man bank director who ends up laughing himself to death. I remember sitting there in the theater, and with the credits, they showed the old man laughing, and then the scrambled letters of his name unscrambled to reveal that the old man WAS Dick Van Dyke. What? How could I have not recognized him? I would have to watch the movie over again to see for real. And so I did.

The missing piece of my story, as I look back, is all that we are able to bring to our stories with distance and hindsight. I was that child afraid to leave home, because it seemed if I stayed in place, everything else would be just fine. My *schoolitis* was likely connected to having a father who was clinically depressed and had even been hospitalized in my childhood. Needless to say, it was a time when this carried an even greater stigma than it still does, and was perhaps viewed by many as a weakness or a failure. He was a kind, intelligent, and imaginative man, a wonderful storyteller, someone who would often say, "This would make a good story," or "This would be a good movie." And he loved teasing and making us laugh. I could not have had a sweeter man for a father. He was tall and handsome, lanky as a young man, with blue-gray eyes and dimples. He had lost a considerable amount of hair in his thirties but dealt with the self-consciousness of it all with good quips for the bald jokes, my favorite being *Grass doesn't grow on a busy street*. And though my mother never owned a marabou-trimmed robe, her love for him was devoted and true. A great and treasured irony of my life will always be that one of his favorite songs, and one I remember hearing him sing, was "When You're Smiling."

It makes a lot of sense that I would have fallen so completely in love with a man whose whole world was built on laughter that I might have first been taken by an episode focused totally on his head and a fear of going bald. I look back on the road map that has led me here, and see all the ways I would offer explanations or connect the dots, were I putting it in a novel. A man is worried about his head and the way he appears to others, and he is seeking help. AND this man also happens to be the same one who provides laughter and thoughts that are dreamy and magical. A gifted writer who knows how to laugh. A kind, good-hearted man who knows how to dance. A practical man who can clean a chimney and also paint beautiful pictures that get washed away in the rain, but if you believe for just a little while, you can jump in and be transported to a painless, happy, often silly, fun-loving place.

The crush is one that, though unlikely when I was five, six, seven, eight, makes total sense. What's more, the characters of Robert Petrie and Bert the Chimney Sweep remain those I would put at the top of my list for humans with their values in the right place. And speaking of place, I also like how they both are so rooted in the routines of their lives, capable of dreaming and imagining, but also completely aware of reality and all the details and responsibilities of the most ordinary days. It's that very honest placement—the swing of the pendulum between comedy and tragedy, the acceptance and honoring of the everyday and commonplace—that brings me to the page as a writer. The last episode of *The Dick Van Dyke Show* ended with Rob Petrie completing his novel; he is forever preserved there in the thick of a good, full life, at the threshold of his dream. I love that. And I will always love Rob Petrie.

Cowboy Jesus

Marianne Leone

The first boy I have feelings for is the cowboy in the picture above my bed. I am seven years old and on the alert for things that might appear in my room at night, summoned by my own juddering fears. The little cowboy on the wall is as pretty as a bride doll and looks down at me coyly with his head tucked into his shoulder. He seems as if he is willing to absorb all of my night terrors. He is shy, like a lot of cowboys. The boy is bare-chested and wears only a brown cowboy hat edged in white against a brown background. I often pretend he comes alive in the picture and smiles shyly at me.

It is all a big mistake. The beautiful blond child in the portrait hanging over my bed is not wearing a cowboy hat. What surrounds his head is actually a halo, and the portrait is of the child Jesus, not a cowboy. I don't want to believe it when my friend tells me this. She says her *nonna* prays to a picture exactly like it. She is know-it-all about it, and I fly into a rage at her smirking face and sneery voice, and tell her to go home.

I love cowboys because they are laconic and chew straw and ride horses and protect people. Cowboys don't say much, unlike my loud and talkative family, who never let me get a word in at holiday dinners.

My mother comes into my room when she hears me yelling at my friend to go home. She tells me, of course, that is the boy Jesus hanging above my bed, and then *she* flies into an unironic rage and yells that she will kill me for telling my friend to go home, and whatsamatter with me, thinking God was a cowboy. She is Italian, unlike normal-speaking mothers, and says *cowboy* wrong, putting the emphasis on *boy*. I am furious with her for mispronouncing *cowboy*, and for not realizing that I love cowboys, and also for refusing my incessant demands for a cowboy outfit. My mother takes my friend downstairs and gives her *pizzelle* and watches her eat and probably wishes my plump, pretty friend was her daughter, and not the skinny, crazy girl upstairs who thinks *Gesù Cristo* is a cowboy.

I don't know how I feel about Jesus. I know I should love him, but I am scared of the way he looks, hanging on the cross and dripping blood above the blackboard in my second-grade classroom.

I mourn the loss of Cowboy Jesus from my seven-year-old life. His full lips and curly blond hair seem to radiate compassion up above my bed, as if he shares my pain at having to sleep alone in a room protected only by stuffed animals. My teddy bear is no help at all from the fireballs that could be hurled by the Wicked Witch of the West, who lives in my closet, or from a possible apparition of the Blessed Virgin Mary that could portend an early death, as it did for the unfortunate Fatima kids. (Only one out of three made it past the age of ten. Look it up).

I had pictured Cowboy Jesus and me growing up and eventually marrying and riding horses together over the plains. Now that I know my future husband is the Lord Jesus, not a cowboy, the only way we could someday marry is for me to become a nun. I think about it for a few minutes, but I don't like the way the convent smells of boiled meat and cabbage when I go there for piano lessons. I couldn't live with the permanent smell of boiled meat and cabbage. Plus, the nuns are married to the spirit of Jesus, a ghostly presence, not an actual man.

When I play house and prepare a lovely pretend dinner on the play stove I got for Christmas, I want my flesh-and-blood husband to come home from work roping cows and shooting rattlesnakes. I want him to pick me up and swirl me around and kiss me when he gets home, not hover above the ground in a long white nightgown with late-night horror-movie blood dripping from his palms.

I switch my allegiance to Spin and Marty, young cowboys on the Mickey Mouse show, but it is halfhearted and short-lived because they are not satisfying boyfriends or pretend husbands. They are just boys who live on a ranch somewhere out West. I admire their snub noses and all–American freckles, but they remind me uncomfortably of the boys I sometimes play with in the neighborhood, the ones who refuse to admit that I won the foot race, or who abandon me when other boys come along to play, and tell me, "Shut up, you're a girl" when I complain, as if that were a real argument ender. No, Spin and Marty probably wet the bed, I tell myself, and move on.

Finally, two long, lonely, mateless years later, I meet my one true love, Sugarfoot. I see him every other week on Tuesdays at seven-thirty. That's when his half-hour show airs on ABC television. After that, my mother makes me go to bed. But it's okay, because Will Hutchins, who is Sugarfoot, is dreamy. He is also my new husband. He is perfect in every way: a handsome cowboy who drinks sarsaparilla, not whiskey. Sarsaparilla is like root beer, and I like root beer, too, so we have that in common.

Sugarfoot, also known as "Tom" in the series, is lanky and blond and gentle and a little goofy. Sugarfoot uses his guns only when necessary; most of the time he just ropes bad guys. But what makes my heart flutter and my breath catch and every other physical emotion that I've read about in the bodice rippers that I've sneaked out of the library. Up the street is the sight of Sugarfoot on his horse in the opening to the show every other week. Tom, my new husband, is not only a cowboy who is perfect at every aspect of cowboying; he is also a lawyer, and in the opening to the show, I can watch him living out my utmost dream: riding a horse *and* reading a book at the same time.

And I can see, by the way he carefully puts his book in the crook of a tree and covers it with his cowboy hat that the book is precious to him, just as my books are precious to me. I love him with all my heart,

I resent Ty Hardin, who hoggishly takes up the alternate weeks in that time slot as the star of *Bronco*. Ty is handsome in the generic, plastic way of a Ken doll, and he knows he is handsome, too. Bronco is more of a sharpshooter than Sugarfoot and gets into more fights. I wish he would ride off into the sunset forever so I could spend every week with Sugarfoot instead of every other week, and I dream of Ty falling into a ravine or getting snakebit or scalped.

Then I feel guilty and wonder if I should go to confession and tell the priest that I had murderous thoughts about a TV cowboy who isn't even real. But Sugarfoot is real.

He is real to me until he isn't anymore. In the summer of the year when I turn thirteen, I swerve away from cowboys to bad boys.

It happens at the drive-in. Every summer, I stay by the ocean with my Aunt Ellie and Uncle Benny, and they go to the drive-in every time the bill changes. Usually I fall asleep during the second film, despite my intention to pinch myself awake if I start to go down. But as soon as the camera soars over Manhattan, and George Chakiris as Bernardo, gang leader of the Sharks, leaps across the screen, Will Hutchins rides off into the sunset alone without even a soundtrack to accompany him. Bernardo fills the screen. His hair is high and black. His features are so exaggerated they are almost a cartoon. He wears red and leans against a wall. He smolders. The deep dimple in his chin makes me think of tongues doing sinful things. He gets stabbed and killed during a rumble, and I weep. My aunt and uncle hear me sniveling in the back seat and laugh. They are Philistines who don't understand tragic, doomed love.

The new soundtrack that plays over and over in my bedroom is *West Side Story*, purchased with my summer blueberry-picking wages. Alone in my by-now-detestably-girly room, drowning in pink flounces and ornamental dollies, I cast myself as Anita, Bernardo's fiery girlfriend, and escape to the sweaty rooftops of Manhattan. The "America" number, with its sultry call and response, is how I learn that sex can be music, too. The whiny laments of the pimply boy singers that played nonstop on my pink radio were background noise, embarrassing nursery rhymes, that belonged to the baby dreams of yesteryear. Now I am in thrall to the taunting and teasing and the unspoken message of Bernardo and Anita's mating dance.

I haunt my local record store and find a solo album by George Chakiris called simply *George Chakiris Sings*. He looks dangerous on the cover, his face half in shadow, wearing a purple shirt. Purple is his color, I think, staring at the cool pose, one that is belied by

Fourteen-year-old Marianne Leone had her eyes on the Beatles when this photograph was taken. Her first love was TV star Will Hutchens. Marianne became a film and TV star herself, having appeared four seasons on *The Sopranos*. She published a poignant tribute to her son, *Jesse: A Mother's Story*, in 2011 and has a new memoir about her own mother.

his dark eyes burning directly at me, promising something that could ignite just between us. But when I put on the album, I am disappointed. I try to learn the songs, to sing along with George, but the Vegas-y numbers belong to my parents' generation. They are cool and jazzy, and there is no passion there, none of the sizzling undercurrent of sex that powered his dance on the roof with Anita.

Slowly it dawns on me that I want to be Anita, and that I like George Chakiris only when he is Bernardo and I can pretend to be his hot girlfriend, Anita. We just don't have anything in common as my twelve-year-old self with George as Mr. Las Vegas.

Inevitably, George Chakiris and I drift apart. Although, as a random side note: many years later, I meet Rita Moreno at a Screen Actors Guild Awards after party—on a rooftop—and am so spellbound by her living presence that I invade her space and touch her face as if I'm Tony, and it's the dance at the gym, and we are the only two people in the room. When I come to my senses, I tell her that seeing her as Anita made me realize you didn't have to look like Sandra Dee to be an actress. She is gracious and overlooks the fact that I touched her face.

After George disappears from my fantasy life, I am swept away by the riptide of Beatlemania that floods the world and washes ashore in the arms of John Lennon, my new true love. John is both a Beatle and an author. I buy a copy of *In His Own Write* and handle it with far more reverence than my *Saint Joseph Daily Missal*. I look down on my hysterical seatmates at the Paramount Theatre, screaming like seagulls when they show *A Hard Day's Night*. I'm not a screamer, just a silent admirer in love with a married man.

Years later, after I have moved on to actual flesh-and-blood boyfriends, I relocate to New York City with one of them. We are going to become actors. After we break up, I take an acting class and am partnered with a newcomer to class. On his first night in class, the new arrival performs a monologue that causes my teacher to murmur, "Does this guy know how good he is?"

We both come up for a new scene at the same time, and that Rubik's Cube of fate throws us together as partners. Our teacher assigns us an impressively difficult scene from a Eugene O'Neill play, *Mourning Becomes Electra*, where we will portray an incestuous brother and sister. The newcomer is tall, lanky, and doesn't say much. He has dirty-blond hair and looks like he should be chewing on a straw. I find myself staring at him while distant chimes of recognition ring in some adolescent, tucked-away corner of my brain.

We go to a coffee shop to discuss the scene. He gives money to street people on the way to the restaurant. He pronounces *naked* as *nekkid* and tells me about raising Hereford cattle and almost choosing that life. He knows how to ride horses and rope calves. The curve of his lips is mesmerizing and somehow familiar. I invite him to my apartment for dinner. He fixes my rickety table. We spend more and more non-scene study time together. He is diffident and takes forever to kiss me. I introduce him to my friends. He is bashful but fits in with my starving-actor crowd.

After hearing about his cowherding skills, a jokester friend teases him, singing the theme to *Sugarfoot*. At that moment, I become dizzy because of the swirling energy of the time tunnel I'm in. I want to ask him if he ever read a book while riding his horse. I want to watch him drink root beer. I want to find out the color of his cowboy hat, if it was brown and edged in white light. He smiles shyly at me. I know then that I remember him, and that I love him with all my heart.

Yeah Yeah Yeah

John, the Thinking Girl's Beatle

SUSAN LILLEY

Once upon a time, in a sleepy, citrus-scented neighborhood in Orlando, Florida, an awkward preteen girl waited. As a child growing up in the '60s, she carried a growing, tingling suspicion that life was about to change. She moped for no reason. She yearned, but could not place the object of her yearning; it was something elusive, flickering just out of sight. As it turned out, her awakening was sudden, intense, and unexpected. Her vague dreams crystallized into a full-on, life-changing psychosexual explosion, all because her parents made her watch a one-hour variety show on television…

One chilly evening in February, the Lilley family was gearing up for the usual Sunday night ritual: burgers on the grill, then good old mid-century American TV! *Lassie*, followed by *The Wonderful World of Disney*, then *Bonanza*, my dad's favorite Western. My two younger brothers and I were in the grip of fascination about the start of a three-part Disney drama, *The Scarecrow of Romney Marsh*. So imagine our horror when our parents announced over dinner that we were going to have to miss the harrowing adventures of Scarecrow that night.

Dad filled his wine glass with Chianti and calmly stole a Tater Tot from my plate as he spoke. "Listen, you all. We must watch *The Ed Sullivan Show*. Something big is going to happen tonight."

Ed Sullivan! To us, that show meant a parade of jugglers, acrobats, opera stars, hideous talking puppets, and Borscht Belt comedians whose jokes we did not get. A roar of outrage came at him from three open mouths in various stages of chewing, but there was no eroding the unified parental front.

"We've had phone calls about this from people who KNOW," Mom said placidly. "Whatever it is—some group from England, I think—I am not going to miss it. And neither are you."

DVR technology was decades away, and a one-TV home was the norm in average, middle-class, suburban America. An altar-sized hunk of serious furniture, the television set was the focal point of our recently remodeled "Florida room"; it sat next to the rarely-used fireplace. After the unthinkable announcement, my youngest brother, John, fled to his bunk bed in tears. Bubba (yes, many Southern families do have a Bubba), the middle child, checked out my reaction, which was to go get a Nancy Drew mystery for escape from whatever was about to be forced on us. By the time Ed Sullivan was standing in front of his curtains at eight p.m., all three of us were ensconced on the beige cushions of the carved-bamboo couch, devouring peace-offering bowls of vanilla ice cream covered with Hershey's chocolate syrup. We were about to meet the Beatles.

The first song, "All My Loving," brought the entire family to silence. Then Paul sang the ballad "Till There Was You," from my parents' favorite musical, *The Music Man*. Dad was impressed, and Mom was starting to swoon. By the time they got to "I Want to Hold Your Hand," I had unconsciously but thoroughly made the leap from bookish little girl to dreamy-brained, preteen romantic, all in one hour.

I wasn't sure what had hit me. Sure, I was aware of popular music and even had a little 45 collection started, with such treasures as "Sukiyaki," "My Guy" (by the great Mary Wells), "Another Saturday Night," and an Australian novelty song I adored called "Tie Me Kangaroo Down, Sport." I owned a pink plastic record player decorated with cartoon drawings of teenagers twisting the night away, all suddenly rather irrelevant on Monday morning, February 10, 1964.

Over the next weeks and months, my entire generation coalesced into a group obsession that crossed state and national boundaries and already had a name in the mainstream media: Beatlemania. The most acute symptoms included feeling faint and tearful when gazing at collected pictures of John, Paul, George, and Ringo from fan magazines that flew off the racks at local drugstores. My first love was Paul (statistically predictable), but in truth, it wasn't just the star-crush factor. This music hit kids my age with a perfect-storm wallop as adolescence began to rev up, and the remnants of the somnolent Eisenhower era began to dissolve before our eyes.

Dad dutifully bought the album *Meet the Beatles!* at our local record store, and I bought new singles as fast as they were released. I saw *A Hard Day's Night* five times in one day. We played those discs until the grooves practically melted, until the stylus required coins on top to ride the beloved tracks into our ears again and again. We could not get enough of them. We began to look outward, beyond our families and schools, and inward, to ideas and dreams that were to define our paths all the way to adulthood.

Music, the most ephemeral of arts, is culturally perhaps the most powerful. Every generation has its liberating sound, and I feel lucky to have been swept into this particular moment. Boys in my grade started, awkwardly at first, to try to express their ineffable emotions in music. As rock critic Dave Marsh explains in his book *The Beatles' Second Album*, singing might have previously been a suspect activity for boys of that age, but "when John Lennon howls the lyrics to 'Please Mr. Postman,' it's as if he is playing football, tackle, no pads." Just like that, it was now cool for even the manliest of young men to wail their own yearnings, guitar in hand.

As a teenager in Florida, Susan Lilley felt the lure of the "thinking girl's Beatle," John Lennon. Today, Susan is a poet and essayist, still living in Florida.

While male garage bands sprouted up like dandelions, girls gave legitimacy to the sex appeal of the Beatles and British Invasion wannabes in their own backyards. We also began to identify strongly with the coming wave of new women artists, who, like the R&B and folk gods now co-opting the wave of change, entranced us with their female take on the new reality. When Marianne Faithfull delivered "As Tears Go By" on the music show *Shindig*, I felt a tidal wave wash over my girl-brain. Same with Joan Baez, Diana Ross and the Supremes, and Cass Elliot and Michelle Phillips of The Mamas & The Papas.

My friends and I loved Detroit soul, blues, folk, California surf, and all the British Invasion bands. But the release of a new Beatles album was a holy event. *Rubber Soul* was lip-synced at every sleepover in junior high. *Sgt. Pepper* ran day and night the entire summer of 1967, with a bit of time out for Jimi Hendrix. *Magical Mystery Tour* formed the sun-dazed dreams lived on the deck of my friend Sue Ann's pool, and *Help!* was the first official in-car music blasted on the tape deck when we got our street freedom as licensed drivers.

All-weekend listening parties fueled with stolen parental booze and occasional pot were devoted to *Abbey Road* and then the *White Album*, each work seeming more life changing and masterful than the last. It was as if the Beatles were morphing with us through experience, taste, politics, growth, and change.

By this time, I had made the emotional journey of crush-devotion from Paul McCartney to John Lennon, whose darker tones in the Beatles' work and whose public persona were thrilling and inspiring in a new, more adult way. John was my older-teen crush, and I began to hear what he was saying beyond the music. He was a serious feminist and a peace activist, and he walked the walk. And *my God*, was he sexy. The persistent nasal Liverpool accent, the gravel in his voice, along with the intimate nuances built into his songs were a downright incendiary combo. Seriously, just listen to "Happiness Is a Warm Gun" and see if you don't shiver. And those round glasses, the sheer grittiness and frankness he brought to both his public life and the music—a true artist, and my more appropriate young-adult heartthrob. He wasn't "cute"; he was brainy and honest and fearless and human.

Recently, I saw Paul McCartney interviewed in a small venue on a local college campus, and he told stories about his writing partnership with John. He allowed as how John always added the darker vein to whatever song they were working on. In the chorus of "Getting Better," one of the more poppy, optimistic songs on the incomparable *Sgt. Pepper* album, John answers Paul's cheerful lyrics about things getting "better" all the time with the dour and realistic line that they can't get "no worse." The fact that they worked against each other this way created that tonal ambiguity many of us find so rich and satisfying in the songs.

In bittersweet timing, the group disbanded just as my cohort of youthful fans graduated and entered new ritualistic passageways. I pulled college all-nighters to Paul McCartney's album *Ram*. When I was going through my first divorce, John Lennon was shot while I was daily inhaling solace from his and Yoko's new *Double Fantasy* album. I don't know if I cried more for John or my own doomed marriage. Again, I felt the inner earthquake of an era ending and new things coming,

Music is still great, by the way. To hell with curmudgeons who love only the past. I am constantly thrilled with new wonders as they pop up on the scene, and if I had some Lana Del Rey, or Daft Punk's *Random Access Memories* on vinyl instead of in my iPod, believe me, the grooves would have been worn away over the last couple of years. It's fabulous, but not so personal. Even my kids admit that for their generation, there has been nothing quite like the Beatles and all they brought with them. Nothing.

Sometimes, the emotional weight of this particular life soundtrack is almost too much to carry. But we're happy to do it. This music is ours. And John will always be both an icon and a lost love to me.

Now I Need a Place to Hide Away

Ann Hood

It is difficult to hide from the Beatles. After all these years, they are still regularly in the news. Their songs play on oldies stations, countdowns, and best-ofs. There is always some Beatles anniversary: the first number-one song, the first time in the United States, a birthday, an anniversary, a milestone, a Broadway show.

But hide from the Beatles I must. Or, in some cases, escape. One day in the grocery store, when "Eight Days a Week" came on, I had to leave my cartful of food and run out. Stepping into an elevator that's blasting a peppy Muzak version of "Hey Jude" is enough to send me home to bed.

Of course, it wasn't always this way. I used to love everything about the Beatles. As a child, I memorized their birthdays, their tragic life stories, the words to all of their songs. I collected Beatles trading cards in bubble-gum packs and wore a charm bracelet of dangling Beatles heads and guitars.

For days, my cousin Debbie and I argued over whether "Penny Lane" and its flip side, "Strawberry Fields Forever," had been worth waiting for. I struggled to understand *Sgt. Pepper*; I marveled over the brilliance of the *White Album*.

My cousins and I used to play Beatle wives. We all wanted to be married to Paul, but John was okay too. None of us wanted Ringo. Or even worse, George.

It was too easy to love Paul. Those bedroom eyes. That mop of hair. Classically cute. When I was eight, I asked my mother if she thought I might someday marry Paul McCartney.

"Well, honey," she said, taking a long drag on her Pall Mall. "Somebody will. Maybe it'll be you."

In fifth grade, in a diary in which I mostly wrote, *It is so boring here*, or simply, *Bored*, only one entry stands out: *I just heard on the radio that Paul got married. Oh, please, God, don't let it be true.*

It was true, and I mourned for far too long.

Of course, by the time I was in high school, I understood my folly. John was the best Beatle: sarcastic, funny, interesting looking. That long, thin nose. Those round, wire-rimmed glasses. By then I didn't want to be anybody's wife. But I did want a boy like John, someone who spoke his mind, got into trouble, swore a lot, and wrote poetry.

When I did get married and then had children, it was Beatles' songs I sang to them at night. As one of the youngest of twenty-four cousins, I had never held an infant or babysat. I didn't know any lullabies, so I sang Sam and Grace to sleep with "I Will" and

"P.S. I Love You." Eventually, Sam fell in love with Broadway musicals and abandoned the Beatles.

But not Grace. She embraced them with all the fervor that I had. Her taste was quirky, mature.

"What's the song where the man is standing, holding his head?" she asked, frowning, and before long I had unearthed my old *Help!* album, and the two of us were singing "You've Got to Hide Your Love Away."

For Grace's fourth Christmas, Santa brought her all of the Beatles' movies on video, a photo book of their career, and *The Beatles 1* tape. Before long, playing "Eight Days a Week" as loud as possible became our anthem. Even Sam sang along and admitted that it was arguably the best song ever written.

Best of all about my daughter the Beatles fan was that by the time she was five, she already had fallen for John. Paul's traditional good looks did not win her over. Instead, she liked John's nasally voice, his dark side. After watching the biopic *Backbeat*, she said Stu was her favorite. But since he died before the Beatles became famous, she would settle for John. Once, I overheard her arguing with a first-grade boy who didn't believe that there had been another Beatle.

"There were two other Beatles," Grace told him, disgusted. "Stu and Pete Best." She rolled her eyes and stomped off in her glittery shoes.

Sometimes, before she fell asleep, she would make me tell her stories about John's mother dying, how the band met in Liverpool, and how when Paul wrote the tune for "Yesterday," he sang the words "scrambled eggs" to it.

After I would drop Sam off at school and continue with Grace to her kindergarten, she'd have me play one of her Beatles tapes. She would sing along the whole way there: "Scrambled eggs, all my troubles seemed so far away."

On the day George Harrison died, Grace acted as if she had lost a friend, walking sad and teary-eyed around the house, shaking her head in disbelief. She asked if we could play just Beatles music all day, and we did. That night, we watched a retrospective on George. Feeling guilty, I confessed that he was the one none of us wanted to marry.

"George?" Grace said, stunned. "But he's great."

Five months later, on a beautiful April morning, Grace and I took Sam to school, then got in the car and sang along with "I Want to Hold Your Hand" while we drove. Before she left, she asked me to cue the tape so that as soon as she got back in the car that afternoon, she could hear "You've Got to Hide Your Love Away" right from the beginning. That was the last time we listened to our Beatles together.

The next day, Grace spiked a fever and died from a virulent form of strep. Briefly, as she lay in the ICU, the nurses told us to bring in some of her favorite music. My husband ran out to his car and grabbed *1* from the tape deck. Then he put it in the hospital's tape deck, and we climbed on the bed with our daughter and sang her "Love Me Do." Despite the tubes and machines struggling to keep her alive, Grace smiled at us as we sang to her.

At Grace's memorial service, eight-year-old Sam, wearing a bright red bow tie, stood in front of the hundreds of people there and sang "Eight Days a Week" loud enough for his sister, wherever she had gone, to hear him.

That evening, I gathered all of my Beatles music—the dusty albums, the tapes that littered the floor of my car, the CDs that filled our stereo—and put them in a box with Grace's copies of the Beatles' movies. I could not pause over any of them.

Instead, I threw them in carelessly and fast, knowing that the sight of those black-and-white faces on *Revolver*, or the dizzying colors of *Sgt. Pepper*, or even the cartoon drawings from *Yellow Submarine*, the very things that had made me so happy a week earlier, were now too painful even to glimpse. As parents do, I had shared my passions with my children. And when it came to the Beatles, Grace had seized my passion and made it her own. But with her death, that passion was turned upside down, and rather than bring joy, the Beatles haunted me.

I couldn't bear to hear even the opening chords of "Yesterday" or a cover of "Michelle." In the car, I started listening only to talk radio to avoid a Beatles song catching me by surprise and touching off another round of sobbing.

I tried to shield myself from the Beatles altogether—their music, images, conversations about them—but it's hard, if not impossible. How, for example, am I supposed to ask Sam not to pick out their music slowly during his guitar lessons?

Back in the '60s, in my aunt's family room with the knotty-pine walls and Zenith TV, with my female cousins all around me, our hair straight and long, our bangs in our eyes, the air thick with our parents' cigarette smoke and the harmonies of the Beatles, I believed there was no love greater than mine for Paul McCartney.

Sometimes now, alone, I find myself singing the lonesome lyrics to "I Will." I sing to Grace, imagining her blue eyes shining behind her own little wire-rimmed glasses, her feet tapping in time. It was once my favorite love song, silent now in its *White Album* cover in my basement.

How foolish I was to have fallen so easily for Paul while overlooking John and George, to have believed that everything I could ever want was right there in that family room of my childhood: cousins, TV, my favorite music. But mostly I feel foolish for believing that my time with my daughter would never end.

Or perhaps that is love: a leap of faith, a belief in the impossible, the ability to believe that a little girl in a small town in Rhode Island would grow up to marry Paul McCartney. Or for a grieving woman to believe that a mother's love is so strong that the child she lost can still hear her singing a lullaby.

"Now I Need a Place to Hide Away" by Ann Hood originally appeared in the New York Times *on February 26, 2006, and is used here by permission.*

George

Lise Haines

In 1964, the Beatles played the International Amphitheatre in Chicago. The press conference took place in a building meant to hold cattle, next to the stockyards. Smells of hay, manure, and blood filled the air. My sister and I stood in a deep underground hall—a passageway to all things young and unconscious—waiting to get into the interview.

Our parents were reporters, and my mother had roped our upstairs neighbor, another reporter covering the concert for *Time*, into letting us tag along. Jon was a Canadian-born man who looked like a Beatles promoter in his impeccable slim suits. He was married to a fashion model, and she had loaned me a minidress with a target stitched on the front along with a pair of vinyl boots. She ratted my hair up like my sister's and applied thick mascara to my lashes. On the other side of a door in that hall were the Beatles, and we were girls living and dying to see them, but Jon couldn't get us in.

Life Lesson 1: Barge Through Doors.

I should have risked falling through the center of my young, nervous self, tumbling and dropping at George's feet as he drew on a cigarette. But I was still tame, willing to follow rules.

Even the Beatles had a kind of order then—the haircuts, the suits, the concerts. Popular glossies helped us understand their personalities like fortune-tellers. Paul was the sweet one, John the intellectual, Ringo quiet and easygoing, George the sexy one, the soulful one. Something like that. I chose George.

Seated in the Amphitheatre, we watched as they came onstage and did their cheeky, endearing thing. We sort of heard their music, but not really. I didn't want to scream, but eventually I did because it felt odd not to. We were deaf for three hours afterward, pouring out of the big cattle doors. And this was our kiss from the angels: I got to *not hear anything* for hours, unlike other girls who had full hearing and little else. I had sacrificed my senses to George Harrison.

In a movie theater that year, we watched *Hard Day's Night* and cried. Maybe that was the moment that fixed my loyalty. In two seconds of film, George toyed with the strap on a dancer's costume, as if he might slip this down her shoulder. I clutched the velvet seat but didn't see the way the dancer looked—the irritation she expressed that George was troubling her, treating her, perhaps, more like a mannequin than a real woman. But on that first run, in a small Chicago movie theater, maybe the one where Dillinger was gunned down, it was about George's face, his ability to raise his eyelashes like a heavy theater curtain and express desire. This was seduction to girls who had never been seduced.

The winds swept off Lake Michigan, and the Beatles appeared again at White Sox Park the next year. We screamed into the sky. In that way that each Beatles album echoed some moment in the collective unconscious of my wild and wandering generation, we became aware that apples are meant to be bitten, and we possessed something exotic and untamed. Up North, we chased their limousines. Down South, they burned Beatles albums, the smoke of memorabilia coiling in the air. Because the road through the '60s was not only riddled with love, but sinkholes, washed-out turns, arrests, beatings, lynchings, and assassinations. This was the road that tore down a war and traveled over the Edmund Pettus Bridge.

It would be wrong to say I lost my mother so George lost his, or that the Beatles broke down so I could break down. The fact that he was given coffee laced with LSD had nothing to do with the tiny dot I was told to put on my tongue. George Harrison did not hit the road so I could put my thumb out and travel along our western border, until a man in Oregon with a pickup told me he had a gun in his glove compartment. George wasn't someone to mimic or echo or copy. He was a trace element, something I had already ingested when I first heard "I Want to Hold Your Hand."

I listened to the *White Album* over and over in college, until someone tapped me on the shoulder and told me to play it backward because the number nine was streaming in my unconscious. When the Beatles broke up, I saw Ravi Shankar, some called George's sitar teacher, in concert with the Mahavishnu Orchestra. I had found my way to the writing program at Syracuse, where I read Bishop and Sexton and wrote poetry. Walking in on a housemate one afternoon, I found her lit up in half lotus, eyes closed, palms resting in her lap. She was a flutist, someone who understood discipline, and she sent me over to the Transcendental Meditation place so I could learn to *sit*. A couple of the Beach Boys had stopped in the center that afternoon, and their teacher, the Maharishi, had received the Beatles in India like traveling princes. I took the required white handkerchief, piece of fruit, and thirty-five dollars out of my drawstring bag so I, too, could be transformed.

My wandering slowed when I reached San Francisco, where I began to learn something about gurus. Satchidanada had posed in *Vogue* with the model Veruschka; Santana sat at the feet of Sri Chinmoy; Baba Hari Dass lived in the hills of Santa Cruz and spoke to his disciples using a chalkboard; Rajneesh had orgies and ninety-three Rolls-Royces; Muktananda was known for his mastery of yoga; the fierce Yogi Bhajan saw through his disciplines as if they were as light as turban cloth, though he was nearly blind. They went through the flower fields of a culture and picked us for their odd bouquets.

George did the Concert for Bangladesh in Madison Square Garden, and I moved into an ashram in the Mission District. I had my head shaved, woke at four in the morning to make a strong black tea so I could stay awake to meditate. George began to chant to Krishna.

I thought I wanted to sit and drift, play the *tanpura*, and reach Nirvana in a monastic fugue. But the world intruded constantly. The ashram was a grand home on Twenty-Fourth and Dolores that had four stories and wood paneling throughout. The paneling had to be oiled, the kitchen scrubbed down, meals prepared, bills paid. We taught yoga classes throughout the day and evening, and I worked at Bank of America with my quarter-inch of hair, turning my weekly paycheck over to the ashram.

Lise Haines was one of the lucky fans to see the Beatles in person at the Chicago Amphitheatre in 1964, well before she posed for her senior annual. A celebrated fiction writer, Lise has lectured at Harvard and served as a senior writer in residence at Emerson College and is still a George Harrison fan at heart (photograph by Sienna Haines).

All of the food stamps in the city were sent to the Mission District branch to be counted and batched, and on Fridays I helped count them late into the evening. I got only a small lunch from the ashram cook, and having been up at four a.m., I walked in a dizzy, exhausted state up the steep climb of Dolores Street toward home. When I got in the door, the oak paneling gleaming too brightly, my head pounding, I was greeted by one of the women in the ashram. She pushed an envelope into my hands, pleased to share a secret. Inside were black and white strands of hair. She explained that she had pulled the guru's hair from the bathtub drain catch and cleaned it from his hairbrush, and now she would place this on her personal altar.

It's possible I laughed and then apologized. She was a sincere, kind woman, and who was I to say? But in that moment, I arrived at a clear knowing that life will always be full of shedding and death, maintenance and repair, blindness and extraordinary sight. I didn't need to hide my love away to know something mystical or true.

George was fifty-eight when his body gave out. He couldn't drive his cancer away. He couldn't prevent a man from breaking into his house with a knife.

Life Lesson 2: Don't Make Humans into Gods.

He had a son. I have a daughter.

Sienna is staying at my apartment for the holidays, designing a video game while I work on a novel and tease out this essay. On her computer, she pulls up a project she did for one of her college classes. It's based on an Emily Dickinson poem, and it looks like a Cornell box, a three-dimensional object. I tell her I have a wall for this beauty if she needs a place to hang it. She laughs and tells me it's made with code—it isn't real—sort of like our fireplace, a video of logs burning and crackling on the TV screen. I think George spent a lot of time considering *Māyā*, the nature of illusion.

I convey something about the virtual reality I found myself in when I was her age, and I share occasional facts about George as I dig them up, looking for any odd connection or overlap, things I never knew. After the early days, he wasn't my obsession, at most a thread that resided out of sight. Not exactly a *Kalava* or *Janeva,* but an impulse some of us have to see that family and art are the prayer.

I read that his ashes were sprinkled in the Ganges near the confluence of the Yamuna and Saraswati Rivers. The sacred, dirty Ganges where the past, the present, and the future float by.

I put "I, Me, Mine" on my computer. My daughter and I sing a little as we work. We've had a good dinner, a walk in the snow, and she talked about her plans for after college. I am happy to have her home as her journey begins.

Life Lesson 3: This.

Groovy's Hat

Marianne Gingher

The soundtrack of my early teenage years begins with Elvis's sumptuous crooning of "Love Me Tender," followed by Ricky Nelson's doleful "Lonesome Town," to which I first dance cheek-to-cheek with a boy, Bill Teague, at Linda Hattaway's party in sixth grade. I remember everything. The smell of the starch in his mother-ironed shirt, the prickle of his crew-cut against my ear. Then somebody puts on Chubby Checkers' "The Twist," to knock the romance out of us. I love moony wailings best, like "Where the Boys Are" by Connie Francis. But I never feel more alive than when I dance to one-hit wonders like Little Eva's "Locomotion" or the Orions' "Wah-Watusi."

My mind is saturated with songs. You'd think that with so much great American music I might feel disloyal tuning in to what deejays in 1964 dub the British Invasion. But if listening to "I Wanna Hold Your Hand" on the car radio is treason, I am ready to be expatriated. My blood turns spangly, my heart kabooms. By the time I've heard the flip side of the record ("She Was Just Seventeen"), I am criminal with desire. They are singing about *me*. I am *almost* seventeen.

I rush right out and buy the album *Meet the Beatles*. It has all their pictures on the cover, and that's when I begin to sort out my preferences and give my heart to Ringo Starr. I love his droopy eyelids, his pillow lips, the grin that wobbles between attitudes of smirk and aw shucks. Of the foursome he's the shaggiest and most Teddy bear-like. Teenage girls *think* they want boyfriends, but what they really want is something snuggly that won't disappoint, betray, or judge them, like a pet—or stuffed animal. Ringo! He looks so … *possible*. If he weren't famous, he *would* be.

It is a crazy thing to be in love unrequitedly, stirring your heart into emotional soup that's not on anyone's menu. It's as close to the flames of martyrdom as you can be without getting fried. I'm in a drab little folk trio called "Two Thorns and a Rose." We mostly sing songs covered by Peter, Paul, and Mary. I idolize Mary Travers. I want to sing like her; I want to swing my limp, stick-straight hair the way Mary does, and dye it corn silk blonde. But I don't want to make out with her. I want to make out with Ringo Starr.

Fat chance that will ever happen. But, no matter. The white-hot intensity of my flame contrasted with Ringo's cool obliviousness, gives me an urgent holy feeling, like a nun marrying Jesus. That I am burning for him, my heart bleating like a sacrificial lamb, while Ringo has 85,000 girls lined up ahead of me, only makes me feel more pure, more stoic. This becomes the pattern of a lifetime: setting myself up for romantic torture and doom.

Yet, in spite of a lopsided love, the miserable, dateless world of my high school experience feels sunnier because of Ringo's drumbeats. Up until now, rock and roll has been dominated by greasers, rockabillies, and the throbbing dance music of Motown. To my ear, the Beatles' harmonies sound more velvety. Entire complex stories unfurl from their lyrics. I don't know about marijuana in the mid-'60s, but the Beatles get you high before all that other stuff becomes accessible. They are more sing-along than dance-along, greatly appealing to a wallflower like me. They are a phenomenon nobody saw coming and nobody can emulate—although the Monkees try, Herman's Hermits try, even the Dave Clark Five gives it a shot. Peter Paul and Mary manage to parody them in their hit song "I Dig Rock and Roll Music."

Then, the summer after I turn seventeen, I meet a boy who resembles Ringo, and am instantly smitten. Truthfully, I sort of *make* him look like Ringo. I can blur my eyes a certain way and, voila! He *does* have bedroom eyes like Ringo's, a distinctively wonky nose, and he wears his chestnut brown hair long and moppish, too. He and his college roommate like to sing Beatles' songs in the stairwell of their dormitory where the acoustics intensify the harmony. My boyfriend plays the piano, not the drums. But, hey, he can make the piano *sound* like drums.

Fall, 1965. My college friend, Carilee, who everybody calls "Groovy," is from Boston, closer to big city opportunities than I am in Dullsville, North Carolina. She's seen the Beatles perform live at Shea Stadium where the fans go berserk and tackle one another, fighting to snatch clods of grass the Fabulous Four have walked on, then *eating* those clods. I am in awe of Groovy. She wears mini-skirts the size of napkins. She's the only

Marianne Gingher's friend Carilee Martin in May 1969, groovin' over Ringo Starr (Salem Academy & College Archives). Marianne, a professor at UNC–Chapel Hill, drew on her teen idol days for two of her books: *Bobby Rex's Greatest Hit* and *Teen Angel and Other Stories of Wayward Love.*

freshman allowed to take a studio art course without taking Principles of Design first because already she paints like Bonnard, her favorite Impressionist. She uses oil paints, not the hip new modern medium, acrylics. Groovy plays guitar and has a Joni Mitchell voice—like, if a feather could sing. She's wackily resourceful. For instance, one weekend she sneaks off to New York to meet a friend and for three days, because she blew all her money on the train ticket, eats nothing but chocolate birthday cake. She tells stories about her crazy mother and her 85-year-old *father.* Nobody has an 85-year-old father. She says that during her growing up years, he ate all his meals in his study with the door locked. She or her crazy mother would carry up a tray for him and leave it outside the door. She calls him Birdy. Her whole life seems like the stuff John Lennon and Paul McCartney write songs about. Lucy in the Sky with Diamonds. Eleanor Rigby. She's in love with Ringo, too, and we bond over that.

Groovy and I create a ritual that continues through college. It begins our sophomore year with the release of *Rubber Soul.* As soon as we hear some radio deejay playing the hit single "Michelle" and announcing the album's availability, we cut class, and walk downtown to the closest record store and buy it. We spend the rest of the day in our dorm rooms, celebrating the release, blowing off all our classes, even art lab, listening to the music over and over until we know every lyric and can sing along, even harmonize.

I get married in a fever, age twenty, after my sophomore year, to the boy who looks like Ringo Starr. We rent a cracker box house near the college and, and while he works as a public school teacher, I stay in school. It's a pretty turbulent time, 1967. Already, the U.S. has dropped more bombs in Vietnam than during World War II. Rioting in the ghettos escalates, described by black leader Rap Brown as "a dress rehearsal for revolution," and claiming that violence is as American "as cherry pie." At the movies, if the headlines aren't bloody enough for you, there's *Bonnie and Clyde* and *In Cold Blood,* saturated in gore; Over 700,000 people march up Fifth Avenue to protest the Vietnam War; Muhammad Ali, refuses induction into the Army on the grounds of being a conscientious objector, is denied that status, given a $10,000 fine, slammed into prison, and stripped of his Heavy Weight Champion title. New fads include tall boots, mini skirts worn with maxi coats (every girl wants to be super-thin like the British model Twiggy), jogging, and psychedelic art. Hipster vocabulary includes: "guru," "blow your cool," "head shop," "narc," "ballsy," and "peacenik." The Beatles (and Ringo) are everywhere, their newest album *Sgt. Pepper's Lonely Hearts Club Band* topping the chart and introducing the world not only to electronic rock but to rock music aspiring to be classical via full symphony orchestrations.

By 1967, since I'm married and living off campus, we can play *Sgt. Pepper's* at full-volume, the speakers shuddering, and sing at the top of our lungs. When my husband comes home from work, he joins in, too. We cook hamburgers and crack open beers and sing long into the dark. Sometimes we link arms, a trio of Beatlemaniacs, and dance all over the house and out into the weedy front yard. Who owns a lawnmower? The Establishment. The people who start wars and hate rock and roll mow their lawns. Not us. Don't trust anybody over thirty—that's our mantra. We'll never be thirty. Never. My husband has grown a mustache similar to the one Ringo now sports. Facial hair for young men is in vogue, but like all fads associated with the counterculture, it suggests anarchy to the Establishment. Before long, the principal at his school orders him to shave off the mustache, and to keep his job, he complies. We keep falling off the tightrope of idealism into the land of sheep. This is the way you eventually get to be thirty.

We celebrate the release of the famous *White Album* in 1968 and *Abbey Road* in 1969. It's the end of the Beatles—the band breaks up after *Abbey Road*—and the end of college for us.

In the spring of 1969 our college hosts an event, an annual ritual for graduating seniors called Hat Burning. Students design and construct paper hats that symbolize carefree youth and trivialities and give the hats to partners. The hats are required to be wearable, but they don't need to be fancy. Ideally they call to mind the spirit and personality of the person who wears them, and their designs are kept secret until the hats are gifted to their recipients. Groovy and I make hats for one another.

Brainstorming her hat, I leave my homework in the dust. I can hardly think of anything else. Not my exams, not my senior art show I'm supposed to be building frames for. The hat … how to make the hair, the nose? The hat I construct is big, three-dimensional, colorful and funny. When it's finished, I can hardly bear to hand it over: a gigantic replica of Ringo Starr's head. Groovy gasps. She hugs me, then settles the Ringo hat atop her head with reverence, like the crown of our friendship it is. "I can't bear the thought of throwing him into the fire," she says. "Do I have to?"

"We're graduating," I say. "We're supposed to put away childish things."

"Never," she says.

I wish I recalled the hat that Groovy made for me, but I can't, perhaps because I worked so hard on the one that I made for her, that it became a hat that served both of us, that linked us. A hat that stood for a time in our lives when we gave ourselves in full-throated pleasure to the joys not only of wallowing in song but in radiant possibilities. The gauzy wonderment of those years was like a chrysalis. Our wings were still incubating. Beyond the confines of our privileged innocence, the world was waiting to challenge our flight and to chew us up.

We couldn't imagine the future. Our present was as deeply immersed in fantasy as any yellow submarine. We wouldn't have wanted to know where we were headed, the disappointments and losses in love, work, the deflations of hope, ambition, the suffering. In time my marriage to the boy who looked like Ringo ended. Then, in her fifties, Groovy developed a rare progressive form of aphasia that affected her ability to communicate. Once she couldn't remember a particular word, she lost all memory of the physical thing itself. We were sitting in a Boston restaurant one day when I commented on the beauty of the china plates. Only I said, "Isn't this china pretty?" She gave me a blank look. "China is a country," she said.

The last time I visited her, her husband suggested we play a Beatles album.

"What's 'Beatles'?" she asked. He got up from the table and put on the CD. Her face brightened. She could no longer sing the lyrics, but in seconds she was humming the music perfectly. We all hummed along. We even harmonized.

Not long after, she was sitting on the floor of her art room, cutting up magazines. It's what she did all day to entertain herself while her husband was at work. There was no purpose to the cutting. She wasn't making a collage. She must have enjoyed the repetitive motions of the scissors, the physicality of them, the process of doing. She no longer painted because she could not remember the images she wished to paint. If she smelled smoke, she did not understand it as a danger. Perhaps she had forgotten the word for smoke. When her husband called to tell me she had died in a house fire, he speculated that it was because she forgot the way to her front door. Or maybe what a door was.

On Hat Burning Day, there are speeches. All doors are flung wide open for us. We can go anywhere. Do anything. Be courageous and fierce and determined. We line up in the quad, don our paper hats and parade beneath a canopy of swishy campus oaks and maple trees, arriving at the smoldering pyre. One by one, we lift the hats from our heads and cast them into the flames. I watch Groovy hesitate, then bravely unseat Ringo from her forehead and toss him into the flames. Ringo burns as quickly and as completely as all the rest, but I also think, the brightest.

The Stuff Daydreams
Are Made Of

Hank Phillippi Ryan

I'm not sure where I found the instructions. There was no Internet in 1964, so probably they were in a magazine or maybe a library book. To make a crepe-paper rose, you cut petals and smoothed each center, then twisted them around a pencil. Something like that. Then you affixed each petal to that thin green florist tape, somehow, and then twisted green crepe paper to make the stem. Somehow.

I needed to learn how to make a rose, because I had a date—an actual date—and Jim (not his real name) and I were going to a concert. A Paul Simon concert. Two weeks away.

I had to plan. Paul Simon needed to know—*needed* to know!—that I could not live without him. So I got it into my head that I should give Paul roses. But how? Back then, even teenager me knew a bouquet of real roses was impractical and impossible and besides, way more expensive than my allowance (A dollar a week? Maybe five? But that included lunch money) could bear.

So paper rose it would be. If I could give him this perfect rose, he would look at me and understand that his music and his words had changed me. Had saved me.

Without Paul? I knew I would have been doomed. Doomed as only a fourteen-year-old girl could be. Doomed as only a needy, bookish, misfit, teenaged girl could be.

This was rural Indiana, so rural that you couldn't see another house from our house. My sister and I used to ride our ponies to the library, get a saddlebag full of books, then read them up in the hayloft of the barn behind our house.

I had no friends, except for the characters in those books.

One day at school—we called it junior high, though today it's called middle school—they voted on the class superlatives. I was not voted Most Popular, or Most Likely to Succeed, or Best Dressed. I was voted Most Individual.

Most Individual. Sure, *now* that's great. Now that means unique and special. Innovative and powerful. Then? It was disaster. *Di-saster.*

I knew what it meant. It meant most we-don't-want-to-sit-with-you-at-lunch. Most unlike-everyone-else. Most loser. They put my picture in the school paper upside down to show how truly weird I was.

I came home in tears, red-eyed and vowing never to go back to that stupid school again.

I stomped up to my bedroom to sulk and plan how I was going to leave town, change my name, change *everything*, and get cooler shoes and better hair.

You have to picture the bedroom I shared with my sister. My parents had decorated it in white and pale blue, so pretty, all little flowers and scrolly woodwork, sweetly feminine wallpaper—blue and white, bandbox clean, with flecks of shiny stuff. Nina and I plastered every square inch of it with Beatles cards and posters, affixed, to my stepfather's intense and unending chagrin, with Scotch tape.

Anyway … I stomped upstairs, vowing revenge. Flipped on the almond plastic Sylvania radio to my beloved Top-Forty station. And out came the voice of Paul Simon.

I stared at that radio as if I could see Paul, watch him sing. As if that song and that voice, melodic and gentle and understanding, were only for me. He sang his song "I Am a Rock."

I sang it, too, getting it perfectly as it came to the chorus for the third time. I sang it at the top of my lungs. *I don't need to be like you*, I thought, *I don't need friends, just like Paul doesn't. I don't need a date to the stupid prom, either, because I am fine. Completely fine.*

Then he sang about how islands never cry. And I sobbed. And then I stopped.

I had a record player, of course, with a flip-up top and felt turntable, and I went to the Lyric Record Store (how'd I get there?) and bought (possibly with my mother's credit card, but we won't discuss that) the first Simon & Garfunkel album, the first one I remember at least, *Sounds of Silence*. And I brought it home, and there, again, Paul claimed my heart.

"Hello Darkness, My Old Friend." And I was his old friend; yes, I was, and he knew it.

Paul knew me. He must. And look at that cover! Paul, nebbishy but brilliant. Maybe there was hope? Maybe there was hope for *Most Individual*?

I wrote poetry, too, and devoured books, and tried to understand that being different was not only acceptable, but powerful. And when Jim (not his real name) invited me to the Simon & Garfunkel concert (his mother would drive us), I knew I needed to show Paul how much I cared.

I made that one perfect rose. I created one, then another, over and over, to make it special and memorable and important and perfect. Just like his songs. He would connect with me, just as I'd connected with him.

Garfunkel? Sorry. Not so much. He was talented, sure, but seemed whiny and pushy and too obviously trying to take the spotlight from my Paul. Also, did I say whiny? Teenagers can be so harsh, and I am sorry, Art. But later, so much later, my husband told me a story. As a prelaw student, he'd worked at a law firm in New York one summer, doing head-splittingly boring research about some intricate and impenetrable lawsuits involving oil fields. His colleague, a guy who was supposed to be sharing the workload, was, according to my husband, doing absolutely no work at all. Instead, he spent every second of every day writing something on a legal pad, intently and passionately. My husband finally got courageous enough—or frustrated enough—to ask what the young man was doing. Arthur showed him. He'd been copying, squiggle for squiggle and curlicue for curlicue, a ten-dollar bill. He'd been drawing the currency.

"I hate this job," Art said. "My friend and I are musicians, and we just made our first record."

"Great," my husband said. And back then, thought, *What an idiot.*

You know who that was, of course. Art was always the flaky one.

The only S & G song I didn't like as a teenager was "Homeward Bound." It baffled and upset me. They were griping about being famous? They appeared in front of cheering crowds and got to take airplanes and have fans and stay in hotel rooms with little soaps, and yet they were singing about wanting to be "Homeward Bound"? Home was the only place I did not want to be; I wanted to be in the world and making a difference, and … "Homeward Bound" I simply did not understand.

But that was only one song. The rest were my gospel. My first Paul Simon concert was at Clowes Memorial Hall in Indianapolis; recently I confirmed the exact venue on the Internet, and there it was, 1967. I was sixteen by then. I don't remember one second of the music. And as memories go, maybe it's better that I don't remember. I found an old *Indianapolis Star* newspaper story about it. The reporter portrayed the concert as headlined by the Sandpipers, "who found themselves on the top of the charts with their hit 'Guantanamera'" playing "with" Simon & Garfunkel. My guy didn't even get top billing.

Still, I'm sure it was wonderful. And I do remember Jim and me waiting at the stage door for my Paul to come out. I needed to give him that rose. But the universe did not arrange for that. Jim's mother arrived. Paul never did.

I kept the rose. Although it did not survive my road trip to college, my affection for Paul Simon did. Somehow his songs continued to parallel my life. I left home—*hurray!*—and hit the spooling-out highway into an uncertain future.

I was empty, like Paul, and aching. And I certainly didn't know why. But Paul sang it, and I understood. And it was about love, too, wasn't it? And purpose? To look for America and for our destiny and for the reason we exist. Budding writer me realized that song didn't even rhyme! Paul was telling me again that it was okay to be different. Valuable to be brave. We were all on a road trip then, right? And when Kent State happened and blew up all of our lives, what did Paul come up with then?

He was my—all of our!—bridge over troubled water. I went into politics and journalism, deciding to be a bridge, to be passionate and compassionate. I felt him singing to me again. I knew it was my time to shine. Were my dreams on their way?

How could he know that?

Why do we have such crushes, anyway, as young women? I certainly had no thoughts of marrying Paul Simon—I'm smiling as I write that. I'm not sure what I would have said if I'd actually met him. The point was: Here was a person who seemed to understand teenager me. He was not a high-cheekboned heartthrob (though I also had a crush on Henry V, but that's another story). He was a not a cover boy. But he was someone intense and poetic who would never criticize me, never yell at me, never ask why I got only an A-minus and not an A. Who wouldn't ask why I never had dates. Who would never say things like "I'm not criticizing you, honey. I am only observing." Who would not go ballistic if I was simply trying to save money by piercing my own ears with a match-sterilized needle and a cork. Who would not be "horrified" that I had cut off one side of my hair in a do-it-yourself Sassoon. (I mean, hey, it was a look. Apparently, for me, not a good one.)

It wasn't that Mom didn't understand my crush. She was lovely and smart and stylish, and I think of her often. I wish I could tell her she was right about the Sassoon thing. She had a Teen Idol of her own, she'd once confessed. She skipped high school one day to see Frank Sinatra at the Circle Theater in downtown Indianapolis. "We all went," she confided. "He was so handsome." (I didn't understand that, not then. *That* guy?) But she didn't make fun of me, as my stepdad did, when I cried over the Beatles. (I also tried to make my hair look like theirs, which was even less successful than the DIY Sassoon.)

Hank Phillippi hankered for Paul Simon during her teen years in Indianapolis. A best-selling fiction writer and one of Boston's top on-air reporters, Hank hopes to see Paul Simon during his 2018 farewell tour.

Maybe a Teen Idol is something—someone—to have for our very own. The stuff our daydreams are made of. Who will always say and sing exactly the right thing, be there in our heads as we walk to school, be there at night as we imagine our still-uncertain futures. Never disappoint us, never dismiss us. Always call. Always be a date for the "big dance."

We grow out of them, in the romantic sense. Teen Idols become favorites, or classics, or even—*sigh!*—oldies.

I got married. And then divorced. And then Paul did, too, didn't he? And although twenty-something me worked in Washington, D.C., because the universe loves irony, my first TV reporter job, in 1975, brought me homeward bound (I just thought of that) to Indianapolis.

Oh, still crazy after all these years.

As I grew into a reporter and writer, I began to listen to his songs in another way. Not only how could he *know* that, but how could he *write* that? How did he think? How do I think? How do I reach clarity and innovation and drama? How do I tell a story? Where do the ideas come from?

I teach classes about that now, about creativity and our thought processes, and the goose bumps that come when a good idea hits. "You'll know it when it happens," I've told students. "It'll just sound right. One word, one incident, one gem of a moment will feel like a whole story. Why does that happen? Who knows?"

Then I heard an interview with Paul Simon, and he described his process almost the same way. I'll hear a sound or a rhythm, he told the interviewer, and it just sounds like an entire story.

Something like that. Paul Simon and I write the same way? How can that be?

Then I discovered even more similarities. I have no idea, when I begin a novel, how the story will end. I can type Chapter One, and know there are four hundred pages to go, and somehow have faith that the rest of the story will emerge. Paul Simon, it turns out, writes that way, too.

He's said, "It's like walking on a path, and not knowing what's coming next. You turn the corner and there's a surprise. And that's fun."

Hey, Paul, I think so, too. Life's like that, too. I've heard him in concert several times now, and have never forgotten about that rose. I wish I could have given him a thank-you gift. Because he's given me so many.

As my own career evolved, I toured for my novels in airports and hotels, in one-night stands in bookstores, with crazy-early flights and impossible schedules and iffy accommodations.

I cherish it, every bit of it. But one day, after two weeks on the road, I was slogging through the mean concourses of O'Hare Airport, happy, yes, because who doesn't love a book tour? But bedraggled and tired and … what was that other emotion? I tried to name it. And there it was. I was homesick. I wanted to go home, where my husband was waiting.

Unbidden, a song went though my mind as I was dragging my roller bag past the endless gates. I heard Paul's voice in my head singing it, that song I'd never liked. That song that, as a teenager, I'd never appreciated. "Homeward Bound."

And I got it; in that random moment in the chaos of travel, I understood what he had been trying to tell me all those years. That life is crazy and rewarding and a journey. We should be incredibly grateful for what we get to do and say. And for what we get to sing.

When I Fell for Dylan

Susan Shapiro

On my first date with David, he drove me home in his silver Camaro with white Canadian plates and a Bob Dylan bootleg in the cassette player. I'd never heard of Dylan or bootlegs before.

"Listen," he said.

The guy sang in a weird scratchy howl, almost whispering how everything about me was "bringing him misery."

"Good line," I declared. "Too bad his voice sucks."

I was a private-school ninth-grader who'd secretly get stoned alone and read confessional poetry until dawn. David was pre-med like my father, and from a Jewish family in Windsor, Canada, forty-five minutes away from where I lived in suburban Michigan. He took me to my first Dylan concert at a nearby stadium, where we drank vodka and smoked hash. The performance confirmed that his scruffy, messy-haired musical idol could not sing. He mumbled, so I could barely even make out the lyrics he was croaking. He was tall, Jewish, and sarcastic, like David. No wonder.

David had a weird sense of humor, describing me as his "old sea hag," who had "violent eyes and breeder's hips," which for some reason seemed hysterical. Was he trying to emulate the irreverence of his musical idol?

For my fifteenth birthday he bought me a gold heart necklace. Instead of a card there was a note, handwritten on his brown stationery. It was lines from "Like a Rolling Stone," about a lonely rich girl. Was he sending me a message? Both David and Dylan's words hit too close, working on different levels.

One muggy August midnight, we parked at Orchard Lake, two miles from my parents' house. Lakes were our hotels in those days. We smoked strong Jamaican weed, made out on a blanket spread on the damp sand. I slapped a mosquito on my arm, too many bugs. The small speedboats docked by the pier rocked and swayed in the murky water. I'd never been in love before. I was terrified that he didn't feel the same way.

"I'm not so good at emotional connections," I admitted.

"Let's just have a physical one," he said. "I don't like your personality anyway."

I laughed, thinking what my mother told me about sex: "First it hurts and you bleed. Then it gets better."

In his back seat, I lay down. He climbed on top. His coarse hands rubbed my breasts, legs, pulling down my jeans and panties; I let him this time. He went for his wallet. "The rubber," he whispered, fumbling before he crawled back on top of me. I wrapped my legs around his waist and tugged his hair. I'd heard guys liked it when you pulled their hair while you were doing it. He locked my hands over my head, pushing into me. Then he collapsed on top. My foot was falling asleep. Why was he stopping now? "It's over?" I asked. "That's it?"

"You're not supposed to say that," he laughed. "I'm sorry, too fast." He'd done this before, I knew.

It didn't hurt, but maybe I was too stoned and missed everything. "At least I lost it," I said.

"Glad I could be of service." He opened the car door and stood up.

"You sure we did it right? Mom said I was supposed to bleed." I got dressed. With my clothes on, I suddenly felt vulnerable. "Listen, if you don't really want to be together.... I mean...," I started to say, but I was crying.

"Hey." He came closer, twirling a strand of my dark hair around his finger. "Do you think I'd put up with your insanity if I wasn't in love with you?"

I'd played out every possible scenario—one night stand, platonic pain, eternal hatred—it had never occurred to me that our feelings could be mutual. Now what? We did it all the time, everywhere. My mother and David were right; it got better. He brought me a book of writings and drawings of Dylan. It mixed romantic sagas with angry sexism and misogyny that I pretended I liked. Really, I couldn't imagine love twisting into such dark emotional disasters, as in "One of Us Must Know," "Just Like a Woman," and "Idiot Wind." What was wrong with this guy?

Eventually my mother asked, "Have you been intimate with David?"

"You mean sex? Yeah, since last summer."

She cried for two weeks, then said, "Well, the Goodman women were always hot-blooded." (She evoked her maiden name in times of trauma.) I loved the way that sounded, as if I were suddenly the member of a secret Russian tribe. But then she kept worrying that David and I were going to run off and elope.

"Don't be silly. I'm only fifteen," I said, thinking it was cute that sex and marriage were linked in her mind.

"I met your father when I was fifteen," she said one night, serving David and my father brisket and lamb chops and spare ribs and potatoes. "David looks a little like him, don't you think?"

I wanted to marry him, too, but chose my own metaphor. The rubbers he brought came in little blue plastic capsules. I collected the empties in a bag I kept in the basement. When he was gone, I sneaked down and glued them together, making a blue plastic house. (My mother had chosen white brick, a garden in the front yard.)

The only thing I loved more than David was my early acceptance to college. One piece of paper proved I was smart. David went to grade thirteen, a Canadian requirement. Luckily, his hip father encouraged his son's romps with an American college girl in the city that my unhip father deemed "The People's Republic of Ann Arbor." Every Friday night my freshman year, David showed up at my dorm room, bearing roses and presents: a new Dylan album we'd play, a T-shirt that said "Instant Foreplay," a charm bracelet with a gold "S" pendant. I didn't like jewelry, but I wore anything he gave me and kept the flowers on my dresser for weeks after they'd died.

My sophomore year, he started college in London, Ontario, three hours away. I worried he'd find a new girlfriend. Yet I was his date for his kid brother's bar mitzvah. I borrowed my mother's black satin dress. "Now that's a classy dame," his father said, winking, while the Canadian cousins asked me to slow dance to "Sunrise, Sunset." When somebody asked my favorite song, I was surprised to answer, "Like a Rolling Stone."

David always said, "If you want, you can see other guys." I took that to mean I could fool around with anybody I felt like on weekdays, but I kept my weekends (and naked body) reserved for him. One afternoon, returning from a make-out session at my classmate Brad's, I found a letter under my door, with lyrics from Dylan's "You're a Big Girl Now." I ended it with Brad.

The summer before senior year, a blue-capsuled rubber must have broken. I was two weeks late. My world came tumbling down. He said, "We could get married." Though we'd been together five years, I couldn't imagine having a baby at nineteen, in nine months, in May. Postponing getting my diploma would mean I wasn't smart, after all. I booked the first abortion they had, in two weeks. That Saturday, David drove me to a nearby hospital and paid for it. I woke up from the anesthetic, hallucinating that the doctor standing over me was my father.

"Are you going to tell your mother?" David asked on the drive home.

"I'm not telling anyone." I stared out the window at the blocks of torn-down buildings as he turned onto the highway. It was a dark, rainy August day. Usually a fast driver, he was going slowly, playing a tape, the song "You're Gonna Make Me Lonesome When You Go."

"You hungry?" he asked, reaching into the paper bag between us and pulling out the triple-decker salami hero he'd bought at the hospital cafeteria. Since we found out, he'd been feeding me popcorn at the movies, bringing over fried chicken and pizza. I couldn't wait to get back to school to starve.

"No." I stuck out my tongue.

He took a bite of the sandwich, got mustard on his chin. I wiped it off with a napkin. "When do your classes start?" he asked. "When do you register?"

Usually a man of few words, he was trying too hard to make conversation; we'd switched roles. The new black snakeskin boots he'd given me for my birthday weren't worn in yet; they hurt my feet.

"Still want me to come up next weekend?" he asked, pulling into the driveway of my parents' white house as night was falling. The porch light went on; my mother was home. I nodded, not sure. He didn't come in.

She opened the door. "Why didn't you invite David in? I put out some Nutter Butters."

"I have to go pack for school."

"I put a new nightgown in your room for you to take. Black, your favorite, I think it's morbid. Don't roll it up in a ball like you did last time."

"Thanks." I avoided her eyes, sure that it showed on my face. The hot-pink wallpaper in my childhood bedroom, which had seemed mod when I chose it at eight, made me dizzy. Getting on the scale, I saw that, in a month, I'd gained nine pounds from David's food, as if he wanted to replace the loss, replenish me. I picked up the nightgown, low-cut and lacy, just what I needed now, a sexy nightgown from my mother. I took the Percodan David gave me with diet soda. Turning off the lights, I lay down on the hot-pink bedspread. "We could get married," he'd said.

But I didn't want to move to Canada, marry, and have children now. I wanted to live in Manhattan after I graduated, to be a writer. The big city was too much for a Windsor boy. To him I was the big city. As a car pulled up the driveway, I ran to the window, catching the flash of silver, hoping David changed his mind and returned. It was just my father's Cadillac. I felt empty, like I'd lost my baby and my only lover in the same second. I lit a cigarette, turned up the tape of David gave me. "I Want You" played.

When David opened the door to my Ann Arbor apartment a week later, he walked into a loud, crowded party, everyone tripping on magic mushrooms.

"Who are all these clowns?" he demanded.

I knew he hated having a lot of people around, but I'd invited them anyway. We went to my bedroom. He tried to hold me, but I didn't want to be touched. I was still bleeding; nobody had told me you bled for ten days. I moved closer, wanting to hold him, and said, "Maybe we need time apart."

Why was he leaving? I wanted him to leave. I'd never been so torn. After he walked out, I locked my door.

Everyone was gone in the morning. I was sweating, the long nightgown my mother gave me tangled around my thighs. The collar was too frilly; it made me itch. I ripped off a line of lace, the way religious Jews tore a piece of clothing when in mourning.

I didn't speak to David for six months. Then a letter came with more lyrics, another puzzle. "Visions of Johanna."

"Does this mean you still love me?" I called to ask him.

"It's complicated."

"David, it's me," I pleaded. "You can tell me…"

Everything's ruined." He sounded tortured.

"It doesn't have to be ruined," I said. But it was.

At two a.m. one autumn Friday, I impulsively drove my orange Cutlass four hours to his university in the middle of the night to ask why he was sending me cryptic typed-out lyrics. He never really answered, though he admitted that he was engaged to Eva, the petite girl under his covers in the other room. With her sleeping in his bed, I cried in his arms on the living-room couch. Then I drove home, sobbing to the Dylan bootleg set he'd made me over the years, surprised to find that I knew the words to all the songs by heart.

Dear Miss Joni Mitchell

Marjorie Hudson

Dear Miss Joni Mitchell,

They tell me you had a stroke a few years back, Miss Joni, and it almost took your voice away. Tough soaring genius, you are philosopher and chanteuse combined, chronicler of love for a generation of women. Impossible that you should ever leave us.

Here's the fan letter I never wrote to you, the one I really couldn't write until now. 'Cause I owe you, Miss Joni, big time. The entire female population of the U.S. and Canada and maybe France owes you. At least, the ones who ever wanted to be artists of some kind.

Ladies of the Canyon

It started in high school, like most obsessions. I was a preacher's kid, awkward and lanky, going to a school way too rich for my blood, outside Washington, D.C. My parents' house was full of serious study, political activism, beige walls.

At Robin's house, I was a spy in the house of cool. Robin had all the albums. She was from California. She lived in a modern '70s suburban bungalow, low and lean, with an automatic coffeemaker, handmade pottery, and real garlic in the kitchen. Robin wore Lee jeans and peasant shirts and had the most freckles I had ever seen on a person, and the most joyful smile. What did we have in common? A restless feeling. A need to be anywhere but here.

I was Bohemianish, Joni, because I didn't fit in, but also because it was cheaper to wear jeans. Thank God the style in the '70s was clothes that were worn out and slightly strange. I had that covered: granny glasses and a cloud of dark frizz, scruffy cargo jeans, my grandmother's black velvet cape with a gold brocade clasp. I had learned to hide myself in costume. Don't all artists do that until they are ready to emerge, full-blown, from the chrysalis of their own invention?

One day after school, Robin pulled out an album, the cover an explosion of gold and orange and red and green, of what could have been hair and could have been flowers, surrounding the figure of a woman, doodles like multicolor dreamclouds surrounding her head. A flock of birds assembled to form words in the sky: *Song to a Seagull*.

"Joni Mitchell." Robin said.

But I was still staring at the cover. The colors were mesmerizing, the swirls of line like a maze containing many secrets.

"She paints her own covers," Robin said. Then she pulled the big black vinyl record out of its sleeve and put it on the record player. *Pop. Hiss. Music.*

The music was just like the doodle: mesmerizing, multicolored, with your rich, impossibly high, girlish voice, Joni, dipping and rising like a hallucination, weaving in and out of complex rhythms, internal rhymes, quick-slide major and minor keys. You warbled, looped, and spiraled upward like stairs, then back down, dizzy, settling on a low clarinet note, whispering secrets, and harmonizing with a ghostly twin of your own voice. The songs were stories: about mermaids and freedom, about lonely women, about men who ached to learn how to love, about adventure and beauty, about betrayal and imagination. There was even a song named "The Dawn Treader," like the name of the magical ship in my favorite C.S. Lewis Narnia book of all time. Had you read those books, Joni? Had they saved your life as they had mine? Already I felt I knew you. But you were so much cooler than I would ever be.

"Sisotowbell Lane" was my favorite: a song about neighbors and tea and rocking chairs, wheat fields and well water and pickling jars, far from the city. It wove a world full of colors and dreams and warm intimacy, a place where people loved easily. A place I'd never been but suddenly believed existed. Your official website now explains what I didn't know then. "Sisotowbell" was your secret code for "Somehow, in spite of troubles, ours will be everlasting love."

Robin and I could not resist singing along. Our small, thin voices were no match for yours, Joni, my dear. We squeaked along a few steps behind, hitting a note now and then. If we blasted the volume, it sounded okay.

A few days later, Robin brought out your next album, *Clouds.*

"It's a self-portrait," Robin said, handing me the cover.

So this was what you looked like: electric blue eyes, straight blonde hair, long, thin fingers holding an enormous red flower with great delicacy. There was a frightening clarity in the direct stare of your eyes.

Miss Joni, I knew then I was nothing like you. You were unattainably beautiful and strange. I was strange. But I was hiding in it. You wore your strangeness like a flag.

When Robin and I listened to *Ladies of the Canyon,* your next album, I began to believe that I could find a place like that canyon in Southern California, where women gathered and made art together and celebrated each other's eccentricities, from antique finery to compulsive bread baking. Did it have to be in California? Joni, that was so very far away.

That spring, Robin and I began our life of adventure—hiking the Appalachian Trail, riding bikes out along the river, farther and farther from home, from childhood, from our families. When your songs came on the car radio, we sang along, Joni, again masking our cracked, imperfect voices by blasting the volume. On the high soprano parts, we could barely hear the squeaking sounds in our throats, a sound like metal chains straining on playground swings ridden too high. We wanted to live like you. We wanted love and romance. We wanted to be free.

The next year, Robin found a boyfriend named Chris and proceeded to break her heart over and over on his body. While Robin flew off with her new love, I dreamed a life of adventure that might include a place where I was not alone, a place where I knew how to be in this world.

I started skipping school, hitching into DC. Looking for something real. I got a crush on a guitar player who played blistering Crosby, Stills & Nash songs and had a tiny girlfriend with a beautiful, big voice and straight brown Joni Mitchell hair. He helped me find a guitar to buy. I started teaching myself to play, singing along in my wheedling voice to simple five-chord songs like "House of the Rising Sun." My crush had taught me five chords.

That summer, my cousins and I sat on a farmhouse porch with our guitars, picking out tunes. In a family photo, my hair is long and straight, Joni Mitchell style.

Blue

Winter 1971. I'm laid out on a mattress and pillows on the floor of a derelict house on Wyoming Avenue in Adams Morgan with a houseful of gay men and my new partner in adventure, Jeanne. Jeanne knows these guys from a health-food store in Georgetown where she used to work. We're crashing with them while their house gets renovated and until our next housesitting job comes through.

Somebody is passing a spliff around. The air has turned hazy blue, and I'm not sure who these people are, who I am. Someone says, "This new Joni Mitchell is amazing." There is the hiss and pop of needle on vinyl. And your voice slides up into the blue smoke, just like your face on the album cover, and it fills with curling song.

Your songs are stories about writing songs, drugs, lost children, lost friends, adventures in Paris, parties in Spain, bars in Greece. They are about lost love, found love, love that's not quite good enough, love that must be given up for art. Dear Joni, you've been out in the world, having adventures without me. I still don't know how to love. I've been playing at being free. But the songs in this album seize me like no others.

"It's okay to be sad," your songs tell me. And I am. Very, very sad.

I've been traveling, too: hitching up and down the East Coast. Living with hippies who are all older and way cooler; huddling in chicken sheds, in attic rooms, in my down sleeping bag, lugging my backpack and guitar wherever I go. You've been escaping fame, living with a man you call Cary in a cave in Matala.

I have learned how to smoke cigarettes. I smoke pot when I run out of cigarettes. And I've been thinking there might be something really, really wrong with me.

I don't seem to know how to talk to people, especially boys. I've never had a boyfriend. Jeanne has hooked up with a guy from the farm collective we worked for last winter. Joni, you've had many lovers by now. I can read them in the liner notes; they all sing in your band. David Crosby, James Taylor, Graham Nash. They inhabit your story-songs.

You weave a story about a restless wind blowing in from Africa, and I sense that all your adventures have turned flat. Mine too.

I'm still a virgin. In spring, I will hitch to New Haven and arrange my deflowering by following a biology grad student to his bedroom. He will give me several orgasms. In the morning, I will fly away.

The Last Time I Saw Richard

It's 1973, and I've finally given up the road and succumbed to college, Joni. My mother has tricked me into it by letting me sign up for art and philosophy classes over the summer. I'm drawing portraits of friends, studying existentialism in French: Sartre, Ionesco. I've got a mad crush on a man named Richard, who is extremely lanky and cool, with a hank of bushy black hair, and who is engaged to Charlene, a sleek leather-and-lace co-ed from New Jersey. When Richard invites me to dinner at his apartment, I know better. But I go anyway. I am beginning to learn how to be a fool for love.

To my great surprise, Richard makes me pasta, then turns on music and dances with me. I know he doesn't know me. I know he will never love me. I know this because I can hardly speak around him. When we make love, he's so lovely and sweet that I come and come, and then I cry and can't stop crying, convulsions like orgasms, wave after wave, "What's wrong?" he keeps asking, as if he really cares. But I know his life will never include me. I leave his apartment the next morning, fully fucked and miserable.

Standing outside, squinting in the sun, I suddenly remember I have an appointment to get my student ID. I don't have time to brush my hair. My face in that picture is blurry, my mouth open, cheeks flushed, like someone who just got up from her bridal bed.

Richard has a bachelor party a few weeks later. A bunch of us crash it and sleep on the floor. In the morning, someone has put a video camera on endless loop. Richard and Charlene. Richard and Charlene. Richard and Charlene.

Later I will find myself hum-singing "The Last Time I Saw Richard," with its Detroit bar that may as well be in New Jersey, its barmaid in fishnets and bow tie, its jukebox dreams. But the thing is, Joni, in this story, I'm Richard, the dashed romantic sitting in the bar, playing sad love songs. And in the end, so are you, Joni. So are you.

My romances are not living up to your standards, Joni, your "Sisotowbell Lane" perfections, your full-body devotions. I am making it up as I go, keeping it all inside, a stumbling fool. But at least I know you are on that same lonely road, spilling your life like an open wound.

The Hissing of Summer Lawns

1976. Twentieth and S Streets, the Chateau Thierry Apartments. I'm listening to *The Hissing of Summer Lawns*, at top volume, in my one-room roach hotel. The album cover is a montage: silver cityscape, a green field, and Africans in breechclouts carrying an enormous snake. You've been experimenting, shagging your way into jungle music and jazz, exposing the heart of LA as the drug scene turns to heroin and coke, the rhythms of the incessant sprinklers like the beating hearts of sad, beautiful women.

"Yes!" I want to say, "I know!" All around me, friends are falling into addictions—money, drugs, sex. Poppies weave through one of the songs; their petals fall like jazz riffs, spittle on sidewalks, discarded needles.

You've built an anthem to an American city on a hill, a judgment on Cain and all his descendants, and you've invited the warrior drummers of Burundi to lay down your rhythm track, Rousseau to paint a barmaid, drug dealers to inhabit your lyrics. I've been taking Images of Women in Literature, and your songs feel like a musical exposé of the exact place I live, caught between freedom and too much freedom, which feels a lot like loneliness.

I live nowhere near LA. But I, too, have settled in a city: DC, the boho part near Dupont Circle. Here is where I will learn to toast a sesame bagel and put real butter on it. Here is where I live alone with a cat and eat toast and oranges for breakfast, lunch, and dinner if I want, just like on a Chelsea morning, but there's no lover to share it with. My guitar is in the closet, molding. I'm waiting tables and cooking at the local hippie bar, working my way through school, telling people to drink up, closing time, just like that waitress in Richard's song.

It's hot as blazes this summer, Joni, and I've got no air conditioning, just a fan in the window open to the street, and the dry heat of LA in your music melds with the swamp heat of Washington, and the drums from your "Jungle Line" call to the conga drum line pounding up from Dupont Circle. I blast it louder.

One night, the entire second floor catches fire, and with my cat in my arms, I escape, barefoot and wearing a 1940s movie-star nightgown, all tucks and lace, which I bought at an estate sale on Sixteenth Street. "You sure know how to dress for a fire," someone says in the dark.

I've attracted the attention of the primo neighborhood drug dealer. He comes to visit me while I sear onions at the restaurant, my face sweaty and my frizzled hair kerchiefed, glasses steamed, toe socks and sandals, my new feminist camouflage.

Later, at the bar, I tell him about D.H. Lawrence, and how he thought men hunt women the way they hunt animals. I sit on my bar stool and turn my coaster in circles, wondering if he thinks I'm crazy, wondering why I'm telling him this. He is a handsome man with a sense of brute power in his arms and chest. He turns and looks at me over his beer glass as if he knows exactly what I mean, as if he's been listening, listening in the forest, and he knows now where the prey is.

At home, I listen to "Edith and the Kingpin," your song about a woman falling prey to a coke dealer. At work, just as in the song, people come and tell me stories about this man: he's been to prison, he dumped a redhead, he's a coke head, he's killed a man.

I listen to "Boho Dance," Joni, and twist my mouth with the irony of it all. I live in the heart of a Bohemian flowering in 1970s DC, and I've finally figured it out: Bohemian just means poor and arty. Your clothes are not supposed to be any good unless you got them from the estate sales of dead women. Still, I've been playing at glamour, haven't I, in my estate-sale nightgown? Just like you, Joni, with your bit of lace along the seams.

Inspired by Joni Mitchell, Marjorie Hudson jams with her cousin Jeff in 1971. Marjorie recalls her Bohemian "Joni" days with affection (photograph by Anne Anthony).

The highest aspiration of most of my restaurant cohorts is to score some pot and smoke it behind the dumpster on their break. My hope is to graduate college and get a real job. I have your "Boho Dance" conversation on endless loop in my head, Joni: *I fit in here; I'll never fit in here.* And Joni, you're right there with me, confessing that you'll never be a street person, grubbing in the dirt, but you'll never be a glam queen, either. You're just strange and true and full of yearning.

In a year, I am living with the man from the bar. We don't talk much. But he is kinder than anyone I've ever known. He brings me presents. He takes me fishing. He gives me a puppy. He takes beautiful care of his apartment, filling it with antiques and Chinese rugs. Then he starts smoking crack. He throws me out with all my stuff in a black plastic bag in the hall.

At last I'm having romantic adventures, Joni. But that sweetness of "Sisotowbell Lane"? I haven't seen that yet. Seems like you've walked away from there, too, and now there's something hard-edged in your lyrics, your voice. No more magic. Your spooky, clear gaze is turned on us. Reality has taken the both of us over, like snakes in Eden.

Sisotowbell Lane

I get my real job, an editor for a nature magazine, the perfect job, except I work nights and weekends and have to get up before dawn to walk my dog. By October 1984, Joni, I'm burned out. You've gotten tired of LA, sold your Laurel Canyon place, and bought a place in British Columbia where you can hide.

I ditch it all, too, move to a new place, a rural place, far away from the city. I fall in love with it, full body, my Sisotowbell Lane, with pickling jars and fields, well water and whippoorwills. When I meet my husband, we are both wrecked on the shores of love. We drink too much. But we also laugh. Love feels easy with this man; it falls through my cracks to my hidden places.

On our wedding day, there is so much sweetness that it leaks from our eyes, tears rolling down our cheeks as we stare at each other through the ceremony, a small breeze lifting a makeshift pennant in the heat by the pond. Someone roasts a whole pig that day, starting at nine a.m., and wafting in the hickory smoke from the coals comes the sound of women's voices ringing out from the tape player in the cook's truck: Emmylou Harris, Dolly Parton, and Linda Ronstadt. *Trio*: the showcase country album of the year.

I have not listened to your music, Joni, in a long time. The album I got was just before I left the city: the one you did with Charlie Mingus. You were experimenting again. I couldn't believe you loved Charlie Mingus the way I did. You had stopped breaking your body and heart over and over again. Or at least you'd stopped singing about it.

I've given it up, too.

Sometime in the 1990s, in the quiet of a nurturing life, I begin to write. A story flies out of me about a man who breaks his body over and over on the rocky shores of loving other men; a story flies out about a cook who never does what he truly loves; a novel flies out about a runaway girl hiding out in a hippie restaurant. The stories ask the question: What became of the Bohemians, the sad, lost ones, the drug dealers, the drums of Dupont Circle? The rhythms of your song-stories, your strong, shape-shifting voice, Joni, infuse my imagined worlds.

You have been teaching me to be an artist: someone who begins to be comfortable in her own skin with her own expressions; someone who is strong enough to finally share her life with someone else, whole body, and still thrive in her artistic life. A clear-eyed woman who loves.

Little Green

In 2003, my father dies, and for the first time, I start spending time alone with my mother. One night, we're watching a PBS special about your life, Joni. You talk about "Little Green," the song to the baby you gave away when you were very young, and the story that now opens like an unexpected flower is the story of your lost daughter finding you. How happy you look! It is as if the great sadness, the wound that made you need to pour your pain out, has now suddenly healed.

"We had a fundraiser with her," Mom says.

"*What?*"

"I think they call it a house concert. She came and sang. It was about thirty people. This was back in the '70s. I don't know where you'd run off to."

I turn and stare at my mother. "Joni MITCHELL?" I say. "You sat next to Joni Mitchell and never told me?"

"I didn't know you liked her."

I can't believe it. The queen of cool, my mentor in all things lovely and real and Bohemian, singing for my earnest Methodist parents and their peacenik friends. It isn't possible. It isn't fair.

Turns out it isn't true. It was the activist singer Judy Collins, who no doubt sang your songs that night, Joni, the early popular ones that she also recorded: "Both Sides Now," where, in confessing the fool, you are enduringly wise; or "The Circle Game," your mind caught in time like a young woman caught in amber, her understanding of life wise for her years, sweet and full of a child's yearning for the mystery of adult life. I can see it: cheerful, soulful Judy Collins raising money for a good cause, pleasing everyone, not rocking the boat, filling the room with her lovely voice, something pure and unwounded about her, despite her own troubles. Of the two of you, Joni, she is the singer my parents could better understand.

That night, I finally tell my mother about my two abortions. I have never told her anything deeply true about my life before. I've been hiding it all. I tell her that after trying for years, I have long since given up on having kids. But the healing gift that has come to me, Joni, is a red-headed stepdaughter who is so beautiful, people stop on the streets to touch her hair.

A few years back, I went to an artist colony where I didn't fit in. One night after dinner, fueled by wine, I mentioned to some painters my discovery of your early performances on YouTube.

"Yes!" they said. "Joni Mitchell!"

I flipped open my laptop and tuned you in, like a radio. We watched your tender young self get introduced by Johnny Cash, strum your zither, and raise your strong, high voice in a song about a bar in Paris, France, and your home in California. Yes, we sang along. We didn't care how we sounded. We were filled with the joy that lives inside you.

Not long ago, Joni, I began a ritual of early walks up the hill next to our farm. My small dog and I sprint and walk, sprint and walk, in the palm of predawn, fields and woods around us, the intimate embrace of land. Sometimes the world is completely still but for my breathing.

One morning I start whisper-singing in the dark, and what comes out are your songs: "A Case of You," "California," "For Free." My voice has gotten stronger. I hit most of the notes. The early morning air cushions my mistakes in its velvet cloak of darkness. I remember all the words.

More than once, at the top of the hill, there has come a moment: The sun rises and seagulls fly over my head, hundreds and hundreds of them, unexpected so far from the coast, gilded and black-tipped like messengers from another world.

And this is what I know: Since I was a tender fool of a girl, Miss Joni, you've been beside me, breathing, in the deepest part of my mind, the part where patterns are made and kept in the pre-emergent dark of night. You've been companion of the road, touching me with chords and words that invite me to feel, the way a finger touches parts of the body when making love—this, and this, and this.

You've taught me it's okay to feel it all, joy to misery and back again. Life with you beside me has never had beige walls. It has gold-floss clouds and blues so deep they rip the earth.

Last I checked, you were still alive. I'm listening to you now. I imagine you at home in your retreat in British Columbia, maybe lying on rocks like on the *For the Roses* inside cover, naked to the rush of waves. Feeling it all. Whatever's next. Bring it on.

Followed by a Moonshadow

My Secret Life with Cat Stevens

Morgan Callan Rogers

I didn't start my crushing-on-pop-stars career with one of the Beatles, like so many twelve-year-old girls did. There were rules about which Beatle you could pick. If the Beatle you loved had already been spoken for by another friend in your group you had to move on to another Beatle. I could have loved John, but he would never have been mine without my getting into a pissing match with Linda Smith, who claimed him first. I wound up with Ringo, although it felt like he and I were the nonromantic couple on a double date. Not that he was subpar; on the contrary, he was a hell of a drummer, voted number fourteen on *Rolling Stone*'s list of the "100 Greatest Drummers of All Time." He was also the only blue-eyed Beatle. But when I settled into bed at night and tried to fantasize about him, all I pictured was his sad eyes. It was not a turn on.

Imagining a relationship with a sexy man who may as well have lived on Mars was not unique to me. Junior high school was hormones on wheels. Awkwardness caused by a growing awareness of previously taken-for-granted body parts made sane communication with a member of the opposite sex almost impossible. As a result, lots of confused and lonely girls preferred to put their frustrated romantic notions into imagined relationships. It was easier to love a nebulous teen angel who never had pimples, greasy hair, or body odor.

The popularity of the Beatles spawned a plethora of musical idols ripe for the imagination's picking. A few years after my tepid relationship with Ringo—our split was mutual, and we're still friends—I turned my attention to brooding Neil Young and his band, Crazy Horse. I loved the album *Everybody Knows This Is Nowhere*. The songs "Cinnamon Girl," "Cowgirl in the Sand," and "Down by the River" were my favorites. Neil had such a plaintive coyote voice, along with deep, dark eyes and a "Heal-Me" soul. I wanted to be his cinnamon girl, or any spice he preferred. But after a while, I grew tired of his moodiness, my fickle imagination changed its mind, and his voice warbled like a soggy dirge in the night.

After Heal-Me Neal, I switched direction and fell for Keith Moon, the balls-on crazy drummer for The Who. I pictured all the girls saying to me, "Oh, he's such a devil," to which I would retort, "At home, he's just a sweetie! He makes me breakfast in bed and we laugh SO hard!" But our breakfasting days were cut short when he died from a drug overdose at thirty-two.

When I was seventeen, it was a very good year. I eschewed my fantasy boyfriends for a real boy. I fell in love with him at first sight, as he did with me. On our third date, he asked me to marry him, and I said yes. Our feet didn't touch the ground for a while, until I began to have an inkling of my real self, of the person who lived inside of the person who was so comfortable living within the walls of her imagination. I thought about college and about opportunities, about what I might want to do with my life. Then I thought about love and about disappointing this boy, who I did love. But when I spoke to him about these doubts, he cried. No one had ever openly expressed how bereft he might be, were I to disappear from his life. I did love him, and wasn't that enough? We would work it out. So, we married at nineteen.

We settled into playing house in an apartment on a hill in a tiny Maine town in the back of beyond. He sold clothes in a store downtown. I worked as a grocery clerk a couple of villages over. I didn't say anything to him when the reality of my mistake hit me like a ton of bricks. Instead, I retreated inside myself, hoping something would change, and I would love him again. I didn't understand that marriage took work. My parents' marriage had always been a good one, or so it appeared. They never let their children see what happened behind the scenes. I thought marriage was about cooking dinner at night and settling into leisure chairs to watch television. I didn't know how to function as a wife, let alone a wife who had doubted she wanted to be married in the first place.

Not loving reality so much at all, I returned to what had always worked for me. I fell head over heels in imaginative love with Cat Stevens. Steven Georgiou was his birth name. He was a British citizen by birth, but he had Greek and Scandinavian ancestries— wild, curly, black hair, dark, soulful eyes, and a sensitive, pale, Byronic face half covered by an ebony beard. He had known tragedy, living the life of a pop star when he was struck down by tuberculosis and he spent a year in recovery. While there, he had an epiphany and began writing songs directed at me, a lonely, chubby, twenty-year-old woman happier in her head than in her life. He sang to me in "How Can I Tell You?"

I have a vivid recollection of staring out the picture window of the apartment my boy-husband and I shared and looking into the white winter woods, sick with longing for Cat. Of course, he and I would find each other. Of course, we would meet. Even though he lived in England and allegedly dated Carly Simon, I was the one he was waiting to find. It was I that he was waiting to find. I was certain that someday soon, he would traipse up into the wilds of Maine, find this nondescript apartment on the top of a hill in the little town, know psychically where I lived, knock politely (because he was British, and he didn't want to harm his slender hands), then take me away, as he sang in "Moon-shadow." Yeah baby. Oh yeah. I waited for Cat and my marriage withered on the vine.

Evidently so was my husband, because he not only had an affair of the heart; he had an affair of the loins. I came out of my Cat-swoon long enough to express outrage and hurt. But later on, squinting back through the wrong end of a telescope, I know that I had to take much of the responsibility for agreeing to a marriage that never should have happened.

My husband and I divorced. It took a while to sort myself out, but when I finally entered the real world, I became a writer, melding reality and fantasy. When I write fiction, my They do not retreat to a chair after supper to submerge their souls within the confines of a TV screen.

I still love Cat Stevens. I bought his every album, and I treasured every song. I know it was madness to replace a real human being with the fantasy of loving Cat, but he kept me company during a lonely, confusing time, and I will always be grateful for that.

I'm not sure how teenage girls today can create a mystery around the rock musicians they fall for. Part of my loving Cat back then had to do with the mystery of him. I was only fed carefully crafted publicity created to boost his image. I could imagine our fantastical love affair without random paparazzi shots of him appearing on the Internet as he stumbled out of a club with some tousled starlet, or walked down some street holding a tall latte, a cell phone, and car keys. That information wasn't available to me, then, and I'm glad it wasn't.

Decades ago, Cat Stevens converted to Islam. He changed his name to Yusuf Islam, and (true story) several years ago, he was detained at the Bangor International Airport in Maine under suspicion of being connected to a terrorist organization. Those suspicions never amounted to anything serious—not surprising, considering that this is the man who wrote "Peace Train." This was the man who celebrated love and nonviolence. This is the man who keeps a little piece of my heart to this day.

When I heard about the incident on the news, I dipped into a present-tense, ever-ready fantasy.

I am working security at the airport, and they bring him into my office. Somehow, we are left alone for a few precious minutes.

We look at each other for a little while.

"It's you," he says to me.

"Yes, it is," I say.

"You're beautiful, just as I knew you would be," he says.

"You are as handsome as I remember you," I say.

Each of us smiles at the same time.

"Are you happy?" he says.

"I am," I say.

He begins to hum the tune to "Moonshadow," and I harmonize with him as I open my office window. His shackles fall from him as he stands up, puts his hands on both sides of my face, kisses me, and then slips through the open window and flies away.

Cher Bliss

Lesléa Newman

It was sure to be the New York moment of a lifetime. Cher, singer of "I Got You Babe," "Half-Breed," and "Gypsys, Tramps & Thieves"; Cher, of the sultry, sexy voice and sultrier, sexier body; Cher, one of the first women to show her belly button on TV and to call David Letterman an asshole (in public anyway); Cher, mother of Chastity and widow of Sonny (Mary Bono who?); that very Cher was going to be signing copies of her book, *The First Time*, at the Barnes & Noble on Sixth Avenue in Chelsea. It was just too good to be true.

Now, anyone who knows me knows my pet peeve is the celebrity-turned-author. I am sick of people who can't put a sentence together being paid mega-amounts of money for books they didn't even write. How would Madonna feel if I got paid more money than she'd ever see in her entire life to lip-sync "Like a Virgin"? But forget all that. We're not talking your run-of-the-mill celebrity here. We're talking Diva. We're talking *Cher*.

Cher, whom I had admired, adored, perhaps even lusted after, and definitely envied since I was a teenager. Back then, I'd have given anything to have Cher's straight, waist-length hair instead of my frizzy, shoulder-length mop; Cher's small boobs, tiny waist, and sky-high legs instead of my short-waisted, flat-footed, *zaftig* body; and Cher's cheek-bones that always looked like she was sipping through a straw, instead of my chubby cheeks that looked stolen from a chipmunk. I'd have given anything to wear one of Cher's shimmery, glittery gowns that was designed by Bob Mackie to conceal practically nothing and reveal practically everything. And truth be told, though several decades had passed, I still felt that way. So who cared if Cher had been paid a gazillion dollars to write/not write a book? Like the rest of us authors, part of her job was to schelpp around, meeting her fans and hawking her wares, which meant that at this time tomorrow, I would be in the very same room as Cher, only a pen's length apart. Oh, be still my heart!

The evening before the great event, I called the bookstore. "Yes, Cher will be here," the bookseller said. "She'll start signing at twelve thirty sharp."

"What time should I arrive?" I asked.

"We open at nine."

"I'll be there." I hung up and dove into bed for my beauty sleep. At eight thirty the next morning, I left my pied-à-terre and started walking up Sixth Avenue. I arrived at Barnes & Noble at nine fifteen. There was no evidence of a line anywhere. I even had time for a cup of coffee. Just to be sure, though, I asked at the information booth.

"Cher? Oh yes, she's still coming. You buy your book first, then get on line outside."

Lesléa Newman met Cher at a booksigning of the singer's memoir, *The First Time,* an apt title for her star-struck encounter. Today Lesléa is a star author in her own right.

Outside? I quickly made my purchase and left the store to join the mob of fans snaking around the block. "Did you really get here at nine this morning?" I asked the woman up front.

"No," she said. "I got here at nine last night."

I made my way to the back of the line, which was full of gay men, much to this self-identified, proud fag hag's delight. I joined a crowd of especially fetching fellows, figuring if I was going to stand out in the cold for two hours, I might as well enjoy myself. "What did you do, take the day off?" I asked the boys.

"I lied to my boss," said one whose name was Scott.

"What about you?" I asked the guy standing next to him.

"I am his boss," he replied, extending his hand. "I'm Rob. And this is my boyfriend, Tony."

"I'm Brent," said an unusually pretty lad.

"I'm Deanna," said the woman to my right. "I don't even like Cher."

"You don't?" The crowd was ready to pounce.

"No. I'm here for my friend Rocky. He met her once, years ago."

"He met Cher?" Deanna, who was almost dog meat two seconds ago, was now the envy of the crowd.

"She was trying on shoes in Bloomingdale's," Deanna said. "And she asked Rocky what he thought of them. I'm sure she'll remember. Look, here's his picture"

As we all gathered around to gawk at Rocky, a panhandler came up to us. "What are you on line for?"

"We're here, we're queer, we're waiting to see Cher!"

"Cher? Sonny died. Oh Lord have mercy, Sonny *died*." The panhandler started moaning and groaning until a cop shooed him away.

At noon some people from the bookstore came out and handed us The Rules. "Huh," I muttered. I'd been signing books for over a decade, and I'd never had any rules. But this was Cher, and her rules were as follows:

1. Cher will sign only two items. (For the mathematically impaired, two means two books, two CDs, or one book and one CD.)

2. Cher will write only her name. She will not write a personal inscription.

3. Cher will not sign any memorabilia, and you may be asked to surrender such items at the door. ("Not on your life." Rob clutched his 1965 Sonny and Cher *Look at Me* album to his chest. "They'll have to kill me first.")

4. Cher will not pose for any pictures.

As everyone contemplated the rules, I thought of the rules I would like followed at my next book signing:

1. Everyone must buy multiple copies of each one of Lesléa's books. (For the mathematically impaired, multiple copies means six or more.)

2. Lesléa will personally inscribe your book if you pronounce her name correctly.

3. Lesléa will not sign any memorabilia, and you may be asked to surrender these items, as well as your jewelry, at the door.

Lesléa will be happy to pose for pictures, but only for Hollywood agents.

At exactly twelve thirty, the line started inching forward, and the press descended upon us. "We're from WSLEEZ." A reporter thrust a microphone in Scott's face. "Would you switch teams if Cher would go out with you?"

Scott rolled his eyes. "Dearheart, I don't want to sleep with the woman. I just want to go shopping with her."

"What about you?" The reporter turned to me.

"I wouldn't have to switch teams," I told him and waved right into the camera. "Hi, Mom!"

Two hours later, my little group finally entered the bookstore. Deanna went first. "Do you remember Rocky?" she asked.

Cher studied the picture. "I'm sure I do," she said, "but I don't have my glasses." Oh, how gracious was the Goddess!

Brent went next. Cher signed his book and then blew on the ink. "Be careful, baby, it stays wet for a while." Brent swooned and crawled out on his knees.

Rob and Tony presented Rob's album together. "There's no fan like an old fan," Cher said, signing away.

Then it was my turn. I thought of all the things people had said to me at book signings. *I like your work. You're not as good looking as your photo. Is your hair real?* I didn't want to sound like an idiot. But what could I possibly say? "Cher," I whispered.

"Yes?" Oh, that voice!

"I … I," And then to my tongue-tied horror, I burst into tears.

"It's okay," Cher said, reaching out her hand. Should I kiss it? Press it to my breast? Thank God, I came to my senses and shook it. Then a guard politely showed me the door, which I floated through. In fact, weeks later, my feet have yet to touch the ground. Who cares if I waited six hours to spend six seconds with my idol? I'm still in Cher Heaven, and I'm never washing my right hand again.

Piece of My Heart

LESLIE LAWRENCE

No giant poster on my bedroom wall. No rushing the stage to touch the hem of her bell-bottom. I was never really the idolizing kind. Too cerebral? Too full of myself to bow to another? Too sternly warned by my father about the dangers of losing one's head in a crowd? In any case, I was already well past the most idol-prone stretch of my teens in 1967. After the Monterey Pop Festival, critic Richard Goldstein declared in *Vogue* that Janis Joplin was the "most staggering leading woman in rock." Yet ask me who my Teen Idol was, and she's the one who leaps to mind.

Alter ego? Shadow self?

Sometimes I feel like my little dog who is so full of love and longing he can hardly contain himself.

This is what I wrote in 2008 when instructed by Facebook to say something about myself.

Re-reading the words right afterward, I wondered: Is this how I want to present myself to ... God knows who?

Yes, I thought, for the *love and longing* part.

Maybe not for the *can hardly contain herself* part.

Even so, the words felt true and, with a defiant shrug, I let them stand.

Almost ten years later, they stand there still.

Born smack in the middle of the twentieth century, as a *pre*-preteen in Queens, NY, I heard the music my older sister played. I loved "Wake Up Little Susie" and "Splish Splash, I Was Takin' a Bath." Small, sensitive, often scared, I could be spunky, too, and clownish. I enjoyed imitating Elvis doing "Hound Dog" and Jerry Lee Lewis wailing "Great Balls of Fire" (pompadour flying). When, in 1960, "The Twist" blew the lid off the tamped-down '50s, I was just ten, but I still remember my older cousin's training method: Hold a towel behind your back, and swivel as if you're drying your behind.

"She Loves You (Yeah, Yeah, Yeah)." Hard to believe the Beatles' cheerful harmonies seemed so revolutionary then, but after *should be glad*, all of us let loose with a high-pitched, fluttery "wooooooooo" that rattled the windows in our eighth-grade school bus.

I really liked them, I wrote in my ninth-grade journal, after watching the Beatles on Ed Sullivan. That was it. A measured, temperate soul I was most of the time—a dutiful student, too. *I have to cut out articles on what Goldwater and Johnson think about nuclear power.*

Last Friday, I went to a dance at my temple, I wrote. *The tramps and hoods went extremely wild and were disgusting. I danced too, but not like that.*

Whatever **not** *like that* was, I doubt it was much fun. Some people, it seemed, just knew how to dance. I had to stand next to my sister in front of the mirror that spanned our dining-room wall. *Slow ... slow ... quick, quick, slow....* Maybe it was the mirror messing up my left-right sense. Maybe I just had no rhythm. Though eventually I mastered these few steps, for years I remained a self-conscious, rule-bound teenybopper.

Then something happened. A lot of things, I guess, out in the world and inside me: The Civil Rights Movement gained momentum. I started writing a little poetry. MLK and RFK were assassinated. "Mr. Tambourine Man"—that pained, throaty crooning became my new beautiful. I started visiting art museums in Manhattan, and I gained a taste for gloomy foreign films. I went to a Rolling Stones concert and *lost my head in the crowd,* just as my father feared, standing not just on the Academy of Music seats but climbing onto their wobbly arms, shrieking as if I were being electrocuted.

In the summer of '66, I went with a group to the Blackfoot Reservation in Montana, where I rode bareback through the foothills and met a family who hung their meat on a laundry line. The next summer, I lived with a family in Naples, Italy, where men on the street frightened me with their relentless ogling. I flirted with anorexia. As a junior in high school, I performed in our class's subversive remake of *Alice in Wonderland* (*Alice in Greenwich Village!*). Protests against the Vietnam War accelerated. As a senior, I tried pot and, in the arms of my muscled boyfriend, tripped out on *Sgt. Pepper.* Visiting Oberlin College as a prospective student, I heard Ravi Shankar play music with no beginning or end. That summer, as a counselor for what we then called "retarded and disturbed" children, I inched toward *menschdom,* learning to be less afraid of the broken and deformed.

And then, during Oberlin's freshman orientation, I found myself at a dance party in the aptly named Wilder Hall. *Slow ... slow ... quick, quick ...* didn't go *entirely* out the window, but within an hour or so, I was no longer its slave, nor the smug prude of my journal. I doubt I danced *like that,* but I danced *almost* as if no one were watching. In fact, no one was! My big revelation: I was not the only, nor the most interesting person in the room! In fact, *everyone* at Oberlin was interesting—especially the shaggy-haired male poets and Marxists, but also the upright Midwesterners, the Quaker pacifists, the skinny guys with Coke-bottle glasses, who'd been brutalized in high school but were respected here for their brilliance and wit. I was intrigued even by the prep-school kids— I'd never met one before—and by the international students and the Afro-Americans, as they were briefly called.

My junior high had been well integrated, but my classes there were not at all. My high school had a black student-body president, but he was one of only a handful in a school of close to five thousand. That night at Wilder, the Afro-Americans hosted and DJ'ed. The room heated up. High on starting anew in this magical place, I discovered I had a bit of rhythm after all. Shedding a crusty layer of inhibitions, I fell madly in love with dancing.

Released that August of '68, within a couple of months *Cheap Thrills* placed number one on the charts. I don't recall the moment I first heard Joplin sing. I don't remember buying the album or getting it as a gift. I only know it was a favorite among my modest collection. I'm surprised now to learn that "Cry Baby," "Me and Bobby McGee" and "Mercedes Benz" came out later. I must have eventually owned *Pearl* as well. No matter. "Summertime" was there and, on side one, track four, the number that rooted most deeply in me: "Piece of My Heart."

Up until then, the female singers I liked—Mary Travers, Diana Ross, Leslie Gore, Petula Clark, Dionne Warwick, Judy Collins, Aretha Franklin, Mama Cass, Joan Baez—they always felt other, distant. Either they were black or blond or British, too pretty or skinny or fat or perfectly groomed—and their voices just too damn good. But Janis! (In my heart we are on a first name basis.) With her impish smile and wild mop, like me, she was a bit of a ragamuffin. She struggled with her skin and her weight. I look at photos now and think she's adorable, but the frat boys in Austin campaigned to vote her "the ugliest man on campus." Scarred by that, by being an outcast in Port Arthur, where she was called "nigger lover," she liked to act tough, invincible. As for her voice—I adored it, but was it "good"?

More like a "shovel scraping bare rock."

Poet Wendy Drexler's words in "Janis Joplin at Monterey," they get at what got to me: the effort in that voice, the digging down to the bottom of herself, the pebbly roughness there. For some reason, the word "gauziness" comes to me, though probably it's entirely wrong. I don't mean thin or diaphanous. I mean mesh-like, as in containing tiny holes—nano-moments of absence, interstices full of mystery and longing.

An insomniac as a child, I would relieve the boredom by making sounds. One night I discovered I could slow down enough to hear individual pellets of sound. Why this thrilled me so, I'm not sure, but I kept sputtering and sputtering until my parents ordered me to go to sleep.

Teetering between silky and raspy like the teeth of a saw, Janis's voice often sounded on the edge of destroying itself. I didn't know about the blues then. Didn't know how much Joplin had been influenced by Bessie Smith and Billie Holiday and many others. I didn't know much about jazz, either, though I knew and loved "Summertime." My parents had the *Porgy and Bess* album, and a little chorus in my grade school performed a Gershwin medley ("Fascinating Rhythm," "Let's Call the Whole Thing Off"). In sixth grade, I chose Gershwin as the subject for a required report. He was Jewish, I learned, like me. Janis may have represented the grittier, illicit world I was drawn to, but "Summertime" provided a bridge back to that sturdy, sunlit house in Queens.

Of course, Joplin's "Summertime" was her own. She stretched out the notes, added extra syllables, messed with the timing, with just about everything. "Artistry" wasn't a word I knew then, but I was already interested in it—in art of all kinds and in what made some of it better than others. How did they do it—those artists, mostly men? They seemed to know something I didn't, *have* something I didn't. But Janis had it. So maybe…?

In her portrait on the back cover of *Cheap Thrills*, her face is tilted upward, her mouth is open. Her right hand clutches the mic; the fingers on her left are spread apart. Those fingers—not quite straight or evenly spaced—they're awkward, straining. The world is watching, but her eyes are closed as if she's laboring to give birth. That nakedness, that bravery, that willingness to give it all away! In them I sensed a place I wanted, needed to go.

What I do remember is dancing in Harkness, the co-op known for the wildest parties. I've been at Oberlin at least a few months now, maybe more. Tonight, I'm dancing near the floor-length windows—maybe with someone, maybe not—dancing with at least twice the abandon I had that night at Wilder. Probably

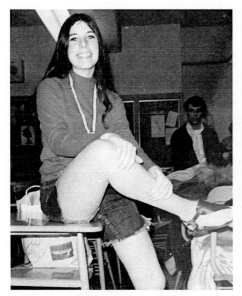

Leslie Lawrence was already into dance in her pre-Janis Joplin days. In 2014, she was still feeling Joplin vibes in a modern improv class. From left: Arlene Barnard, Donna Newman Bluestein, Emile Tobenfeld, Leslie Lawrence. Lawrence's 2016 memoir is aptly titled *The Death of Fred Astaire and Other Essays from a Life Outside the Lines.*

I'm a little stoned, but mostly, it's those initial guitar chords followed by that voice: Oh, come on! from the woman so full of love and longing she can barely contain herself.

Nor can I. Desire? Hurt? Defiance? Whatever it is, it's too much. I want to shed my skin, turn myself inside out. My daring moves, they're thrilling but scary, too—sometimes wild and free, sometimes steely and tense, bordering on the grotesque. At the edge of my ability, I'm dizzy, disoriented. I could fall, crash into the windows, careen out of orbit, explode like a star.

That's the point, really—the lure. To dissolve, disappear. But then I might want myself back!

I wasn't yet even thinking about becoming a writer, but dancing to Joplin was teaching me about every artist's struggle: maintaining that tricky balance between freedom and control, abandon and discipline.

I still don't fully understand that anthem, "Piece of My Heart," or its enormous appeal. Sure, it had that hard-hitting, driving, erotic rhythm, and I liked the idea of being the women Janis sang about in the song, yet in practice, I wasn't good at it. For one, I was still officially a virgin, saving myself for love. And early in my Oberlin life, when I visited the counseling center about some boyfriend problems, the kindly Father-Knows-Best therapist asked me, "Do you think you make your men feel like men?" His implication was easy to discern: I needed to be more careful with the male ego. Chastened, it would be another couple of years before I had language for my percolating feminist instincts.

Yet if there was something abject in Joplin's pleas to "take it" and "break it," weren't they also defiant dares, with a hint of feline hiss and a sly "darling" tacked on there at the end!

All I know is that at some point I stop dancing. Maybe the song is over? Maybe I just need a break? I head toward the doorway that leads to a hallway. Really, this is the part I remember best. I've stopped walking—maybe to talk to someone or simply gather myself. Ask myself: What was that?

Am I still here? Still me?
I'm sweaty, exhilarated—happy but shaken by the danger I sensed.

In the summer between my sophomore and junior years, I lived in Cambridge, Massachusetts, with fellow female Obies in an unfurnished apartment beneath what we soon learned was some sort of call-girl ring. I spent most of the time at my boyfriend's. I loved this man. A whip-smart, sweet Midwesterner, he was a campus leader at Oberlin, a radical socialist who believed that the goal of the revolution was to create a world where men—and women!—could hunt in the morning, fish in the afternoon, read poetry after dinner—or something like that. The point: It was hard believing in art during such political times, but he gave me permission; in fact, he encouraged me. Soon he'd be going to divinity school, his pass out of Vietnam, and I, having declared myself an English major, would be heading to London for my junior year abroad. For now, my guy was working in the Stride Rite shoe factory. I was working in the credit department of the American Biltrite Rubber Company, a job so boring I endured it only by reading poetry in the bathroom stall.

What do I remember from that Joplin concert, August 12, 1970? Harvard Stadium's steep stone steps, the arches, the enchanting resemblance to the Roman Colosseum. No matter that our seats were high in the bleachers, Joplin filled our vision, strutting and stomping across the stage, devouring the mic, slugging Southern Comfort from the bottle, boa flying. Maybe I was disappointed "Piece of My Heart" wasn't on the program, but who could complain? "Mercedes Benz" was there and "Try (Just a Little Bit Harder)" and "Summertime"—all spectacular. No one could have guessed this would be her last performance.

> *I never seemed to be able to control my feelings, to keep them down.... [B]efore getting into this band, it tore my life apart. When you feel that much, you have superhorrible downs. I was always victim to myself. Now though, I've made feeling work for me.... Man, if it hadn't been for the music, I probably would have done myself in.*

This was Joplin talking to the critic Nat Hentoff in April of '68.

I heard the news on BBC radio, October 4, 1970. Sixteen days earlier, I'd heard the same news about Jimi Hendrix: fatal heroin overdose. Hendrix was a huge deal in London; he'd spent enough time there to have his own flat (next door to where George Frideric Handel had lived). The newsmen kept calling him a genius. My muted reaction to his death made me feel out of step. In the case of Joplin, it was the opposite. Her '69 solo performance in Albert Hall had the famously reserved Brits dancing in the aisles. But Joplin never settled in London, and although her death was still big news there, my reaction felt bigger.

> *Here again, as with that memory at Harkness, the most vivid part has me walking—my way of defying any emotion big enough to paralyze me? I'm walking, but then I'm not. In this case, I'm stalled under a wide archway separating living room from foyer. My head feels sloshy, my stomach heavy. I make myself take deep breaths.*

Not Janis! I'd just seen her! Maybe I had felt a slight queasiness over all the booze and bravado. Still, this seemed impossible. And if it was true—what did it mean for me?

I'm embarrassed now by how quickly I slid from shock and grief over Janis to fear for myself, but that's how I remember it. My father once told me he worried I'd someday "go off the deep end." *Worrywart!* I thought. But now his fear didn't seem so farfetched. I wasn't big into drugs or booze, and I didn't have anywhere near the guts, not to mention talent Janis had; still, the hair, the spunk, the smile, the granny glasses I'd adopted, the tough act I must have sensed was guarding the softness inside? Whatever it was, I felt akin. And though most of this was barely conscious, I took her death as a warning: *Find a way to make your feelings work for you, or else.*

That year in London, I traveled all over the UK and twice made it down to Greece, where I slept in the famed hippie cave quarters on Crete. I discovered a Trinidadian dance class near Covent Garden. In service of my plan to become a high school English teacher, I observed in a gritty London school. But mostly, I read Shakespeare plays and British novels. It took thousands of pages and close to a year, but one rare sunny day in spring, I sat in the yard of the suburban cottage my Oberlin friend and I shared with three young men from China. I remember a pear tree, but I see now there's mention of a pear tree in *To the Lighthouse.* Maybe that confusion says it all: Great literature transports.

Woolf wasn't the first woman writer we read. There were, after all, Austen, the Brontës, George Eliot, and more. But Woolf! Although I didn't make the connection at the time, like Joplin, she could stretch out a moment (a sentence, a phrase) and fill its interstices. By honoring the microscopic movements of the mind and heart (of women, no less!) Woolf gave me the courage to think that these thoughts and feelings might be worthy. If ever I were to write, I thought, that was how I'd want to do it.

And write I did—often with a fearlessness and eventually with some skill that "made my feelings work for me." First, poetry in college. Then—after a brief stint teaching high school—short stories, eventually two novels (still unpublished), and finally, my first book, a memoir in essay form: *The Death of Fred Astaire: And Other Essays from a Life Outside the Lines.* As I skim my output over almost forty years, I see that Janis never left me. Only once, in the relatively recent essay "Wonderlust," do I find her mentioned explicitly; she's first on a list of things I find beautiful: "The fissures in Janis Joplin's bluesy voice."

But I also wrote a whole novel about an aspiring jazz singer without realizing that my interest in daring singing began in earnest with Janis. Here, my protagonist, Bayla, is recounting her impressions of Bette Midler's voice after attending her concert in the early '80s:

> *Big … and probably on its way to ruin, but I loved the holes in it when she got all slow and raspy. Those tiny punctures in the vowels pulled me right in.* [It was Midler, after all, who played Joplin in *The Rose.*]

And here Bayla is describing one of her singing lessons:

> *I tried to do it as Damon* [her teacher] *taught me—thinking of a rope, spinning. I'm out there, way out, about to fly off into the wild blue but I don't—because there's a rope. But I don't collapse or drop down either—because of that force, centrifugal, centripetal whichever….*

On May 5, 2016, as I brushed past the counter that holds my envelopes ready for mailing, something caught my eye: a particular stamp I had, without much thought, placed on a particular envelope. The stamp? An Uncle Sam-sanctioned commemorative: Janis Joplin's smiling face, rose-tinted grannies, bangle-covered wrist, boa-topped mop—inside an arch à la (the original) Madonna and Child, all framed by psychedelic lettering. The envelope? Business-sized, addressed in bold print to Medicare, and inside: *my* check.

Who would've thunk on either count! I grabbed my camera.

For years after signing on to Facebook, I more or less ignored it. Then, in 2015, the year I turned sixty-five, the year *The Death of Fred Astaire* was accepted for publication, I was told by just about everyone that if I wanted to sell this book, I'd better get down with the social-media program.

My post: the photo of the stamped, addressed envelope with these words:

> Surely, in my youth, I thought often of the future but, somehow, neither this stamp nor this check, let alone their ticklish proximity, ever crossed my mind.

The sentiment seemed to strike a chord. *Likes*? 93.

Who knows what it is about fissures, punctures, crevices, gaps? Ever since discovering them in the sounds I uttered before sleep, those spaces between have beckoned me. Disruption, disjunction—they're as crucial as the stuff that surrounds them. Both absence and presence. To be *and* not to be? Like Janis, long gone but now gracing a Forever Stamp. Like me, writing about the girl I was, from the perspective of the woman I've become. Letting go and holding on at the same time.

Bobby Orr

Suzanne Strempek Shea

"Watch out!"

My mother flung out her arm and knocked me back to the sidewalk. The big blue car I'd almost stepped in front of rolled smoothly past us and down Causeway Street. We'd traveled so far, and I'd waited so long for this day, my mother reminded me. We were almost at the door of the Boston Garden, and now I was going to get myself killed.

"But, but..."

"But what?"

"But that was Bobby Orr!"

I was thirteen years old, an absolute nut for the Boston Bruins.

This was 1972, two years after the team had won the Stanley Cup for the first time since 1941, and one year after its unsuccessful defense of it. But I was no fair-weather fan. I'd long before caught the bug from my father, who grew up playing hockey on the Chicopee River that marked the end of his dead-end Chicopee Falls Street. He dated my mother at Springfield Indians games in the Eastern States Coliseum, where team owner and former Bruin great Eddie Shore regularly stalked around, shining a flashlight in the faces of fans brazen enough to put their feet up on the chairs in front of them.

Winter nights, I'd fall asleep listening to our radio fuzzily picking up the Bruins games on Boston's WBZ. In time, we purchased and hooked up in our attic a huge television antenna that was shaped like an arrow and pointed in the general direction of the other end of the state, and Boston. With the dawn of cable, we got our first clear and regular pictures of the Boston Bruins in action. My passion shifted into full gear.

I read everything I could about the team. I collected the cards, saved for the magazines and the yearbooks, monopolized the titles owned by the library. I kept scrapbooks, one solely for columns by the former *Boston Herald American*'s D. Leo Monahan. I memorized the players' middle names, hometowns, birthdays, and those of their wives and kids and pets. I knew that Ken Hodge had a pool shaped like his number eight. That Derek Sanderson's father once kept a jar of stitches collected from his son's face and body during junior-hockey days. I committed to memory career stats and could go head-to-head on Bruins trivia with any boy.

While my sister was up in our room applying her first brushes of makeup, I was down in the cellar, paying homage to my hero goalie, Gerry Cheevers, by painting on my street-hockey mask the same type of stitched-up scars adorning the one that covered his face. As my sister curled her hair with orange-juice cans, I happily emptied more for her, working toward the dozen labels I'd need to get a free Bobby Orr poster offered by Minute Maid.

When it arrived, I tacked it above my bed, above the team color picture clipped from the Sunday *Globe* that previous fall. Below it, I dreamed of attending an actual game. But tickets those days were impossible for mere mortals. So I did what I had heard other desperate souls did: I prayed. And I wrote my congressman.

Actually, he was my state representative, the only politician I knew of in our neck of the woods, a guy named Al Lolas over in neighboring Monson. I knew that his work brought him to the State House in Boston, so I dropped him a note asking if he had any way to get tickets while he was there.

With a kid's undying optimism, I soon began checking our mailbox daily. Nobody but I believed I'd find anything in there. Then one day I actually did: three tickets wrapped in Al Lolas stationery. Bruins vs. Penguins.

He didn't even bill me.

The Saturday took ages to arrive. After a morning of shopping, my parents and I found the Garden. Its bricks glowed golden. A train roared on the tracks overhead. And Bobby Orr drove past.

We were on his trail in an instant, running across the street and into a wide alley next to the building. There, the shiny silvery-blue car backed into a space. The door opened. Out stepped my first-ever in-person legend.

In the photo my mother quickly snapped, twenty-four-year-old Robert Gordon Orr is impossibly young. He wears natty game-day dress: a three-piece gray suit topped by the muskrat coat, which I actually had a news clipping of him purchasing. He watches as I place on the hood of his Cadillac El Dorado the box of Jordan Marsh blueberry muffins we'd purchased earlier in the day. I hand him a Filene's bag, which he autographs in pencil, his right hand making the same looping signature as the fake one imprinted inside my worn copy of his 1970 picture-book bio *Orr on Ice*. I don't remember a conversation. That's how it is when you're truly stunned.

Thirteen-year-old Suzanne Strempek (Shea) watched Bobby Orr sign his name on her box of Jordan-Marsh muffins on the hood of his Cadillac that he had parked near the old Boston Garden. Suzanne still muses about Orr from her writing desk in Palmer, Massachusetts.

It was a good win. The Bruins whipped Pittsburgh 6 to 3. But we viewed the victory from lousy seats. Far, far below us skated the little black-and-yellow-and-white dots that were Espy and Cheesy and Shaky and Turk. And my good pal Bobby Orr. But I didn't complain about a thing. As I knew well, the Garden officially could hold 15,009 people. That day, my parents and I were the three at the end of the number. And I felt like an incredibly lucky one.

It turned out that hockey would bring me my other important crush, one that's continued for forty-three years. The fall after I met Bobby, I entered high school and quickly began to realize that the weekly paper in my little Western Massachusetts town never covered my new school's hockey team. I, of course, loved hockey, and also was falling for some of the boys on the team. That they rarely won made no difference: I thought they should be on page one every week. When I gathered my courage and marched to the newspaper office to complain, the man behind the counter offered the only solution: "If you go to the games, why don't you write the stories?" I began to, and also realized that *Springfield Daily News* dropped on my doorstep each afternoon also never contained any stories about the Palmer Panthers. At the next game, I asked who was the reporter for that city paper, and was pointed to one of the higher rows of seats and a shaggy-auburn-haired guy holding a notepad. "Why don't you ever write about the Palmer Panthers?" was the first thing I ever said to the guy who would indeed go on to write about them, who would then get my foot in the door at his newspaper to both write and photograph throughout high school and college, and who cheered me on when I got a full-time reporting job there right out of college. And after ten years of being a very dear friend, Tommy Shea stood with me at an altar in my little Western Massachusetts town and slipped my late grandmother's wedding ring onto my hand. All I can say is it pays to complain.

One morning in 1998, while driving from the Sumner Tunnel to the expressway, I traveled up the ramp and spotted the startling sight of the Garden in mid-demolition, one entire end of the sad seventy-year-old structure chomped open by the wrecking crew: the end of the building where I'd been seated for that first Bruins game, the end that edged the alley that held the parking space where a big shot once was kind to a speechless fan.

I nearly missed the exit I needed, the sudden one that leads to Cambridge and gives height-phobic people like me their last chance to bail before heading over the frightening Tobin Bridge. I took the right and shivered from the surprisingly disturbing sight of the death of a building I'd been in only a handful of times, a space now holding no more than light and dust and air, and nothing less than the gilded memories of countless star-struck kids.

Originally published in The Union-News, *Springfield, Massachusetts, Thursday, June 25, 1998.*

What Would Chrissie Do?

Katie Hafner

We all must wonder on occasion what it would be like to have been born in another time and place. Victorian England, perhaps, with its refined sensibilities. Or Paris in the 1920s. But whenever I start to muse along these lines, I like to remind myself that if I hadn't been born precisely when I was, I wouldn't have grown up witnessing the phenomenon that was Chris Evert.

In the early 1970s, when the Internet was but a glimmer in the eyes of a couple of computer scientists, news still managed to travel, and the world quickly became besotted with "Chrissie," the unflappable Fort Lauderdale teenager whose two-handed backhand resembled Carl Yastrzemski's home-run swing at Fenway Park.

I was thirteen in 1971, when I first heard about her, and I, too, got caught up in the Chrissie craze. Not only did I find her tennis a wondrous thing to behold, but I was star struck by her appearance: slender, tanned arms and legs and long, straight, brownish-blonde hair, which she parted in the middle, put back in a flat ponytail, and often topped off with a ribbon. Chrissie was, I decided, not merely the perfect tennis player, but the most perfect of all human specimens.

I lived in awe of Chrissie's tennis playing, to be sure: her flawless execution of the fundamentals; her exquisite footwork; the way she watched the ball onto the racket; and, of course, her mind-boggling consistency. But still more, it was her aura of calm that kept me enthralled. How, I used to wonder, could one person maintain such impeccable composure?

If it's true, as I once heard someone observe, that we bring one hundred percent of who we are onto the tennis court, I imagined Chrissie's life a sea of calm, with only the politest of words exchanged across the family dinner table, barely a facial expression in evidence. I doubtless constructed this fantasy to counter the bedlam in which I was growing up in Amherst, Massachusetts, in a large and dysfunctional blended family, the days punctuated by loud, ferocious fights between my father and stepmother. As I lay in bed listening to the escalating disputes downstairs, in my mind's eye I saw Chrissie tucked in bed in her pin-neat Florida bedroom, in the sleepwear version of her ultra-feminine tennis outfits: a set of light cotton pajamas with a pale pink top scalloped at the hem. Knowing Chrissie was out there keeping chaos at bay gave me faith that I might slay my own adolescent dragons.

In the warm months and even well into the cold ones, I escaped to the local clay courts—Chrissie's preferred surface, I might add—where I hit the ball with my boyfriend, who was, like me, addicted to tennis. We both played singles on our high-school team. His idol at the time was the blustery Jimmy Connors, and once Jimmy and Chrissie started dating, we imagined ourselves their New England doppelgängers. We rooted for each other. We spray-painted stenciled *W*'s on the strings of our Wilson rackets. My best friend sewed me a tennis dress that looked exactly like something Chrissie would wear, replete with ruffle-fringed undergarment.

I also became a Chrissie scholar of sorts, spending hours at a time in the UMass library studying back issues of *Tennis Magazine*. I learned about the origins of her two-handed backhand (when she started playing at age five, she lacked the strength to control her racket, so her father eventually suggested she start hitting her backhand with both hands). That two-handed backhand added a crafty quality to her game, allowing her to disguise where she was headed with her shot. I learned that her parents were loving disciplinarians. They believed in hard work, possessed old-fashioned values, and held their kids to high standards. Chrissie described herself as having been a shy child who simply craved something she could be good at.

Just before a match, she said in one interview, she took her mind into what she called "a state of nothingness," her own brand of meditation. That state followed her onto the court, where, with each point, she became completely immersed in the task at hand. Among sports psychologists, that mental zone has come to be known as "relaxed focus." Whether winning or losing, she just pushed a stray piece of hair out of her eye and got on with the next point.

Not only did Chrissie famously show no emotion, but she never threw a hissy fit, berated an umpire, or so much as challenged a line call. This, she said in an interview in the early 1980s, was because "tennis is not worth making a scene over." Known for her honest self-appraisals, she added that she wished she could say she refrained from making scenes because of the effect such behavior would have on kids. (She was, after all, a role model for thousands.) But that would have been disingenuous. "The reason I don't act up," she said, "is that it's not in me to show that part of myself. I don't wear my heart on my sleeve."

Many people criticized her for precisely this quality. She was dubbed the Ice Maiden. My theory is that they secretly loved her all along, but tennis fans often griped that they preferred, say, the buoyant cheer of Evonne Goolagong, the intensity of Martina Navratilova, or the histrionics of John McEnroe. Anyone but Little Miss Metronome. But I knew there was a great deal more to Chrissie than met the eye. She kept emotion out of the equation while playing, not because she was emotionless (what young woman void of emotions would get romantically entangled with Jimmy Connors, of all men?), but because she knew that was her key to winning matches. And just for the record, watch old videos of Chrissie's most intense matches through the years, and you'll see a delicate fist pump or two.

I also studied her televised matches. I could see that behind the milkmaid façade lurked a killer instinct. She was a baseline artist through and through, which in and of itself can be a test of sheer endurance. In the time it took Chrissie and Tracy Austin, another expert baseline player, to finish a point, Joyce Carol Oates could have written an entire novel. She took every ball that came to her and hit it hard and hit it clean. And she aimed her balls, landing them with uncanny regularity right at the opposite baseline, from corner to corner, until her opponent began to disintegrate. Then, the minute she got a short ball, she punished it, creating an impossible angle and opening up the court for a put away shot.

There are many Chris Evert matches that remain etched in my brain, lo, these many years later. But the one that taught me all about true grit was my very first introduction to her. It happened in 1971, and she was not yet seventeen, playing against Mary-Ann Eisel, a top American player. In the match, she fended off not one or two match points, but *six*. I had never seen anything like her poise. Even when she was struggling, her respect for the decorum of the game trumped everything. All of this at age sixteen.

Chrissie could do all of this and still be polite and gracious. When she lost, which was seldom, she fairly bounded to the net to shake her opponent's hand. One story that has always stuck with me was that of a match she lost to Evonne Goolagong. Not only did Chrissie run to the net the moment the last point was played to congratulate Goolagong, but at the awards ceremony afterwards, spotting Evonne's coach, she congratulated him, too.

I was an erratic player in high school, easily flustered. I lost far more matches than I won. I tried my best to internalize the lesson Chrissie was teaching an entire generation of players. In lieu of drama (and our team had drama to spare), I tried stone-faced stoicism. At every disappointing turn in a match, I would say to myself, "What would Chrissie do?" Sometimes it worked. But more often than not, it simply reinforced what I already knew: Everything that Chris Evert managed to do on the tennis court was hard. Which was why she was Chris Evert and I was, well, a normal teenager whose tennis would mature into little more than a wholesome hobby.

Eventually Chrissie's ponytail gave way to a short shag cut, with a brief French-braid period, and her lean limbs grew sinewy and muscular. She began wearing more austere outfits. I missed the frilly dresses and the ingénue look, but went along for the ride, all the way through her rivalry with Martina Navratilova, which spanned fifteen years and more than eighty matches. Martina seemed to be the one player who could shake Chris Evert's exacting confidence on the tennis court. ("You can't fake confidence," Chrissie once said.) I admired Martina but continued to adore Chrissie.

Chrissie's personal life didn't interest me. But it did worry me. When she and Jimmy Connors got engaged, I hoped it wouldn't distract her too much. When they broke up, I was relieved. And when she married the tennis player John Lloyd, I worried that his gutless game would rub off on her. It didn't, of course. But she did divorce Lloyd and married the skier Andy Mill. In 1989, she retired. She was thirty-four. I was thirty-one. We both started having kids, and for a couple of decades, we lost touch.

Chrissie re-entered my life a few years ago when I started watching more tennis on television and there she was, a commentator! I had always known she was eminently sensible, but now I see that she possesses a trait I had never given any thought to: she's smart. Invariably, her commentary is right on the money. She avoids nonsense and filler, and floats pithy gems of wisdom ("As I'm always saying to my kids, get your first serve in.") in a tone that makes this viewer take note. Sometimes I lose interest in the match and just wait for the next thing Chrissie has to say. And all seems right with the world.

Pretty Brown Girl
with Big Brown Eyes

DARLENE R. TAYLOR

In the photograph of Barbara, my father's youngest sister, is prom queen. Poised and assured, arms at her side, she is confident, I know. She's completed the journey from notebooks to perfume. Glamorous, with satin gloves that cover her elbows, a crown on her head, and pearl earrings, she looks out with doe-like eyes look at what I imagine to be the crowd watching her. She's a pretty brown girl with big brown eyes. I have those eyes, my dad says.

Mom looks off to the side, away from the photographer, when she poses for a picture. She's not shy. She believes it's a better angle or avoids red eye when the camera flashes. Flipping through the pages of *Ebony* and *Cosmopolitan* in the hairdresser's chair, where I'm waiting for my press and curl, I notice that none of the women in the photographs looks away. The *Jet* centerfold girl in a bikini looks back at me. Long curls on her shoulder, hand on her hip, barefoot, a toe in the sand, she smiles with her head back.

On the table next to the hairdryer is a stack of magazines. *Jet* also comes in the mail at home. Jermaine Jackson straddles a chair on the August 31, 1972, issue, his Afro a perfect halo. The headline says he "Becomes Idol of Teenagers."

Diana Ross's bright eyes catch my attention because there are so many Diana Ross and the Supremes or Diana Ross photographs. I know she is beautiful, because only the prettiest women and girls get in magazines.

Diana Ross is my Teen Idol and helps me find the beauty in my own face. The superstar is in nearly every magazine in the hair salon: *Ebony, Essence, Jet, Look,* and *Life*. Not only is she beautiful, she wears the best fashions: sequined evening gowns; matching dress-and-overcoat ensembles; hats trimmed in leopard print; and glittering, strappy sandals. She's on the cover of *Jet*, April 8, 1971, sporting a curly Afro and holding a guitar. The caption reads: "The New Diana Ross." She's dressed in a jumpsuit that seems as if it was peeled from a silver-white snake. There's another more recent *Ebony* from November 1972. That caption is "In New Movie: Diana Ross Relives Life of Billie Holiday." Arms raised, the signature Lady Day gardenia in her hair, Diana Ross wears a pearlescent white halter gown and gloves above her elbows like my Aunt Barbara's. When we leave the hair salon, I flip through magazines in the drugstore and grocery store and see more Diana Ross smiles.

Because my Uncle Earl is a photographer, there are many pictures of me growing up. And, of course, every year at school there is the obligatory class photo.

139

In seventh grade, when I hear the school photographer is coming, I don't want the press-and-curl ponytail Mom usually tells the hairdresser to do. Ponytails make me feel like a little girl, and I want to look grown-up. I like Diana Ross's curly 'fro. On Friday after school, I wash my hair. A friend tells me to roll my hair and keep the rollers in all weekend for tighter curls. So I aim to do just that.

When Mom is away from the house, I go to her room and sit on her dresser bench. The dressing table is beautifully curved, with a dark wood stain. Mounted to it is a matching mirror. Bottles of perfume and powder puffs are neatly arrayed on a mirrored tray. Another tray holds miniature lipsticks and sits off to the side next to a crystal lamp. I spend half an hour in the mirror, carefully parting my hair in even squares, wrapping the strands on sponge rods, and snapping the pink rollers in place. I pull at the corners of my eyes, imaging them narrow. Would I be pretty with differently shaped eyes? I don't dare play in Mom's eye shadow. I remove the tops from the lipstick tubes. Between the shades of red, orange, and pink, I select one and rub the tip across my cheek and lips. I poke out my lips like Diana Ross blowing kisses to fans. My mouth looks as if cinnamon bubblegum exploded on my face.

I go to Mom's closet and take out her shoeboxes. I put on Mom's crocodile pumps and step in front of the full-length mirror and turn side to side. I'm skinny. There are no bumps in the front of my sweater. I wear a bra just because. It's my under-the-sweater fashion statement. My feet seem big, and my toes point outward.

When Mom gets home, I'm playing cards with my brother, with the television watching us. She cooks and serves dinner, and I sit at the table with rollers in my hair. Dad doesn't say anything, but Mom tells me the rollers are too tight and will break my hair off. I tug on them and say I feel fine. I disagree with her on small things like rollers as I'm trying to figure out my wants and what's going on with my hair and body.

Saturday comes, and I'm on the couch, my head resting on the cushy arm. There are only two television shows I care about, and they're on Saturday mornings: *Soul Train* and *The Jackson 5ive*. The cartoon is a rerun of Diana Ross meeting Michael Jackson and his brothers. Miss Ross comes to Gary, Indiana, to do a concert. A pink snake hidden in a bouquet of flowers frightens her. Rosey, the snake, belongs to Michael. Rescued from the reptile, Diana Ross invites Michael to her concert. She ends up hearing a performance when the Jackson brothers pick up the band instruments in the empty theater and play. Michael's boyish charm in "ABC" comes alive with psychedelic stripes, clouds, and hearts falling from pink-and-blue skies. The Jacksons dance. Michael sings about a love that he, like me, is too young to know. I mean, we're twelve years old. Diana Ross applauds and invites them to get in touch with her music company in Detroit when they've grown up. After a night of big dreams, they drive to Detroit in Tito's jalopy. They trick their way into the studio.

Reluctantly, I get off the couch and remove the rollers when Mom says we're going shopping for an outfit for the class photo. I finger comb my curls, trying not to disturb them too much. I tie the rollers in a scarf and tuck them under the sofa. I don't overly complain about missing what happens when the Jacksons get to Detroit and Diana Ross makes their dreams come true. But I know what happens because I've seen all the shows in the series, and a few years before, Motown released *Diana Ross Presents the Jackson 5*. Hearing my mom's key ring jingle, I turn off the television set.

Mom and I get into the car, and she drives to the Wheaton Plaza shopping center.

Darlene Taylor in 1972, already into her Diana Ross fixation. Now a writer and cultural arts advocate, she still holds Ross in high regard.

What I know about glamour comes from Mom's closet and magazines. I want a pantsuit I saw a girl in *Jet* wearing. It won't be easy to find, I imagine. And I believe Mom won't buy it. She wears pants more than skirts. But I'm thinking she'll pick out dresses with lace on the collars and puffy sleeves, so I pout.

Mom parks; we get out of the car and walk across the parking lot. When we pass a fountain, I watch the steel shapes that jut from the water. Mom offers me a penny to wish on. I toss it into the water. It quickly sinks and settles on a pile of other pennies.

We go to the girls' section of the Woodward & Lothrop department store, and immediately I see a two-piece knit set I have to have. I grab it and show it to Mom. It's green, which Mom says is a nice color. I try it on. Mom doesn't look convinced. She says the bell-bottom pants are too long. But I say the top, a lightweight ribbed knit, fits fine. The sleeves are snug against my arms. The front panel of embroidered fruit hides my flat chest. I look at myself in the mirror, then Mom.

"Is that what you want?" she asks.

I nod. I know how to sew, but she says she'll hem the pants.

Mom pays for the outfit and lets me carry the shopping bag out. I swing the bag, walking through the parking lot. In the car on the ride home, I'm holding my prize on my lap, considering whether I should hang the set in the closet or lay it on the foot of my bed until Monday, when I'll wear it to school. I get home, put on the pants, and stand straight while Mom pins the hem. When she finishes, I set out the outfit on the bed. Then I immediately roll my hair again.

Monday is picture day. I dress in my new knit suit. I undo the rollers and toss them on my dresser. I finger-comb the curls. Mom brings me a wide-toothed comb and Afro pick. She helps me with the curls in the back. I want a part in the middle of the crown of my head. It's crooked when I do it. Mom fixes it for me. She uses the pointy end of the comb and slides a straight line perfectly in the center between my eyebrows.

When I get to school, I notice my friends in skirts and blouses. Some are wearing slacks and a blouse. I feel self-conscious. Suddenly, the knit pants feel too tight. After the photograph, I put my coat on and don't take it off until I get home.

Sometime during that first year of middle school, fashion relaxes and girls wear pants more often, even jeans. When I join the gymnastics team, leotards with jean skirts or pants are my wardrobe. I'm rushing, usually to the gymnasium, after history and Spanish class. Next, I join the school newspaper staff and wear cutoff jeans to wash cars for fundraisers to pay for printing and supplies.

Mom doesn't say much about my dressed-down look of jeans and T-shirts and sneakers. By the time the junior-high prom comes, Mom looks at her plain daughter and offers me lipstick. I guess I don't seem interested, but she nudges me to look at the makeup on her dresser. Fashion Fair face powders, blushes, eye shadows, mascara, and lipsticks are on display like a Woodward & Lothrop cosmetics counter. She must've gone shopping, I'm thinking. Mom picks up a tube of lipstick and turns the casing until a tangerine stick appears.

"Is there a color you think you like?" she says, showing me a wheel of colors.

I like the frosted copper but don't say so. I shrug, then say, "I don't like red."

"You don't have to do red. Red is too old for you. There's pink, and then there's this one," Mom says, pointing to a small tube. She hands it to me, saying, "Want to try it?" She looks at me, expecting some excitement.

I take the tube from her hand.

"It's ok to wear a little lipstick," she says. "Not every day. But you're growing up, and it's okay to wear a little."

Mom wears coral. It looks pretty on her. I'm thinking how it almost blends with her copper skin. Her hair is a mass of dark curls. She's chic in slacks and a contrasting top. I like that look on her.

In the mirror, I see my hands. I stare at my fingernails and notice how ragged, short, and uneven they are. I peel them with my teeth, walking home from the gym. Mom's nail tips are slightly round and glow with a neutral shade of polish.

Mom wants me to have experiences and things she couldn't have when she was my age. I see it in her face and the way her smile softens when I tell her what I don't want. I see it in the bend of her head when she fishes through the drawer and gets a nail file. I hear it in her voice when she asks me, "Is that the one you want?" It's as if she's holding my hand, guiding me on wintery stairs. She's holding a lipstick tube, but speaks with a "Careful on the steps" worry. I hear the worry when she and dad talk about the new school I said I want to go to that's outside of our neighborhood. I'll have to take the bus to get there.

My sixteenth birthday makes me aware of another change: the question comes more and more about what I want to do when I grow up.

Mahogany is in the movie theaters, and Diana Ross splashes the covers of magazines with her portrayal of the pretty brown girl with big brown eyes from the South Side of Chicago, Tracy Chambers, who journeys from a department-store secretary and night-school art student to fashion model in Rome. In knits that hug her slender frame, rhinestones on her velvet lashes, and a new hairstyle on every page, Diana Ross makes me aware that style is about a young woman finding herself, loving herself, and making her future.

In high school, I'm trying to fit into a new environment and meet new people. High school seems a fashion show. The senior girls dress in heels, panty hose, and dresses. Their dresses hug their waists and curve at their bustlines and hips. Future power people, many of them go to work in a program that places high schoolers in government agencies. It gives them their first experiences in the workplace. They look so grown-up in their fashions inspired by *Mahogany*.

At the lockers, it seems every girl is talking about boys and what the boys are saying about them. I didn't understand the high-stakes boy-girl friendships. Besides the time after a Jackson 5 concert at the Richmond Coliseum when I argue that Michael Jackson would like me better than my cousin, I don't think about what a boy thinks of me. But between-classroom hall-locker chatter changes that. "Pretty for a brown girl," I hear some say as they pass. "Too skinny," I also hear.

In *Mahogany*, as Tracy Chambers, Diana Ross is told she doesn't have the right body. I'm narrow and flat-chested and no longer on the gymnastics team, so I understand when Tracy sasses back. But I'm too shy and uncertain of what pretty is to sass.

Besides, being that skinny brown girl with big brown eyes isn't too bad for Diana Ross. After all, she kisses and is loved by the Hollywood hunk of the '70s, Billy Dee Williams. Everybody loves Billy Dee. *Jet* magazine calls him a matinee idol. I hear ladies in the hair salon swoon about Billy Dee. At school, the boys say they want to be Billy Dee, with his slicked-back hair, mustache, smooth walk, and way with the ladies. With his good looks, love for his woman, and gentle hand extended like a prince from the fairy tales, he's the guy the girls want to marry. In fact, twice in film—in *Lady Sings the Blues* and *Mahogany*—Billy Dee Williams loves Diana Ross and wants to marry her.

In the '80s, preparing for a photo shoot is no easier than for those old class photos. My hair is teased. My eyes covered with Ray-Ban sunglasses. I'm wearing high heels, torn jeans, and a faded T-shirt. I lean my head back while balancing on a plumbing pipe that juts out of a wall in an alley near Dupont Circle in Washington, D.C. The photographer tells me to give attitude. Easy for him to say. He's on a sidewalk and wearing running shoes. I don't have attitude. I'm trying not to fall. I flash a big smile.

"That's not the look," he says.

Not the look? I adjust and close my mouth.

Again he says, "That's not the look."

I'm trying. I'm holding myself with the confidence of Olga Korbut on a balance beam, and he's still not pleased.

"Relax," he says. Then he tells me to think of someone with attitude. He calls out a few names of disco-music queens and models from fashion magazines: Iman and Grace Jones.

The photographer in front of me is best known for advertising shots of corporate logos on a headquarters' building, fruit for a health-and-nutrition awareness campaign, and pets for animal-care brochures. But he prefers shooting portraits in natural settings. He tells me to lean back, and I tilt my head backward and strike a pose. I think of Diana Ross. Me tottering on the sewage pipe tries to mimic the *Diana* album cover. She pouts without seeming angry. She's sultry in a fresh-out-of-the-shower way. Her wavy, damp hair is combed through. Even in faded jeans and a bleached T-shirt, Diana Ross is fiercely glam. I feel like Diana Ross on the *Love Child* album, with the Supremes in a city alley where graffiti marks brick walls. Except this sun-drenched, stuccoed wall I'm standing near is an untouched backdrop, like new snow on an early morning before children head to school.

"Yes," the photographer says. The camera shutter hums open and shut in a series of fast clicks.

I clench my teeth. He laughs at me. I'm holding my body still. I don't laugh when he laughs. I'm thinking, *Take the darned picture.*

There's one photograph I keep on my makeup table: a photograph taken my senior year in high school. To me, it frames the perfect moment of knowing myself.

I spend my last year of high school at a school for dreamers like me, who want to be writers, photographers, and graphic artists. Style is casual and comfortable. Jeans, T-shirts, and sweaters. Oversized denim jackets. Motorcycle boots and sneakers. It's all about what's inside you.

A classmate, a guy who lives in a downtown neighborhood hard hit by the riots of 1968, finds beauty in the everyday things he sees. He turns the camera on me. He doesn't ask me to smile or pose or give an attitude that I don't have. I'm wearing lip gloss and mascara and jeans. Lost in thought, I gaze at the Potomac River, staring into the current, wondering about what's next for me. I want college, a writing career, and like Tracy Chambers, I want to see Rome.

Good Guys

Lisa Williams Kline

I didn't sit at the "cool" lunch table at Wiley Junior High. I wasn't part of the seventh-grade in-crowd, so I wasn't in on the plan concocted against our Spanish teacher, Señor Valderas, until the very last minute.

Someone came up to me after lunch and said, "Every time Señor Valderas turns his back to write on the board, one person is going to go out the back door of the classroom, and then everyone else is going to move down one seat until nobody is left in his class. Pass the word."

On the way to my locker, I became quite anxious trying to decide whether to participate. First, I was a devoted rule follower, terrified of getting into trouble. I had once participated in a coordinated pencil drop and found myself drenched in cold sweat. Second, and most important, my favorite show, *The Man from U.N.C.L.E.*, with my idol, Illya Kuryakin, was on that night, and if I got into trouble I might not be allowed to watch it.

Every week, my brother and I had to receive special dispensation from our parents to stay up past our bedtime to watch the escapist tongue-in-cheek spy series.

"Illya Kuryakin!" I squealed at the beginning of the show each week, with swooning seventh-grade drama, giving his name the flourish of the character's alluring accent.

"Napoleon Solo!" my fourth-grade brother shouted with equal zeal. We'd throw ourselves on the floor, our chins in our hands, a few feet from our small black-and-white set (everyone else in the neighborhood had already gotten color), and slip into the world of spies.

Illya Kuryakin's and Napoleon Solo's names had exactly the right number of syllables, and they rolled off the tongue with incredible ease. Now that I'm an adult writer, I have to laugh at the fun those writers must have had creating those mellifluous names.

The writers must have had fun with the acronyms of U.N.C.L.E. and its diabolical nemesis, T.H.R.U.S.H., too. U.N.C.L.E. stood for United Network Command for Law and Enforcement, the international spy organization with headquarters located in the back of "an ordinary tailor shop" in the East Forties in New York City. T.H.R.U.S.H. stood for the Technological Hierarchy for the Removal of Undesirables and the Subjugation of Humanity, which to me today strikes a suddenly more chilling note. Agents from T.H.R.U.S.H. were always kidnapping scientists to get them to do their nefarious work for them.

Each week, Illya Kuryakin and Napoleon Solo executed white-knuckle spy missions while maintaining effortless, deadpan James Bond banter. (Ian Fleming was one of the producers). Illya wore an incredibly sexy black turtleneck with his gun holster buckled over one shoulder. Not only was he clever, resourceful, and unflappable, he had an accent to die for. His character was supposed to be from Russia. He was played by actor David McCallum, and I now realize that his accent wasn't Russian but Scottish. At age thirteen, I didn't notice the difference.

Illya had a lean and wolfish face, with a shock of Beatle-length blond hair. I liked him better than Napoleon Solo, who was too suave for me. Illya was aloof, *mysterious*. He rarely showed emotion. In my mind, his most attractive characteristic was that he seemed a little bit shy, like me. He was not a defector, like Mikhail Baryshnikov; Illya was still a Russian citizen. Yet, could he remain loyal to his mother country and still do his humanitarian spy work? Did he leave a Russian girlfriend behind? These questions were never answered, which only ratcheted up the intrigue. In my fascination with him, I was not alone. David McCallum received more fan mail than any other MGM star between 1964 and 1968, the years when *The Man from U.N.C.L.E.* was on the air.

Even though my brother and I had endured years of school drills, crouching under our flimsy desks in case of attack from our Russian enemies, Illya in my mind could never be a "bad guy." The Russian *government* was our enemy. Illya Kuryakin was a "good guy" in every way, and I could still have a crush on him.

The men from U.N.C.L.E. were always helping the kidnapped scientists escape from T.H.R.U.S.H., but I never had any fear that my father, who was a scientist, would be kidnapped. We lived a serene life on the bucolic Wake Forest University campus in Winston-Salem, North Carolina. Dad had gone to school on the GI Bill after serving on a submarine in World War II. He had seen his share of war and danger, but now strolled across the peaceful green campus to teach his classes and do research in the lab. Our only nod to the Cold War was the fallout shelter in our basement, which Mom at first stocked with canned vegetables. Eventually, it became a cinder-block storage room full of junk. In Winston-Salem, Southern decorum was paramount, but the community was multicultural for a city of its small size. Dad's colleagues in the physics department came from all over the world—India, China, Israel, and the Netherlands—and had multiple religions and accents. Growing up on the college campus, I assumed that people of all nations lived together in harmony, as in the physics department, and I was long an adult before I realized this wasn't true.

I liked reading and writing, and remember studying *Green Mansions* and *Animal Farm* and *1984* and *Lord of the Flies* in English class, with themes of revolution, human rights, and environmental responsibility that I was probably too young to understand. I attended a sort of magnet school that was integrated from the beginning, and I had been taking Spanish since third grade. My foreign-language skills, in spite of my fascination with Illya Kuryakin's accent, were sadly lacking.

That day of the planned escape, as we noisily piled through the door of Señor Valderas's Spanish classroom, there was a palpable, almost breathless, excitement and anticipation. I still had not decided what I was going to do. Watching *The Man from U.N.C.L.E.* was a highlight of my week, and I did not want to endanger that in any way.

"*Buenos dias, estudientes,*" said Señor Valderas in his monotone voice. "*Sientese, por favor.*" Señor Valderas had a beautiful accent. He was pale and balding, and I found it curious that he always wore a shabbily elegant three-piece suit to class while other teachers dressed more casually. His wife, Señora Valderas, taught Spanish at the high school. We heard she was stricter and more vivacious.

Even to my seventh-grade eyes, Señor Valderas's heart was not in the job. He seemed to be in a trance most of the time, inches away from collapsing from exhaustion every day. He often forgot to mark things wrong on our papers and gave us better grades than we deserved. If people were clowning around in the back of the class, Señor would pretend not to notice. He wouldn't even call them down. When it happened, he would turn his back and begin to write long lists of verb tenses on the board. I wondered about this. How could he not notice that one kid was shooting a paper football across the room and yelling, "Heads up, Huffstetter!"? As an adult looking back, I realize that Señor Valderas's lack of reaction was a combination of pride and despair. But we were only thirteen.

We waited with bated breath for Señor to turn his back to write on the board. He droned on and on, his despair and hopelessness seeming to envelope him like a cloud as we recited verb tenses. Some of us deliberately stumbled on the tenses just to alert him that we might need extra drills using the board. At last, he turned and picked up the chalk.

There was an audible, collective intake of our breath as the student on the end closest to the door ducked out into the hall. I happened to be in the back row; he seated us in alphabetical order, and my last name was Williams. A few people moved down one seat. Others snickered. Señor did not turn around.

A second person ducked out the door, serenaded by more chuckling, and more people moved down. Everyone seemed euphoric with this escape from authority. An empty seat beckoned beside me.

The kid next to me gave me a meaningful look.

My heart beat like a parade drum. There was much I didn't understand at that time: the difference between a Russian and Scottish accent; the themes of *1984*, *Green Mansions*,

Lisa Kline was about 13 and living in Winston-Salem, North Carolina, when her idol David McCallum ended his four-year run on *The Man from U.N.C.L.E.* Today Lisa lives in Davidson, North Carolina, and writes books for young people.

and *Animal Farm*; the inhumane way that so many people around the world over the centuries had been mistreated when I had been so loved. But I did know that I was not a rebel.

I stayed in my seat and continued to recite the verbs. I pretended not to see the exasperated glances of my fellow students.

Someone crawled over me and moved down, giving me a dirty look. A few more people ducked out. I have no idea what they did for the rest of the Spanish period. Went down the hall to the bathroom and smoked, probably. Señor Valderas, when he at last turned back around, gave no indication that he noticed they had left. Aloof to it all, he turned no one in.

But the revolution against Señor Valderas fizzled. There were enough students, like me, who would not leave the classroom that the plot failed. And it wasn't only because I didn't want to miss *The Man from U.N.C.L.E.* on TV that night. Maybe it was because I was a cowardly rule follower. Or maybe, because both of my parents were teachers, I couldn't show a teacher disrespect.

I was not a secretive kid, so that night at dinner, I told my parents and my brother about the scheme to escape Señor Valderas's classroom.

"I bet you chickened out," my brother said.

"How do you know?" I said.

"We know you," teased my father.

It was then that my parents told me that Señor Valderas and his wife had escaped from Cuba when Castro took over. He had been a lawyer, and he and his wife had to flee in the dark of night, leaving everything behind. Teaching Spanish had been the only jobs they could find here. We took the globe down from the bookshelf, and our parents showed us where Cuba was.

"So why did they have to leave?" I asked. In my protected life, I could not even imagine a place so dangerous you'd have to escape.

"I suppose they refused to become communists," my mother guessed.

As I was cleaning up the dishes, I thought about my giddy classmates escaping from Señor Valderas' class that day, and I wondered what Señor Valderas's escape from Cuba must have been like. Did they have to pay someone to take them? Did they get shot at, like the scientists on *The Man from U.N.C.L.E.*? I understood why he didn't turn anyone in. And I had a glimmer of understanding about why he was sad: He missed his home.

"Who's finished with their homework and ready to watch *The Man from U.N.C.L.E.*?" my father said now, scooping chocolate ice cream into four bowls.

"Me!" my brother and I shouted at the same time, and we lay on the floor, in front of the TV.

The moment I'd been waiting for all week had arrived. The exciting opening music for *The Man from U.N.C.L.E.* swelled, and we watched Illya Kuryakin skillfully land a helicopter to help a scientist from the international public health service escape from the clutches of T.H.R.U.S.H. As I sat with our family, safely ensconced in our den, beside the green and peaceful campus, with our fallout shelter just below us, I hoped Señor Valderas and his wife had someone like Illya Kuryakin to help them escape from Cuba.

Years later, I would move away from the South and fall in love with and marry a man with a similar family story of escape. His grandfather, Nathan Zagoria, escaped from Russia in 1918 during the pogroms, in the engine room of a cargo ship, with his little brother Max. Two boys, headed for America, leaving the rest of their family behind. The man who was supposed to bring them food for their journey took their money and left. For days, they licked the sweating water pipes in the engine room to survive. Finally, a crew member found the boys, gave them food, and smuggled them into New Jersey. That brave story is one of the many reasons I fell in love with my husband and his family.

His grandfather's escape reminded me of Senor Valderas' escape from Cuba. Even though Illya Kuryakin was a TV character, in helping people escape from intolerable circumstances, he portrayed values that my family and my husband's family hold dear. Having a crush on a character from a country I had been taught was our enemy helped me to redefine the "good guys" and the "bad guys," which I think has helped me over my lifetime to see the world in a more open way.

Julie on My Mind

Mary Granfield

The Mod Squad was the coolest show on TV in 1972. At its center was a trio of improbably attractive young cops in Los Angeles. All had tangled with the law before being recruited by their boss, an enterprising police captain, to work as plainclothes detectives instead of serving jail time.

Peggy Lipton played Julie Barnes, a troubled young woman picked up for vagrancy after fleeing San Francisco, where her mother worked as a prostitute. Michael Cole played Pete Cochran, a disaffected youth collared for car theft after being banished from his parents' Beverly Hills home. Clarence Williams III played Lincoln "Linc" Hayes, one of thirteen siblings in a black family who got caught up in the violence of the Watts riots.

When I was twelve, it didn't strike me as unusual that one of the stars was black, even though I lived in a 98 percent white town where the son of McCoy Tyner (of the John Coltrane jazz quartet) was one of the few minorities at our high school. All three stars were cool, but Linc—a gap-toothed, Afro-sporting dude—embodied a coolness that was through the roof. According to Wikipedia, *The Mod Squad* was one of the first shows to feature African Americans as stars. Moreover, it was "groundbreaking in the realm of socially relevant drama" as it dealt with such issues as domestic violence, drug dealing, slumlords, abortion, the antiwar movement, and racism.

Of course, as a kid watching the show in the early '70s, I couldn't really appreciate its groundbreaking nature. But I was riveted by Julie, who was unlike any other female I'd watched on screen. She wasn't adorable, funny, feisty, or mind-blowingly sexy. Granted, she was absurdly beautiful for someone we were supposed to believe was a cop, but the same was true for many TV actors. The key thing was that the show didn't make a huge deal about Julie's being female. She was just a girl (sorry, people, this was years before "woman" was commonly used) doing a tough job alongside the boys.

Let's travel back in time, shall we? Below is a sampling of the leading TV ladies of that era:

- Ann Marie in *That Girl*: adorable, eager to please;
- Mary Richards of *The Mary Tyler Moore Show*: cute, funny, feisty;
- The girls of *Gilligan's Island*: Ginger (va va voom!), Mary Ann (cute, eager to please), and Mrs. Howell (ditzily funny and whose actual non–TV brother we met at a neighbor's annual Christmas party, and who harangued us about his being Natalie Schafer's brother);

- Agent 99 on *Get Smart*: smart, cute, and sexy;
- Sister Bertrille in *The Flying Nun*: sweetly bumbling, adorable (she could FLY!);
- Samantha in *Bewitched*: feisty, adorable (she worked MAGIC!);
- Jeannie in *I Dream of Jeannie*: eager to please, mind-blowingly sexy (she also worked MAGIC!).

Unlike her cohorts, Julie's gender wasn't an in-your-face thing. It was a whisper amid foghorns. She was the polar opposite of Jeannie, a bosomy, harem-pants-clad genie whose sole purpose in life was to please her "master." Julie's wardrobe was functional; it didn't scream style or sexiness. She had a boxy leather jacket and prim turtlenecks. (Okay, she occasionally wore miniskirts, but so did we all back then.) Everything about her was low-key and understated. You weren't constantly distracted by what she was wearing, which was as it should be for an undercover sleuth nabbing swindlers and rapists. Her shoes? Thank God, we hardly saw them. But I'll bet they were practical, in case she had to sprint after some greasy perp.

She seemed to be making no effort to please anyone. Her face was unsmiling, and her hair hung glumly around her face like faded curtains. No sprayed flip-do for her! Julie didn't have time for curling wands; her hair was no-fuss wash and wear. She couldn't have been more different from the perky, coiffed Samantha on *Bewitched*, who worked her magic with a nose wiggle. If Julie Barnes and Sister Bertrille ever found themselves stuck in an elevator, Julie would have waited serenely for the rescuers while the nun fumbled with her wimple in an attempt to fly up through the escape hatch, to the canned hilarity of a laugh track. Julie wasn't trying to be anything; she simply *was*.

I have a mortifying memory of trying to be adorable. I was at the house of a kind woman who sometimes watched me after school while my mother worked. Although I was a moderately cute child, for some reason, I wanted to be *way cuter* to impress this woman, whose own son resembled a hairless rabbit. Somewhere I found lipstick to draw rosy circles on my cheeks. I don't recall anything else about this incident—whether I got the reaction I desired or not. All I remember is *how hard I tried*. I was only seven! What was driving me? Julie Barnes's non-trying came as a revelation and a relief.

Even more unusual, she was a moody character who gave off a depressive vibe. It made sense, as Julie came from a dysfunctional home, but it also mirrored the turbulence of the early 1970s. Just think of the popular films of the day: *A Clockwork Orange, Deliverance, The Last Picture Show*, and *The Exorcist*. Not to mention the political turmoil around Watergate, desegregation, busing, and the Kent State shootings. Seeing a psychiatrist went from shameful to stylish; suddenly, it was hip to discuss your Freudian analysis at cocktail parties, à la Woody Allen.

Those of us watching Julie could almost—almost!—imagine ourselves in her place, doing courageous work in a slippery world. We, too, were moody girls with serious stuff on our minds. We resented those Neanderthals who'd pass us on the sidewalk, ordering us to smile as if it were their birthright. That *never* happened to Julie. Her colleagues spoke and listened to her respectfully. Neither Pete nor Linc would have dreamed of (well, *maybe* in their dreams) patting her on the butt or commenting on her "nice tits." (In any case, she barely had tits. Neither did we! Only Sister Bertrille's breasts were as unobtrusive.)

At the other end of the spectrum, Jeannie's master constantly condescended to her, and why wouldn't he? His exasperation with the situation—having this eager, empty-headed concubine foisted upon him—was the show's comic premise. The actress, Barbara Eden, had little to do except pout and fume sexily, draping herself across pillows while waiting to be let out of her bottle. Even the spunky newswoman Mary Richards—the most professional of these leading ladies—was talked down to by her boss, Lou Grant, an old-guard sexist, and even more infuriatingly, by the harebrained Ted Baxter. One of the jokes underpinning *Bewitched* was that Samantha was smarter than her dim-witted husband, yet nonetheless had to put up with his patronizing behavior, which she did with many a fetching eye roll.

Another thing that set Julie apart was that *she hardly talked at all*. She let Pete and Linc do most of the gabbing while she frowned in concentration or stared off into space. I can't emphasize enough how weird this was: Julie was quieter than any other TV female was permitted to be. While I can't remember a single plot from *That Girl,* I do recall Ann Marie's desperate chatter. Mary Richards, Sister Bertrille, Agent 99, and Jeannie spent a lot of screen time explaining themselves to uncomprehending men (or in the sister's case, to the mother superior.) Julie seemed not to feel that same pressure to justify herself. Her thoughts were mysterious.

There was something deeply thrilling about *The Mod Squad,* and while I couldn't have articulated it back then, I now think that it partly had to do with the racial barrier the show crossed by featuring a black star. My friend John, an ardent *Mod Squad* fan, remembers that the chemistry between Julie and Linc was "smoking hot." He recalls in particular one episode in which she had to pretend to neck with Pete—her white colleague. "It was painfully obvious to me," John says, "that she would have much preferred to partner up with Linc instead."

As a 16-year-old in New Canaan, Connecticut, Mary Granfield idolized actress Peggy Lipton. Now a writer based in Massachusetts, Granfield still recalls her *Mod Squad* days.

She eventually did get a chance to kiss Linc, but only after Aaron Spelling, one of the show's creators, insisted upon it, despite network resistance. One script called for Linc to give Julie "a friendly kiss," which ABC executives wanted to cut, fearing an outcry. One of the earliest interracial kisses on an American TV had taken place on *Star Trek* in 1968, so this was still fairly taboo in the popular culture. Wikipedia quoted Spelling as follows: "'You can't do that,' I was told. 'You can't have a black man kissing a white girl.'" However, after he dug in his heels, the studio heads relented. "But they warned me I'd receive thousands of complaint letters," Spelling recalled. "I didn't get one." That Julie had no problem kissing a black man became even more evident when Peggy Lipton married the musician-producer Quincy Jones in 1974.

Julie Barnes showed me a different way of being female in the world. You didn't have to knock yourself out to impress guys with your cuteness or sexiness. You didn't have to smile unless you felt like it; if you were sad or depressed, you didn't have to pretend otherwise. You also didn't have to get romantically involved with—or work with—jerks who underestimated your intelligence. You had a right to expect equal treatment in your personal and professional life. You didn't have to fill every silence with your own nervous chatter. Finally, you didn't have to try so hard to please anyone other than yourself.

Despite this newfound wisdom, my pre-teen self gave in to societal pressure: in eighth grade, I became a Pop Warner cheerleader. Did I enjoy watching football? Uh, no. Did I like jumping around in a short skirt, doing cartwheels, and shouting inane cheers while being ogled by male spectators? Not especially. I'm glad to say that, after one season of this charade, I came to my senses and quit. Julie would have approved.

For many years, I wore my hair the way she did: long, straight, and parted in the middle. Because I was fortunate enough to have straight hair when it was popular, I never had to fuss with it much. In fact, I never even got into the habit of blow-drying it.

Once, when I was a sophomore in high school, I went to a salon and came away with a disastrous cut that required elaborate blow-drying and curling with a hot wand. If I skipped those steps and let my hair air-dry after washing it, it hung limply around my face, as unflattering as a helmet. I can still remember how self-consciously I sidled through those hallways.

It felt liberating to allow my hair to return to its natural state. Julie's unstyled hair—not to mention Linc's Afro—sent a signal to young women and men across the racial spectrum in the 1970s that there was no need to force their hair into the unnatural and time-consuming styles that had been de rigueur for their parents and grandparents.

The worst thing about my hair now is that I have to dye the roots every three weeks, an investment of time and money that—for most of my life—I was able to avoid. One of these days, I'm going to let nature take its course and let the gray usurp the brown. But … something holds me back. Maybe I'm waiting for a *Mod Squad* reunion in which Julie, Linc, and Pete join forces as intrepid senior citizens, hot on the trail of pension-fund embezzlers and Bernie Madoff types. If I could see Julie with her lovely, lined face framed by silver hair, I just might be able to make the leap. *That* would be cool.

Rescue Me

Leslie Pietrzyk

My twentieth birthday loomed, and I was angsty. I wanted to be a teenager forever, though I couldn't express why; my teen years weren't particularly remarkable or especially pleasant. But twenty sounded to me then ancient and heavily symbolic: Not A Child. An Adult. Responsibilities and nothing but death and taxes ahead. I'd obsessively read and reread *The Catcher in the Rye,* and what I wanted most was Holden to save me from falling off the edge of this cliff.

The other problem with my birthday was that it fell in late June, always lost in the out-of-school summer shuffle, a circumstance I bitterly resented.

The one person I could count on to remember was my true-blue high-school friend, whom I'll call Jenny. "I have a surprise for your birthday," she promised. Like many of our classmates, she had stayed behind in Iowa City to live at home and attend the local university, while I left for Chicago, ill-prepared for preppie smart kids speaking a foreign language—Choate, Boca, Shaker Heights, AP English—and their pompous fussing about how Chicago pizza was slop compared to pizza in "the City," which I finally translated: *New York City.* I assured myself they were all phonies who couldn't possibly understand me. I had applied to two colleges, the local university and this one, which in my town was viewed primarily through the lens of Big Ten football and so considered a weakling cream puff, everyone's favorite visiting team for homecoming. I'd had no idea what I would be walking into, and I was floundering.

I was uneasy there, but now I was equally uneasy in Iowa, amidst the people with whom I'd graduated high school, and my friends—including Jenny—with whom I'd worked with at the movie theater, selling popcorn. This summer, I was maniacally earning money, darting between four movie theaters, begging for any open shift. In this pre-multiplex era, three theaters were downtown single screens, and one, the Englert, retained some of the glamour of its youth, having been built in the glory days of pre–Depression-era movie palaces, when a theater seated hundreds. A spiral of alluring stairs wound up to a secluded balcony, and red velvet curtains cascaded across the screen.

This was a summer of blockbusters, as summers are, and floating from shift to shift— matinee here, Saturday there—I encountered *Caddyshack, Urban Cowboy,* and the movie that defined my summer, *The Empire Strikes Back,* which arrived at the Englert as I started up there and didn't leave until after I returned to school. For us, then, it was the second episode of the saga, the immediate sequel to *Star Wars,* notable for the dark revelation pounding us at the concession stand nightly, penetrating a haze of popcorn grease and exhaustion to bash through the tattered velvet draping the doorways: "I am your father," followed by gasps from every audience, even the prepared, as those words gut-smacked them. It was the secret, yes, and the knowledge of a dangerous and conflicted path ahead, but also it was a rare flash of adult understanding: that submerged below this surface story, below every surface story, lurked layer upon difficult layer, secrets we might not wish to acknowledge. Depths existed beyond what we saw.

When the very first *Star Wars* movie came to the Englert, Jenny and I had been in high school, starting our friendship. We rode the bus downtown, paid for our tickets with quarters, agreed upon seats midway through the half-full theater, and as the lights dimmed, we both stared ahead at the screen with an absolute lack of expectation. Impossible to imagine now, but back then there were no trailers leaked to YouTube with artful precision, no social-media frenzy, no merry-go-round of interviews and yuk-yukking with a parade of two-bit TV hosts. News came from our paper, *The Des Moines Register*, which focused on rain forecasts, hogs, and soybean futures. We weren't immersed in celebrity culture, and anyway, no one in *Star Wars* was a celebrity. The movie had maybe been on the cover of *Time* magazine, stacked on my parents' coffee table. That was why Jenny and I went—that, and because that was what we did when we were sixteen and not driving: dive into the fantasy of movies.

"A long time ago in a galaxy far, far away…" These modest, lowercase blue letters invited us to settle into this fairy tale, this comforting story where good—in the end—triumphs over evil. Like "once upon a time," where the bad things that happen are always set right. That's the pact we—young girls, children—believed in. Utterly. So it was unsurprising that after watching the movie, we let others be blown away by the special effects, let others stress over the battle for the moral heart of the universe. The two of us stumbled out of the dark theater, bodies in one world, minds in another, and our eyes locked with recognition, our mouths landing on the same two words we exhaled: *Han Solo.*

Han Solo. The swashbuckling space pirate with a heart of gold, played by Harrison Ford, a bit player, a Hollywood carpenter as the legend went, whose most notable prior role had been a handful of screen minutes as drag racer Bob Falfa in George Lucas's 1973 classic ensemble movie, *American Graffiti*. Han Solo and his feathered hair, rock-star-tight black leather pants; bromancing empathy for and understanding of Chewbacca's fearsome moans; those devil-may-care eyes, those eyes we saw as grey-with-an-e-never-an-a, those eyes; his insolent smirk, a confident gleam assuring us he'd artfully get any old jalopy gassed up with crumbs and rubber bands—the *Millennium Falcon* or your dad's Ford; Han Solo, who no way was compromising for the cause, who was in it strictly for the dough until, sigh of relief, he was committed; swapping insults with our feminist warrior role model, Princess Leia (it was a sign of true love; we got it, how teasing meant "yes" in our world of "check box if you like me" notes passed during math); Han Solo, our hero, piloting the *Millennium Falcon* into the fray with that bold *yahoo!* and saving the day, rescuing civilization, proving to girls like Jenny and me that bad boys were good, that bad boys would change, that a noble cause and a feminist warrior role model with two oversized cinnamon buns of hair could work these miracles. Han Solo was the man to Mark Hamill's Luke, a boy who was exactly like the boys around us: pale, conflicted, worrying, weak Lukes, all of them mere plot points buckling before the vast and grand adventure that was Han Solo. Of course, two shy, bookish high-school girls brimming with undefined and endless yearning would alight upon the shining knight in every once-upon-a time-tale. Rescue *me*, Han Solo, I thought; rescue *me*, Jenny thought.

She and I rewatched *Star Wars* countless times, and the movie played in town at least a year, long enough that it moved from the cavernous Englert to the modest, two-screen mall theater where Jenny and I found high-school jobs slinging popcorn. She worked the night of its last showing in Iowa City and cried—long before the everlasting life of Netflix, On Demand, or even videos. When would we see Han Solo again?

Now! This summer, the year I turned twenty, with *The Empire Strikes Back* ensconced at the Englert. Let Luke turn darkly complicated ... let Yoda arrive on the scene cute and wise ... and let Han Solo forever be Han Solo, extricating himself from tricky situations with charm and skill and the confidence of *je ne sais quoi*. Perhaps the most memorable Han Solo scene in this movie was when he and Leia had been caught, and he was about to be dipped into a vat of something that would freeze him. As they eyed imminent death, there was a passionate kiss, and then our feminist warrior role model broke down and confessed that she loved him. "I know," he said. An entire theater howled in approval of this classic bad-boy dodge. It was an easy laugh on the screen, though by then Jenny and I both felt deeply the exquisite pain (and addictive pleasure) of loving real-life boys who would not love us back, boys with whom we worked at the movie theater, who endured our awkward, fruitless flirting night after night.

During long, late hours of intense discussion, we argued that Han Solo not saying he loved her left him free to love us. His fictional status felt mysteriously surmountable and irrelevant, while neither of us acknowledged the true problem here, that Han Solo was one more cookie-cutter image of a Peter Pan man, the emotionally withholding, irresponsible, and adorable rapscallion who loved mind games and himself and maybe winked the way of some reckless tomboy down the street, but never, never loved little you. Still, if he was out rescuing all of humanity, you were part of that, right? Maybe that felt good enough.

On my birthday, Jenny picked me up around ten, after my second shift at the Englert. We both worked nights, so our plans always unfolded in the dark. Since high school, we had often stayed out until four or five on weekends; we were so dutiful that our parents trusted us, so quiet that it's possible they didn't notice our absence. We would talk and talk and talk, the two of us alone or with our movie-theater friends, just talk and talk some more.

"I have a surprise," she told me. "Someone special wants to come celebrate your birthday."

I flashed on the withholding boy of my dreams, but she was sick of hearing about him, and I was sick of talking about him. I was sick of him, really, almost physically sick, but I couldn't let go. And he wouldn't come to celebrate me. He wouldn't think of me at all, not on my birthday, not ever, even though I thought about him every day. I still remember his middle name now, and how to spell it.

I said his name, put a question mark after it.

She scowled as the traffic light changed, and she accelerated the car. "Better," she said.

She drove to City Park, the oldest park in town. Nothing special really, but it had been a semi-special-occasion destination in my childhood because our side of town contained newer, more modern parks that were a walk away instead of a drive. This park was older, more deeply established, bordered by the river, sprinkled with huge trees wider than a child's arms could wrap around. The swings were different from the gentle swings

Sailing through her Harrison Ford days, 16-year-old Leslie Pietrzyk had no inkling she would become a lauded fiction writer. She is a Ford fan to this day.

in our park because they creaked along giant iron-loop chains. There was a rickety merry-go-round corralling faded wooden horses; the abandoned tracks of a former kiddie train ride tracing an oval through overgrown grass; an alarmingly tiny (and still pungent) cement platform remaining from a too-small cage for bears that lingered too long; and plenty of open-air shelters with picnic tables and charcoal grills for weenies, burgers, and s'mores. A swimming pool for summer, an ice skating pond for winter. The park officially closed at ten or eleven or dark, but no one kept us from slowly winding along the one-way, one-lane road. Something sharp panged my gut as I felt childhood slipping beyond me, symbolized by this park, abruptly mysterious now, transformed by the shadowy dark, and I understood that being an adult allowed entrance into this altered nighttime world.

We stopped at the first set of swings, and we plopped down and swang; I'm sorry, but a child never says "swung." So simple: pump your legs, soar, maybe try to "marry" by swinging in exact unison. Leap into the sky, tumbling on the grass when you don't land on your feet. See who jumps off farthest, who swings highest. Feel your beating heart match the rhythm of your pumping legs.

Then she led me to a picnic shelter and said I should close my eyes and wait a minute. My ears and body suddenly tuned into all that surrounded me: elm leaves whispering, a distant burr of Dubuque Street traffic, the sensation of insects circling the light-bulb dangling from the shelter ceiling, a stick snapping, the lost roar of those neglected caged bears, the kiddie train's toot-tooting, my ice skates slashing a frozen pond, the lumps of the swing chains gripped within two tiny fists, and that metallic smell of my palms after, her car trunk opening and closing, footsteps.

"Just because you're twenty, it doesn't mean you have to grow up," she said. "Open your eyes."

She presented a clutch of twenty balloons anchored by ribbon—red, purple, blue, yellow, green—all the colors balloons were supposed to be before they morphed into garishly anonymous silver Mylar. We would be children forever, she assured me, both of us, together. There was cheesecake, my favorite. Probably a gift—a stuffed animal? A card. I cried mostly because of the balloons, which I kept for the rest of the summer in my basement bedroom, where I barely was because I spent that much time working. I clung to those balloons after the helium dissipated and they thudded into a huddle on the floor, after the air leaked out and they shriveled and sagged into rubbery rags, clammy to the touch in the dank humidity. I clung to them after my mother wondered when I would "throw that junk out," wondered why anyone my age wanted limp, broken-down balloons. I loved those balloons. I loved that party. I loved that magical gesture and swinging together "married" in the dark. I loved this friend.

And this: "Oh no!" she exclaimed as we ate cheesecake off paper plates at the picnic shelter. "Where's our special guest?" and I can't believe I thought his name again, but I did, and she said, "Wait, what's this?" and she handed me something she pretended to find on the picnic table. "I think he left you this message," she said.

A baseball-card-size collector's card of Harrison Ford captioned in bold red ink, all caps: SPACE ADVENTURER HAN SOLO! He was mid-action, firearm poised and ready for the danger heading his way, that cocky gleam in his grey-with-an-e-never-an-a eyes, the skintight pants, the Robin Hood white tunic shirt, chest peeking through the deep V of the neck line, a leathery vest, holster at one hip, my hero, our hero, the man who would rescue us or rescue me or break our hearts while he was saving humanity.

On the back, on pasted white paper in blue ballpoint, with the tidy cursive hand-writing I could never forget thanks to letters arriving at college, notes poked through high-school locker slats, birthday cards and postcards mailed to every address I've ever had, the handwriting of this forty-year friendship:

Leslie,

I'm sorry we can't be together on your 20th birthday, but I am involved in a dashing adventure right now, and have to finish what I've begun. I hope to see you soon, however. Until then, take care, and don't forget about me.

Love,
    Harrison

I love those commas, used (mostly) properly. I love that we would assume Han Solo understood comma usage. I love that he signed "love" to me, even though I didn't have giant buns of hair and was no one's feminist warrior role model. I love that he knew, somehow, that I would be okay, that Jenny and I would be okay. That watching a friendship endure over time is reason to turn twenty and then some.

Later, years later, we learned words for some of the things we had witnessed during our high-school years: that our high school principal was a drunk and a danger, but that no one took action to get him fired; that a thirty-five-year-old man should not shack up with our sixteen-year-old friend; that instructing students to randomly choose books from The Canon and read them quietly during class was not teaching American literature or in any way preparing us for a world where "Choate" exists; that even if the only Latino in your school agrees that "Chico" is a fun nickname, it's not; that "fag" is not the right word for anyone, particularly not the beautiful boy with the soulful eyes who died of AIDS six years after graduation.

You learn that because someone evades talk about home life; because someone declares everything's "fine" when asked certain questions; because you never see parents beyond the back of a head, quickly glimpsed; because listening means more than simply registering the exact words spoken; because of learning all *that*—once you're an adult, you learn that things actually may *not* have been fine back then. I should have done something, you will think.

But no. You were waiting for the *Millennium Falcon*. Waiting for Han Solo. And so an adult may eventually forgive the choice you made without knowing that it was a choice: to save yourself, to escape to college and onward, uncertain exactly why it was you were going, or where you would end up, or who would make this journey with you.

I Should Have Married
Michael Jackson

SUSAN WOODRING

When I was nine years old and in the fourth grade, my family moved from Clare-mont, California, to Greensboro, North Carolina. This transition brought on a number of challenges. The language was, first of all, different. All my life, the word *hey* had been used as a prelude to something else, usually a summons or a request, as in "Hey, Susan, come here!" When my classmates said *hey* to me in North Carolina, I stopped, waiting for the rest. But there was nothing else, just *hey*. Translation: *Hi*. There were also *y'all*, *fixin' to*, and *mash*, as in *mash that button to make the elevator go*.

We had not yet plunged into long division in the California version of the fourth grade. In California, our teacher read to us every single day after lunch. That was how I first encountered beloved classics such as *Island of the Blue Dolphins*, *My Side of the Mountain*, and—the best—*A Wrinkle in Time*. Pencils and paper were provided. In North Carolina, on the very first morning, my parents had to scramble to find pencils for my sisters and me. We ended up with used pencils with lopsided, half-eaten-up erasers from my dad's work. They were cylindrical rather than hexagonal, and they were painted white with logos and slogans touting various insecticides and other helps to the modern farmer. Our new house wasn't ready yet, so we were staying in an apartment. The building was gray, I remember, and there were lots of windows. The floors were all linoleum tile, even the living room. The landscape around us was hilly. The January version of gray in North Carolina, which is green blanched with naked tree limbs, left frost on the grass early in the mornings. Muddy. The grocery stores were called Winn-Dixie and Food Lion. Food *Lion*, as in circus, as in the African savanna, as in *roar, roar*, went the lion at the zoo. *Dixie*, as in whistling. Everything was weird. Everything was wrong.

My mother hated this move. She and my father had argued about it. She was giving up friends, her job, and favorites particular to Southern California: the ocean, Disneyland, birds of paradise in her front-yard shrubbery, lime and lemon trees in the back. A hot tub. It was the eighth time she'd moved to accommodate my father's work.

My older sister was halfway through her freshman year in high school. She had been a band nerd; now, she was from California, and everyone knew what that meant: easy sunshine, easy everything else. The druggiest state in the Union. She had certain stereo-types to overcome. She was sad, but she didn't talk about it. She only complained that here, so far away from trendy LA, the women wore skintight Chic jeans. They still feath-

160

ered their hair back. She came home from school and sat in that crummy, cold-floored living room and stared at the television screen as she ate through a box of Twix bars. I yelled at her to stop hogging them.

My dad, in a new office, a new job—he'd made it to the company's headquarters at last—came home every day in his suit and tie, with his briefcase, and offered encouragement. He smiled thinly. This wasn't so bad, was it? Was it? At least we had a company car. At least we were at the company's headquarters now. We would never have to move again.

This was the fifth time my family had moved in my lifetime, and though I only remembered three of those moves, I had learned the importance of making friends right away. This was the first order of business, more important than figuring out long division. Right away there was a girl named Temple who helped me with the long division. But then my teacher, Mrs. Graham, moved me to another spot, and now I was sitting next to a black girl named Tracey. This was 1984, and Tracey and I soon bonded over our longings for high-top Reeboks and Cabbage Patch Kids. Mrs. Graham had us working burlap needlepoint, and I chose to draw a skunk on mine. Tracey laughed at my skunk, told me I was crazy, but then came around. It didn't look so bad. She was doing a pair of ladybugs, even though it violated two rules: you could draw only one animal, and it had to be an mammal. I told Tracey *she* was crazy. At recess, we stood on the swings. We never played dodgeball. *Never.* I described to her the playground I'd left behind in California: tetherball and swinging monkey bars. We ate lunch every single day outside, I told her. My mother packed me Twinkies and Fruit Roll-Ups. We had earthquake drills. Tracey was impressed with all of this, with the exotic nature of an earthquake drill. She laughed at me for wearing shorts beneath my dresses. She wanted to know all about coyotes. She confessed to me: She was in love with Michael Jackson. She wanted to marry him.

I was nine. In three years, I'd have my first real kiss. In one year, I would have my first peck on the cheek. It would happen when I was in the house alone—the house we were waiting for now. I'd been playing with Barbies at the foot of my closet when my little fifth-grade boyfriend and his friend bicycled to my house to play soccer in the front yard. In the eighth grade, I would suffer my first heavy-duty relationship with a boy named Stiles, whom I'd won from another girl because of a harem costume I wore to my friend Meredith's Halloween party. In high school, I would fall in love with a boy with black, curly hair, who bore an endearing if a little unsettling resemblance to Rick Astley. Rick Astley's sweet, pale, freckled face set inside a nest of black curls. That boyfriend, named Quinn, danced the "Foxy Lady" for me.

So, love was coming for me. But that day, in the fourth grade, while we chatted over our burlap needlepoint, I told Tracey she was crazy.

"You so crazy!" We hooted until Mrs. Graham hushed us. We were to work quietly. "You crazy," I whispered to Tracey, and she shook her head, smiling at her own audaciousness.

I did like Michael Jackson. Actually, I was a big fan. This was partly because, among nine-year-old girls, crushes are as contagious as colloquiums, and partly because this was 1984. You couldn't avoid Michael Jackson in 1984. *Thriller* had come out a year or so earlier, but it was just gaining momentum among little girls in North Carolina. Most afternoons, Mrs. Graham took us to the cafeteria after lunch had been cleaned up and led us in aerobics; we jump-jacked and windmilled and jogged in place to "PYT: Pretty Young Thing," "Beat It," and even "Billie Jean," which probably would have caused quite a stir among fourth-graders, if any of us had really listened to or understood the lyrics.

"It's about a crazy fan," my older sister explained to me.

We were in our house now, and it was spring, and my mother had purchased artificial birds of paradise to poke into the houseplants and pretend they were real, and my younger sister had a mean third-grade teacher but seemed to be faring okay, and we had a dog now, Charlie, the sweetest mutt you'd ever know, and Shelley, my older sister, seemed to be Doing Okay.

"A crazy fan," she said, "and an unwanted pregnancy." She laughed, fluffing her hair up in the back. "It's called *slut*."

She was five years older, so she was, of course, the authority on everything. Shelley knew things. She knew how to sharpen an eyeliner pencil over the toilet so the shavings wouldn't make a mess, and she knew how to hold the tip to a lit match to soften it, make it go on easier. She knew how to cuff jeans, which was about to become hugely important as the '80s rushed on. My sister could tie a cherry stem, so long as it was long enough, in her mouth. This was something I never mastered, though I learned the eyeliner thing, and, years later, how to make warm artichoke garlic parmesan dip, Shelley's specialty.

She said Christie Brinkley married Billy Joel because she wanted a normal, not-particularly-good-looking guy. She said nobody knew Boy George's true gender; he/she kept that a secret. No one had ever even seen this "person" use the bathroom. She said my thighs were starting to get chunky. She said she had loved being an only child; those five years were the best of her life. Jill and I came along and ruined everything. She said my face was getting oily. I needed to start using acne pads. She made her predictions: "You're going to have big boobs," she told me. "Someday." (She turned out to be wrong—very wrong—on this point.)

Back then, however, on the subject of Michael Jackson, she reminded me, "I've seen him. In real life."

This had happened in Disneyland, when we still lived in California. She was a freshman in the Claremont High School marching band, a band of some repute, and they'd been invited to march in a procession of some sort. Afterward, the band students had some free time at the park, and my sister went off with her troupe of friends to ride Magic Mountain over and over again. Michael Jackson, my sister claimed, was on the ride, just a few rows ahead of her. When he was getting on, he waved at them. "Hello," he said in his Michael Jackson little-boy voice. He smiled.

This may have been the first time I doubted my sister. I suspected she had invented the Michael Jackson thing, maybe not maliciously or with any real design to deceive. I think it happened the way this kind of thing so often happens: We catch a glimpse of something that could be, and we simply believe it into existence. It becomes our story. We believe it, and now it's ours.

When I told Tracey the story of my sister and Michael Jackson on Magic Mountain, she again told me I was crazy. I told her it was true. It happened, I said. My sister brushed elbows with Michael Jackson. The Prince of Pop. The Big MJ.

Not that Shelley was herself a fan. She was a little older and thus much more mature, and instead had fallen in love with Bon Jovi. My Michael Jackson phase, plus the fact that I wanted to be a writer and a teacher when I grew up, was the beginning of her pronouncing me weird. Really weird. Like, throwaway weird.

"Really?" she said. "Michael Jackson?" It was the poster tacked up on my bedroom wall showing him reclining on his side with a tiger cub on his knee. Tracey kissed hers, but I wasn't ready for that. I studied his face. He really seemed to be looking at me. He seemed very calm. Well rested. He was at ease, I think, with the baby tiger. Michael's pressed white suit. But years later, after he died, I would Google that same image, and what would strike me was how very unknowing he seemed. Like the rest of us, he had no idea what was coming. His life, like all of ours, was made of tiny, every-minute decisions. This minute follows this follows this. From this perspective, it's easy to see. Our lives are all made of the same stuff. None of us knows anything for sure. We just keep going.

I tried to ignore Shelley's mocking tone. I liked Michael. I knew he was black. So what? I knew my friend Tracey was black, too. We were on the same team, somehow. He was hanging on my bedroom wall. He moonwalked on TV, broke up a poolroom brawl with dancing. He turned into a werewolf, lit up sidewalk squares with his feet. He danced the way he did, like nobody else has ever danced, as if things like gravity and the certified boniness of bones didn't apply to him. He talked like Mickey Mouse. He was sweet in that way. He was a child, like one of us. A child, but also a star. A colossus, and black, but tiny, fragile.

"I'm proud of you," my father said. He meant about being friends with a black girl.

Shelley, I remember, looked away at that moment, when my dad said that. It was back at the apartment, in the early days. We were walking to the car; my dad was going to drive us to school that day. It could have been that she was simply thinking of something else. Probably, she was distracted by the problems in her own life, all the obstacles and uncertainties that awaited her that particular school day.

I lost touch with Tracey over the summer. By the time fifth grade began, I had a new best friend, and Tracey was no longer at our school. I also lost touch with Michael. The *Thriller* craze ended, and I bought a Madonna tape. Cyndi Lauper. By the time I was in middle school, I was in love with a different Michael: Michael Hutchence of INXS. "Devil Inside." Yes, indeed.

Michael Jackson had become a joke. He burned his hair, kept dancing, kept singing, kept altering his appearance in increasingly odd ways. He bleached his skin and thinned his nose until it began to literally fall apart. He married Lisa Marie Presley, then Debbie Rowe. Allegations came to light. He was removed from Neverland for his court date, and I was absolutely disgusted, seeing this enfeebled, shrunken man, accused pedophile, limping palely along in his pajamas under a big black umbrella held against the usual sunshine of an everyday, beautiful, blue-skied, bright California morning.

It wasn't until he died that I thought about marrying him. I was a homeschooling mother and wife, thirty-five years old, living in a small town—very small—in western North Carolina. That weekend, my then-husband had taken our two young children, aged three and seven, camping so I could do some home improvement. My plan was to paint two rooms and a hallway in two-and-a-half days. I'd made my selections: a light taupe for the living room, a mustardy yellow—but not too brown—for the kitchen, and an almondy shade of white for the hallway. I'd already had the paint mixed at my father's favorite paint shop, and I was off. Michael Jackson had died the day before, an accidental overdose of the kind of medication only anesthetists typically administer. That day, my radio was on while I painted, and they played a ton of Michael Jackson songs. The DJs pontificated: What to make of this particular tragedy? A megastar, arguably the most successful, best-known musician of my generation. A one-man freak show. A disgrace. A picture of invention and re-invention, of breath-catching pageantry. A brilliant costumer. A peacock. A man who danced with such fluidity, such precision, such ease; no one danced like Michael Jackson. A criminal. A child abuser. A joke. A plastic-surgery junkie. A heart-hurt little boy. Sad Peter Pan case. One of the commentators, a member of the media who had followed MJ's career for many years, explained that Michael Jackson could never have been a pedophile. Impossible. Jackson, this man claimed, had been asexual. All of his sexuality came out in his dancing.

Also on the news: South Carolina governor Mark Sanford had found his soul mate at an open-air dance spot in Uruguay. But he would try now to fall back in love with his wife. Everyone seemed to be having a good time with this one. Mark Sanford's Argentinian soul mate. *Soul mate. As if,* the world was saying. *Soul mate. Sure.*

Two-and-a-half days had seemed like a wealth of time. I had planned on getting the painting done, plus I had an appointment for a haircut that afternoon, and I was hoping to rise early the next day and get some writing done. But the taupe was too pink, and so I had to head back to the paint shop. It was clear by late morning that I was not going to make my hair appointment. I stopped only to eat a couple of chocolate-chip cookies, because to actually cook anything or even to slap together a sandwich seemed like too much trouble. I drank coffee and Diet Coke. I kept the radio on. My knees hurt from crouching to get the floorboards. There was sunbeam-yellow paint in my hair. It was summer, hot. My husband called to tell me our three-year-old was not cooperating. I felt guilty, as if it were somehow my fault that my son was not the happy little camper his father had hoped he would be, and I also felt annoyed. What the hell had he expected? I spent all day, every day with these children. I was a writer and a former teacher. Now, I homeschooled. I wrote math problems on individual-sized whiteboards. I did laundry. There was *always* something in the dryer that needed folding and putting away. This was the first time in a long time, years maybe, that I had been alone for any stretch of time.

I hadn't stayed Tracey's friend. Or Michael's. I could cry, thinking about it. It was impossible, in this moment, for me to imagine changing my current situation, and so I was left to rethink my past. I wanted to go back, fix everything. Lisa Marie had not been any kind of help to Michael, and certainly Debbie Rowe hadn't either. Debbie Rowe was just a normal person. Now, standing on a stepladder in my kitchen, sweaty and sticky with paint splotches on my arms, my fingers, I realized that it should have been me. I could have saved him. I should have married Michael Jackson.

I *could* have. This seemed wildly, chaotically reasonable. I mean, why not? I'd given up on him many years ago; I'd given up on a number of things. I could have done things differently. Sometimes, it seems very odd to me that I've been assigned a life with choices and everything. I don't feel qualified to make these decisions. I'd like a teacher or some other kind of authority to come along with a red pen, tell me how to fix everything.

By the next morning, I had a headache squeezing at the base of my skull, and my hair was clean but wild. I'd washed it the night before and gone to bed with it wet. My dad showed up at eight with two coffees from McDonald's and a paint roller. He took one look at me and told me to go to bed. He'd finish up. Later, I asked him if he remembered my friend Tracey from the fourth grade. He thought so. Did he remember that Shelley had once encountered Michael Jackson? In real life? A million years ago. Before everything. Before *Thriller,* even. I told my dad that Jackson's father used to call him "Big Nose." Did he know that? No wonder he started in on the plastic surgery. No wonder he got carried away. Some people need the constraints of time and money in their lives, I said. It can be a bad thing, too much of either. I said, Remember when we first moved to North Carolina, and I put his poster on my wall? It's just sad, I told him. Didn't he think it was just really sad?

By the time I woke from my nap, my walls were perfect; Dad had fixed all of my mistakes. My headache was still there, but dimming. My husband and children were due back soon, so I sat on the front steps to receive them. I was still thinking about what would happen if we could go back and unmake Michael a star, how sometimes what we want most is the worst thing for us. What if we unmoved to North Carolina? My sister never had to leave the famed Claremont High marching band. My mother got to keep her birds of paradise.

Some months later, I told one of my closest writing friends my theory about how I could have saved Michael Jackson. I had had a couple of glasses of wine, and we'd been talking about insane little things. She looked at me for a moment and then nodded. She conceded that I might have been a good influence on him. She said, "I could watch him dance all day."

I agreed. I wish I knew how to moonwalk, I told her. I wish I could dance like that.

Cry, Baby

KATE KASTELEIN

The entire back wall of my uncle's convenience store was floor-to-ceiling shelves of VHS tapes. Patrons took their selections along with bags of chips and six packs of beer to the cashier, who swapped the Styrofoam-filled cardboard boxes for the actual tapes, each in a brown box with a bright orange "Be Kind, Rewind!" sticker affixed to the front. This was before streaming, before DVDs, and before chain movie-rental stores. Back then, movie distributors sent promotional materials directly to tiny-store owners across the country.

There were too many posters for one little store to display, which is how my brother ended up with a life-size cardboard cutout of Arnold Schwarzenegger in full *Terminator* gear, and I with a movie poster for *Cry-Baby*, starring a young, handsome Johnny Depp. I was twelve and too young for *21 Jump Street*, too young for *Cry-Baby*, but when I saw Johnny's dark, broody face, that was the poster I wanted, not *Home Alone* or *Pretty Woman* or *Gremlins 2*.

In the poster, Amy Locane lies on a pink bed with her pink capri-clad legs straight up in the air. On the wall next to her hangs an enormous poster of Johnny Depp. His hair is greased back, the popped collar of a leather jacket just visible around his neck. A single tear slides down his cheek. The words *He's a doll. He's a dreamboat. He's a delinquent,* written in turquoise script fill space between Locane's legs and Depp's face. The poster for this John Waters film is obviously a send-up of '50s greaser movies, but twelve-year-old me didn't know that. I thought it edgy and profound. I don't remember if I saw *Cry-Baby*, and if I did, it didn't matter; I knew what would happen. It happened in *Grease* and *Dirty Dancing*. Bad boy meets good girl, and they fall in love, and more important, good girl gets bad-girl cred.

I did not want to be a good girl. Around the same time I put up the *Cry-Baby* poster, I received a scholarship to attend a writers' camp hosted by Johns Hopkins University. I told my classmates I had to go to a special summer school, so great was my despair at being recognized for intelligence. Later, I spread a rumor about myself that I stayed back in kindergarten, and therefore had an extra year to learn things, which was why I won so many awards for high scores on tests.

For some reason, it didn't occur to me until much later to sabotage myself by not trying in school. Perhaps what I needed was a bad boy with a heart of gold. I set to work finding my own bad boys: the boys who dropped out of school or hung out in the smoking area in leather jackets. Tall, blond boys with Mohawks, musicians who flicked cigarettes

166

from their porches directly onto their parents' lawns. Boys who played Dungeons & Dragons, who smoked pot and had tattoos. I didn't date all these boys, but I surrounded myself with them, an army of golden-hearted bad boys. My plan worked. I was no longer a good girl.

When I was sixteen, I met a dark-haired, dark-eyed boy with high cheekbones and a soft voice, not unlike Johnny Depp. When I was twenty-two, I married him and remain so today.

I saw *Edward Scissorhands* in our tiny downtown theater. I went with my cousin and hiked up the steep steps and paid five dollars to sit in ripped-up red velvet seats in a flat-floored, un-air-conditioned hundred-year-old building. The air hummed with Spree candies, which kids flicked as hard as they could around the theater by snapping them between their fingers and thumbs. An occasional gummy bear slapped onto the screen, but not too often; the movie would have been shut down if too many got stuck there. I sat transfixed by the strange and beautiful Edward Scissorhands, Johnny Depp transformed into a monster was still the most gorgeous man I'd ever seen.

The scene where blonde-wigged Winona Ryder as Kim danced in the ice shards as Edward snips a sculpture out of a block of ice is still one of my favorites. IMDb describes Edward Scissorhands as "a gentle man, with scissors for hands." Johnny was now a man who could slice his girlfriend to bits, but didn't. In real life, he and Winona Ryder dated, and when they split, he changed a tattoo on his arm from "Winona Forever" to "Wino Forever." Edgy and funny, a little dark but not too mean. Bad boys are a social construct, I learned. Even with scissors for hands, their hearts were gold.

My infatuation with Johnny Depp wasn't obsession, as some of my star-struck friends' crushes were at the time. Sure, I had a picture in my locker and the poster on my wall, but I didn't buy all the magazines he was in or rush to see every movie. The interviews I saw revealed what I had dreamed about him to be true; he was smart and weird, like me. He started wearing glasses over his dark eyes, and I wondered if he really needed them. I decided it didn't matter, because he was a man who thought, correctly, that he looked fantastic in glasses. Johnny was not only someone I wanted to date, but someone I would love to hang out with in general.

My crush on Johnny entered a new level when it was revealed he was to play Hunter S. Thompson in *Fear and Loathing in Las Vegas*. Thompson, the off-kilter author of two of my then-favorite books, *The Great Shark Hunt* and *Fear and Loathing in Las Vegas*, was as much of an intellectual crush as Johnny was a romantic one. A literary bad boy, Thompson was famous for "gonzo journalism" which usually involved excessive drinking and drug use, and then infiltrating and writing about cultural phenomena like the Kentucky Derby or the Hells Angels. Johnny prepared for the role by moving into Thompson's basement. He spoke about their friendship at length on the late-show circuit, and in one interview he discussed their similar ideology and Johnny's fear of becoming commodified as an actor.

It struck a chord with me, I was struggling with whether to pursue my dream of becoming a writer or go to business school and take over the family car dealership. I took that interview to heart, and though it took a few years, I backed away from my family's path and onto my own.

When Thompson committed suicide in 2005, I read that Johnny paid for his funeral, which included Thompson's cremated remains being shot out of a cannon, as instructed in his will. It is rumored to have cost three million dollars and was a very golden-hearted final gift from one bad boy to another.

Johnny slipped off my radar. His movies came out, and I saw some, but none stuck with me. *Inside the Actors Studio* interviewed him in front of their largest crowd to date. He wore beat-up jeans and a Carhartt jacket and smoked hand-rolled cigarettes one after the other, while he shyly peeked out from under a curtain of hair. When the audience clapped or responded positively to various accomplishments that John Lipton, the interviewer, mentioned, Depp thanked them sheepishly. He was a man still uneasy with his fame. I was happy to see him, as shy and tough and golden as ever.

When Disney cast him as Captain Jack Sparrow in *Pirates of the Caribbean*, millions of moms happily took their kids to watch their former Teen Idol in the lead role. Even that role was quirky and smart, dark but kind. In an interview with IGN, Johnny said Jack Sparrow was inspired by both Keith Richards, guitarist for the Rolling Stones, and Pepé LePew, the amorous cartoon skunk who wouldn't take no for an answer. Jack Sparrow was a dark and dangerous pirate, but that heart of gold remained intact.

> *Do you think he did it?*
> *Who did what?*
> *Johnny Depp!*
> *The dog-smuggling thing in Australia?*
> *No. His wife said he beat her up.*
> *Shit.*

My best friend texted me first thing one morning before I had coffee, let alone switched on my computer. The text was like a bucket of ice-cold water down my back. Johnny had been in the news more lately. He'd left his partner, Vanessa Paradis, after fourteen years, and started dating his young costar Amber Heard, whom he married. They'd gotten into trouble for bringing their dogs into Australia on their private jet, and released a bizarrely staged apology video a few months before. I hadn't paid much attention to the entertainment news in a while. Amber Heard had accused Johnny of verbally and physically abusing her on numerous occasions, and had placed a restraining order

Deep into Depp, 20-year-old Kate Kastelein was living in Damariscotta, Maine (photograph by Tabitha Onorato). Today Kate lives in the same town—she's shown here on the stairs of her slightly-haunted house.

against him. Did I think he did it? No way! The Johnny I knew wouldn't do that. He wouldn't hurt anyone, not even with his scissor hands. He was the bad boy with the heart of gold, a pirate hybrid of a guitarist and a cartoon skunk. My reaction to the accusation was immediate. It was obvious to me there was no way he would do such a thing.

I watched a few newer interviews with him. Gone were the long hair and beat-up jeans. Now he wore three-piece suits that reminded me of the Mafia. He flung his arm over the back of the chair and answered questions without a hint of modesty or shyness. I did not recognize this man. I had never been the victim of domestic abuse, but knew many women who had. After the shock of the news settled, my quick response to dismiss the allegations, based only on my perceived familiarity with a celebrity, scared me. I did not know Johnny Depp. Yes, he'd guided me toward the golden-hearted bad boys I'd befriended and loved over the years, and all had been as funny and smart and kind as the boys in the movies. None had grown from bad boys into bad men. But I knew them and drank coffee with them and talked about books and music with them in real life. Just because they were good didn't mean Johnny was. At the least, I had no real frame of reference to make such a strong judgment as to his guilt or innocence. If, based on a movie-star crush constructed out of movie posters and late-night television appearances, I could so quickly discount a woman who said she'd been abused, what did that say about me?

Heard dropped the charges and Johnny was not convicted of spousal abuse. The couple was legally divorced and released the following joint statement: "Our relationship was intensely passionate and at times volatile, but always bound by love. Neither party has made false accusations for financial gain. There was never any intent of physical or emotional harm." One can spend hours reading the evidence for either side of the story. For me, it's not about his guilt or innocence, but my reaction to the allegations.

Johnny Depp is not the characters he plays in the movies, the bad boys with hearts of gold, though he's crafted a career and a public image to coincide with that persona. The power of his harmless bad boy image carries the weight of adoration from millions of women; some, like me, have had a candle burning for over two decades. When someone has been in your eye for that long, you feel as if you know a little bit about him. But you don't really.

A few years ago, a frayed wire in my parents' attic caused a fire. The house was saved, but the attic was destroyed. Among the knickknacks that didn't make it was a box labeled "Kate's childhood." Among other things, it contained the *Cry-Baby* movie poster. If it hadn't been lost, maybe I would have retrieved it and hung it on the wall of my office. Maybe it would have been hanging there when the allegations broke, but it wouldn't be anymore. The torch I'd carried in my own golden heart had been snuffed out.

Confessions of a Would-Be Duran Duran Groupie

Caitlin McCarthy

Spring, 1984. I was on the edge of fourteen, about to graduate from a Catholic junior high school. Sporting a Princess Diana haircut, I had already graduated into my first full-blown celebrity crush: John Taylor of Duran Duran.

MTV entered my house in 1983. I immediately spotted John in the onslaught of Duran Duran videos and knew we were destined to be together. A Ouija board even confirmed this fact during a sleepover at my best friend Jennifer's house. (She was going to marry John's bandmate Nick Rhodes, so it was perfect; we could all travel the world together.)

I started sneaking hydrogen peroxide into the bathroom at home, so I could streak my bangs blond like John's. My mother hit the roof when my brown hair started to turn orange and yellow (and not in a cool punk way). I blamed it on the sun.

I hung a *Tiger Beat* poster of John in the back of my closet so I could see him in the morning when I put on my school uniform. (If I were of legal age, this image probably would have thrilled him!)

I scoured every teen magazine for updates on John and wondered when he'd leave dreary England and come to my dreary hometown—Worcester, Massachusetts—to support his band's latest album, *Seven and the Ragged Tiger*. We had so much in common. I was sure of that. I didn't even mind that his first name was really Nigel.

Finally, the big announcement came over local radio: Duran Duran would play the Worcester Centrum on March 14, 1984. I had never been to a rock concert before, but I was sure as hell going to this one, even if it meant bringing my non–Duranie big sister Erin with me as a chaperone.

My teen mind immediately shifted into overdrive: How could I meet John? The thought of staking out his hotel didn't occur to me. I was truly innocent back then, in a way young teenagers aren't these days. I thought of sending him a letter, but I didn't have his address. It'd never get to him on time if I mailed something to his record label.

Then brilliance struck. I'd write an editorial for Worcester's *Evening Gazette*, which would be sure to attract John's attention. Everyone reads newspapers, right? (Insert laughter here.) In the fifth grade, I had published poems in the newspaper's "Happy Time" section for kids. But by sixth grade, I had outgrown that and started writing editorials in the "Time Out" section for adults (not to be confused with porn, thank you very much). The newspaper and I had a relationship. Maybe it'd help me start a relationship with John!

During math class, I tuned out Sister I-Forget-Her-Name and wrote an opus to Duran Duran in my notebook. Instead of making John the focus, I branched out and detailed the entire band's fabulousness. That way, no feelings would be hurt, and the guys would all support my "relationship" with John.

Below is my opus in its entirety (yes, I saved it):

Duran Duran: One of the Greatest

While reading the "Time Out" section of the paper I was happy to find a long overdue article on one of the greatest groups of the past four decades, Duran Duran. The music, lyrics, videos—it all fits together to form a well-balanced band.

Duran Duran has been criticized for relying too much on expensive videos and their handsome good looks. For one thing, no matter how expensive a video is or how good looking you are, it will not put you on top of the music charts. You have to have talent and determination, which Duran Duran definitely possesses.

The group has frequently been compared to the Beatles, due to the group's large success and the reactions of their fans. The press has dubbed Duran Duran as the "Fab Five" as opposed to a certain "Fab Four." Simon Le Bon has been quoted at a press conference, "We're interested in writing our own history, not writing somebody else's." And to me, that is what makes success.

Caitlin McCarthy
[Address Removed]
Worcester

Much to my surprise, the "Time Out" section not only ran my editorial, it put a thick black box around it. I realize now that someone at the newspaper must have found my comments cute. But as a young teen, I believed that a guardian angel was helping my cause by making sure the item was highlighted so the band would see it when they rolled into town. Back then, the newspaper published the addresses of people who wrote editorials. I thought John could use it when calling 411 to get my number, because he'd be dying to speak with the author of this insightful editorial. I envisioned myself meeting John backstage at the Centrum and maybe, just maybe, getting my first kiss from him. (I never thought about what else could happen with John … remember, I was a painfully naïve thirteen-year-old.)

Duran Duran played Worcester that March. I was there, in the Centrum's nosebleed section with Jennifer and my snickering sister Erin. I never met John because he never called me. Sigh.

But my editorial *did* trigger responses from other people. Female teen Duranies from the Worcester area started sending me letters at home, saying they loved the band, too. I started penpalling with them, and eventually we created our own Duran Duran fan club. We'd meet at each other's houses and watch the band's music videos on the VCR, pausing the tapes occasionally so we could "Ooh" and "Aah" over certain guys. (John got the most requests.) The "Rio" video was a particular favorite of ours.

Many years later, John Taylor married Amanda de Cadenet (the British photographer, author, producer, and talk-show host), and then married Gela Nash (one of the co-founders of Juicy Couture). He never married me. I'm still writing, though—for the big screen as well as TV and blogs. So John, if you ever read this, I don't expect you to divorce your wife. But a kiss on the cheek, after all this time, would still rock my world.

Postscript: In 2016, I saw Duran Duran twice in concert—thirty-two years after the Worcester Centrum gig. Both tickets came courtesy of Jeanette, Duran Duran superfan and wife of one of my high-school classmates. Jeanette and I had connected at my twenty-fifth high-school reunion in 2013 and bonded over our Duranie pasts. Unlike me, Jeanette had met the band on several occasions and travelled to various parts of the east coast for shows. I even caught a glimpse of Jeanette on TV, front row (of course!) at one of their concerts, when *CBS Sunday Morning* ran a segment about Duran Duran in 2015.

I first tagged along with Jeanette to the Mohegan Sun Arena in Connecticut, when Duran Duran was supporting their fourteenth studio album, *Paper Gods*. My seat was on the floor, on "John's side" (thanks, Jeanette!), but not front row. When John stepped out on the stage, I flew back in time—only now I had an iPhone in my hand. Dodging security, I weaseled my way up to the front row and snapped a picture of him towering above me. Yes! I had documented the moment of seeing my Teen Idol up close, in real life—before security asked me to return to my seat. Like a teenager, I grudgingly listened to authority. Several rows back, I still had a great view of John, and thoroughly enjoyed the show.

Jeanette and I later attended an after party up in a suite at the Mohegan Sun Hotel, with women (from New England and beyond) whom Jeanette had befriended during her Duran Duran adventures. I showed them my picture of John, and they shared photos from the Mohegan Sun Arena and other concerts over the decades. I even met a woman who had attended the same Worcester Centrum show that I had. I found myself thinking that Duran Duran was fortunate to have such amazing superfans. Everyone was inclusive, upbeat, and *normal*. They all had lives outside of their love for the band. Attending concerts was their "hall pass" from family and career responsibilities.

A Duran Duran fan to the core, Caitlin McCarthy sported big hair in college. Given a chance to see the band live, she'll gladly go. Today Caitlin is a teacher and award-winning screenwriter.

At my second Duran Duran concert in 2016—this time at the Xfinity Center in Massachusetts—I discovered that Jill, one of the Mohegan Sun gals, was only a few rows away from me. We met up in the aisle for a hello and selfie before the band came on. I was as thrilled to see Jill as I was to see Duran Duran. Like my young teen days, the band had a way of connecting me with others.

That year, *Salon* named Duran Duran "the hottest tour of the summer"—and it was. At every show, Duran Duran acknowledged its past while blazing new trails with cutting-edge music. But for my generation (Gen X), Duran Duran will always be our Teen Idols.

You never forget your first love.

Songs That Make the Young Girls Cry

My Life with Manilow

STEPHANIE POWELL WATTS

In the dim mists of time, there used to be businesses called video stores dotted all over the American landscape. A body entered such an establishment and rented a video tape of a movie or television series or even a concert. There were signs all over these stores with the lyrical admonishment to be kind and rewind your tape before you returned it. I know, I know, it sounds highly implausible. Like you, at my fingertips I have access to all kinds of services that I can rent or buy in seconds. I can watch movies from the phone in my pocketbook. But just a few short years ago, streaming and downloading and viewing platforms were the stuff of science fiction to most of us. Back in the day, in the '80s, you walked into a video store and searched the rows of movies, wandered through the aisles like a pathetic Indiana Jones, and scoped out some kill to drag back to your dark cave and your sofa.

One Christmas holiday, my mother and four brothers and I went to one of these fabled stores to load up on movies. I should say here that we were all Jehovah's Witnesses at the time and did not celebrate the holiday. That meant that we would not be visiting other family members who celebrated. We would not be going to church services or parties or other events to herald the season. It would be just the six of us in a small house for several long, empty days. We had to have some diversion to beat back the depression of feeling like the last people on earth, so we each got to choose a video to take home. In my wanderings, I came upon a section of taped live concerts. At that time, I had never been to a live show, unless you count the folk singers who came to our school for an assembly, or the choir at my grandmother's church. In my memory, there's a clean, warm light, a mote-free spotlight focused on the cover of a single video case. Time slows; there is no sound except for the contented hum of the universe. I like to think I was in my best jeans, dark blue on one side and rad stone-washed on the back, though I can't be sure about this. My eyes are directed (no, led) to a blue case at the bottom of the white wire shelf. The picture on the video is of a blond, bell-bottomed man in a white, rhinestoned onesie, gold chain dripping from his neck, his prominent nose leading his joyous face in profile, his fingers arched in mid-play over the keys of a grand piano: *Barry Manilow Live in Concert*. Merry Christmas to me!

While finding the video was serendipitous, I had discovered Barry Manilow long before that day. *Discover* is a strange word. How can you discover someone whom scores upon scores, thousands upon thousands of people already know? But I love the idea that a song or a place, a person or an idea can break through all the clutter of your mind and be birthed into a new thing, daring and fresh, infinitely interesting to you. I have my mother to thank for my introduction to Barry. She was the primary discoverer of his oeuvre. You might be thinking, how does a black woman stumble into the musical world of Manilow? A better question might be how could she avoid him? On the radio, on *Dick Clark's New Year's Rockin' Eve* specials, in every department store known to humans in the '70s and the '80s, Manilow ruled. I'm sure his net dragged in fans far and wide, and my mother came to the fold without a struggle, with me and my brothers in tow.

Imagine this: It is early in the morning, before light on a school day. From some place deeper than memory, I hear music, then a man's mellow voice, more pleasant than powerful, curling around my head. I stir, not wanting to get out of bed, but the familiar lyrics layer into my brain like snow in a shaken globe. In that place between sleep and realization of the day, I begin to mouth the lyrics I know by heart. Before I realize it, I am on the way to the kitchen with the chorus of "Weekend in New England" spilling from me and into the room. How many mornings I woke up with Barry Manilow, I can't truthfully confess. This is not a tell-all that everyone knew about us. It would be no exaggeration to say we spent years together—or enough time for every member of my family to know all of the greatest hits and most of the B sides. In fact, one of my brothers made a cassette tape of his own renditions of Barry's hits. I will call him Brother X. Nothing kills street cred like a cassette of you singing Manilow. If we did not love Barry from the start, we grew to love him from his proximity to us, from his sheer insistence on being in our lives, from his inextricable intertwinement with our too-short youth. We all loved him in our own ways, but I loved him most. Our love was intimate for sure, no less powerful or significant for its chasteness.

I have heard for at least thirty years, and long before Barry announced it himself, "You know he's gay, don't you?" Gay? Straight? What does his sexual orientation have to do with anything? The object of desire for young girls is someone as sensitive and as pretty as we are. He or she listens and understands, and might be our best girlfriend if given half a chance. It is the rare preteen or teen girl who wants sex. Girls mimic the roles of seductress and temptress trying to become the object of somebody's appreciative gaze, because that's what they've seen in life and television (or in their hundredth viewing of "Despacito"). Sex might be a means to an end and a way to get what they really want: to be noticed, then admired, and finally adored. My relationship with Barry fits this bill perfectly. His songs promise me that I am known and seen, always remembered, singular and unique in the world. Isn't that what we all want to hear?

Now, I know what you are probably thinking: Manilow has become synonymous with schmaltzy lyrics; big, over-the-top music; notes wrung dry of all emotion; songs with smashing-wave crescendos about lost, ruined, or unrequited love. If you are thinking this, you could be forgiven. Way back, years ago, it was an easy joke to make fun of Barry Manilow. He was too earnest and loving and too sincere to be taken seriously. '80s television encouraged us to laugh at his brand of lowbrow, uncomplicated love. And why not? Big emotion has always been associated with women, and anything too closely allied with women and women's desires is easy to mock and discount. It didn't help, of course, that Barry was a memorable physical type: stick-thin with a huge nose (a perfect detail for the caricaturist) that launched a thousand comic bits. But those big songs were the stand-ins for the tumult in my thinking that I didn't have the language to reveal. Those songs were my mother's feelings, too. She carried the original Manilow gene and passed it to me. While I was just waking in those long-ago mornings, my mother had been up for who knows how long, preparing for the day, a couple of cups of instant coffee already downed by the time her own singing began. My mom sang along with Barry about their shared heartbreaks and loves gone so wrong, about too many failed attempts at happiness. My mother was young then, just in her early thirties. When you are young and lonely, with hope and little else, you want to hear someone else's keening, his cries of great despair, her disappointment about her complete and utter inability to make life work. But young people need to know that others see and understand their suffering. They don't yet know the relief, but also the sadness knowing nothing lasts forever, even the weight of their pain. They don't know yet that life, even a very good life, is a series of attempts, as Barry himself might say, of "Tryin' to Get the Feeling Again."

Sounds like sad songs, right? Oh they are. Do not be misled. If you get to the end of a Manilow song with a dry eye, I don't know how you live without a functioning heart. But my mother needed the certainty and reinforcing power of someone else's pain to endure her own. I think she loved the routine of the morning music, too. Once my parents divorced, we lived in more than a dozen places in a few short years. Sometimes we moved to a new town, but often we landed just a street or two from where we started. My mother was convinced and convincing, and sold us on the idea that if we were able to find the right address, we would find the right life. I didn't know this at the time, but this scenario plays out with single mothers and their children all over the country. When you are on the move, a natural reflex is to cling to routine and to the unchangeable little artifacts or rituals that mean stability and home. Enter the songs of Barry Manilow.

It has been years since I lived with my mother, and years since those early-morning record-player reveilles. Back then, I did not get to see Barry Manilow perform live and in person. In fact, I was grown and long moved out from my mother's house when I saw his show for the first time. The concert was billed as a night of music and passion in East Rutherford, New Jersey. And, believe me, it did not disappoint. The audience was almost entirely white, full of middle-aged and older white women, coupled gay men, my dear friend Alex, and my husband. I counted two other people of color (at least two who were obviously people of color) in the arena. It was December, almost Christmastime, and the stage was decorated with wreaths, oversized ornaments, and pine boughs, but Barry sang only one Joni Mitchell holiday song. It was Christmas, but this was not a Christmas show. Barry knew we came for the hits, for the songs that were the sound-

Now an acclaimed novelist and a winner of an NAACP Image award, Stephanie Powell Watts grooved to Barry Manilow as a teenager.

track of our childhood and young adulthood. We wanted the old songs that brought back the old times. I thought of my mother many times that night and the hard, hard days when we all were young, days I didn't know then were good ones. Barry sent one of his dancers into the audience looking for someone to join him. We held our breath when Barry scanned our faces. One lucky fan was pulled on stage to sing with and be serenaded by Barry while the rest of us marveled at her good fortune—she re-enacted a dream we'd all played out a thousand times.

I have a seven-year-old son now. His piano teacher tells me to play music for him—all genres, she insists. It is his early engagement with music that will form his lifelong musical vocabulary. I play classical and jazz standards for him, of course, but I also make sure he knows Michael Jackson, early rap, Prince, the tempting Temptations, the Carpenters, '50s rock 'n' roll, Duran Duran, Emmylou Harris, and anything else I think he might find intriguing. He loves it all. He is without discrimination in anything; everything is good—a beautiful quality that has to fade as he ages, but one I'll miss.

One day, I heard him singing at the kitchen counter.

"What are you singing?"

"I think it's called 'Copacabana.'"

"How do you know that song?"

"I heard you sing it."

Of course, I have played Barry Manilow for him. But not everything. I want to save the hard stuff for when he's older. I'll save the pain for when he needs it.

"I like that song," he said.

You are my son, of course you like that song, I wanted to say. What I did say was, "Keep singing, honey."

Torch and torch songs passed.

Oh, Misha

Ann Rosenquist Fee

Thirty-five years after the fact, I'm starting to forgive Mikhail Baryshnikov for not drifting down the marble staircase of the Auditorium Theatre into the post-rehearsal reception which a bunch of people like me and my friend Shaun Olson had paid sixty dollars to attend. Actually, Shaun's mom had mailed a check, and then after an agonizing wait, we'd received our American Ballet Theatre Open Rehearsal and Reception passes in the Olsons' mail. I'm fine now. It's all good. At this point I can see that the experience had its gifts, maybe in fact the greatest possible gift, i.e., the eventual birth of my life-and-art motto: "Unrequited is underrated." Which, I mean, you can feel free to use for yourself, as long as you credit Mikhail Baryshnikov and the heartbreak he inflicted on Shaun and me that afternoon in 1982.

For most of that school year, Shaun and I had taken turns borrowing Baryshnikov's biography from the library. I don't remember how it was that we'd happened upon that book or on him in the first place. Maybe it was some public television special. I honestly don't recall how either of us got turned on to this unlikely heartthrob—unlikely for two awkward teenagers who were in choir and band but not dance—certainly not dance—as we were safely and squarely outside the graceful-athletic-willowy-popular toe-shoe set. But it happened. And we fell hard.

For me, that mostly meant waiting to watch shows on PBS and reading that biography over and over. But for Shaun it was different. Shaun's family was fancy, and that meant they lived in a world that was actually connected to the same world in which Baryshnikov lived. Shaun's family lived in a refurbished building that was formerly not-a-house; I can't remember exactly what it was—a hospital or a library or something like that. They subscribed to magazines that were not *Reader's Digest*. In Shaun's house, there was potpourri in the bathrooms, flaked and in spray form. The Olsons ate rolls with dinner, and they ate them first, passed around in a basket. First. Before the rest of the food. So, of course, it was Mrs. Olson who blew my mind with the casual announcement that if we could round up the cash and permission from my mom, she would take us to an open rehearsal of the American Ballet Theatre, featuring Baryshnikov as the lead in *Les Sylphides.*

And we would see him. We would see him, and he would naturally also see us, because following the rehearsal was a champagne reception. That probably wasn't capitalized on the passes themselves, but it was very much capitalized in my mind's eye and my pounding heart.

On the day of the rehearsal (and reception), I wore a gray wool blazer and plaid pencil skirt from my sister's closet. Plaid, but not schoolgirl plaid. A pale and subtle plaid, plaid like almost tweed. Vaguely collegiate. Also, nude panty hose and black shoes, both of which I usually wore only to perform in choir concerts. They were too hot, itchy, and formal for a regular school day, which was how we spent the morning, Shaun and me, sitting through eighth grade as if we were just regular people and not people who would be traveling downtown that afternoon for up-close, in-person mingling with our muse.

It was a long morning. Exceptionally long. Agonizingly long. I passed the time by thinking through my plan. Probably, most likely, I would stand at the bottom of the stair-case in the Reception room, not obnoxiously at the exact bottom of it, but nearby. Prob-ably leaning on a wall or banister or pedestal or plant stand, with one hand on my hip. Probably that would be my left hand, and my right would go around the glass of cham-pagne. Despite the risk of being mistaken for a collegiate patron of drinking age (see: tweed), I would decline in favor of sparkling cider, but I'd definitely take it in the would-be champagne glass. Which would probably be a wide, shallow one, not a flute.

Additionally, when Baryshnikov arrived and moved from guest to guest to thank us for coming, I wouldn't talk right away. I would follow his face with my eyes, which were lined in Wet-n-Wild navy, plus a pink shadow which you wouldn't think worked with the tweed, but I felt it was a demonstration of integrity to let my eye makeup indicate my actual age. I wasn't out to deceive. Nor was I out to seduce. This was about art, about assuming my rightful place in the constellation of creatives with whom Baryshnikov was known to partner, crisscrossing disciplines and defying conventions. If anyone could understand the sacrifices I'd made to be able to enroll in both choir and band for the past three years, it was him. When he looked at me, I would smile (lips closed over braces). Depending on how long that first eye contact lasted, I might also nod in a way that would let him know I appreciated and understood his work.

Even if it took several interactions in the course of that one-hour Reception, the nod was the thing. I'd be able to say it all through that. I just needed that moment to take place, and then I would know we'd connected, that he would know that I knew, and I would linger in his mind and he in mine (more than before), and who knew how we'd inspire each other going forward? Who knew how long before we'd be making sweet, sweet art? Us. Mikhail Baryshnikov and me.

During the rehearsal, Shaun and I held hands, hard. We had to. We both needed something to keep from shaking or levitating or something in between. Or, at least, I did. We leaned forward as far as we could over the railing of the second balcony. Barysh-nikov was far away, but that was fine. It was all I could stand to know I was in the same room with him, sharing air, watching the shape of him twist and soar. It's possible that I was too far away to hear the actual sound of him, the pound of his feet when he landed, but I heard it anyway. My senses felt sharp and open, and where they left off, imagination and true love picked up the slack. We probably also weren't close enough to see his sweat, but I saw it anyway; I saw it with great empathy and understanding. Others might have had to move closer to perceive that much, but I knew what I knew without needing to disturb his personal space. I knew he was sweating. My own legs were freezing. They were panty-hose Popsicles bouncing up and down with readiness to make something—anything—with that force. I couldn't dance, but I was a section leader in choir and got excellent grades in art and in anything to do with writing. I knew something would work. Misha was known for innovation. Surely, during the Champagne Reception, we would connect. He would see the potential in me. And my next get-out-of-school-early note from home would be a full-on exemption from junior high, straight to somewhere else. Someplace high off the regular ground.

There weren't any stairs at the Reception. The guests were just a bunch of people who looked like they'd paid to be there, too, or else they worked at the Auditorium Theatre. Shaun or I must have asked somebody with a name tag when the dancers were coming, and they must have explained that that wasn't part of the deal at the sixty-dollar level. I don't remember how that crushing news was delivered, or at what point it happened in the course of the hour-long event, which was supposed to have afforded me multiple opportunities for the eye contact that would launch the agenda for the rest of my life. I don't remember the face or tone of voice or anything about who set us straight, but I'm sure it was a staffer, because what I do remember quite clearly is paging through the *Playbill* on the ride home, in the back seat of Mrs. Olson's car, reading every name in the lists of staff and board members. Also reading and re-reading the donor list and thinking, why would all these people give money if they already knew they'd be holding a plastic cup in a side room with a bunch of other regular people? Who were they, who were any of them, the donors and the people who had titles like Development Assistant? Developing and assisting what? What?

I also don't remember what day of the week it was. Looking back, I hope it was Friday, because who wants to go to school the day after that, after having expected to ascend or at least levitate but ultimately just drinking some punch and getting dropped off at home in a damp, smelly blazer? I'd expected to return the blazer to my sister's closet with something like generosity, like I'd be gifting her the lingering smell of the Reception, and it would be a blast of exotic sophistication such that her closet had never experienced. As it was, the blazer just stank like me, and its return to the closet was a humiliating little grace note to the night. Which I wish had been a Friday, but it's more logical to figure it was a Thursday, because anyone who's anyone in arts administration knows that's when you do open rehearsals. Weekdays. Paper the house.

Thirty-five years after the fact, I am comfortable slinging terms like "paper the house," because I'm the executive director of a small nonprofit arts center, Southern Minnesota's only art gallery, arts-education space, and live-music/literary-arts venue. I fundraise, and then I proofread my own donor lists in my own performance programs and hope like hell I spelled everybody's name right just in case they read the list, which they won't, because no one does. Additionally, thirty-five years later, I have an exquisite artistic collaborator in my friend Joe, who is my bandmate and not my romantic partner, a fact which is basically the foundation of our brand. I don't have data to prove this, but I am one-hundred-percent confident that the reason we've grown a fan base over ten years of performing together is because people are anything from irritated to intrigued to relieved by the fact of our non-coupleness. We have great harmonies and a broadly appealing song selection, mainly 1970s AM Radio Gold and originals that embody that aesthetic— but my hunch, reinforced by occasional feedback from strangers during breaks ("I just have to ask ... because I can tell, you're not a couple, you get along too well for that ... but ... you two ... what *are* you?") tells me it's our flagrant and refreshing display of rock-solid unromanticness that's the draw.

Same for my writing. I have an MA in literary criticism and an MFA in creative writing, two rigorous programs which had me first voraciously dissecting and then creating literary erotica that pretty much involved zero actual sex. My obsessions as a critic

Baryshnikov captured the imagination of Ann Rosenquist (Fee) when she was a teenager in Illinois sipping 7-Up. Now a writer, performer and arts center director in St. Peter, Minnesota, Ann still muses on her near-meeting with Misha.

and later, as a writer, were stories in which "erotic" was a function of anticipation without consummation. You read that right. Two graduate degrees devoted to the build, the tease, the tee-up, the ache, the place where thoughts and sense of self both disappear into a million tiny quakes of desire. Is she/are they? Can we? Would you? You don't get to know. Do the stories win contests, steal the show at open mics, land on the pages of a literary journal now and then? Yep. Unrequited is underrated.

Would I have immersed myself in arts administration or developed a musical partnership known regionally as "the duo that's not a couple but their posters always look like one of them is about to file for divorce," or built up a collection of both published and rejected pieces of flash fiction riffing on the theme of sexless sexiness, had Mikhail Baryshnikov not broken my heart by not coming down any goddamn stairs? I really don't think so. My artistic and academic curricula vitae are too full of testaments to the agenda he set. I have no choice, at this point, but to be grateful.

Fortunately, I'd realized this by the time I got to touch and talk with the man. It was the third or fourth time I'd seen him perform since the Auditorium Theatre. On each occasion, I'd been able to afford progressively better seats. This time it was White Oak Dance Project in Minneapolis. The best seats were ninety dollars. I could do that, provided I went alone. My husband, Scott, was down with that. We made a plan to get drinks and dinner before, and then Scott would tour around the city during the performance, ready to pick me up after. But not right-away after. Only after I'd handed Mikhail Baryshnikov a rose wrapped in a calla lily leaf, purchased that afternoon and stashed carefully under my theater seat during the show. I'd heard from an arts administrator friend that if you waited on a sidewalk outside the stage door, around the nondescript side of the building, Baryshnikov would eventually exit and sign autographs. I spent the show—the whole up-close two hours of it, watching him sweat as I knew he would, hearing the floorboards of the stage creak and moan every time he landed—thinking through my plan. Hand him the flower, ask for an autograph, make clear with eye contact that I was indeed available for coffee, and not in the future but in fact right now. Tonight. If he asked. I'd made that clear to Scott, and he was down with that, too. It's like when you have a celebrity-pass deal with your spouse, except for me, it wasn't sex. I wasn't out to seduce. I was out to make art, still, after all these years.

Baryshnikov exited the side door eventually, about three hours after the show. Most of the moms with ballet-dancer daughters, toe shoes in hand for autographs, didn't stick it out. I did. And eventually there he was in a white linen suit, not much taller than me, light, like light coming from his eyes and through his skin. Light like the way person looks when you've seen his own muscles lift him high in the air, and you'd swear he could do it again right now, or you yourself are about to lift off the ground, or both. Light like the way a person looks when he's come through space and time as your guiding force, but he doesn't really know that, and you're both just here on the sidewalk. I gave him the rose wrapped in a leaf, which he handed to his bodyguard. I don't know what I said, probably nothing, because words weren't in my plan, and I've tried to twist that fact into reassurance that it's better that the coffee date didn't happen. Hasn't happened, yet.

A few years after the sidewalk encounter, I had a long layover in New York, and I left the airport solely to walk about a million blocks with my carry-on luggage to the newly leased office space of the Baryshnikov Arts Center. I wasn't expecting a sighting or anything like that; I just wanted to see what the lobby looked like. Through the glass door, I watched the receptionist answer the phone. "Baryshnikov Arts Center." That's how she spent her days, saying that. Envy kept me from walking through the door. Also holding me back was the fact that I had no reason to be there.

Today, if asked by the receptionist, I think I'd be ready to say that I'm in an acoustic duo that would very much like to collaborate on a modern dance piece elevating such AM Radio Gold selections as Melanie's 1971 "Brand New Key" or Sammy Johns' 1973 "Chevy Van" to the full artistic statements they could be. Or that I run a small arts center known for inviting well-respected creatives to come exhibit or perform in a medium relatively new to them, and wow, wouldn't it be perfectly unexpectedly transgressively Baryshnikovian to show up and do his thing in a small Midwestern town? Or I might say I have some short stories that might interest Misha. This might be most appealing, seeing that he's getting older and none of my stories require leaping. Most of them don't even need movement. He could just stand there, slightly off-center on a bare stage, and read my work aloud, daring the audience to feel the dance in his voice. Lots of stories, Misha, I have lots. Some with thighs and sweat. Any one would make an excellent *pas-de-deux*.

What a Feeling

Lee J. Kahrs

I fell in love with Jennifer Beals on a brown plaid couch in the dark family room of a school friend one December afternoon in 1983. The Chicken McNugget was just born, and Sally Ride was the first woman in space. I was seventeen, and up until I saw *Flashdance*, I was more interested in sports than in boys … or girls.

My friend lived three blocks from school in a small house with olive-green shag carpeting and dim lighting. The centerpiece of the living room was a huge color TV encased in a heavy wooden console replete with cabinet doors on each side where you could store all those state-of-the art VHS tapes. It probably weighed three hundred pounds.

In my house, a fifteen-inch black-and-white TV lived on a cart under the orange Formica island in our kitchen/family room. It was rolled out and turned on for special television-viewing events, like Tuesday nights on ABC, with *Happy Days* and *Laverne & Shirley*, and the annual airings of *The Wizard of Oz* and *The Sound of Music*.

Color TV was magical, and that is why I went to that girl's house. She also had cable TV, and there, sitting on the shag rug, eating Cheetos, and drinking Coca-Cola, I gazed upon Jennifer Beals in *Flashdance*, and I made the most important realization of my young life: I was a lesbian.

Up until that night, my only crush was on my best friend. She never knew, and I didn't know much more than that. I had kissed a boy once and didn't really like it, so never pursued that option further. Then I saw Jennifer Beals.

Those liquid brown eyes, that creamy, caramel skin, that pouty mouth—I was enraptured. Beals was probably the reason I have always favored brunettes. I don't remember anything else about that evening. I don't think I spoke for the hour and forty minutes the movie was on.

It didn't matter that the film's premise was fairly unbelievable: an eighteen-year-old female welder who works at a steel mill by day, and as a burlesque-bar dancer by night, has a dream to become a professional ballet dancer. Her name is Alexandra, but she goes by Alex. She appears to have no family. She has an elderly mentor named Hanna, a woman of indeterminate Eastern European descent, who was a ballet dancer back in the day. They go to the ballet together, and Hanna urges Alex to apply to the dance conservatory.

Alex deflects the advances of her handsome boss, played by Michael Nouri, but eventually succumbs to his charms. But even that was fine with me. He was as taken with Beals' character as I was. I would have had the same dumb look on my face as I sat across

183

from her in that fancy restaurant, staring at her faux front of a tuxedo shirt with nothing underneath as she used lobster more as an aphrodisiac than an entrée.

But he blows it and lets slip that he pulled strings to get her that audition, and she, furious, gets out of the Porsche in some tunnel in Pittsburgh and walks home. Ever the gentleman, he follows her all the way home in his Porsche with the flashers on.

Then the elderly mentor dies, and Alex sinks into a deep depression, stops training, and starts smoking, shutting everyone out. It's only when Richie, the burger-flipping comedian from the club, asks for help rescuing their friend Jeannie from the clutches of the low-life scum with a skankier dance club that Alex breaks out of her depression. They perform an intervention with Jeannie and Alex realizes she must pursue her dream because not everyone can.

The final scene was completely believable to me, when Alex nails the audition melding ballet, hip-hop, and break dancing in front of a panel of humorless, tweedy judges, forcing them to blow their noses and realize she's something special.

So Jennifer Beals was incredibly sexy, and watching her in that film opened up, for the first time in my short life, a true understanding of pure physical attraction. But there was something else.

I was drawn to Beals' character because of her artistic pursuit and her independence. She lived alone in a renovated warehouse in Pittsburgh decades before it was fashionable in Pittsburgh or Brooklyn or anywhere else. She shopped at thrift stores and wore creative ensembles of her own design. She was driven but scared, talented but stubborn. I could relate. I wanted to be a writer but had no idea how to proceed, and I was anxious to go to college and be on my own.

Lee J. Kahrs's passport photograph captures her preppy self at 17, the year she discovered Jennifer Beals—an episode that profoundly influenced her life. Lee now edits a small newspaper in Vermont.

Still, driving home after the movie that night, the image of Beals sitting braless in a torn, off-the-shoulder sweatshirt was burned into my brain. I realized I was attracted to women, not men, and I was excited. It explained so much.

And then I got scared. As sheltered as I was growing up, I knew being gay was not generally accepted, and I knew my Catholic mother would not be happy. As time went on, I purchased the wildly popular *Flashdance* soundtrack on cassette, the songs instantly conjuring the scenes from the movie in my head, allowing me to relive the Beals experience again and again. I stayed closeted for another five years until my mother and I had that conversation, and it was a decade more before my family really came to terms with my sexuality.

Jump to 2003. I'm out and proud and living in Vermont and working as a newspaper reporter. I started to hear rumblings about a new show coming to Showtime called *The L Word* about a bunch of high-end lesbians living in Los Angeles. And who was starring in this lesbian lovefest? None other than Jennifer Beals, all grown-up and looking fabulous. I was floored. Could it be that my teenage crush and the catalyst for all things gay in my life would actually play a lesbian on cable TV? It was too good to be true.

There was never any oversaturation of Jennifer Beals after *Flashdance*, which made her all the more appealing to me when she re-emerged on the small screen in *The L Word*. She didn't go on to make bad made-for-TV movies. She didn't get caught up in some sordid tabloid gossip. She never got regrettable plastic surgery. After *Flashdance*, she made a few more movies, then disappeared for twenty years. She graduated from Yale, took up photography, got married. In the 1990s, she was diagnosed with several serious autoimmune illnesses, so she started practicing yoga and cross-training, seeking out alternative medicine and focusing on nutrition to improve her health.

She divorced and remarried, then in the midst of rebooting her acting career, gave birth to a daughter in 2005. Jennifer Beals has lived her life on her terms, and having her drop out of the limelight only made her more attractive when she returned.

There have been other idols in my life, many of them men I wished to emulate, like Ernest Hemingway and James Bond. In the end, all that got me was twenty years of alcoholism and a rakish personality. Sure, I was drawn to Jodi Foster and Kristy McNichol, but they were tomboys like me and not feminine enough for my tastes, even before I knew I was gay, even before I knew what that meant.

Jennifer Beals came along at precisely the right time to help me figure myself out, so I will always hold a small torch for her.

And for the record, my wife is a brunette.

Dear MJ

A Love Letter, Late

Shara McCallum

There are images that stay: the glittering, single glove extended, the black fedora tilted to obscure the face, the telltale opening drum beats and baseline of "Billie Jean," the poplocking action of a leg bent at the knee and flicked up at a right angle toward a hip before refinding the floor, the sudden gliding of the boyish man who would be a king moonwalking across the stage.

Ten years old, I had lived in the U.S. for a little over a year in 1982, when Michael Jackson's *Thriller* was released. I was on the cusp of adolescence, about two years after the album's initial release, when the fixation with MJ took full possession of me. MJ was part and parcel of my transition from Jamaican to American and from girlhood to womanhood.

I don't recall exactly when or why or how I acquired the LP; I just know the record was a fixture of daily life in 1983–84, the year I was eleven turning twelve. Even now, I remember the look and feel of the album as if it had been in my hands not five minutes ago: Michael on the cover in an unforgettable white pantsuit, black button-down shirt opened to offer a glimpse of his hairless chest, Michael sprawled in such a way to suggest languor, Michael with one or two Jheri-curled locks glancing his brow, Michael with his dark eyes penetrating the very depths of my soul. Or so I thought.

Each day of sixth grade after school, I'd rush home to gaze into those eyes for hours, holding the album jacket while the songs played over and over, flipping back and forth between liner notes and inset photos, always returning to the cover image. Hearing was bound up with seeing and touching. My daily dose of *Thriller* meant not just tracing my fingers absently across the record sleeve, but doing so to possess the whole of the sensory experience. Turning the rectangular piece of cardboard in my hands, it was as if I thought I could make the music come alive and will Michael into being, in the flesh, inside my grandparent's Miami townhouse.

The act of listening to *Thriller*, as with other albums I had on replay in my youth, was also ritualistic. It involved lifting the record player's needle to set it down deliberately and carefully onto the vinyl surface of the record, meant waiting for the scratching sound that preceded each song to yield to MJ's vocals and inflections and the music's backing and instrumentation. The act of listening left me adrift from time, yet more aware of each instance through the music. My mind was under a spell, neither jumping backward to irritably examine the previous hours and my missteps and failures, of which I kept a daily tally in my head, nor springing forward to feel the future's uncertainty burbling inside of me. The act of listening to MJ absorbed me, and I was rapt by and wrapped inside his voice each day of my twelfth year on the planet. I anticipated each sigh and inhale of air that left MJ's lips and punctuated the notes as if they were my own breath. I knew each note not only by heart but as if these notes were my own heart, whose contours were a continent and I its first explorer.

In July of 1984, the summer between elementary and junior high school, my aunt drove me the five-and-a-half-hour ride from Miami to Jacksonville to watch MJ perform with his brothers at the Gator Bowl in the so-called "Victory Tour." Packed into the stadium with over forty-five thousand fans, I, too, screamed at requisite intervals throughout the concert and would erupt in fits of tears, much to my aunt's bewilderment. The idea that I was at a live event was, in retrospect, more fiction than fact. Given the distance from my seat to the stage, MJ was either a doll-sized man and barely visible to my naked eye, or he was a fuzzily transmitted figure brought overly close to my face by binoculars my aunt had brought in anticipation of the problem, or he was an oversize giant, lit large on the screen above the stage set, a screen that broadcast the performance to an eager and devoted audience who had ironically come to witness him in person.

When I'd asked to attend the show in Miami, my grandparents hadn't been obliging. The concert tickets were very expensive—reason enough for our family, who did not have much means then for luxuries. After the reality sank in that I wasn't going to the Miami show, I had become forlorn and dejected. When three new shows in Jacksonville were announced, my grandparents and aunt relented and undertook the considerable effort and expense. I was one of the lucky girls going.

My aunt had warned me we didn't have great seats, but it turned out once we arrived at the stadium they were worse than even she had thought. We followed the directions of usher after usher, urging us to keep climbing till we arrived at our seats, in the *very last rows* of the stadium, in the bleacher section perched so high above the stage and field-turned-seating below. I felt a touch of vertigo in looking down. My disappointment was visible, and my aunt apologetic, but I quickly assured her I couldn't have cared less. And I really didn't care once I reoriented myself and the feeling of light-headedness passed. Maybe it was just nerves causing that queasiness after all. I was finally and actually this close to my beloved Michael in this moment of my real life.

When I attended the "Victory Tour" in the summer of 1984, my commitment to MJ went way beyond that of a casual fan of *Thriller.* Over the year or so since its first twinge, obsession had strengthened its grip. I'd gone back in time to the days of the Jackson 5, was listening as often to those early recordings of him and his brothers and to his previous, fifth solo album, *Off the Wall,* as I was to *Thriller.* I'd read every biography I could find that recounted Michael's early life in Gary, Indiana, growing up a Jehovah's Witness with an overbearing father who pushed the children into show biz. Joe Jackson had Michael, at the age of five, and his older brothers playing the "Chitlin' Circuit" initially, before they worked their way up to better and better gigs. From the scaffolding of his story, I'd fully constructed the details of Michael's innermost self. I believed that despite (or because of) his success and his fraught relationship with his father, Michael was trapped inside his own sadness. I'd identified in him the markings of what I was beginning to connect to myself: we were outsiders. This was the foundation on which I'd built our imaginary relationship.

There were plenty of differences and obstacles that, to any rational person, would have signaled the impossibility of any real relationship transpiring. Age alone, to start: he was twenty-five, and at twelve I was less than half his age. Oh, and there was that one other minor inconvenience: I had no chance of ever meeting him. The probability of it happening was about as close as you get to zero. The Jacksonville concert should have only highlighted the insurmountable nature of the divide between us.

Any one of these details, or all of the signs, if I'd read them, might have rid me of the deluded conviction that what I felt was true love. But no matter what logic anyone presented to me to make reason prevail in my consciousness, I was stubborn and steadfast in my refusals and dismissals of the evidence. Where MJ was concerned, I had lost my mind. "I'm not only going to meet MJ, I will marry him," I announced repeatedly to any family member or friend who was kind enough to keep putting up with me when, at every opportunity in conversation, I would find a way to bring him up. With all the certainty a twelve-year-old girl can muster, I believed in my heart of hearts MJ and I would forever be together. With all that age's earnestness, mixed with the dawning of desire in me, I had convinced myself—was one hundred percent certain, in fact—I would save him from a world that misunderstood him.

There are hints of sadness in *Off the Wall*—notably in the ballad "She's Out of My Life." But in many cases now, it's clear I was imposing a feeling of alienation onto MJ's fuller body of work, or drawing upon a smattering of the earlier songs to make the case in my head that the man even needed saving. The song that best bolstered my argument was "Ben." Released in 1972, the year I was born and when Michael was fourteen, "Ben" was the first of MJ's solo releases that would end up at number one. "Ben" struck a chord, not only in me, but in many, many other people, it seems. With its plaintive melody and lyrics, the song suggests that one person can lift another out of his or her inherent aloneness. The song was a hit that endures.

I would not only play it but also sing it to myself repeatedly.

Of course, I should mention the song is literally about the story of a friendship between a boy and a rat. But my capacity for metaphor, for willfully missing the forest for the trees, was a force in me already at twelve. Leaping past such particulars as who the characters were in "Ben" was no more a problem than sustaining the fantasy world I lived in, where MJ and I were together, nor did any of it strike me as odd or funny. Whenever I sang the song, it was very simple: I played the role of the boy, and MJ became the cast-aside, mistreated rodent.

I was nothing special in loving MJ. I can easily see that now. Virtually every girl my age at that time, in the era of *Thriller*, was in love with him. As much as I can see this now, I believed the opposite at twelve. Upon falling to pieces and refusing to eat dinner after hearing the news that he'd been burnt in an accident while filming a Pepsi commercial, I was sure I was the only girl in the world who was experiencing such piercing grief. I put my faith in the flimsiest of facts; that I obsessed over his recovery or vicariously felt his suffering was all the proof I needed that MJ and I had a special bond and were fated to be together.

Why at twelve did I look to find such overblown and dramatic emotional responses as proof of love? Why did I feel compelled to mount a case, based on myopia, that my beloved and I were destined for one another? It's really not that complicated. In fact, it's terribly ordinary and clichéd. Such adolescent and particularly gendered ideas of romance and love in our culture are like lice. Young girls, impressionable as all young people are, simply pick up these messages on love, which then spread rapidly in their own fanciful imaginations.

Look at any fairy-tale princess story, rom-com, or reality show, and you'd have to be obtuse to miss the lesson: "Love" is apparently fated, mysterious, sudden, and all-consuming. If you heed the culture's vast quantity of relationship advice on heterosexual pairings, the role of the boy may be to rescue the girl physically or financially, but hers is a far superior moral and spiritual mission: She is there to save him from the very depths of himself. In many of the most prevalent plots, knowing the other person hardly factors into whether or not you should invest yourself in this kind of an undertaking. In fact, stopping to consider such a trifle could muck things up. According to the stories, real intimacy, the kind that comes from the more painstaking, slow work of trying to know another human being, is *not-love*, is blasé and *boh-ring*.

Desire is complicated. I'm not quibbling with that. In some measure, desire is predicated on our tendency, ability even, to objectify another. It is some part projection of the craven part of our nature onto the one we crave. It is

Before she became an award-winning poet, Shara followed the Prince of Pop. Today Shara is an expert in Caribbean literature and her latest book of poetry is *Madwoman*.

some part never fully knowing and partly obscuring the person we desire, of exchanging for a second the one in front of us for a person we've conjured through our wanting. But how much a part of love is this aspect of desire? Does it merely inflect or overwhelm what we know as love?

When I've seen footage of teen girls fainting at the sight of Elvis or screaming and crying over the Beatles, I understand myself and my attachment to MJ as part of some cultural pantomime that is for most young girls, perhaps, harmless as a passing fancy. But left to take root, or in excess and kept apart from a fuller understanding of love, this kind of desire seems to me not harmless at all. It becomes a weed and threatens not only the person who understands love and attachment in this way but also the one who is the recipient of such attention.

For those of us who claimed to love MJ, especially in the days of *Thriller*, our collective obsession wasn't love but rather the definition of *fanaticism*: cultish and crazed. Over the years following *Thriller* and up to his death, many of us watched the way MJ crumbled and was mangled by our "love." His constant need to reimagine himself in whatever ways the culture seemed to be telling him he ought to be was apparent on a physiological level and also hinted at something much deeper having gone awry. I won't profess to know or understand what really happened to the man who was Michael Jackson, or to be able to separate the myth from the person who lived, or to be able to answer the questions that increasingly swirled around him regarding the universe in which he resided. But I know, from the outside looking in, that MJ's world and how he saw himself within it seemed ever more disturbed and disturbing.

What I wonder still, now that he is gone, is if he would have chosen the frenzied levels of adoration he received if he could have understood from the start what he was risking. I still sometimes think of the person he might have been, were he not battered by the wishes of too, too many others. He was a child, then teen, then young adult being everywhere seen and desired. At the height of his fame, he was the most recognizable human being on the planet, and this in a pre–Internet, pre-social-media age. With his adolescent, developing identity being forged at the same time he was existing in countless people's imaginations—his own perhaps being drowned out or becoming stunted—how much of a fighting chance did he have?

After my year of *Thriller* and loving MJ, I all but stopped paying attention to him. His later music barely made a dent in my consciousness, with the exception of a few songs like "Smooth Criminal," the video for which as much as the song I still adore. But quickly after that year ended, and for years later, when I'd happen to catch a news story or clip of an interview or MJ in performance, I mostly looked away. If I tried, I couldn't dredge up my schoolgirl feelings, once so intense. I couldn't for a long time understand that girl I'd been, so divorced from reality and truth, and I felt mostly embarrassment when I thought of her mawkishness and obsessions.

As I grew up, my love for MJ had come to be replaced by something else then: pity and even horror—less noble feelings I'm not proud of whenever they arise in me, as I think they are feelings that allow us to hold another person at arm's length, to reassure ourselves we are not bound up in his failings, or that we are altogether different from him. In the decades following *Thriller*, whenever I'd look at MJ, all I could see was our "Man in the Mirror" ever more lost in a maze of endless reflections. Increasingly, I saw a person eclipsed by some of the most troubling aspects of our culture, and I was left with more questions than answers:

What exactly had our preoccupation with and worship of money and fame done to him? How much had the straitjackets of race and masculinity in the United States warped who he was?

I understand better now why MJ left my brain when he did; that stage of adolescence is one I moved past. But it still seems strange that the exit of someone who had undone me so completely was so sudden and final. It was as if one morning I woke and he had vanished, the memory of how I'd once felt about him like a dream, elusive and dissolving at the edges.

When MJ left the stage of my young-girl heart, my tendency to fall in love with an idea of a person, rather than the person in front of me, didn't come to quite as sudden an end. Throughout my adolescence, I continued to hold less-than-ideal concepts of what being in love means, albeit trying ideas out on boys and men who were somewhat closer to me. For a long time, I was in love with being in love more than with the object of my affection. As much as anything else, I wanted to dwell inside desire, inside that feeling of wanting and never having.

Well into my late teens and till my early twenties, when I met the man who is now my husband, I also had the bad habit of falling in love with boys and men who were unlikely or unable to return my attention, who were attached to someone else, or were way too old for me anyway, or were gay. I could romantically attach myself to another person, it seemed, only from the safest of distances. Standing on one side of a chasm, I could fling and fling my affection across the rift, knowing that my love would never reach the intended or come back.

My sense as a young girl that MJ was lonely and trapped inside of his loneliness was probably a not-too-far-off-the-mark insight into some part of who he was. But identifying and fixating on this sadness and calling that *love* had never been about saving him. I question that altruistic idea underpinning the standard interpretation of the girl's role in the conventional stories as much as any other part of the tales of desire and love we spin. Even if I had such a misguided notion at twelve, now I think that much of that time, I was looking at MJ in the way we observe light refracted through water, hoping to better see and understand my own path.

Sending My Representative

Whitney Houston and Black-Girl Perfectionism

DOLEN PERKINS-VALDEZ

I once had a friend who would use the phrase "sending my representative" to describe how she sometimes presented herself to the world around her. It always seemed to me to be a flip invocation of W.E.B. DuBois's classic interpretation of black duality. I suppose it should come as no surprise that this woman is no longer in my life; perhaps she sent her representative to me as well? Maybe both our representatives were interacting with each other? This notion of the presented self is a dizzying concept, but not an inconceivable one.

My mother owned a beauty salon in Memphis, Tennessee, in the 1980s, so I had early exposure to the labor behind black women's outward appearances. At nine years old, I already understood how much time and effort we put into our grooming. It was not unusual for clients to keep weekly standing appointments. And though it was a relaxing and social space, there was no denying the physicality of taming black hair. Curl rods, relaxers, hot combs, Jheri curls, wraps. We endured what were sometimes painful procedures, all in an effort to present ourselves to the world in what we considered a respectable way.

I had a head of hair so thick that in fifth grade the mean girls nicknamed me "Bush." I jumped in a salon chair every chance I got, in order to try to tame it. And to this day, I love the thrill when the chair is turned toward the mirror and I can see, finally, after all those hours, that I have been transformed into someone different. Sometimes when I change my hair, people do not recognize me. There is something thrilling about that, about being a chameleon. And part of the sisterhood of black beauty salons is that we keep each other's secrets. We tame our manes in private, then step out of the salon onto public stages, where we project the looks of our inner desires.

In the summer of 1985, I was twelve and just about to start junior high. My favorite song was Whitney Houston's "The Greatest Love of All," and I knew every word. I didn't have to write down the lyrics, because it was played on the radio all day long. It seemed as if every girl I knew learned to sing "I Wanna Dance with Somebody (Who Loves Me)." It was all about children and the future, so of course the lyrics were an instant teen classic.

We sang it in church. We sang it in school. We sang it a cappella. We sang it with the instrumental. We sang it for holidays. We sang it for pageants. In our community, we called it being "on program." If there were some kids on program that year, it was probable that somebody would be singing Whitney. In the same way that R. Kelly's "I Believe I Can Fly" became the black children's anthem a decade later, Whitney's song represented the hopes and dreams of black girls and boys. The vocals were relatively easy to imitate. The lyrics were inspirational. Plus, Whitney was respectable. Our parents loved her because she was a good girl.

If you've always been surrounded by role models, then you probably don't understand what it's like to not have any. Back then, in the mid–'80s, there were not a lot of black girl Teen Idols. In the sports world, there was Debi Thomas, the talented Olympic ice skater. On television, black girls like me watched *The Facts of Life* primarily due to the presence of roller-skate- and braces-wearing "Tootie," played by actress Kim Fields. When *The Cosby Show* began airing in 1984, Tempestt Bledsoe and Lisa Bonet became our sisters. That same year, Vanessa Williams was crowned the first black Miss America. In 1987, Jodi Watley broke away from the group Shalamar to record as a solo artist, clad in Madonna-esque lace skirts. We'd grown up with Janet Jackson as "Penny" on the 1970s television show *Good Times*, so when her album *Control* was released in 1986, it felt like our own personal declaration of independence from our families.

This may seem like a sizable list, and in my memories it was an exciting decade, but it does not at all compare to the number of Teen Idols available to white girls at the time. It is also smaller than during the 1990s, when the numbers of black teenage stars would begin to expand, in some part due to the success of *The Cosby Show*.

Now my daughters have *Black Girls Rock* and Black Girl Magic, but when I was young, we did not have anything like that. In the 1970s, our mothers hunted uselessly in stores for black dolls, while we styled our hair like Farrah Fawcett's flip or in an asymmetrical version of the mushroom. In the 1980s, we searched for black girls to emulate. Whitney Houston appeared on the cover of *Seventeen* in 1981, years before she rocketed to superstardom as a singer, and it was a rare and welcome sight.

I'm drawn to the years between 1985 and 1989, because it is the period during which my own innocence overlapped with Whitney's. Although she was nine years my senior, it still feels as though we grew up together. Part of the allure of celebrities is that we think we know them, so of course I understand that I am speaking about Whitney's representative, not the actual woman. Still, I think there is something to probe here.

Sometimes it is difficult to remember Whitney Houston's happier times. Things turned out so tragically, so mind-numbingly horrific for her and her family, that the earlier image of the bright-eyed twenty-one-year-old who stunned the country with her talent and poise gets washed out.

I will never forget painfully watching Whitney Houston appear on the 2005 reality television show *Being Bobby Brown*. In the third episode, she was flipping through a magazine, and she came upon a photo of Beyoncé. "Just beautiful," she whispered under her breath. "She really is lovely." I was struck by the graceful compliment from an aging pop superstar to a junior star who everyone could already tell was headed for extraordinary heights. Still, I couldn't help but wonder what she felt—a sense of replacement? A passing torch? Once, Whitney was our Beyoncé—successful, gifted, beautiful, and the kind of crossover talent that drew pride from blacks and admiration from whites. Whitney was the first major crossover artist since Michael Jackson, and broke records as the best-selling black female pop artist of all time.

When I was younger, we watched white shows primarily for the black characters. Tootie on *Facts of Life*. Diahann Carroll on *Dynasty*. Gary Coleman and Todd Bridges on *Diff'rent Strokes*. As far back as the 1950s, *Jet* magazine published a "Television" page in its back section listing the names of blacks appearing on television that week. It was not uncommon for them to list the single black performer appearing on an otherwise all-white show. For people under the extraordinary pressure to be good and representative Negroes, role models played a crucial role in our communities. It was impossible to be a Teen Idol without also being a role model. For us, they were one and the same.

Whitney emerged into the public eye at a time when positive black celebrity representation was crucial. And I wanted to be just like her. Both of us were tall and model-thin. Neither one of us could dance very well. We'd both been raised in the church. Well, I wasn't a singer, but like many black girls of my time, I tried to imitate her voice and sing along.

Anyone who has delved into the problematics of being a "model minority" can easily see the cracks in this fantasy. I remember the moment Debi Thomas, an ice skater known for what was then a difficult "triple toe-triple toe" combination, stumbled in the 1988 Olympics. Like many of my black girlfriends, I was at home with my family that evening, watching her perform live on television. Debi was very good, a serious contender for the gold medal that year. She began by skating a beautiful program, and when it was time for the final routine, I remember feeling as if my chest would burst with anticipation.

In Whitney Houston mode, Dolen Perkins (Valdez) posed for this portrait at her Memphis high school in 1990. Dolen, a writer on faculty at George Mason University, will always love her idol.

Not long after the beginning of her long program, she stumbled. And stumbled again. It was heartbreaking. I was watching with my family, and I remember crying. Debi's tumble wasn't just her mistake. It was an error committed by every black girl watching. Even though she took home a bronze medal, becoming the first black American athlete to ever medal in the winter Olympics, we grieved that she had failed to skate perfectly.

This anxiety about black-girl perfectionism was not new. Weeks before the end of Vanessa Williams's reign as the first black Miss America in 1984, it was reported that compromising photos of her would be published by *Penthouse* magazine without her consent. At the time, she was twenty-one years old. It was a devastating moment for her, but it was also crushing for us black girls who were busy outrunning stereotypes. We witnessed time and time again our heroines become fallen heroines, often held to different, higher standards than their counterparts. Because there were so few black female celebrities, their mistakes were magnified.

This was the stage Whitney walked onto in 1985. Every step she took was the step of a nation. Every clear note that came out of her throat came out of ours. She was musical royalty, our black American princess, daughter of Cissy, cousin to Dionne. In 1985, a critic for the *Globe* proclaimed hers "a voice that can scale mountains." In May 1986, just a little over a year after her debut album, the *New York Times* labeled her "Pop's New Queen." She was just twenty-two years old.

And I loved her.

At twelve years old, I was five feet eight inches and a size four. Whitney was also five feet eight inches and a size four. When she performed, she wore elegant dresses. I loved to wear dresses, too. What was unique about Whitney was that she did not use her sex appeal to draw attention to herself. In a review of a run of sold-out performances at the Roxy, the *Los Angeles Times* wrote, "her old-fashioned, ladylike demeanor was wonderfully refreshing." They called her "extremely un–Madonna." It was this wholesome packaging of her that solidified her standing as a powerful role model.

It is probable that this refined look was not merely the vision of Clive Davis, her mentor at Arista Records; it also reflected her conservative upbringing. Cissy Houston, Whitney's mother and a longtime gospel star, clearly had an interest in Whitney representing the family well. The notion of dressing up in one's "Sunday best" has always been intimately connected to the history of black respectability. Whitney was an all–American girl. She gave us hope, taught us to value our talents and to let those gifts speak for themselves.

It was perhaps inevitable that she would disappoint us. Who can maintain such perfectionism? So Whitney did what so many of us do: She split into two. One life, public. The other, private. The public life in all the wigs and carefully applied makeup and long gowns. The private life, with her friends and family from New Jersey. I will not fall into the trap of terming these selves as false versus authentic, but I think it's reasonable to assume there were parts of her she never let the public see. When she began dating "bad boy" Bobby Brown and eventually married him in 1992, it was a devastating moment for black girls everywhere. Something cracked in our perception of her. And the innocence seemed both irretrievable and even unwanted by Whitney herself.

But I don't want to cross into the 1990s. I want to remain in the time of her innocence, when the trappings of celebrity and fame were still new, when she was still wide-eyed and filled with promise.

When I was, too.

In 1985, I started junior high school and began to pack my schedule with activities, becoming a cheerleader, a member of the band, and a student-council officer. I believe my decision to try out for cheerleading was a combination of my mother's urging and my desire to be popular. From the very beginning, I was ill-suited for it. I was taller than many of my classmates, and I was ashamed of my thin legs in my cheerleading dress. Yet despite the crushing insecurities of adolescence, I worked hard to be perfect. I took gymnastics lessons in a fruitless attempt to learn tumbling. I strived for straight As. I auditioned for All-West Tennessee Band and earned first chair. And I spent a lot of time in my mother's salon trying to keep my bush tamed.

At the end of that year, I was voted into our class Hall of Fame, though I had to share the title with a white girl. Even with all my successes and the fact that I never got into trouble at school and was considered one of the class leaders, I distinctly recall standing in the dining hall and looking into the face of our middle-school principal as she quietly hissed to me that I was "insubordinate."

Black-girl perfectionism is not often written about, but it permeates our society. A retaliatory answer to the low expectations placed upon black people in general and a complement to the pervasive fear of black boys, black girls often find themselves in a position of overcompensating. Spending hours in the beauty salon is just one facet of this phenomenon. We study harder, work harder, and when we get older we have a tendency to shoulder an extraordinary amount of familial responsibilities. We even strive for spiritual perfection, disproportionately populating black churches.

In the 1970s, the scholar Michele Wallace warned of the dangers of this behavior, calling it the "myth of the black superwoman." More recently, Melissa Harris-Perry has coined what she calls the "crooked room." She claims that many black women "bend" themselves to fit into skewed, crooked rooms that represent societal expectations of us. When black women's personal tendencies toward perfectionism conflate with societal expectations, we begin to step into dangerous zones that can literally affect our mental and physical health.

I was no stranger to this tendency in my junior-high years, even though I had no idea that I was buying into a cultural trap. Black children growing up in the 1980s with strivers for parents knew that the worse thing we could do was embarrass them. We had to make them proud, and being respectable was of paramount importance.

As I looked around for role models, Whitney topped that list. She was black-girl perfectionism personified, and when I looked at her, I saw myself.

An informal poll among my current circle of my friends reveals a strong distaste for Whitney's music. I cannot believe it. How could they not like her early songs? But I remember that by 1986 and 1987, when her second album was released, criticism had begun to emerge. Whitney's recorded music was considered bland and predictable. It wasn't that people commented she was incapable as an artist; they merely felt she was not using her vocal talents to their full capacities.

On the contrary, her live performances were much more dynamic. She revealed more range and depth in live performances than she did in the studio. This was a business decision, but the criticism persisted nonetheless. As a result, a gap emerged between her slick, polished albums and her more vocally dynamic live concerts. It's plausible to infer this gap was a mirror of her public and private selves. The albums represented the public face of Whitney, the image carefully cultivated by her record label and management. In live concerts, Whitney revealed a bit more of her private self, her gospel and R&B influences, her Newark upbringing.

At home, my father teased my mother for using her "Chicago voice." This was the standard-English, clipped-consonant affectation that she reserved for business, a professional voice she'd acquired when she migrated North during her younger years. When it was just family around, my mother's tones grew warm and folksy again. My dad wore a suit and tie every day to his corporate job. On weekends, he casually unbuttoned the top buttons of his shirt and wore an emerald-eyed lion pendant hanging from a gold rope chain around his neck. In the American South where I lived, this need for cultural dexterity was even more pronounced, given the deep class and racial divisions of the 1980s.

At school, I learned it wasn't socially advantageous to shine too brightly. I did not brag about my grades, and I did little to enhance my looks. Though some of this was surely attributable to my desire to fit in with my peers, I think this kind of pressure, coupled with black-girl perfectionism, created a psychic fissure. Like Whitney, I carefully chose the moments when I revealed my talents. Existing in that perpetual state of duality, however, can erode your self-esteem. At least, that's what happened to me. By the time I began high school, my perfectionism had become a shield I used to mask my low self-esteem. It was toxic.

I wonder if Whitney experienced the same erosion.

Well, it seems inevitable that Whitney's disease of addiction would creep into this essay. Like many people, I refused to believe it for a long time. I did not want to see her sick. Yet I could not stop watching images of her on television. It was as if someone else were inhabiting Whitney's body. This was not the Whitney who'd inspired my childhood fantasies of talent and success. This was someone else: a representative sent to confirm our worst nightmares about what was possible when we slipped down the dark slope of self-destructive behavior, when we failed to acknowledge that perfectionism was just someone else's projection.

Still, I loved her. I wanted so badly for her to get well. Although I never blamed Bobby, somehow sensing that such things are never uncomplicated and one-sided, I desperately wanted her to leave him. To stand on her own two feet. To put on her bobbed wig and long dress, and caress a microphone and sing the way she used to. I did not care if it was her public or her private self, her bad music or her good music. I just wanted my childhood Whitney back. If she could redeem herself, I could overcome my own mistakes. We could both shake loose the chains of expectations that bound us, and be confident even in our imperfections.

The state of celebrity must pose a complicated challenge for black women—this endless splitting into more and more selves, always underscored by intense public scrutiny. When I look in the mirror, what do I see? That junior-high-school cheerleader is both a part of me and also an elusive projection. I am refracting even as I write this essay, allowing you to see the self I select on this page, admitting even to myself that there remain unknowable parts of me. Yes, I am sending you my representative. Do you look up to her? Is she good enough for you?

Catch her before she falls.

"Digging for Fire"

1990s' Nostalgia and the Pixies

Heather Duerre Humann

Merriam-Webster's smartphone app defines a *pixie* as "an imaginary creature that looks like a small person and has magical powers." According to *Merriam-Webster*'s thesaurus app, the adjective form of pixie, *pixieish*, means "tending to, or exhibiting, reckless playfulness." The band I idolized in the 1990s was the alternative rock group the Pixies, and they were well-named. Their sometimes cryptic lyrics addressed a strange mixture of topics (family drama, self-destruction, and obsession, to name just a few), and they tackled these themes by making frequent allusions to historical events and mythology. Their music, however, also reflected their interest in popular culture and science fiction, and some of their songs seemed to be making playful inside jokes as well.

Indeed, the band would often embrace humor and silliness, so I was always left with the impression that they never took themselves too seriously. While songs by the Pixies clearly bore the influence of a number of other popular musical groups, their sound was nonetheless unique—so much so that they seemed to defy genre. They were too upbeat to be either grunge or punk rock, but their cynical world view (which came out through their lyrics) clearly positioned the band outside of the realm of pop music. The end result of this combination was that The Pixies forged their own sound.

My devotion to the band began in the fall of 1990, when I traded in the Smiths' *Strangeways, Here We Come* album, which I'd been listening to on repeat since eighth grade, for my first Pixies CD, *Bossanova*. The first song of theirs that I heard (and fell in love with) was a track on that CD called "Dig for Fire." My last vivid memory of listening to a Pixies' song was in late 1999, when I heard "Where Is My Mind?" played during the final scene and ending credits of *Fight Club*. In a way, these two songs bookend the decade for me. Not only do they symbolically mark its beginning and end, but they capture the movement from naiveté to *weltschmerz* that I have come to associate with the 1990s.

As a teenager, much of what I knew about popular music was based on what my friends listened to. Their tastes changed like the seasons, but I, on the other hand, would fixate on a band when I found one I really liked. This is what happened after I heard my first Pixies' song.

The youngest of my group of friends, I was the last one to get my driver's license, so most days I would ride to and from school in a friend's car. I remember that fall day in 1990, when, sitting shotgun in my friend's mom's Honda Accord, I first heard the Pixies. The song was "Dig for Fire," and it was like nothing I'd ever heard before. For one, there was a startling contrast between the lighthearted melody and the song's more serious subject matter.

"Dig for Fire" was clearly a song about self-destruction, and it seemed to celebrate rather than condemn making bad choices. The song's lyrics describe a man who lives in a town near a beach where the singer would one day live. The thought behind the lyrics appealed to me, but I also found the song's use of verb tense interesting. In English, we often denote actions that will take place in the future by using the simple future tense, which is composed of two parts (*will / shall* + the base verb). In contrast, "going to live" (even though it refers to a future event) uses the first-person singular of the present tense (by using the present participle, or *-ing* form of the verb *go*). In this case, however, the verb *go* carries no sense of actual movement. This construction

Heather Duerre Humann cheered for the Pixies as they forged their own sound; in the years since, Heather has forged her own path as teacher and author.

therefore works as another of the ways in which English expresses the future. Both *going to* and *will* are the English language's way of conveying something that will take place in the future, but neither stipulates when the action will take place (it could be happening in ten days or in two decades).

A useful distinction between the two is that *going to* often implies a preconceived intention, whereas *will* is used at the point of making a decision, but again, neither indicates at what point in the future the event will take place. The juxtaposition of conviction and uncertainty set up by the song's use of verb tense spoke to me. The *going to* reflected my certainty that I would move away from the town I'd lived in since elementary school. Similarly, I knew I would one day be a writer (and I also dreamed of living by the beach). What I was less sure about was when those things would happen.

With the Pixies, I quickly moved from having my curiosity piqued to full-blown obsession. *Bossanova*, the CD we'd listened to in the car (and my introduction to the band), was new to me, but it was the Pixies' third album. I wanted to see what else they'd released, and I remember eagerly handing over my babysitting money to explore the band's full discography. Not only did I buy and quickly devour their first two CDs, but I was content to spend many a weekend afternoon poring over the dusty shelves of record stores looking for imports and other hard-to-find compilations of the band's music.

For all my obsessing, I never heard the Pixies perform live. The closest I came was when I got to see Frank Black, the lead singer, perform as part of his solo concert tour in the summer of 1993. The band had broken up earlier that year, and Black Francis, performing under the name Black Frank, was coming to play at the 40 Watt Club in Athens, Georgia.

I had recently moved to Athens. I was living in a dormitory at the University of Georgia, where I was enrolled in summer classes. The local college radio station was giving away tickets to the show. I called in and won two tickets. I quickly placed another call; this one was to my high-school friend who'd introduced me to the band, and she drove up to Athens from suburban Atlanta to attend the concert with me. In some ways, the 40 Watt, an intimate venue on Washington Street in downtown Athens, was the perfect spot to see him perform, and there were definitely memorable moments of that evening, like getting to hear his amazing rendition of "Hang on to Your Ego" from just a few feet away. Nonetheless, there was something disappointing about hearing him perform alone and without Kim Deal and the other members of the Pixies.

Of course, I bought Frank Black's solo album and listened to it on occasion, but I preferred putting *Come On Pilgrim, Bossanova, Live in Hull, Doolittle, Trompe le Monde,* or *Surfer Rosa* on repeat and hearing the full band in all their glory. My choice *du jour* depended on my mood. Though as time passed, certain songs or albums inevitably diminished in my mind, my devotion to the band stayed true for many years. Eventually even this changed, and toward the end of the decade, my obsession with the band started to wane. As my musical preferences shifted, I found other bands that I liked.

Just at the point when I thought I was done obsessing over the Pixies, I rediscovered them via the film *Fight Club*. Since its 1999 release, *Fight Club* has earned a place among American pop-culture iconography. When I first watched the film, however, I was not quite sure what to expect (I hadn't read Chuck Palahniuk's novel on which it's based). The film was still in theaters, and all I knew was that it was "must-see."

There are themes frequently touted in relation to *Fight Club*, such as the film's violence and moral ambiguity, and while I noticed these aspects of the film, they were not what I found most meaningful about it. Instead, I felt a connection to the characters who were searching for purpose in their life. I was working an office job at the time and, much like the office workers in the film, I struggled to see the value in how I was spending my days.

In fact, at the time I felt a real sense of uncertainty about the direction my life was going. By 1999, I had graduated college and was working full time at a bank, but I would stay up late at night to write—sometimes on a borrowed computer—with the hope of one day being published. While I recognized that many others would view this as a waste of time, I actually felt more productive hammering out sentences than I did during the hours I passed at my place of gainful employment. The result was that I found myself considering leaving my good-paying job and the relative stability it offered, to go to graduate school.

As I watched the film, my ambivalent feelings about my life came bubbling to the surface. When, during the closing scene and credits, I heard "Where Is My Mind?" my connection to the film only strengthened. "Where Is My Mind?" is the perfect anthem for that movie, since its surreal quality reflects the mood. At the same time, as a seminal song of the Pixies' career, it serves as a prime example of how the indie-rock band would frequently use lighthearted lyrics to tackle serious subjects, and, in retrospect, I believe that is probably what drew me to their music.

I have heard it argued that teenagers idolize musicians or celebrities because it gives them the chance to emotionally invest in someone without making themselves vulnerable to rejection. While I agree that this explanation accounts, in part, for my teenage obsession with the Pixies, I also feel that the way the band managed to borrow, from others but ultimately make something new, struck a chord with me.

For me, the 1990s were the years that bridged the messy divide between childhood and adulthood. I came of age in the 1990s. It was in that decade that I learned to drive, graduated high school, worked a string of part-time jobs, got my heart broken, traveled across three continents, started trying to get my writing published, graduated college, met my husband, and got my first full-time job. Of course, what also marked the last decade of the twentieth century were events of more far-reaching and global significance: the Gulf War, the advent of the Internet, IPOs, the Columbine massacre, and the Y2K bug.

Just as it remains hard to define the essence of a decade, it is also difficult to express what a decade means to me personally. In the end I believe music shaped the last decade of the millennium for me: the sometimes joyful and at other times somber music of the Pixies, a sound which also captured the quintessence of the 1990s.

Distiple

An Obsession in Ten Albums

LISA BORDERS

Chronic Town

It's early 1983, and a friend lends you a cassette of an EP called *Chronic Town* by a band from Athens, Georgia, called R.E.M. The sound quality of this tape is already slightly shot—it has been passed around a lot—but you like it: jangly guitars, mysterious lyrics, energetic drumming. It sounds nothing like the synthesizer-heavy dreck on the radio, nothing even like the punk rock your college station plays. The black-and-white photo of the band on the back of the cassette is hard to make out, but the lead singer has long, curly bangs that nearly cover his face. He looks interesting.

Murmur

R.E.M.'s first full-length album comes out while you are home from college for summer break. You feel lucky to find it at the crappy record store in the mall near your South Jersey hometown. The songs on *Murmur* don't merely speak to you; they cry out. Listening through the album from "Radio Free Europe" through "West of the Fields" is like surfing an elegant mood wave with a Rickenbacker guitar. You bring *Murmur* back to college, and you and your closest friend fall into a habit of listening to it late at night, after the bars have closed or the parties are over.

In October, R.E.M. appears on *Late Night with David Letterman*. A bowl of popcorn by your side, you settle cross-legged on the floor of your student apartment in front of an ancient television that requires a pair of needle-nose pliers to change the channels, The band launches into "Radio Free Europe"; as soon as you see the lead singer, Michael Stipe, you stop eating the popcorn. His eyes are large and blue; his cheekbones distinct; his lips a perfect Cupid's bow. Ringlets of curly brown hair frame his face and hang in his eyes. He looks as if he stepped out of a Renaissance painting—a Da Vinci, perhaps, or a Botticelli. You barely register the other guys in the band. From that point on, you are not just a fan of R.E.M; you are now instantly, hopefully in love with Michael Stipe. Hopefully because you are twenty years old, and you think that surely there is a way to meet this man, and that once you meet, he will fall as instantly in love with you as you have with him. You are soul mates. You know all this from watching him perform two songs on *Letterman*.

Reckoning

The next album comes out just before your college graduation. You study the liner notes more thoroughly than you ever studied for parasitology or biochem, which is perhaps one reason you are not going to veterinary school as planned. You miss seeing R.E.M. for the first time at a small club in Boston that spring because you really, truly have to cram for a vertebrate physiology exam, a poor decision that will haunt you for the rest of your Stipe-loving life. But the following fall, when you have graduated and are back in South Jersey working on your hometown newspaper and unsure of what to do with your life, you see your favorite band for the first time at the Tower Theater in Philadelphia. The show is shortly before the 1984 presidential election; "Let's get us a new President," is the only thing Stipe says to the crowd for the entire show. Mostly he hides behind his hair. You are even more in love with him now. He hates Reagan, just as you do! And he's shy—no rock star attitude! And oh, the richness of that voice. The sound he creates feels like the exact frequency of your deepest longing.

Fables of the Reconstruction

At the newspaper where you work, you become friends with another reporter who loves R.E.M., too, and understands, though doesn't share, your crush on Stipe. Her boyfriend lives in New York and is a music fanatic and turns you on to the kind of obscure indie magazines that have interviews with Stipe. You start going to the East Village on weekends and collecting these publications, plus any R.E.M. B sides you can find. During this period, you learn much about Mr. John Michael Stipe (or J.M. Stipe, as he is often referred to in early liner notes). Patti Smith inspired him to play music, so you immediately buy Smith's *Wave* and *Easter*. You seek out the artwork of Howard Finster, who illustrated the cover of *Reckoning*. Stipe loves Walker Percy, so you read *Lost in the Cosmos*. The man of your dreams is smart and well-read! And he's a vegetarian and animal lover, just like you are! You imagine the farm where you and Michael will live on the outskirts of Athens, Georgia. It will have a crazy shrub-and-found-artwork maze, just like the one in the video for "Radio Free Europe." The cats and dogs and horses you have both rescued will have room to roam. You will sometimes play Henry Mancini and Hüsker Dü at the same time, because Stipe said in an interview that he did that once.

The new album, *Fables of the Reconstruction*, is a little harder to get into than their earlier albums, but after listening to it eight times you decide it's their best yet. You go see them at the Tower Theater again, dancing so ferociously you feel like you leave your body and float above the stage. You can almost touch Stipe's beautiful face, the delicate lashes. When you tell your friend at work this story, she smiles. When you tell your friend from college, she says, "Michael Stipe is gay, you know." You refuse to believe this.

During downtime at work you write a story called "A Fable," which makes copious use of R.E.M. lyrics to tell a tale of the creation of a god among men, one Michael Stipe.

"Send it to him," says your friend at work, who by now has completely bought into the deliciousness of your obsession. "How could he not answer that? It's so well written." So you send it. You hear nothing back. Years later, you will feel retrospectively lucky that Stipe did not take out a restraining order against you, and you will also realize that your friend's enthusiasm had more to do with her belief in your writing ability than with any chance she thought you really had of meeting Michael Stipe.

Lifes Rich Pageant

The newspaper you are working for in New Jersey has been acquired by a national chain, and when you see that the chain owns a paper in a small town in Georgia not far from Athens, you seriously consider applying. You'll move there, and on your first trip into Athens for supplies—paper towels, lightbulbs, the most mundane things—you'll run into Michael Stipe. Your eyes will meet. It will be fate. He'll carry your lightbulbs home for you.

"On the other hand," says your friend from work, who is getting ready to accept a job offer in Florida, "if you move down there and you never meet Michael Stipe, you'll be stuck covering zoning-board meetings in some crappy little town in Georgia."

You take a job on a newspaper in Massachusetts instead.

The week *Lifes Rich Pageant* is released, you and your friend from college go to T.T. the Bear's in Cambridge to see Miracle Legion, a band that sounds vaguely like R.E.M.

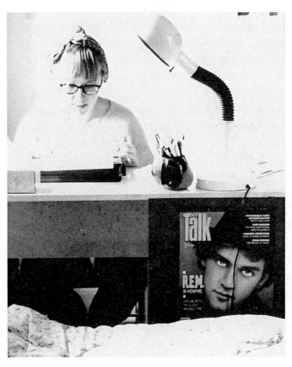 

Lisa Borders' fondness for Michael Stipe followed her to grad school in Philadelphia in 1988. A novelist and essayist, she still treasures her R.E.M. albums.

You find a kitten outside the club and decide to take it home with you. You want to name the kitten Michael, for the love of your life, but you settle on Matthew instead. Because what if you met Michael Stipe, and he came to your apartment, and you had to explain why you'd named your cat Michael? It would be embarrassing. On the ride home that night, the kitten climbs up the back of the driver's seat and perches near the headrest, purring in your ear, while you hear "Fall on Me," the single from the new album, on the radio for the first time. Years later, the cat will gently touch his paw to the speaker when that song comes on your stereo, and you will wonder if he remembers that moment in the car, too.

A few months later, R.E.M. comes to Boston. You go to the show with a guy you've just started seeing, several coworkers from your new job, and your friend from college. Michael Stipe is no longer shy onstage; he's becoming something of a showman. You ditch your boyfriend so you can get closer to the stage, closer to Stipe. He shimmies his slender hips to "Begin the Begin"; he pounds his chest during "Just a Touch," then pulls his T-shirt up, exposing his hairy chest. You scream like one of those bespectacled girls at the Shea Stadium Beatles show in 1965. Seriously, you scream. You just can't help it. Your friends from the newspaper, all male and ten years older than you, find your crush amusing. "He might be bi," your college friend offers, gesturing toward Stipe. Your boyfriend sulks.

Document

You now have enough friends scattered around the country to plan trips around R.E.M. shows, and you go to see the band in Miami, Philly, and New York. But the show you are waiting for is the one in Providence, the one where you got eighth-row seats by hauling your ass out of bed at six a.m. and waiting at the box office. You look forward to this show until a conflict arises: the town meeting for the Southeastern Massachusetts municipality you cover—the biggest event of the year in your boring local-news beat— is scheduled for the same night as the R.E.M. concert. You fret. You ask your music-loving editor friend what you should do. "I guess you have to figure out where your priorities are," he says, and you thank him for the clarity. Your priority is Michael Stipe!

The concert is in a beautiful old theater, and the band never sounded better. Michael Stipe's hair is very long now, pulled into a thick ponytail. He radiates beauty, a beauty beyond the physical. The entire crowd seems to be made up of mega-fans; between songs it's as quiet as a religious service. Though you will spend the rest of that weekend worrying that someone from work might have seen you at the concert, you will always remember that show, and you will never regret missing the Wareham town meeting.

After the concert, you and your friend go to an after party. R.E.M. guitarist Peter Buck is there, and you work up the nerve to tell him how much you love the band. He smiles a genuine smile and thanks you. You are equal parts disappointed and relieved that Stipe isn't there. Disappointed for the obvious reasons; relieved, because what could you say in this context that would be at all meaningful to him? You are now old enough that you no longer believe Stipe would fall, on first sight, as madly in love with you as you are with him. But that doesn't make you desire him any less.

"Now *him*," your college friend says, motioning to Buck after the two of you have walked away, "he's definitely straight."

Green

You have left your reporting job to move to Philadelphia for graduate school in creative writing; one of the short stories you used for your application was about a girl with a crush on the lead singer of a fictional band, a singer who resembles, more than a little, one Michael Stipe. In a few years, it will be your first published story. In Philly, you meet a gorgeous guy with long, curly brown hair. He is nothing if not Stipelike. You fall immediately in love with him. It takes a long time to work yourself into his world, but you manage it, and since he is an R.E.M. fan as well, the two of you decide, on hearing that the *Green* tour is opening in Gorgeous Guy's hometown in the South, that you will go there for spring break and see the band.

Your heart gets broken on that trip, just before the concert. Instead of finding the music comforting, it feels alien to you. This is no longer a reverent R.E.M. crowd; there are teenage girls behind you, chattering about school. Stipe performs with a megaphone, working the stage; he's become a different person entirely, just as Gorgeous Guy, this man you thought you loved, is not who he seemed to be. You look at Stipe and think, *Yeah, I bet he'd break my heart like this, too.* You start hearing the darkness in the love songs, a darkness you have until now blithely dismissed.

You'll never really enjoy the *Green* album after that, and you'll never be sure if it's because the music started going in a poppier direction with that album, or if it's because of the association with Gorgeous Guy.

Out of Time

You are living in Vermont, back in school to learn something more practical than creative writing, but still drafting short stories late at night. You can't say you like *Out of Time* the way you like the older albums, but you can't completely dismiss it, either. It will be the album that wins R.E.M. several Grammys, and you actually tear up watching the awards show. You can't help it; you're proud of your boys, as proud as you'd be if you actually knew them.

You have been long-distance dating a guy who lives in Philly, and at a point near the end of the relationship, you are riding in the car with him, feeling hurt, when "Losing My Religion" comes on the radio. You immerse yourself in the music. A certain lyric in this song—the part about saying too much, yet not saying enough—sums up this relationship you are now in. You softly sing along.

"Maybe I should leave the two of you alone," your boyfriend, who knows of your once-intense crush on Stipe, says. And soon, he does.

Automatic for the People

This album has a song you love—"Nightswimming"—but it also has the first song R.E.M. has ever recorded that you truly hate: "Everybody Hurts." It's sappy and dull and just beneath them. You find yourself gravitating to new music with more of an edge—Nirvana, Nine Inch Nails, the Red Hot Chili Peppers—but it is impossible to think that you might not still be an R.E.M. fan. True, you are no longer so in love with Stipe that you have a picture of him taped near your bed, no longer so in love that you sometimes allow yourself to gently touch your fingertips to his photographed lips as a way to say good-night. You are almost thirty now, and much of your twenty-something identity was wrapped up in having a giant crush on Stipe, on being R.E.M.'s number-one fan. If you no longer like R.E.M., if you no longer love Stipe, then who are you?

Monster

The first bad sign is when your now-elderly cat scrambles from the room on first listen. You try so hard; surely, there's something in this noisy-yet-bland album to like, but damned if you can find it. You go to see the band at one of the large arenas they are playing these days, hoping to be proven wrong. But the magic is gone. Seeing Stipe onstage is like seeing your first love at a high-school reunion. There's fondness, but the longing isn't there. There has been much speculation in the press about Stipe's sexuality, and it hits you, finally, that he probably *is* gay, and that your mid–1980s fantasies of a life with him were not only farfetched; they were impossible, even if you had met him.

So you take the energy you used to put into elaborate fantasies about your future life with Michael Stipe and channel it into this novel you've been thinking of writing. Freed of your Stipe obsession, it seems a large chunk of your brain is now available to sustain the characters and setting of an entire world, the world of your novel. The book will be about music, and R.E.M. will make a cameo, but they are now just minor players in your imaginative life.

You won't like any of R.E.M.'s albums after *Monster*. You will be sustained by other bands, other albums—Counting Crows' and Son Volt's debuts, Wilco, and Neko Case, and Death Cab for Cutie, and Arcade Fire—but none of them will ever have the place in your heart that R.E.M. did. No lead singer, however appealing, will be to you what Michael Stipe was. You are simply too old now, your life too full. This is good, you suppose, but there's something sad about it too.

Now, instead of longing for Stipe, you sometimes long for that girl who loved him so. Whatever happened to her?

But one day, in a new century and a new life, you will hear a radio interview with Stipe, hear him explain that he's bisexual, even hear him quantify his desires. "I'm attracted to three women for every seven men," Stipe says. And something in you stirs. You had a shot after all, you think—at least a thirty percent chance. The girl who once loved Stipe feels her heart quicken. What if you *had* taken that job on that little newspaper in Georgia, and you *had* met Stipe, and he *had* fallen for you? The Stipe-loving girl inside you—as real and as apart from you as the characters in your novels—lets out a little squeal. You smile. That girl will always love Michael.

But you—the forty-something you—now love someone who loves you back. He plays guitar and adores animals and is smart and well-read. He even has blue eyes. He is nothing like the real Stipe, but he's a lot like the Stipe you imagined.

And, it turns out, that's all you ever really wanted.

I'll Never Let You Go

Mary Sullivan

Dear Leonardo,

You know when you told Rose that afternoon on the *Titanic*, "That fire's going to burn out"? You were talking about her passion for life, but I knew you were really talking to me. I was a girl on fire, too. When Rose answered that she was fine, you asked "Really?" And I knew that you knew me. You knew I was trapped, too. *I* was screaming, and no one was listening.

You said, "What I was thinking was, what could've happened to this girl to make her think she had no way out?"

"It's not up to you to save me, Jack," Rose said.

And you answered, "I know, only you can do that."

Soon after that, Rose found you looking out over the ocean, the sun going down in oranges and reds. "I changed my mind," she said. And you told her to close her eyes and step up—and *I did*. I trusted you. I stepped up on the bow of the *Titanic* steaming ahead, and felt your hands on my waist and your fingers in mine. I was flying, the whole world ahead of me. I stepped through the silver screen and opened my arms like wings, and you kissed me. More than anything, I wanted this. I was in love. You, Leonardo, were my first.

The wind in my hair, the setting sun, the powerful sea, the promise of love and adventure ahead, and you were letting me go. For the first time in my life, I was free, completely untethered. This is the memory I have of you. Of us. I, your teenage dreamer, etched you in my heart, my soul, my mind. Forever.

Who doesn't dream of a love like ours? My heart stopped when I saw you jumping on board minutes before departure because you'd won tickets gambling in a card game. My heart pounded when I heard you shout to the sky that you were "king of the world!" I laughed. You had nothing except a sketch pad and the clothes you were wearing!

But you *were* king. You saved me. I was desperate; you know, the teen angst kind—the panicked, suffering young girl standing over dark waters, on the edge of oblivion. You took my hand and pulled me back. Even when I called you crazy, you said politely, "With all due respect, miss, I'm not the one hanging off the back of the boat." And I had to laugh again.

I probably wouldn't have done it. The water was way too cold. But when I was that low, you gave me hope. You made my heart sing. And then you taught me to spit—really spit from the back of my throat, which felt awfully good.

You saw beauty in real things. There was feeling in all your sketches—in a hand, a nursing child, a one-legged prostitute. You found beauty in the ordinary. Then you joined us in the first-class dining saloon when you belonged in third class. Posing in a borrowed tux, you looked so good, *and* you dared to speak the truth. That's when I really knew: when you said, "I figure life's a gift and I don't intend on wasting it."

Then you took me to "a real party," and we danced and drank beer, and I was happy. With you, Leonardo, I was myself. With you, I felt whole. But I also turned everything upside down and out of order in a *Midsummer Night's Dream* sort of way, so I tried to go back to what I was supposed to do, who I was supposed to be, as if my path had been fixed. It would have been so much easier maintaining my status, money, comfort, reputation). Over high tea, I watched the other passengers parading like puppets, acting out roles of proper deportment. Then I knew what I was missing: you were true, and you loved *me*. That's why I changed my mind and found you on the bow of the *Titanic*. Then I was flying into the setting sun, into your hands, your lips, your deep blue eyes. You sketched me wearing only the Heart of the Ocean. After that I was all yours.

"You jump, I jump," you said. You would have died for me. You *did* die for me. I said that I'd never let you go, and I meant it. Our love was not watered down. It was the purest, the highest, the truest. Of course, the movie had to end. My dream stopped, suddenly. You were totally and completely mine, and then a black screen rolled credits. You were gone.

But every night I bring you back. I remember you. I feel you right here beside me.

This is how I keep you mine, Leonardo. This is how I hold on to the dream. Even though my sister said I couldn't, I put your poster on the wall next to my bed. It's the one in which I spread my arms straight out, flying, the moment before our lips touched for the first time. I still lose my breath thinking of it. Your lips soft and wanting—wanting mine. When it's dark and finally quiet in our room, I remember you. Every night in my dreams, I feel you.

I *want* to be beautiful for you. So I am spreading on blue eye shadow and curling my hair before school with my sister. My mother pokes her head in and says, "Don't waste your time dolling yourself up." She pokes in again to add, "Especially for a boy." I have five sisters, and she says it to all of us. Of course, we don't listen. Before I leave for school, I feel your hands around my waist, your face so close I can feel the warmth of your breath. I know you're out there, and today may be the day I find you.

My sister doesn't believe in falling in love. She has no idea. But she believes in fashion and advantage, so after school she covers herself in baby oil and bakes in the sun to doll herself up for the prom. By the time her date comes, she has small, white, bubbling blisters all over her chest, nose, and forehead. He holds out a bouquet to my sister, stares, and swallows.

We all look over at my brother, who is being Evel Knievel. We're supposed to pay to watch him bike over a ramp he's built on the driveway. My mother is the only one who gives him money. The rest of us hide in the bushes and behind windows. My sister and her date get their pictures taken, standing slightly apart. After they leave, my brother wipes out·and cuts his head open and blood spills all over the driveway.

Leonardo, you understand. You didn't grow up with a silver spoon. You were never perfect, never *normal*, whatever that is. You liked to tease and play jokes. You get it. You are R-E-A-L. And you know how complicated life gets. Sometimes I feel like I'm screaming so loud and no one hears me, and I'll never be able to stop all of this boring life stuff. More than ever, I need to escape into a world that is only us. I wish we could simply fly away into the blue. The blue of the sky, the blue of the ocean.

Our love is that pure. When I think of you, I don't smell my younger brothers' dirty diapers or see the supper dishes piled high or the mound of laundry waiting to be folded into thirteen piles. When my mother fills out our school forms, she writes for my father's occupation *builder*, and for her own, *slave*. I see her scrubbing the bathroom, lining up the brown bags with sandwiches, bending over the sink or the stove, steam rising behind her. I hear my dad slurping his oatmeal before heading off into the cold to build his houses. I smell the wood-stove smoke that rises up into our rooms where we lie in bed with hats and scarves on to stay warm at night. And then I remember the streaks of orange blazing through the sky and the blue of the sea. *Our sea. Our Titanic.*

The cold blue ocean—everything comes back to you, Leonardo. I think of us sailing toward the blue horizon. About how little we'd need to have a life together. We'd go to galleries and museums, cafes and bars, and every day would be an adventure. We could have a *real* life. Our perfect love would carry us.

On Sundays at church, when the priest lifts the Eucharist and says, "Take this … and eat it; this is my body," he is talking about a love like ours. Then he holds up the chalice and says, "Take this … and drink from it: this is the cup of my blood." And I am eating *your* body and drinking *your* blood. You are part of me. You *are* me. By dying for me, you gave me reason to live, Leonardo. Our love is more than pure: it is holy.

I wait for the moment I am transported, when all the heat in my body rushes to the top of my head. The organ is playing, and my mother is singing loudly off-key (God doesn't mind). My father nods off, his mouth opening, snoring softly. My younger brother moves a hat on the pew so it's underneath the man in front of him. Another brother pinches my sister hard, and she cries out and then covers her mouth. They are giggling. My father wakes, frowning.

I look at the colored light coming through the stained-glass windows high above. We are one, Leonardo, and we will live to eternity.

Mary Sullivan was a huge Leonard DiCaprio fan as a teenager. Her fascination with coming-of-age stories lives on today in her novels for young adults.

But I am not a patient person. Forever is a long time. It's not easy waiting all day to be alone with you at night. Sometimes I go upstairs and slam the door shut just so I can look at you—at us on the *Titanic*—and get back to that moment. I close my eyes to see you better. But my brothers, all five of them, are so loud. The oldest bought a box of donuts last night and is now selling them for twice the price. The others are screaming, running through the house, one insisting that he's Hulk Hogan. Another ties a rubber band around the hose sprayer on the sink. When my mother turns the water on full blast she is sprayed in the face. From my window, I can see her chasing my brother down the driveway with a Wiffle Ball bat in her hand. The smell of Spam frying rises up from downstairs. This is definitely not my life, Leonardo. My life is there with you.

I never even talked to boys until sixth grade. Like I said, you were my first. They say you never get over the first, and it's true. I lie down beside you and lick the honey glaze off my donut (fifty cents). The confection melts instantly on my tongue. One day, you and I will eat honey-glazed donuts together.

Even though our love is perfect, Leonardo, you are not, and I am glad about that. Truth is, when I see guys who are meticulously groomed, I want to wrinkle their shirts and run my hand backward through their hair. You embrace imperfection. I've seen you in every role you've played. You know what it's like to be on the outside, to be homeless, mentally handicapped, abused, from the wrong family, strung out. And I know you understand and love me exactly as I am. Our love is stronger because we recognize our imperfections.

Leonardo, there is something else. I know I'm not the only one. I see the same poster I have of you beside another girl's bed, and then another, and I wonder if they're dreaming *Titanic* dreams, too. It can't possibly be the same for them, but I feel so betrayed. How many others are there? I don't want to know.

Yeah, I'm hurt. So I find someone else: a bad boy, a rebel without a cause, practically a criminal. It's only a crush, not true love. He's bronzed, squinting at the camera, a cigarette hanging out of his mouth, his shirt open, leaning back, the cool, blue sky behind him. Just enough smile to invite me in. I know it's a game, and he's going to win, and still I fall for it. Because I am wanting, and he's waiting there in his cowboy hat like he doesn't need anyone, hands half-stuck in his jeans pockets, leaning against the fins of an old Caddy. His name was Hud—in past tense, because it is over and I'm sorry.

You, Leonardo, are the one I think of every single day. You are my life.

Like I said, Leonardo, everything comes back to you. Month after month, year after year, every wall I set my bed next to has had your face on it. My dreams have new settings, but they always have you—the memory of us as alive as it was the first time. It is magic, the way you flicker and spark and burn inside me all this time.

I write a story with a character who loves you as much as I do. She becomes friends with a girl named Safia who moves to the United States from Afghanistan, where a love like yours is forbidden. In Kabul, boys try to get hairstyles like yours with the long bangs. The barbers are arrested and flogged, and the boys forced to shave their hair. Bazaars sell *Titanic* shampoo, *Titanic* perfume, *Titanic* vests, belts, and pants, even chewing gum! The movie is available through the black market, but your image is forbidden, like the love you speak to. In my story, when Safia watches *Titanic*, she is changed—empowered. The Afghanis are looking for a way to rescue themselves from oppression. (I am, too.) No matter what the Taliban does, though, it cannot ban this irrepressible idea of love. No one can.

That's why I keep searching everywhere for you, Leonardo. I write stories that aspire to transport us and keep our memory alive. I want what is real, what is true. Like that first time when my heart soared, when you let me fly and I was free.

When it finally happens, I don't expect it. I'm emptied out, close to despair, in a relationship where it seems there is no way out: trapped. In truth, I have almost stopped believing it could happen. But I know this is the real thing because my heart stops and I can't breathe. It's not only because I see your blue eyes, your *Titanic* hair, your boyishness, it's *the feel*, something deep inside that I've been longing for. In flesh and blood. It is spring, and the lilacs are blooming, and we're walking along the Charles River when he takes my hand.

Leonardo, he has your fingers, and he is putting his hands on my waist. He is like you: he treats life as if it were a gift. Every day is new. The water and sky are dark blue with night when he kisses me the first time. His lips are soft like yours, and I know then that this is what you want for me. You want me to do with him all the things I imagined doing with you. I will.

Leonardo, we have come so far. You are no longer on a poster next to my bed, but you'll always be mine. I still dream of you, and when I wake I find you there beside me, breathing. Even as you slip away through the dark, icy waters.

With you, Leonardo, there will always be spaces between us. With him, well, I took his hand and married him.

Love,
Mary

"Bowie"

Diana Goetsch

The first time I saw David Bowie it was a man who took me
to a cinema in Huntington 12 miles from our town
where they were showing *Ziggy Stardust and the Spiders from Mars*,
the concert film with backstage footage of Bowie
during costume changes talking with friends he obviously loved.
He was young, with milky skin, as excited about the show
as his audience—no matter how garish the makeup,
how spiky the hair. He was, that is, an ordinary person
saying, "Wow, isn't this a blast?" saying what I would say.
Soon he'd go back on stage in another skin-tight outfit,
the crowd would spend half a song wondering where his dick was,
before surrendering again, singing along to that big voice
as crisp and thrilling as sanity. He was so full of plain goodness,
yet also a space alien, truly fierce, a little grotesque, though I knew
he was nothing to be afraid of, for I was Ziggy Stardust too.
Soon I'd go away to college, putting distance between me
and the man who drove me to see Bowie. For a while he wrote me
letters mentioning other beautiful men. Richard Gere
was on Broadway playing a gay man in a concentration camp,
the Nazis made him wear a pink triangle, and perhaps, his
letter suggested, I might want to try on that triangle too.
Did I tell you he was my 12th grade English teacher?
His understanding of metaphor was quite limited,
but I'm glad I at least got to Bowie, who was so far beyond
gay or straight, a creature so wildly human
there was no word for him yet, which is why he needed
another planet to be from, a planet I needed to find.

Mary Sue in Search of Lemons

Emlyn Meredith Dornemann

Chapter 1: Girl Meets Boy

You are a thirteen-year-old girl, and you want to be a ninja.

Not the kind of ninja that normal people think about when they think about ninjas. Not the kind who wears all black and assassinates people in the middle of the night. You want to be the kind of ninja that is on *Naruto*. You want to be the kind of ninja who has special ninja powers that say something about your personality. You want to be the most badass ninja of all, because you know you would be, if you were actually a ninja.

Unfortunately, you are not a ninja. You are a thirteen-year-old girl in the real world. The world that's not Japanese-animated.

So you wake up in the morning, and you put on your black T-shirt and black pants and black, studded choker that your aunt thinks is a dog collar because she just doesn't *get it*, and you try your damnedest not to smile, because emotions are not cool. You go to your family computer and dial up the Internet. It is on the Internet that you find the closest thing to being an actual ninja that there is: fanfiction.

You are, of course, very specific about the kinds of fanfic you will read, carefully combing through search results for what you need, because search filters don't really exist on Quizilla.com in 2006. It needs to be second-person, so you can better imagine yourself as the beautiful ninja girl that some other thirteen-year-old girl imagines you to be. It needs to take place in the *Naruto* world, because … *duh*. Finally, it needs to be about Sabaku no Gaara, because he is the love of your life.

Gaara is a side character who is in only a handful of episodes, but you fell in love at first sight. He literally has the *kanji* for "love" tattooed on his forehead, so how could you not? So what if he murders people for fun? So what if he's possessed by a demon? There is nothing that your love for each other can't fix.

Gaara has red hair and dark circles around his eyes, because if he ever slept, the demon would take over and murder everyone. Not that that is too far off from how he normally acts. Thanks to a heaping helping of tragic backstory, his mother died giving birth to him, his siblings never loved him, and his dad was the guy who put the demon in him in the first place. Naturally, he has more than a slight disregard for human life. Oh, and he controls sand. He likes to crush people to death with it.

Your favorite scene is when he uses his ninja magic to wrap an enemy in sand and then lifts them up into the air like a giant, sandy turd, then uses the sand to squeeze them until they explode and rain blood on the battlefield. But no rain falls on Gaara, because he came prepared. He has an umbrella.

Once you find an appropriate fanfic, you sit at the computer with your animated boyfriend for hours. When you have to get off the Internet, you open a bunch of chapters in separate windows and let them load before logging off, allowing the fanfic to be readable offline. You go on the computer and pretend to be typing up a paper for school or something, but actually just spend more time with Gaara. This makes you feel very clever.

You read the romantic chapters more than once:

Your fingers interlaced with his.
He kissed you. His tongue licked your bottom lip and begged for entrance.
He unhooked your bra with one hand.

It all seems so realistic.

Even though you *really* want to, you never read any of the chapters labeled ~*LEMON*~ because that takes you to a page that asks how old you are, and you don't know how to clear Internet history, and y'know, Jesus is watching. Your relationship isn't about *that* anyway. It's always about being with someone who understands you, and being with someone who is understandable but still complicated. You really just run through the kissing fantasy over and over with this red-haired ninja-murderer who, over and over again, finds room in his mean little heart for you.

Chapter 2: The Next Level

Somehow you run out of romantic, second-person Gaara fanfic. You spend a while checking Quizilla for updates, but once you've read all of it, new chapters come slowly. Despite the anonymity of the Internet, you are too shy to ask the authors to post more. So you start writing your own, because that is the natural progression of events.

You sit at the computer and start to type. Then you stop, because you need to find the right font. You settle on something that looks vaguely Asian but is still legible. Kinda. Then you start to type again, and you make your masterpiece.

You've been writing stories for as long as you can remember, but these stories are the most important. These are violent, passionate love stories. These are stories about the life you wish you had: the life where you can kick all the mean people's asses, and kids have power, and suffering is romantic, because if it's romantic, then it means something.

It is in first person, because you don't need second person if you're writing from your perspective. Your original character is a badass ninja. She is also pretty much you, or, more accurately, who you wish you were. She's hardcore overpowered Mary Sue wish fulfillment. And you and Gaara are in love. It starts out rocky, but eventually you melt his heart, because you are both outcast monsters in a way, and your love saves him from his literal demon. It is 175 pages typed, the longest thing you have ever written.

You start posting your masterpiece on a small game website, where your friends can read it. Some of them do. One time you get a comment from a stranger.

You print out the whole thing in the hopes of editing it, but you never get that far. It gathers dust in a green three-ring binder.

Chapter 3: Fanfiction Master!

Eventually you realize what every writer realizes: Your first work is not a masterpiece. You also realize that your love for Gaara cannot be contained in 175 pages. So you start a new masterpiece, and this time you handwrite it, so you can keep it with you at all times. You write before school. You write at recess. You write between classes. You write when you're done with your homework. Sometimes you write while you should be doing your homework. At night, you stay up late and write with a flashlight. You only let it out of your sight to let your friends read it. You dutifully mark the extra-kissy parts PG-13, because you know some of your friends don't want to read that kind of unsavory content. Jesus is watching, after all. They usually read it anyway.

The story starts with Miru, a teenage middle-schooler in the real world. One night, one of the big bads from the *Naruto* universe is able to sense her potential across dimensions and pulls her into the *Naruto* world. When she wakes up, she meets the main characters of the show, and they all love her. Everyone, that is, except the Hokage, the ruler of the village. He has seen her ninja power: She can control invisible strings that she uses to move around and trap her enemies with. Because apparently nobody ever told you about Spider Man. He knows that she is too powerful, and he is afraid of her, and he sends her away. All of Miru's new friends are sad to see her go, but Miru knows she must.

It is in this new village that she meets the sand boy. She meets Gaara. It is not the romantic meeting you expect. He knocks her out and tortures her, because, again, she is so powerful that the higher-ups are afraid. Gaara is just doing what he's told. And besides, killing someone as powerful as Miru would be fun.

He doesn't kill her, though. She's more interesting than he originally thought. So they snuggle, but not before he attaches a device that limits her powers and physically hurts her if she disobeys him. Because good romances have conflict.

Emlyn Dornemann (right) and her cousin Genevieve dressed as their fantasy idols in Milwaukee, 2006. Fantasy still shapes Emlyn's writing.

The story goes on and on. You fill up one notebook, then two, then three, until you've filled seven. Miru and Gaara fall in love, learn to travel between the *Naruto* world and the real one, bring all of Miru's real-world friends over to the *Naruto* side. Miru accidentally gets pregnant through ninja magic (not sex!), and all of the *Naruto* characters get baptized, because, dammit, Jesus is watching. At some point, everyone loses their memories and jump back in time, and that definitely wasn't because the TV show was still running and went in a very different direction from what you predicted. Your love for Gaara even transcends a memory wipe, and you two live happily forever after. You write like there's no end in sight.

This is your masterpiece.

Chapter 4: Re-Animated

You write the last line of your seven-notebook epic-fanfiction during your first week of freshman year. You are a high-school student now. That pretty much means you're an adult. You know that now is the time to put away such childish things, but you need to finish it, so you can close that chapter of your life.

It ends sweetly. You and Gaara return to the real world, and you take him to the park in your neighborhood. The two of you sit on the swings and look at the sky, and you feel hope, knowing the obstacles are over, and you have arrived at happily ever after.

Junior year, you will re-read it and tell your boyfriend that he reminds you of the Gaara that you wrote. You realize now that the Gaara you wrote was not much like the Real Gaara, but you appreciate what your representation means about you. You appreciate that your middle-school boyfriend dreams have come true. You have your own monster now, and you can tame his heart.

It is another several years after this that you realize that the real world is not Japanese-animated, and to have the fantasy of loving a monster is to have control over it. In the real world, you do not have control, and you get a horror story instead of a love story. As you grow older, it is a story you become tired of telling, because every time you tell it, you remember some new twist, and after a while this becomes exhausting.

All you know for sure is this: You loved Gaara and you lived. It wasn't happily ever after, but you lived.

Epilogue: A Real Kind of Love

As an adult, you understand the magic of hindsight. You find your fanfiction adventures slightly disturbing in their romantic implications, but they are still a part of you. They are representative of a person you truly wanted to be. You try to still love them, even if you don't still love the mess of lines and pixels that make up Gaara.

There is one love left over from your fanfiction epic. You still write. You write when you should be sleeping, and you write in coffee shops, because that's what writers do. You write to survive. You write and you write and you write.

There's no way of knowing if you would still be a writer if you didn't write all that fanfic, if you weren't so in love with Gaara and the world he lives in, but you like to think that your stories played their part in stoking that passion.

Those stories were the first time you could not stop writing. Your fingers first itched with ideas on those evenings when you held a flashlight to your notebook and wrote through the night. Even though you never got to see the deserts that Gaara lived in, and you never got to be a ninja, you learned how to escape the real world all the same. You thank your fanfiction every day for introducing you to your lifelong love for the mess of lines that make up each of your stories.

We Were All in Love
with Michael Jackson

Susan Straight

In 2003, I was driving with my oldest daughter, who was fourteen then and scanning radio stations, when I heard a mellow love song. I said idly, "That sounds like what your dad and I used to listen to back in the day."

I didn't tell her we used to listen to songs like that while we lay entwined in the back of his sister's 1975 Pinto, parked on isolated, eucalyptus-darkened roads leading to orange groves or remote fields.

"It's a Michael Jackson song," my daughter said, rolling her eyes. "He sounds like he's choking on a peanut or something." She leaned forward to poke the button.

"Don't change it," I said, listening more closely. I had never heard that particular song, and the shadow of the beat took me back to when Michael Jackson was the innocent, yet sexiest soul singer my friends and I knew, with Milky-Way skin and huge Afro and tender smile and soft voice. He ruled the girls in my neighborhood.

In my Southern California city, and all over America back then, in racially mixed working-class neighborhoods like mine, millions of young girls watched him on television as he clutched the microphone to his chest and bent over with the weight of his love for us, throwing out his brown fingers, pulling the air toward him and moaning the lyrics to "I Want You Back!"

Thousands of girls screamed and swooned the way others did for the Beatles or the Monkees. Those were white girls we saw on television, swooning, in all-white audiences. But Michael Jackson and his brothers, as the Jackson 5, were the dreamboats of black America, and they came to play at the Swing, the biggest auditorium in San Bernardino.

I looked over at the eldest of my three daughters, alone for once in the car with me, and I couldn't figure out how to tell her that in 1978, in these orange groves we were passing just a few blocks outside my old neighborhood, her father and I used to kiss for hours while Michael crooned from the cheap speakers in the door of the Pinto. Michael sang "Show You the Way to Go," his voice growling deep.

"Mom, can I change it now? I don't want to hear this." I glanced over at my daughter's lovely caramel face, her long black hair resting in curls on her shoulders. Her mouth was curled in mild disgust at the airless, soulless, whispery voice. "He's so creepy."

That was a song from his 2001 release, *Invincible*, which sold a hugely disappointing two million copies, and whose failure to appeal to the masses led Jackson to appear with

Al Sharpton in a Harlem parade that ended in Jackson's denouncement of Sony Records and Tommy Mottola as racist and "very very devilish" for their lack of support for him.

My daughter said impatiently, "This song is crap. Nobody listens to anything by him." She looked out the window. "Everybody hates him."

Back then, in 2003, whenever we'd see the first ghostly shadows of his face on television, one of my girls would change the channel very quickly, sometimes even looking away until Michael Jackson was gone. For my younger daughters, twelve and eight, who never knew him as brown like them, as a singer and dancer who could captivate an audience of adults and children alike, he was always a figure of shivery unease and news stories.

But I knew my oldest daughter felt a more intense dislike because she remembered when Michael Jackson looked something like her. Not his childhood or teen self, the one I was in love with, my friends kissing him on the heavy cardboard of album covers. His middle self, the man growing lighter, growing more eccentric, with long wavy hair and sparkly jacket.

He was our idol, my friends and mine. In sixth grade, I was the only white girl in my dance group as we performed on our elementary school stage to "ABC," dancing a twirling, hip-rolling routine to imitate Michael and his brothers, Tito, Jermaine, Marlon, and Randy.

I met my future husband in junior high, and when we were in high school, listened to that eight-track in the orange groves, Michael Jackson's voice deep and catching with emotion, almost like church when he did "Jam." With his wide nose, maple-syrup skin, and that huge natural like everyone else had, he looked like a thinner version of my boyfriend. At school dances, all our hella-tough friends did the robot, the moonwalk, and poplocked to "Dancing Machine." We watched him on *Soul Train*. Let me say that

Susan Straight and her future husband skate into their future on the Venice, California, boardwalk in 1978. Now a revered novelist and professor at UC–Riverside, she hasn't forgotten her love for Michael Jackson.

no guy made fun of Michael Jackson, because the girls would punch him. Jermaine was the cool, handsome, older brother; Tito the quiet one; Randy had something off-putting; Marlon was a little dangerous; but Michael was the one who sang to us.

When Michael went solo, we listened to all his hits. He was the suave, sure voice we danced to at house parties or while cruising. He was safe yet sexy, the favorite among every black woman friend I had. He wasn't James Brown, who we danced to as well, but who was rougher and more political. James Brown wasn't about holding our hands. The Spinners and the O'Jays and the Stylistics were big, but if you asked my girlfriends who they wanted, it was Michael, even as he was reinventing himself with hair products and what we suspected was eyeliner.

If someone had told us that in twenty years, he would be white as a powdered ghost, that he would be repeatedly accused of sexual behavior with children, we would not have laughed. We would have slapped that person around. We would have rolled our eyes and said, "Michael? The one who begs us to come back, to give him one more chance?"

My daughter was rolling her eyes now with real anger over my sentimental refusal to change the station. Michael Jackson was still singing about love, about us giving him butterflies, his voice wavering and floating thinly from the dashboard.

His nose is like a sharp weapon, I thought, *his skin pale as bleached muslin, his hair hanging in quills about his etched cheeks.*

She said vehemently, "Mom! Turn it off! No one wants to hear him. He's so desperate."

All those years of seeing his face stare out from newspaper photos, from magazine covers, from the television screen—she, along with so many other African-American teens, considered this man not just someone who behaved inappropriately with children, but a refutal of her own brown skin—an alien, or a zombie.

This same daughter, when she was two, begged to stay up late and watch the Michael Jackson special on TV. She was entranced by the precise dance moves and silver glove. That's what he was in 1992: the silver glove, the pulled-up heels and spins, but he was so cool that she drew a her-sized picture of him, glove and hat and milky-tea-colored cheeks and wacky joints, and taped it to our back-porch door.

And whenever I tried to tell that story to anyone, she'd say, "Don't you ever tell anyone that I liked him, or even that I listened to him sing!"

Hey, I wanted to say, he was the scarecrow in *The Wiz,* the black musical-movie version of *The Wizard of Oz,* and our Dorothy, played by Diana Ross, trusted Michael Jackson's shambling, cool-dancing character to lead her down the yellow-brick road. He wore a Reese's Peanut Butter Cup liner on his nose as part of his costume: a brown, crinkled cup for a nose for the scarecrow we all loved.

What could he possibly fasten onto that damaged, sharpened nose by the time she refused to hear him? What costume was he wearing by 2003, as himself, a man who lived a fantasy none of us understand? He hung there on our back door for five years, dancing on the wood, until the marker-colors of his skin and clothes faded from the sun, and the true colors of his face faded from surgery and vanity and what we can only diagnose as self-hatred.

That's the unspoken reason my daughter hated him then. She said, "He hated himself so much he made himself into a white guy." And in doing so, he erased someone who bore a resemblance to her.

According to teenage-girl listeners like her, his music represented a pathetic attempt to win over people who wouldn't give him even two minutes. He was popular in other countries, but not in America, where no matter the racial composition of her friends—Chinese-American, Mexican-Scottish, California African American—they listened to Audioslave, Black Eyed Peas, OutKast, and System of a Down.

Back then, she found it hilarious that Justin Timberlake, as white as can be, recreated himself as MJ, replete with glove and spins and hat. A white guy reinventing himself as a black guy who'd transformed himself into a whiter guy.

And my daughter, who can check seven boxes on a racial category list due to her mixed heritage, laughed when white guys tried to impress her by declaring, "I listen to Eminem."

"Really?" she replied coolly. "Why?"

Her favorites at that moment were the Red Hot Chili Peppers and the Clash.

Back then, I told her Michael Jackson never got to be a child himself. He was performing constantly, like many child stars who grow up to have mercilessly unhappy adult lives. I was eleven when I danced to his songs, and he was twelve, already enduring long hours and road trips and endless work.

Maybe that's why he made Neverland, his ranch near Santa Barbara, into a child's paradise—for the childhood he never had. "But why would any kid want to go there?" she said. "Who would want to hang around with him?"

By the time he died, alone in a room, with Propofol slipped into his bloodstream, who loved him? Who danced with him?

That day, we had passed through my old neighborhood, and the song was nearly over. The chorus repeated again and again. We cruised over an old railroad bridge, and I glanced at her, my daughter, produced from the love of her father and me, the two who came of age here in Southern California when the dance floor was filled with huge Afros glistening in the disco lights, our bell-bottoms and fast feet.

Her gold-brown arm was propped on the open window, her black curls moving in the breeze, her full lips not singing. "You used to love him, when he looked like you," I said. "Remember that picture you drew?"

"Yeah," she said, looking out the window, away from the fading voice on the radio. That night, I'd find the old vinyl albums in our house and the picture I'd finally taken off the back door and folded into a memory to keep in a drawer.

About the Contributors

Lisa **Borders** is the author of two novels, *The Fifty-First State* and *Cloud Cuckoo Land*, chosen by Pat Conroy as the winner of *River City Publishing*'s Fred Bonnie Award in 2002. Her stories have appeared in *Kalliope, Washington Square, Black Warrior Review, Painted Bride Quarterly, Newport Review*, and elsewhere.

Breena **Clarke**'s debut novel, *River, Cross My Heart*, was an Oprah Book Club selection. A native of Washington, D.C., she is the recipient of the 1999 award for fiction by the New Atlantic Independent Booksellers Association and the Alex Award, given by the Young Adult Library Services Association. Her books include *Stand the Storm* and *Angels Make Their Hope Here*.

Katharine **Davis** is the author of three novels: *Capturing Paris* (included in the *New York Times* suggestions for fiction set in Paris); *East Hope* (winner of the Maine Writers and Publishers Alliance 2010 award for fiction); and *A Slender Thread*. She lives in southwest Florida and Maine.

Emlyn Meredith **Dornemann** still watches what most people would consider too many cartoons, though she writes much less fanfiction. She has a bachelor's degree in writing from Cardinal Stritch University and recently earned her MFA in popular fiction from the Stonecoast Creative Writing Program at the University of Southern Maine. She blogs at www.sadmagicalcreatures.wordpress.com

Janice **Eidus** is a novelist, essayist and short story writer. Her novels include *The War of the Rosens, The Last Jewish Virgin* and *Urban Bliss*. Her story collections are *Vito Loves Geraldine* and *The Celibacy Club*. Her prose appears in such anthologies as *How Does That Make You Feel, The Oxford Book of Jewish Stories* and *Desire*.

Ann Rosenquist **Fee** is the executive director of the Arts Center of Saint Peter, an art gallery, clay studio and performance venue in southern Minnesota. She is also a vocalist and songwriter with the acoustic duo The Frye, a style columnist for *Mankato Magazine*, and a past teaching artist at The Loft Literary Center in Minneapolis. She blogs about transgression and fashion at www.annrosenquistfee.com

Marianne **Gingher** is a professor of English and comparative literature at the University of North Carolina–Chapel Hill. She has published seven books, both fiction and nonfiction. Her novel *Bobby Rex's Greatest Hit* was made into an NBC movie. She has published widely in magazines and periodicals.

Diana **Goetsch** is a poet. She has published eight collections and her work has appeared in leading magazines and anthologies including *The New Yorker, Poetry, The Gettysburg Review, The Iowa Review, Ploughshares*, and *The Southern Review*. She is also a nonfiction writer and columnist; from 2015 to 2016 she wrote the "Life in Transition" blog at *The American Scholar*, about her gender transition.

Judy **Goldman** is the author of a memoir, *Losing My Sister*, two novels, *Early Leaving* and *The Slow Way Back*, and two poetry collections, *Wanting to Know the End* and *Holding Back Winter*. Her work has appeared in *Real Simple, The Southern Review, Kenyon Review, Gettysburg Review, Ohio Review, Prairie Schooner, Shenandoah* and *Best Creative Nonfiction of the South*.

Mary **Granfield** is a former journalist who earned a master's degree at the S.I. Newhouse School of Public Communications. She worked as a staff reporter at *Money* magazine for three years before leaving to freelance for *People, Glamour, Woman's Day, Family Circle* and the *Boston Sunday Globe Magazine*, among other publications.

Katie **Hafner** is a journalist who writes mainly about healthcare for the *New York Times*. She was a contributing editor for *Newsweek*, and has written for *Esquire, Wired, The New Republic* and *The New York Times Magazine*. Her sixth book of nonfiction, *Mother Daughter Me*, was named one of "Ten Titles to Pick Up Now" in *O Magazine* and made *Parade Magazine*'s Summer Reading List.

Lise **Haines** is the author of *Girl in the Arena*, South Carolina Book Nominee, *Small Acts of Sex and Electricity*, Book Sense Pick, and *In My Sister's Country*, Paterson Fiction Prize finalist. Her stories and essays have appeared in various literary journals. A PEN Nelson Algren Award finalist, she has been a Briggs-Copeland lecturer at Harvard and is senior writer in residence at Emerson College.

Ann **Harleman** is the author of two story collections—*Happiness*, which won the Iowa Short Fiction Award, and *Thoreau's Laundry*—and two novels, *Bitter Lake* and *The Year She Disappeared*. Among her awards are Guggenheim and Rockefeller fellowships, three Rhode Island State Arts Council fellowships, the Berlin Prize in Literature and the O. Henry Award. She can be reached at www.annharleman.com.

Ann **Hood** is the best-selling author of *The Knitting Circle, The Red Thread, Comfort, The Italian Wife* and *The Book That Matters Most*. She is also the editor of the acclaimed anthology *Knitting Yarns*. Her work has appeared in the *New York Times, O, Bon Appetit, The Atlantic Monthly* and elsewhere. She has won numerous prestigious awards.

Marjorie **Hudson** is the author of *Accidental Birds of the Carolinas*, a short-story collection, and *Searching for Virginia Dare*, a creative nonfiction journey. Hudson teaches adult writers in her weekly Kitchen Table Workshops, and she has received fellowships and awards from the Hemingway Foundation, Ucross Foundation, Headlands Center for the Arts and Hedgebrook Retreat for Women Writers. For more information, see www.marjoriehudson.com.

Heather Duerre **Humann** is the author of *Domestic Abuse in the Novels of African American Women* (2014) and *Gender Bending Detective Fiction* (2017), both from McFarland. She has also published numerous articles, essays and book reviews. She teaches in the Department of Language and Literature at Florida Gulf Coast University.

Lee J. **Kahrs** is a newspaper editor in rural Vermont and a creative nonfiction graduate student at the University of Southern Maine. Aside from Jennifer Beals, Lee's influences include 9/11, Joan Didion, Jackson Pollock, Etta James, Patti Smith and James Bond.

Kate **Kastelein** is a student at the University of Southern Maine, where she is pursuing an MFA in creative writing. She writes a little bit of everything—nonfiction, speculative and dark fiction as well as the occasional children's book. Her work has appeared in numerous regional and online publications, including *New England Post, HyperInk*, and *Activity Maine*.

Lisa Williams **Kline** wanted to become a writer ever since second grade, when she wrote and illustrated *The Adventures of Little Horse and Little Lamb* on large-lined paper. She is now the author of eight novels for young people, including *Eleanor Hill*, winner of the North Carolina Juvenile Literature Award, and the five-book *Sisters in All Seasons* series.

Leslie **Lawrence**, a recipient of fellowships from the Massachusetts Artists Foundation and the NEA, has published widely in journals such as *Prairie Schooner, Witness, Solstice, Redbook*, and *The Boston Globe Magazine*. Her memoir, *The Death of Fred Astaire*, was a finalist in the Foreword Indie Book Awards. Learn more at http://leslielawrencewriter.com

Marianne **Leone** is the author of *Jesse: A Mother's Story* and *Ma Speaks Up*. Her essays have appeared in the *Boston Globe, Post Road, Bark, Coastal Living* and elsewhere. She is also an actress who appeared in four seasons on HBO's *The Sopranos* and in films by John Sayles, David O. Russell, Larry David and the Farrelly Brothers.

Susan **Lilley** is a past winner of the Rita Dove Poetry Award and has two chapbooks, *Night Windows* and *Satellite Beach*. Her poetry and nonfiction have appeared in *American Poetry Review, Gulf Coast, Poet Lore, The Southern Review, Drunken Boat, Slipstream, Passager* and *Sweet*, among other journals.

Shara **McCallum** is a Jamaican-American poet, who was awarded a 2011 National Endowment for the Arts Fellowship for Poetry. A professor of English and the director of the Stadler Center for Poetry at Bucknell University, she was awarded the Witter Bynner Award from the Library of Congress.

Caitlin **McCarthy** is an award-winning writer of feature film screenplays and teleplays, including "Wonder Drug," an Alfred P. Sloan Foundation script at the Hamptons Screenwriters Lab, and "Pass/Fail," an original TV drama co-written with Jim Forbes. She is also a multiple Emmy, ALMA, AP and Golden Mic award-winning writer, producer, correspondent and narrator, most notably VH1's *Behind the Music*. Learn more at www.caitlinmccarthy.com.

Jill **McCorkle** is the author of five novels and four collections of short stories. Five of her books have been named *New York Times* notable books. She has received the New England Booksellers Award, the John Dos Passos Prize and the North Carolina Award for Literature. She is a core faculty member of the Bennington College Writing Seminars.

Lesléa **Newman** has published 70 books for readers of all ages including the short story collection *A Letter to Harvey Milk*, the novel-in-verse *October Mourning: A Song for Matthew Shepard*, the poetry collection *I Carry My Mother*, and the children's classic *Heather Has Two Mommies*. Her literary awards include poetry fellowships from the National Endowment for the Arts and the Massachusetts Artists Foundation.

Dolen **Perkins-Valdez** is the *New York Times* best-selling author of two novels: *Wench* (2010) and *Balm* (2015). She was a finalist for two NAACP Image Awards and the Hurston-Wright Legacy Award for fiction. She received the First Novelist Award from the Black Caucus of the American Library Association and received a DC Commission on the Arts Grant. She teaches writing in the American University MFA program and lives in Washington, D.C., with her family.

Leslie **Pietrzyk** is the author of two novels, *Pears on a Willow Tree* and *A Year and a Day. This Angel on My Chest*, her collection of linked short stories, won the 2015 Drue Heinz Literature Prize and was published by the University of Pittsburgh Press. Her short fiction and essays have appeared/ are forthcoming in the *Washington Post Magazine, Salon, Southern Review, Gettysburg Review, Hudson Review, Arts & Letters*, and *Cincinnati Review*. To learn more, visit www.lesliepietrzyk.com.

Amy **Rogers** is a writer for NPR station WFAE in Charlotte, where she is contributing editor for the online food magazine *WFAEats: All Things Food and Culture*. She has been featured in *Cornbread Nation 1: The Best of Southern Food Writing* and many other publications. As an editor, writing coach and workshop presenter, she has worked with hundreds of people to hone their skills and find satisfaction in their writing. Visit her at amyrogers.net.

Morgan Callan **Rogers** lives in the back-of-beyond in the Black Hills of South Dakota. Her novel *Red Ruby Heart in a Cold Blue Sea* was published in the United States, Spain, Italy, Australia and Germany, where it won a Reader's Choice Award. She is at work on a new novel.

Hank Phillippi **Ryan** is the on-air investigative reporter for WHDH-TV in Boston; she has won winning 34 Emmys and dozens more journalism honors. She is also the best-selling author of ten mysteries, with five Agathas, two Anthonys, two Macavitys, the Daphne, and the Mary Higgins Clark Award to her credit. Her newest book is the acclaimed psychological thriller *Trust Me*.

Elizabeth **Searle** is a fiction writer and playwright. She is the author of five books of fiction, including the novels *We Got Him* and *A Four Sided Bed* and the short story collections *My Body to You* and *Celebrities in Disgrace*. She is the creator and librettist of *Tonya & Nancy: The Rock Opera*, which is based on the Harding/Kerrigan skating scandal and has been produced in New York City, Chicago, Boston, Los Angeles and elsewhere. Visit her at www.elizabethsearle.net.

B.A. **Shapiro** has written seven novels (*The Muralist, The Art Forger, The Safe Room, Blind Spot, See No Evil, Blameless* and *Shattered Echoes*), four screenplays (*Blind Spot, The Lost Coven, Borderline* and *Shattered Echoes*) and the nonfiction book *The Big Squeeze*. She has also served as an adjunct professor teaching sociology at Tufts University and creative writing at Northeastern University.

Susan **Shapiro** writes for the *New York Times, New York Magazine*, the *L.A. Times, Elle, Esquire* and www.Oprah.com She is the best-selling author of the memoirs *Lighting Up, Only as Good as Your Word*, and *Five Men Who Broke My Heart*, the nonfiction books *Unhooked* and *The Bosnia List*, and the novel *What's Never Said*. *The Byline Bible* is due out in 2018. Follow her on Twitter at @susansshapironet.

Linda K. **Sienkiewicz** is well-published in poetry and fiction. She has a poetry chapbook award from *Heartlands Today*, a Pushcart Prize nomination in poetry, and three finalist awards and an honorable mention for her debut novel, *In the Context of Love*. She and her husband live in Rochester, Michigan, where they spoil their grandchildren and then send them home.

Michelle **Soucy**'s fiction has appeared in *The Florida Review, Bryant Literary Review, EWR: Stories*, and elsewhere. As an undergraduate at the University of Central Florida, she was an editor of *The Florida Review* and *The Cypress Dome*. She has worked in various aspects of publishing, marketing and technology.

Susan **Straight** has published eight novels, including *Highwire Moon*, a finalist for the National Book Award, *A Million Nightingales*, finalist for the *Los Angeles Times* Book Prize, and *Between Heaven and Here*. Her stories and essays have appeared in a variety of anthologies and newspapers and other publications. She is a distinguished professor of creative writing at the University of California–Riverside.

Suzanne **Strempek Shea**'s eleven books include *This Is Paradise: An Irish Mother's Grief, An African Village's Plight and the Medical Clinic That Brought Fresh Hope to Both* and the novel *Make a Wish but Not for Money*. Her freelance work has appeared in publications including *The Boston Globe, The Irish Times, Yankee* and *Bark*.

Mary **Sullivan** is the author of *Dear Blue Sky*, a middle grade novel for which she won the Chautauqua Literary and Scientific Circle Award. Her other novels include *Stay* and *Ship Sooner*, and she has ghostwritten for the *Beacon Street Girls* series. She received a Massachusetts Cultural Council Grant for Literature, a Rona Jaffe Foundation Award, and a St. Botolph's Award. She was one of the Border's Original New Voices. Visit her online at marysullivan.net.

Nancy **Swan** of Arizona began her writing career late in life. With a box full of short stories and the beginnings of a novel, she decided to apply to the Stonecoast Masters in Creative Writing program. One of her essays appears in *Paper Camera: A Half Century with New Rivers Press*. Her book *Escalanté Moon* won the 2016 Dana Award for Fiction in the Novel. Her website is www.nancyaswan.com.

Darlene R. **Taylor** is a cultural arts advocate in Washington, D.C., and heads a national cultural heritage nonprofit and lovingly cares for an 1860s home. She holds an MFA from Stonecoast and is a fellow of *Callaloo, Kimbilio*, and *A Room of Her Own*.

Stephanie Powell **Watts**' much-anticipated debut novel, *No One Is Coming to Save Us*, was named a Best Summer Read of 2017 by *The Wall Street Journal* and *Washington Post*. Her story collection, *We Are Taking Only What We Need*, won a Whiting Award and an Ernest J. Gaines Award for Literary Excellence. Her work has received a Pushcart Prize and was included twice in *Best New Stories from the South*. She teaches at Lehigh University.

Tamra **Wilson**, author of *Dining with Robert Redford & Other Stories*, is a Road Scholar for the North Carolina Humanities Council and a local columnist. Her work has appeared in *storySouth, North Carolina Literary Review, Epiphany, The New Guard*, and elsewhere. She won the Jesse Stuart Prize for Young Adult Fiction, a Blumenthal Award and was a two-time finalist for the Press 53 Novella Award. She was also a finalist for the Killer Nashville Claymore Award in 2017.

Susan **Woodring** is the author of the novel *Goliath* and a short story collection *Springtime on Mars*. Her short fiction has appeared in *The Cupboard, Passages North, Turnrow* and *Surreal South*, among other publications. Her short fiction was shortlisted for *Best American Non-Required Reading 2008* and *Best American Short Stories 2010*.

Index

Abbey Road (album) 88, 100, 186–191; *see also* The Beatles
"ABC" (song) 220; *see also* Jackson, Michael; The Jackson 5
abortion 107–110
abuse: men 60–64, 168–169, 193; parents 16–23, 56–58, 65–70; relationships 217–218
adolescence 10–11, 16–23, 139–144, 186–191, 214–218; *see also* puberty
adulthood 154–159
The Adventures of a Young Man (film) 12; *see also* Newman, Paul
Afghanistan 211
African American history and culture 16–23
African American women 174–178, 192–197
Agent 99 (fictitious character) 151–152; *see also Get Smart* (TV program)
alcoholism 18–22, 56–58
Ali, Muhammad: draft protest 99
"All My Loving" (song) 36–37, 87; *see also* The Beatles
Allen, Steve 20; *see also The Steve Allen Show*
Allen, Woody 151
"America, the Beautiful" (song) 6
American Ballet Theatre 178
American Bandstand (TV program) 20
American Graffiti (film) 155; Falfa, Bob (fictitious character) 155; *see also* Ford, Harrison; Lucas, George
The Andy Griffith Show (continued after 1968 as *Mayberry R.F.D.*) 78; Mayberry, North Carolina (fictitious location) 78; Pyle, Goober (fictitious character) 79; Taylor, Andy (fictitious character) 78; Taylor, Opie (fictitious character) 78
Animal Farm (book) 146–148
anime 214–218
Anita (fictitious character) 84–85; *see also* Moreno, Rita; *West Side Story* (film)

"Another Saturday Night" (song) 87; *see also* Cooke, Sam
anti-war demonstrations 99, 127
aphasia 97–101
Arcade Fire (musical group) 207
Artful Dodger (fictitious character) 43; *see also Oliver!*
The Arthur Murray Party (TV program) 20; *see also* Murray, Arthur
"As Tears Go By" (song) 88; *see also* Faithfull, Marianne
"As Time Goes By" (song) 55; *see also* Bogart, Humphrey
Asher, Jane: engagement to Paul McCartney 36–37
"Ask Me Why" (song) 32; *see also* The Beatles
Astley, Rick 161
Audioslave (musical group) 222
Austen, Jane 131
Austin, Tracy 137
Avalon, Frankie 79

Bacall, Lauren 50–55; Blenheim (pet King Charles spaniel) 54; marriage to Humphrey Bogart 53; *To Have and Have Not* (film) 52; *Wonderful Town* (play) 54; *see also* Bogart, Humphrey
Backbeat (film) 91; *see also* The Beatles
Backstreet Boys 24, 31
Baez, Joan 88, 128
baldness 79–80
ballet 178–182
Bangladesh 94
Banks, George (fictitious character) 80; *see also Mary Poppins* (film)
Bannon, Hud (fictitious character) 211; *see also Hud* (film); Newman, Paul
Barkley, Heath (fictitious character) 79; *see also The Big Valley* (TV program)
Barkley, Jarrod (fictitious character) 79; *see also The Big Valley* (TV program)
Barnes, Julie (fictitious character) 150–154; *see also* Lipton, Peggy;

The Mod Squad (TV program)
Barry Manilow Live in Concert (video recording) 174
Baryshnikov, Mikhail 146, 178–182; American Ballet Theatre 178; Baryshnikov Arts Center, New York, N.Y. 182; *Les Sylphides* (ballet) 178; White Oak Dance Project, Minneapolis, Minnesota 181
Baryshnikov Arts Center, New York, N.Y. 182
Baxter, Ted (fictitious character) 152; *see also The Mary Tyler Moore Show*
Beach Boys 94
Beals, Jennifer 183–185; Owens, Alexandra "Alex" (fictitious character) 183–185; *see also Flashdance* (film); *The L Word* (TV program)
"Beat It" (song) 161; *see also* Jackson, Michael
The Beatles 16, 22, 27, 32–37, 39, 41, 45, 66, 79, 85, 86–89, 90–92, 93–96, 97–101, 103–104, 119, 126, 171, 189, 205, 219; *Abbey Road* (album) 88, 100; "All My Loving" (song) 36–37, 87; arrival in US (1964) 16, 22; "Ask Me Why" (song) 32; *The Beatles* (album) (also known as The White Album) 88, 90, 92, 94, 100; breakup 94, 100; "Do You Want to Know a Secret" (song) 34; *Ed Sullivan Show* appearance (1964) 22, 34–35, 86–87, 126; "Eight Days a Week" (song) 90–91; "Eleanor Rigby" (song) 99; "Getting Better" (song) 88; "Happiness Is a Warm Gun" (song) 88; *A Hard Day's Night* (film) 35, 85, 87, 93; *Help!* (album) 88, 91; "Hey Jude" (song) 90; "I Me Mine" (song) 96; "I Saw Her Standing There" (song) 97; "I Want to Hold Your Hand" (song) 87, 91, 94, 97; "I Will" (song) 90, 92; "I'm Looking Through You" (song) 36–37; International Amphitheatre

concert, Chicago, Illinois (1964) 93–94; *Introducing... The Beatles* (album) 32–37; "Love Me Do" (song) 91; "Lucy in the Sky with Diamonds" (song) 99; *Magical Mystery Tour* (album) 88; *Meet the Beatles!* (album) 35, 87, 97; "Michelle" (song) 32, 92, 99; *1* (album) 91; "Penny Lane" (song) 90; "Please Mr. Postman" (song) 87; "Please Please Me" (song) 32; "P.S. I Love You" (song) 32–37, 91; *Revolver* (album) 92; *Rubber Soul* (album) 88, 99; *Sgt. Pepper's Lonely Hearts Club Band* (album) 88, 90, 92, 99, 127; "She Loves You (Yeah, Yeah, Yeah)" (song) 126; Shea Stadium concert (1965) 35–36, 98, 205; "Strawberry Fields Forever" (song) 90; "Till There Was You" (song) 87; "We Can Work It Out" (song) 36; White Sox Park concert, Chicago, Illinois (1965) 94; *Yellow Submarine* (album) 92; "Yesterday" (song) 91–92; "You've Got to Hide Your Love Away" (song) 91; *see also* Best, Pete; Harrison, George; Lennon, John; McCartney, Paul; Starr, Ringo; Sutcliffe, Stuart
The Beatles (album) (also known as The White Album) 88, 90, 92, 94, 101; *see also* The Beatles
The Beatles' Second Album (book) 87; *see also* Marsh, Dave (rock critic)
Beck, Jeff 47
"Begin the Begin" (song) 205; *see also* R.E.M. (musical group); Stipe, Michael
Being Bobby Brown (TV program) 193; *see also* Brown, Bobby; Houston, Whitney
"Ben" (song) 188; *see also* Jackson, Michael
Ben Casey (TV program) 71–74, 78; *see also* Edwards, Vince
Bergman, Ingrid 51, 55; *Casablanca* (film) 51, 55
Bernardo (fictitious character) 84–85; *see also* Chakiris, George; *West Side Story* (film)
Bert (fictitious character) 80–81; *see also* *Mary Poppins* (film); Van Dyke, Dick
Bertrille, Sister (fictitious character) 151–152; *see also* *The Flying Nun* (TV program)
Best, Pete 91; *see also* The Beatles
The Beverly Hillbillies (TV program) 77
Bewitched (TV program) 151–152; Stephens, Samantha (fictitious character) 151–152
Beyoncé 193
Bhajan, Yogi 94
The Big Valley (TV program) 79; Barkley, Heath (fictitious char-

acter) 79; Barkley, Jarrod (fictitious character) 79
Billboard 35, 45, 49
"Billie Jean" (song) 161, 186; *see also* Jackson, Michael
birthdays 154–159
bisexuality 202–207; *see also* gender identity; homosexuality
Bishop, Elizabeth 94
Bixby, Rob 63
Black, Frank 199–200; *see also* The Pixies (musical group)
Black Eyed Peas (musical group) 222
Black Francis *see* Black, Frank
Black Girl Magic 193
black-girl perfectionism 192–197
Black Girls Rock! (TV program) 193
black superwoman myth 196; *see also* Wallace, Michele
Bledsoe, Tempestt 193; *see also* *The Cosby Show*
Blue (album) 113; *see also* Mitchell, Joni
Bogart, Humphrey 50–55; "As Time Goes By" (song) 55; *Casablanca* (film) 51, 55; *High Sierra* (film) 52; *The Maltese Falcon* (film) 52; marriage to Lauren Bacall 53; Spade, Sam (fictitious character) 52; *To Have and Have Not* (film) 52; *see also* Bacall, Lauren
Boggs, Kim (fictitious character) 167; *see also* *Edward Scissorhands* (film); Ryder, Winona
Bohemianism 111–118
"Boho Dance" (song) 115–116; *see also* Mitchell, Joni
Bon Jovi, Jon 162
Bonanza (TV program) 78–79, 86; Cartwright, Adam (fictitious character) 79; Cartwright, Eric "Hoss" (fictitious character) 79; Cartwright, Joseph "Little Joe" (fictitious character) 79; Ponderosa Ranch 78
Bond, James (fictitious character) 145, 185
Bonet, Lisa 193; *see also* *The Cosby Show*
Bonnard, Pierre 99
Bonnie and Clyde (film) 99
Bono, Chastity *see* Bono, Chaz
Bono, Chaz (formerly Chastity Bono) 122
Bono, Mary 122
Bono, Sonny 122–124; death 124; *see also* Cher; Sonny & Cher
Borders, Lisa 202–207, 223
Bossanova (album) 198–200; *see also* The Pixies (musical group)
Boston Bruins 133–136; Stanley Cup (1941 and 1972) 133
Boston Garden 133–136; demolition (1998) 135
Boston Herald American 133
"Both Sides Now" (song) 117; *see also* Mitchell, Joni

Bowie, David 48, 213; "Under Pressure" (song) 48; *Ziggy Stardust and the Spiders from Mars* (film) 213
Boy George 162
Boyd, Patti 22
Boynton v. Virginia (1960) 16
Brady, Greg (fictitious character) 79; *see also* *The Brady Bunch* (TV program)
The Brady Bunch (TV program) 79
"Brand New Key" (song) 182; *see also* Melanie (singer)
Brewster, Tom "Sugarfoot" (fictitious character) 83; *see also* *Sugarfoot* (TV program)
Bridges, Todd 194; *see also* *Diff'rent Strokes* (TV program)
Brinkley, Christie: marriage to Billy Joel 162
British Invasion 88; *see also* The Beatles; Herman's Hermits
Bronco (TV program) 83–84; *see also* Hardin, Ty
Brontë sisters 131
Browder v. Gayle (1961) 16
Brown, Bobby: marriage to Whitney Houston 193, 195, 197
Brown, H. Rap 99
Brown, James 221
Buck, Peter 205; *see also* R.E.M. (musical group)
Bukater, Rose DeWitt (fictitious character) 208–212; *see also* *Titanic* (film)
bullying 50
Burr, Raymond 3, 56–59; death 58; homosexuality 59; *Ironside* (TV program) 56–59; *Perry Mason* (TV program) 56–59
busing for school integration 151

"Cabaret" (song) 45
Caddyshack (film) 154
"California" (song) 118; *see also* Mitchell, Joni
cancer 15, 17, 45–49, 67–69
capitalism 65–70
Captain Kangaroo (fictitious character) 77
Captain Kangaroo (TV program and character) 77
The Carpenters 177
Carroll, Diahann 194; *see also* *Dynasty* (TV program)
Cartwright, Adam (fictitious character) 79; *see also* *Bonanza* (TV program)
Cartwright, Eric "Hoss" (fictitious character) 69; *see also* *Bonanza* (TV program)
Cartwright, Joseph "Little Joe" (fictitious character) 79; *see also* *Bonanza* (TV program)
Cartwright family (fictitious characters) 78–79; *see also* *Bonanza* (TV program)
Casablanca (film) 51, 55; *see also* Bogart, Humphrey

Case, Neko 207
"A Case of You" (song) 118; *see also* Mitchell, Joni
Casey, Ben (fictitious character) 71–74, 78; *see also Ben Casey* (TV program); Edwards, Vince
Cash, Johnny 117
Cassidy, David 51, 79; "I Think I Love You" (song) 51
Cat on a Hot Tin Roof (film) 12
cereal-box records 50–51
Cha Cha (dance) 17–18
Chakiris, George 84–85; Bernardo (fictitious character) 84–85; *George Chakiris Sings* (album) 84–85; *see also West Side Story* (film)
Chamberlain, Richard 71–76; *Dr. Kildare* (TV program) 71–74, 78; homosexuality 74–76
Chambers, Tracy (fictitious character) 142–144; *see also Mahogany* (film); Ross, Diana
"A Change Is Gonna Come" (song) 19–21; *see also* Cooke, Sam
Cheap Thrills (album) 127–128; *see also* Joplin, Janis
Checker, Chubby: "The Twist" (song) 97
Cheevers, Gerry 133
Cher 122–125; Bono, Chaz (formerly Chastity) 120; *The First Time* (book) 122; "Gypsys, Tramps & Thieves" (song) 122; "Half-Breed" (song) 122; "I Got You Babe" (song) 122; *Late Show with David Letterman* appearance 122; *Look at Me* (album) 124; marriage to Sonny Bono 122
"Chevy Van" (song) 182; *see also* Johns, Sammy
Chinmoy, Sri 94
The Chords (musical group) 5
The Chronicles of Narnia (book series) 112
"Cinnamon Girl" (song) 119; *see also* Young, Neil
"The Circle Game" (song) 117; *see also* Mitchell, Joni
Civil Rights Movement 16–23, 127
Clark, Dick 20, 175; *see also The Dick Clark Saturday Night Beechnut Show; Dick Clark's New Year's Rockin' Eve* (TV program)
Clark, Petula 128
Clarke, Breena 16–23, 223
The Clash (musical group) 222
Cleaver, Wally (fictitious character) 79; *see also Leave It to Beaver*
A Clockwork Orange (film) 151
Clouds (album) 112; *see also* Mitchell, Joni
Cold War 145–149
Cole, Michael 150–154; Cochran, Pete (fictitious character) 150–154; *see also The Mod Squad* (TV program)

Cole, Nat King 20
Coleman, Gary 194; *see also Diff'rent Strokes* (TV program)
Collins, Addie Mae 20, 22–23; *see also* 16th Street Baptist Church Bombing, Birmingham, Alabama (1963)
Collins, Judy 117, 128
The Color of Money (film) 14; *see also* Newman, Paul
Coltrane, John 150
Columbine High School Massacre, Littleton, Colorado (1999) 201
Come On Pilgrim (album) 200; *see also* The Pixies (musical group)
Communism 65–70
concentration camps 213
Concert for Bangladesh, Madison Square Garden, New York, N.Y. 94
Connors, Jimmy: engagement to Chris Evert 137–138
Control (album) 193; *see also* Jackson, Janet
Cooke, Sam 2, 16–23; "Another Saturday Night" (song) 87; birth 16; "A Change Is Gonna Come" (song) 19–21; "Cupid" (song) 18; death 16–23; "Everybody Loves to Cha Cha Cha" (a.k.a. "Everybody Likes to Cha Cha Cha") (song) 17, 19; "Having a Party" (song) 18; "Only Sixteen" (song) 18; "Shake" (song) 19; "That's Where It's At" (song) 19; "Touch the Hem of His Garment" (song) 21; "You Send Me" (song) 17
Cool Hand Luke (film) 14; *see also* Newman, Paul
Cooley, Melvin "Mel" (fictitious character) 78; *see also The Dick Van Dyke Show*
"Copacabana" (song) 177; *see also* Manilow, Barry
Cosby, Bill 22
The Cosby Show 193; *see also* Bledsoe, Tempestt; Bonet, Lisa; Cosby, Bill
Cosmopolitan 139
Counting Crows (musical group) 207
cowboys 82–85
"Cowgirl in the Sand" (song) 119; *see also* Young, Neil
Crazy Horse (musical group) 119
The Crew-Cuts (musical group): "Sh-Boom" (song) 5
Crosby, David 113
Crosby, Stills & Nash 112
Crowe, Russell 62–64; *Gladiator* (film) 62; Hando (fictitious character) 62; *L.A. Confidential* (film) 62; *The Quick and the Dead* (film) 62; *Romper Stomper* (film) 62
Cry-Baby (film) 166, 169; *see also* Depp, Johnny
"Cry Baby" (song) 127; *see also* Joplin, Janis

"Cupid" (song) 18; *see also* Cooke, Sam
Daft Punk (musical group) 88; *Random Access Memories* (album) 88–89
The Daily Worker (newspaper) 67
dancing 16–23, 178–182, 183–186; *see also* ballet
"Dancing Machine" (song) 220; *see also* Jackson, Michael
Darth Vader *see* Vader, Darth
The Dating Game 3
Dave Clark Five 36, 98
Davis, Clive 195
Davis, Katharine 71–76, 223
Davis, Sammy, Jr. 20
"The Dawn Treader" (song) 112; *see also* Mitchell, Joni
Dawson, Jack (fictitious character) 208–212; *see also* DiCaprio, Leonardo; *Titanic* (film)
"Daydream Believer" (song) 3, 24, 42, 44; *see also* Jones, Davy; The Monkees
Deal, Kim 200; *see also* The Pixies (musical group)
Dean, Jimmy 20; *see also The Jimmy Dean Show*
The Dean Martin Show 27; *see also* Martin, Dean
Death Cab for Cutie (musical group) 207
death, dying, and bereavement 10–15, 16–22, 45–49, 56–59, 68–70, 90–92, 97–101; *see also* grief
The Death of Fred Astaire: And Other Essays from a Life Outside the Lines (book) 131–132
de Bricassart, the Rev. Ralph (fictitious character) 76; *see also* Chamberlain, Richard; *The Thorn Birds* (TV program)
de Cadenet, Amanda 171; marriage to John Taylor of Duran Duran 171; *see also* Taylor, John
Deliverance (film) 151
Del Rey, Lana 88
Depp, Johnny 2, 166–169; *Cry-Baby* (film) 166; friendship with Hunter S. Thompson 167; marriage to Amber Heard 168–169; relationship and breakup with Vanessa Paradis 168; relationship and breakup with Winona Ryder 167; Scissorhands, Edward (fictitious character) 167; Sparrow, Jack (fictitious character) 168; spousal abuse allegations 168; *see also Edward Scissorhands* (film); *Fear and Loathing in Las Vegas* (film); *Pirates of the Caribbean* (film series) 168
depression 81
desegregation *see* segregation
"Despacito" (song) 175
"Devil Inside" (song) 163; *see also* Hutchence, Michael; INXS (musical group)

Diana (album) 143

Diana Ross Presents the Jackson 5 (album) 140

DiCaprio, Leonardo 208–212; Dawson, Jack (fictitious character) 208–212; *see also Titanic* (film)

The Dick Clark Saturday Night Beechnut Show 20; *see also* Clark, Dick

Dick Clark's New Year's Rockin' Eve (TV specials) 175

The Dick Van Dyke Show 77–81; Cooley, Melvin "Mel" (fictitious character) 78; "I'd Rather Be Bald Than Have No Heat at All" (episode) 79; Rogers, Sally (fictitious character) 77–78; Sorrell, Maurice "Buddy" (fictitious character) 77–78; *see also* Van Dyke, Dick

Dickens, Charles 60–64

Dickinson, Emily 96

Diff'rent Strokes (TV program) 194; *see also* Bridges, Todd; Coleman, Gary

"Dig for Fire" (song) 198–199; *see also Fight Club* (film); The Pixies (musical group)

Dirty Dancing (film) 166

disabilities 58–59

"Do You Want to Know a Secret" (song) 34; *see also* The Beatles

Dr. Kildare (TV program) 71–76, 78

Document (album) 205; *see also* R.E.M. (musical group); Stipe, Michael

Dolenz, Mickey 39, 44; *see also* The Monkees

domestic abuse *see* marital violence

Donovan (singer) 39

"Don't Be Cruel" (song) 6, 9; *see also* Presley, Elvis

Doolittle (album) 200; *see also* The Pixies (musical group)

The Doors (film) 62

The Doors (musical group) 39, 61–64; *see also* Morrison, Jim

Dornemann, Emlyn Meredith 214–218, 223

Double Fantasy (album) 88; *see also* Lennon, John; Ono, Yoko

Douglas, Chip (fictitious character) 79; *see also My Three Sons* (TV program)

Douglas, Ernie (fictitious character) 79; *see also My Three Sons* (TV program)

Douglas, Michael (actor) 41

Douglas, Mike (TV talk-show host) 20; *see also The Mike Douglas Show*

Douglas, Robbie (fictitious character) 79; *see also My Three Sons* (TV program)

"Down by the River" (song) 119; *see also* Young, Neil

Drexler, Wendy 128

The Drifters (musical group) 24

Dungeons & Dragons (game) 167

Duran Duran (musical group) 3, 170–173, 177; Mohegan Sun Arena concert, Uncasville, Conn. (1997) 172; *Paper Gods* (album) 172; "Rio" (song and music video) 171; *Seven and the Angry Tiger* (album) 170; Worcester [Mass.] Centrum concert (1984) 170–172; Xfinity Center concert, Mansfield, MA (2016) 173; *see also* Le Bon, Simon; Rhodes, Nick; Taylor, John

Dust Bowl Ballads (album) 65; *see also* Guthrie, Woody

Dust Bowl Era (1931–1939) 65–70

"Dusty Old Dust" (song) 66; *see also* Guthrie, Woody

DuVernay, Ava 20

Dylan, Bob 3, 107–110; "Idiot Wind" (song) 108; "Just Like a Woman" (song) 108; "Like a Rolling Stone" (song) 107, 109; "Mr. Tambourine Man" (song) 127; "One of Us Must Know" (song) 108; "Visions of Johanna" (song) 110; "You're a Big Girl Now" (song) 109; "You're Gonna Make Me Lonesome When You Go" (song) 109

dysfunctional families 65–70, 136

Easter (album) 203; *see also* Smith, Patti

"Easy Come, Easy Go" (song) 50; *see also* Sherman, Bobby

Ebony (magazine) 139

Eckstine, Billy 19

The Ed Sullivan Show 5–7, 20, 22, 27, 34–35, 86–87, 126; *see also* Sullivan, Ed

Eden, Barbara 151–152; Jeannie (fictitious character) 151–152; *see also I Dream of Jeannie* (TV program)

"Edith and the Kingpin" (song) 115; *see also* Mitchell, Joni

Edward Scissorhands (film) 167; Boggs, Kim (fictitious character) 167; *see also* Depp, Johnny

Edwards, Vince 71–74; *see also Ben Casey* (TV program)

Eidus, Janice 3, 65–70, 223

"Eight Days a Week" (song) 90–91; *see also* The Beatles

Eisel, Mary-Ann 138

"Eleanor Rigby" (song) 99; *see also* The Beatles

Eliot, George 131

Elliot, Cass (also known as Mama Cass) 88, 128; *see also* The Mamas & the Papas

The Elvis Presley Album of Juke Box Favorites (sheet music) 8; *see also* Presley, Elvis

Emergency Medical Technicians 54

Eminem 222

The Empire Strikes Back (film) 154–159; *see also Star Wars* (film and film series)

Essence (magazine) 139

Evans, Spin (fictitious character) 83; *see also Spin and Marty* (TV program)

Evers, Medgar: death 16, 20

Evert, Chris 136–138; engagement to Jimmy Connors 137–138; marriage to and divorce from John Lloyd 138; marriage to Andy Mill 138

"Everybody Hurts" (song) 206; *see also* R.E.M. (musical group); Stipe, Michael

Everybody Knows This Is Nowhere (album) 119; *see also* Young, Neil

"Everybody Loves to Cha Cha Cha" (a.k.a. "Everybody Likes to Cha Cha Cha") (song) 17, 19; *see also* Cooke, Sam

Exodus (film) 12; *see also* Newman, Paul

The Exorcist (film) 151

Eyre, Jane (fictitious character) 57

Fables of the Reconstruction (album) 203–204; *see also* R.E.M. (musical group); Stipe, Michael

The Facts of Life (TV program) 193–194; Fields, Kim 193–194; Ramsey, Tootie (fictitious character) 193–194

Faithfull, Marianne: "As Tears Go By" (song) 88

"Fall on Me" (song) 205; *see also* R.E.M. (musical group); Stipe, Michael

fan fiction 214–218

"Fascinating Rhythm" (song) 128

Father Ralph (fictitious character from *The Thorn Birds*) *see* de Bricassart, Ralph, Rev.

fathers and daughters 65–70, 80–81, 164–165

Fatima, Our Lady of 82–83

Faulkner, William 10–12

Fawcett, Farrah 193

Fee, Ann Rosenquist 178–182, 223

Fenway Park, Boston, Mass. 35, 37, 136

Fields, Kim 93–194; Ramsey, Tootie (fictitious character) 193–194; *see also The Facts of Life* (TV program)

Fight Club (book) 200

Fight Club (film) 198, 200

Finster, Howard 203; *Reckoning* (album) cover illustrations 203

first loves 10–15, 107–110, 120–121

The First Time (book) 122; *see also* Cher

Flashdance (film) 183–185; Long, Hanna (fictitious character) 183; Owens, Alexandra "Alex" (fictitious character) 183–185; Plasic, Richie (fictitious character) 184; Szabo, Jeanie (fictitious character) 184; *see also* Beals, Jennifer

Fleming, Ian 145

Flipper (fictitious character) 79

Flipper (TV program) 79; Ricks, Sandy (fictitious character) 79

Flying Nun (TV program) 151–152; Bertrille, Sister (fictitious character) 151–152

"For Free" (song) 118; *see also* Mitchell, Joni

For the Roses (album) 118; *see also* Mitchell, Joni

Ford, Harrison 154–159; Falfa, Bob (fictitious character) 155; Solo, Han (fictitious character) 154–159; *see also American Graffiti* (film); *Star Wars* (film and film series)

forgiveness 65–70

Foster, Jodi 185

Foxy Lady (dance) 161

Francis, Connie 97; "Where the Boys Are" (song) 97

Franklin, Aretha 128

Freedom Rides, 1961 16

friendship 16–22, 45–49, 71–77, 97–101, 111–113, 154–159, 160–164

From the Terrace (film) 12; *see also* Newman, Paul

The Fugitive (TV program) 79

Funky Chicken (dance) 16, 18

G. Fox & Co. 33

Gale, Dorothy (fictitious character) 221; *see also The Wiz* (film); *The Wizard of Oz* (film)

Garfunkel, Art 39, 47, 102–106; Clowes Memorial Hall concert, Indianapolis, Indiana (1967) 104; "Homeward Bound" (song) 104, 106; "I Am a Rock" (song) 103; legal career 103; *Sounds of Silence* (album) 103; *see also* Simon, Paul; Simon & Garfunkel

gender identity 162

General Electric Theater 20

Generation X 173

Georgiou, Steven *see* Stevens, Cat

Gere, Richard 213

Gershwin, George 128

Get Smart (TV program) 151–152; Agent 99 (fictitious character) 151–152

"Getting Better" (song) 88; *see also* The Beatles

Gillespie, Leonard (fictitious character) 72–73; *see also Dr. Kildare* (TV program)

Gilligan's Island (TV program) 150; Grant, Ginger (fictitious character) 150; Howell, "Lovey" Wentworth (fictitious character) 150; Summers, Mary Ann (fictitious character) 150

Gingher, Marianne 97–101, 223

Gladiator (film) 62; *see also* Crowe, Russell

Goetsch, Diana 213, 223

"Goin' Down the Road Feeling Bad" (song) 70; *see also* Guthrie, Woody

Goldman, Judy 5–9, 223

Goldstein, Richard (rock critic) 126

Goldwater, Barry 126

Gomer Pyle U.S.M.C. (TV program) 79

gonzo journalism 167; *see also* Thompson, Hunter S.

Good Times (TV program) 193; Woods, Millicent "Penny" Gordon (fictitious character) 193; *see also* Jackson, Janet

Goolagong, Evonne 137–138

Gore, Leslie 128

gospel music 19–23

grandmothers 74–76

Granfield, Mary 150–153, 224

Grant, Lou (fictitious character) 152; *see also The Mary Tyler Moore Show*

The Grapes of Wrath (book) 66

Grease (film) 166

"Great Balls of Fire" (song) 126; *see also* Lewis, Jerry Lee

Great Depression 65–70

"The Greatest Love of All" (song) 192–193; *see also* Houston, Whitney

Green, Karl 29; *see also* Herman's Hermits

Green Mansions (book) 146–148

Gremlins 2 166

grief 10–15, 16–23, 45–49, 56–59, 90–92; *see also* death, dying, and bereavement

Griffin, Merv 20; *see also The Merv Griffin Show*

Griffith, Andy 78; *The Andy Griffith Show* 78; Mayberry, North Carolina (fictitious location) 78; Taylor, Andy (fictitious character) 78; Taylor, Opie (fictitious character)

"Guantanamera" (song) 104; *see also* The Sandpipers (musical group)

Gulf War (1991) *see* Persian Gulf War (1991)

Guthrie, Woody 3, 65–70; death 68; *Dust Bowl Ballads* (album) 65; "Dusty Old Dust" (song) 66; "Goin' Down the Road Feeling Bad" (song) 70; Huntington's disease 68; "Talking Dust Bowl Blues" (song) 70; "This Land Is Your Land" (song) 46, 66, 68; "Tom Joad" (song) 66

"Gypsys, Tramps & Thieves" (song) 122; *see also* Cher

Hafner, Katie 136–138, 224

Haines, Lise 93–96, 224

"Half-Breed" (song) 122; *see also* Cher

Hamill, Mark 155; Skywalker, Luke (fictitious character) 155; *see also Star Wars* (film and film series)

Handel, George Frideric 130

Hando (fictitious character) 62; *see also* Crowe, Russell; *Romper Stomper* (film)

"Handy Man" (song) 8; *see also* Taylor, James

"Hang on to Your Ego" (song) 200; *see also* The Pixies (musical group)

Happening (TV program) 46

"Happiness Is a Warm Gun" (song) 88; *see also* The Beatles

Happy Days (TV program) 183

A Hard Day's Night (film) 35, 85, 87, 93; *see also* The Beatles

Hardin, Ty 83–84; *see also Bronco* (TV program)

Hari Dass, Baba 94

Harleman, Ann 3, 56–59, 224

Harris, Emmylou 116, 177; *Trio* (album) 116

Harris-Perry, Melissa 196

Harrison, George 32–37, 66, 87, 90–92, 93–96; *Abbey Road* (album) 88, 100; "All My Loving" (song) 36–37, 87; arrival in US (1964) 16, 22; "Ask Me Why" (song) 32; assault (1999) 95; *Backbeat* (film) 91; *The Beatles* (album) (also known as The White Album) 88, 90, 92, 94, 100; cancer 95; death 91, 95; Concert for Bangladesh, Madison Square Garden, New York, N.Y. 94; "Do You Want to Know a Secret" (song) 34; *Ed Sullivan Show* appearance, 1964 22, 34–35, 86–87, 126; "Eight Days a Week" (song) 90–91; "Eleanor Rigby" (song) 90–91; "Getting Better" (song) 88; "Happiness Is a Warm Gun" (song) 88; *A Hard Day's Night* (film) 35, 87, 93; *Help!* (album) 88, 91; "Hey Jude" (song) 90); Hinduism, exploration of 94–96; "I Me Mine" (song) 96; "I Saw Her Standing There" (song) 97; "I Want to Hold Your Hand" (song) 87, 91, 94, 97; "I Will" (song) 90, 92; "I'm Looking Through You" (song) 36–37; International Amphitheatre concert, Chicago, Illinois (1964) 93–94); *Introducing... The Beatles* (album) 32–37; "Love Me Do" (song) 91; "Lucy in the Sky with Diamonds" (song) 99; *Magical Mystery Tour* (album) 88; *Meet the Beatles!* (album) 35, 87, 97; "Michelle" (song) 32, 92, 99; *1* (album) 91; "Penny Lane" (song) 90; "Please Mr. Postman" (song) 87; "Please Please Me" (song) 32; "P.S. I Love You" (song) 32–

37, 91; *Revolver* (album) 92; *Rubber Soul* (album) 88, 99; *Sgt. Pepper's Lonely Hearts Club Band* (album) 88, 90, 92, 99, 127; "She Loves You (Yeah, Yeah, Yeah)" (song) 126; Shea Stadium concert (1965) 35–36, 98; "Strawberry Fields Forever" (song) 90; "Till There Was You" (song) 87; "We Can Work It Out" (song) 36; White Sox Park concert, Chicago, Illinois (1965) 94; *Yellow Submarine* (album) 92; "Yesterday" (song) 91–92; "You've Got to Hide Your Love Away" (song) 91; *see also* The Beatles; Lennon, John; McCartney, Paul; Starr, Ringo
"Having a Party" (song) 18; *see also* Cooke, Sam
Hayes, Lincoln "Linc" (fictitious character) 150–154; *see also* The *Mod Squad* (TV program); Williams, Clarence, III
Heard, Amber 168–169; marriage to Johnny Depp 168–169; spousal abuse allegations 168–169
Heart of the Ocean (fictitious jewel) 209; *see also Titanic* (film)
"Heartbreak Hotel" (song) 9; *see also* Presley, Elvis
Helen of Troy 66–67
Help! (album) 88, 91; *see also* The Beatles
Hemingway, Ernest 185
Hendrix, Jimi 39, 88, 130; death 130
Hentoff, Nat (rock critic) 130
Herman's Hermits 1, 2–4, 24–31, 79, 98; "I'm Henry the Eighth, I Am" (song) 24–25; "Jezebel" (song) 27; "Mrs. Brown, You've Got a Lovely Daughter" (song) 24, 26, 31; "Rattler" (song) 27; *There's a Kind of Hush All Over the World* (album) 27; "There's a Kind of Hush All Over the World" (song) 24–25, 29–30; *see also* Green, Karl; Hopwood, Keith; Leckenby, Derek; Noone, Peter; Whitwam, Barry
"Hey Jude" (song) 90; *see also* The Beatles
"Hey, Mister Sun" (song) 50; *see also* Sherman, Bobby
High Sierra (film) 52; *see also* Bogart, Humphrey
"Him or Me—What's It Gonna Be?" (song) 45; *see also* Lindsay, Mark; Paul Revere and the Raiders
Hinduism 94–96
The Hissing of Summer Lawns (album) 114–116; *see also* Mitchell, Joni
Hobbes, Thomas 40
hockey 133–136
Hodge, Ken 133

Hogan, Hulk 211
Holliday, Billie 128, 139, 143
Home Alone (film) 166
"Homeward Bound" (song) 104, 106; *see also* Simon & Garfunkel
homosexuality 59, 74–76, 122–125, 175, 183–185, 203–207, 213; *see also* bisexuality; gender identity; lesbianism
Hood, Ann 90–92, 224
Hopwood, Keith 29; *see also* Herman's Hermits
"Hound Dog" (song) 6, 126; *see also* Presley, Elvis
"House of the Rising Sun" (song) 113
Houston, Cissy 195
Houston, Whitney 192–197; addiction 197; *Being Bobby Brown* (TV program) 193; "The Greatest Love of All" (song) 192; "I Wanna Dance with Somebody (Who Loves Me)" (song) 192; marriage to Bobby Brown 193, 195, 197; *see also* Brown, Bobby
"How Can I Tell You?" (song) 120; *see also* Stevens, Cat
Huckleberry Hound (fictitious character) 77
Hud (film) 12, 211; Bannon, Hud (fictitious character) 211; *see also* Newman, Paul
Hudson, Marjorie 111–118, 224
Hullaballoo (TV program) 27
Humann, Heather Duerre 198–201, 224
"Hungry" (song) 45; *see also* Lindsay, Mark; Paul Revere and the Raiders
Huntington's disease 68
Hüsker Dü (musical group) 203
The Hustler (film) 12; *see also* Newman, Paul
Hutchence, Michael 163; "Devil Inside" (song) 163; *see also* INXS (musical group)
Hutchins, Will 82–85; *see also Sugarfoot* (TV program)

"I Am a Rock" (song) 103; *see also* Simon & Garfunkel
"I Believe I Can Fly" (song) 193; *see also* Kelly, R.
"I Dig Rock and Roll Music" 98; *see also* Peter, Paul and Mary
I Dream of Jeannie (TV program) 151–152; Jeannie (fictitious character) 151–152; *see also* Eden, Barbara
"I Got You Babe" (song) 122; *see also* Cher; Sonny & Cher
I Love Lucy (TV program) 78; Mertz family (fictitious characters) 78; Ricardo family (fictitious characters) 78
"I Me Mine" (song) 96; *see also* The Beatles
"I Saw Her Standing There" (song) 97; *see also* The Beatles

"I Think I Love You" (song) 51; *see also* Cassidy, David
"I Wanna Dance with Somebody (Who Loves Me)" (song) 192; *see also* Houston, Whitney
"I Want to Hold Your Hand" (song) 87, 91, 94, 97; *see also* The Beatles
"I Want You Back" (song) 219; *see also* The Jackson 5; Jackson, Michael
"I Will" (song) 90, 92; *see also* The Beatles
ice skaters 193–195; *see also* Thomas, Debi
"Idiot Wind" (song) 108; *see also* Dylan, Bob
"I'm Henry the Eighth, I Am" (song) 24–25; *see also* Herman's Hermits; Noone, Peter
"I'm Looking Through You" (song) 36–37; *see also* The Beatles
"(I'm Not Your) Steppin' Stone" (song) 48; *see also* Paul Revere and the Raiders; Sex Pistols
Iman (model) 143
"The Impossible Dream" (song) 46
Impressionism 99
In Cold Blood (book and film) 99
In His Own Write (book) 85; *see also* Lennon, John
In the Context of Love (book) 63
interracial friendship 160–164
interracial kissing on television 153
Introducing... The Beatles 32–37
Invincible (album) 219; *see also* Jackson, Michael
INXS (musical group) 163; "Devil Inside" (song) 163; Hutchence, Michael 163
Ironside (TV program) 56–59; *see also* Burr, Raymond
Ironside, Robert T. (fictitious character) 56–59; *see also* Burr, Raymond
Islam, Yusuf *see* Stevens, Cat
Island of the Blue Dolphins (book) 160
Italian families 82–85

Jackson, Janet 193; *Control* (album) 193; Woods, Millicent "Penny" Gordon (fictitious character) 193; *see also Good Times* (TV program)
Jackson, Jermaine 139, 220–221; *see also* The Jackson 5
Jackson, Marlon 220–221; *see also* The Jackson 5
Jackson, Michael 140–141, 143, 160–165, 177, 186–191, 193, 219–222; "Beat It" (song) 161; "Ben" (song) 188; "Billie Jean" (song) 161, 186; burn injuries (1984) 188; child abuse accusations 163–164; "Dancing Machine" (song) 220: death 222; Gator

Bowl concert, Jacksonville, Florida (1984) 187; "I Want You Back" (song) 219; *Invincible* (album) 219; "Jam" (song) 220; marriage to Debbie Rowe 163–164; marriage to Lisa Marie Presley 163–164; "Man in the Mirror" (song) 190; Neverland Ranch 163, 222; *Off the Wall* (album) 187–188; plastic surgery 163–164, 221–222; "PYT: Pretty Young Thing" (song) 161; scarecrow in *The Wiz* 221; "She's Out of My Life" (song) 188; "Smooth Criminal" (song) 190; *Soul Train* appearance 220–221; *Thriller* (album) 161, 186–190; Victory Tour (1984) 187; *see also* The Jackson 5

Jackson, Randy 220–221; *see also* The Jackson 5

Jackson, Tito 140, 220–221; *see also* The Jackson 5

The Jackson 5 (musical group) 140–141, 143, 186–191, 219–222; "I Want You Back" (song) 219

The Jackson 5ive (TV program) 140–141

"Jam" (song) 220; *see also* Jackson, Michael

Jamaican immigrants 186

Jane Eyre (book) 57

Japanese animation 214–218

Jeannie (fictitious character) 151–152; *see also* Eden, Barbara; *I Dream of Jeannie* (TV program)

Jehovah's Witnesses 174, 187

Jerk (dance) 16

Jesus 82–85, 214–218

Jet (magazine) 139, 141, 194

The Jetsons (TV program) 78

Jett, Joan: "Just Like Me" (song) 48

Jewish families 65–70

"Jezebel" (song) 27; *see also* Herman's Hermits; Noone, Peter

The Jimmy Dean Show 20; *see also* Dean, Jimmy

Joad, Tom (fictitious character) 66

Joel, Billy: marriage to Christie Brinkley 162

Johns, Sammy: "Chevy Van" (song) 182

Johnson, Lyndon B. 126

Jones, Davy 2–3, 38–44, 45, 48, 61, 79; Artful Dodger (fictitious character) 43; Broadway career 43; "Daydream Believer" (song) 3, 42, 44; death 42–44, 48; Fort Myers, Florida concert 40–42; "Valleri" (song) 42; *see also* The Monkees

Jones, Grace 143

Jones, Indiana (fictitious character) 174

Jones, Quincy: marriage to Peggy Lipton 153

Joplin, Janis 126–132; *Cheap Thrills* (album) 127–128; "Cry Baby" (song) 127; death 130–132;

Harvard Stadium concert, Cambridge, Mass. (1970) 130; "Me and Bobby McGee" (song) 127; "Mercedes Benz" (song) 127, 130; Monterey Pop Festival (1967) 126; *Pearl* (album) 128; "Piece of My Heart" (song) 128–130; postage stamp 131–132; "Summertime" (song) 128, 130; "Try (Just a Little Bit Harder)" (song) 130

The Jordanaires (musical group) 6

"The Jungle Line" (song) 115; *see also* Mitchell, Joni

"Just a Touch" (song) 205; *see also* R.E.M. (musical group); Stipe, Michael

"Just Like a Woman" (song) 108; *see also* Dylan, Bob

"Just Like Me" (song) 48; *see also* Lindsay, Mark; Paul Revere and the Raiders

Kahrs, Lee J. 183–185, 224

Kangaroo, Captain (fictitious character) 77

Kastelein, Kate 166–169, 224

Kelly, R. 193; "I Believe I Can Fly" (song) 193

Kennedy, Edward M. 67

Kennedy, Edward M., Jr. 67

Kennedy, John F. 16–17, 20, 22, 24; assassination 16–17, 20

Kennedy, Robert F. 127; assassination 127

Kent State Shootings, Kent, Ohio (1970) 104, 151

"Kicks" (song) 45; *see also* Lindsay, Mark; Paul Revere and the Raiders

Kildare, James (fictitious character) 71–74, 78; *see also* Chamberlain, Richard; *Dr. Kildare* (TV program)

Kimble, Richard (fictitious character) 79; *see also* The Fugitive (TV program)

King, Martin Luther, Jr. 16, 20, 127; assassination 16, 20, 127

Kline, Lisa Williams 145–149, 224

Knievel, Evel 209

Korbut, Olga 143

Krishna 94

Ku Klux Klan 66

Kuryakin, Illya (fictitious character) 79, 145–149; *see also* The Man from U.N.C.L.E. (TV program); McCallum, David

The L Word (TV program) 185; *see also* Beals, Jennifer

L.A. Confidential (film) 62; *see also* Crowe, Russell

"La La La (If I Had You)" (song) 50; *see also* Sherman, Bobby

Ladies of the Canyon (album) 111–113; *see also* Mitchell, Joni

Lady Sings the Blues (film) 143; *see also* Holliday, Billie; Ross, Diana

Lassie (TV program) 79, 86

The Last Picture Show (film) 151

"The Last Time I Saw Richard" (song) 113–114; *see also* Mitchell, Joni

Late Night with David Letterman (TV program) 202–203

Laughton, Charles 5–7

Lauper, Cyndi 163

Laverne & Shirley (TV program) 183

Lawrence, D.H. 115

Lawrence, Leslie 126–132

The Lawrence Welk Show 7

Leave It to Beaver (TV program) 79; Cleaver, Wally 79; Rutherford, Lumpy 79

Le Bon, Simon 171; *see also* Duran Duran

Leckenby, Derek 29; *see also* Herman's Hermits

Led Zeppelin 39, 47

Leia, Princess (fictitious character) *see* Organa, Leia (fictitious character)

Leitch, Donovan *see* Donovan

Lennon, John 2, 33, 36, 43–44, 85, 86–89, 90–92, 93, 99, 119; *Abbey Road* (album) 88, 100; "All My Loving" (song) 36–37, 87; arrival in US (1964) 16, 22; "Ask Me Why" (song) 32; *Backbeat* (film) 91; *The Beatles* (album) (also known as The White Album) 88, 90, 92, 94, 100; death 43–44; "Do You Want to Know a Secret" (song) 34; *Double Fantasy* (album) 88; *Ed Sullivan Show* appearance (1964) 22, 34–35, 126; "Eight Days a Week" (song) 90–91; "Eleanor Rigby" (song) 99; "Getting Better" (song) 88; "Happiness Is a Warm Gun" (song) 88; *A Hard Day's Night* (film) 35, 85, 87, 93; *Help!* (album) 88, 91; "Hey Jude" (song) 90; "I Me Mine" (song) 96; "I Saw Her Standing There" (song) 97; "I Want to Hold Your Hand" (song) 87, 91, 94, 97; "I Will" (song) 90, 92; "I'm Looking Through You" (song) 36–37; *In His Own Write* (book) 85; International Amphitheatre concert, Chicago, Illinois (1964) 93–94; *Introducing... The Beatles* (album) 32–37; "Love Me Do" (song) 91; "Lucy in the Sky with Diamonds" (song) 99; *Magical Mystery Tour* (album) 88; marriage to Yoko Ono 44, 88; *Meet the Beatles!* (album) 35, 87, 97; "Michelle" (song) 32, 92, 99; *1* (album) 91; "Penny Lane" (song) 90; "Please Mr. Postman" (song) 87; "Please Please Me" (song) 32; "P.S. I Love You" (song) 32–37, 91; *Revolver* (album) 92; *Rubber Soul* (album) 88, 99; *Sgt.*

Pepper's Lonely Hearts Club Band (album) 88, 90, 92, 99, 127; "She Loves You (Yeah, Yeah, Yeah)" (song) 126; Shea Stadium concert (1965) 35–36, 98; "Strawberry Fields Forever" (song) 90; "Till There Was You" (song) 87; "We Can Work It Out" (song) 36; White Sox Park concert, Chicago, Illinois (1965) 94; *Yellow Submarine* (album) 92; "Yesterday" (song) 91–92; "You've Got to Hide Your Love Away" (song) 91; *see also* The Beatles; Harrison, George; McCartney, Paul; Starr, Ringo

Leonne, Marianne 82–85, 225

lesbianism 74–76, 122–125, 183–185

"Let's Call the Whole Thing Off" (song) 128

Letterman, David 122, 202–203

Lewis, C.S. 112

Lewis, Jerry Lee 126; "Great Balls of Fire" (song) 126

Life (magazine) 139

Lifes Rich Pageant (album) 204–205; *see also* R.E.M. (musical group); Stipe, Michael

"Like a Rolling Stone" (song) 107, 109; *see also* Dylan, Bob

"Like a Virgin" (song) 122; *see also* Madonna

Lilley, Susan 86–89, 225

Lindsay, Mark 45–49; "Him or Me—What's It Gonna Be?" 45; "Hungry" 45; "(I'm Not Your) Steppin' Stone" 48; "Just Like Me" 48; "Kicks" 45; Pink Puzz (pseudonym for Paul Revere and the Raiders) 47; *see also* Paul Revere and the Raiders

Lipton, Peggy 3, 150–154; Barnes, Julie (fictitious character) 150–154; marriage to Quincy Jones 153; *see also* The Mod Squad (TV program)

Liszt, Franz: "Liebesträum" 3

Little Eva: "Loco-Motion" (song) 97

Little Feat (musical group) 47

"Little Green" (song) 117; *see also* Mitchell, Joni

Live in Hull (album) 200; *see also* The Pixies (musical group)

Lloyd, John 138

Locane, Amy 166; *see also* Cry-Baby (film)

"Loco-Motion" (song) 97; *see also* Little Eva

Lolas, Al 134

"Lonesome Town" (song) 97; *see also* Nelson, Ricky

Long, Hanna (fictitious character) 183; *see also* Flashdance (film)

The Long, Hot Summer (book and film) 10–12, 15; *see also* Newman, Paul

Look (magazine) 139

Look at Me (album) 124; *see also* Cher; Sonny & Cher

Lord of the Flies (book) 146

"Losing My Religion" (song) 206; *see also* R.E.M. (musical group); Stipe, Michael

Lost in the Cosmos (book) 203

Love Child (album) 144; *see also* Ross, Diana

"Love Me Do" (song) 91; *see also* The Beatles

Love Me Tender (film) 6; *see also* Presley, Elvis

"Love Me Tender" (song) 5–6, 9, 97; *see also* Presley, Elvis

Lucas, George 155; *see also* American Graffiti (film); The Empire Strikes Back (film); Star Wars (film and film series)

"Lucy in the Sky with Diamonds" (song) 99; *see also* The Beatles

Lupino, Ida 52

Madoff, Bernie 153

Madonna (singer) 122, 163, 193, 195; "Like a Virgin" (song) 122

Magical Mystery Tour (album) 88; *see also* The Beatles

Maharishi Mahesh Yogi 94

Mahavishnu Orchestra 94

Mahogany (film) 142–144; Chambers, Tracy (fictitious character) 142–144; *see also* Ross, Diana

The Main Street Rag (magazine) 63

The Maltese Falcon (film) 52; *see also* Bogart, Humphrey

Mama Cass *see* Elliot, Cass

The Mamas & the Papas 88; *see also* Elliot, Cass; Phillips, Michelle

The Man from U.N.C.L.E. (TV program) 78–79, 145–140; Kuryakin, Illya (fictitious character) 79, 145–149; McCallum, David 145–149; Solo, Napoleon (fictitious character) 78–79, 145–149; T.H.R.U.S.H. (Technological Hierarchy for the Removal of Undesirables and the Subjugation of Humanity) 145–149; U.N.C.L.E. (United Network Command for Law and Enforcement 145–149

"Man in the Mirror" (song) 190; *see also* Jackson, Michael

Man of La Mancha (play and film) 46–47

Mancini, Henry 203

Manilow, Barry 47, 174–177; *Barry Manilow Live in Concert* (video recording) 174; *Dick Clark's New Year's Rockin' Eve* (TV program) appearances 175; homosexuality 175; "Weekend in New England" (song) 175

March on Washington for Jobs and Freedom (1963) 16, 20

March Street Press 63

Marie, Ann (fictitious character) 150–152; *see also* That Girl (TV program)

marital violence 168–169

Markham, Martin "Marty" (fictitious character) 83; *see also* Spin and Marty (TV program)

Marsh, Dave (rock critic): *The Beatles' Second Album* (book) 87

Martin, Dean 27; *see also* The Dean Martin Show

Martin, Timmy (fictitious character) 79; *see also* Lassie (TV program)

Mary, Blessed Virgin, Saint 82–83

Mary Poppins (film) 80–81; Banks, George (fictitious character) 80; Bert (fictitious character) 80–81

Mary Sue (stereotypically idealized fictitious character) 214–218

The Mary Tyler Moore Show 150–152; Baxter, Ted (fictitious character) 152; Grant, Lou (fictitious character) 151; Richards, Mary (fictitious character) 150–152; *see also* Moore, Mary Tyler

Mashed Potato (dance) 16, 18

Mason, Perry (fictitious character) 56–59; *see also* Burr, Raymond

McCallum, David 145–149; Kuryakin, Illya (fictitious character) 79, 145–149; *see also* The Man from U.N.C.L.E.

McCallum, Shara 186–191, 225

McCarthy, Caitlin 170–173, 225

McCartney, Paul 2, 32–37, 87–88, 90–92, 93, 99; *Abbey Road* (album) 88, 100; "All My Loving" (song) 36–37, 87; arrival in US (1964) 16, 22; "Ask Me Why" (song) 32; *Backbeat* (documentary) 91; *The Beatles* (album) (also known as The White Album) 88, 90, 92, 94, 100; "Do You Want to Know a Secret" (song) 34; *Ed Sullivan Show* appearance (1964) 22, 32–37, 86–87, 126; "Eight Days a Week" (song) 90–91; "Eleanor Rigby" (song) 99; engagement to Jane Asher 36–37, 90; Fenway Park concert 35, 37; "Getting Better" (song) 88; "Happiness Is a Warm Gun" (song) 88; *A Hard Day's Night* (film) 35, 87, 93; *Help!* (album) 88, 91; "Hey Jude" (song) 90; "I Me Mine" (song) 96; "I Saw Her Standing There" (song) 97; "I Want to Hold Your Hand" (song) 87, 91, 94, 97; "I Will" (song) 90, 92; "I'm Looking Through You" (song) 36–37; International Amphitheatre concert, Chicago, Illinois, 1964 93–94; *Introducing... The Beatles* (album) 32–37; "Love Me Do" (song) 91; "Lucy in the Sky with Diamonds" (song) 99; *Magical Mystery Tour* (album) 88; *Meet*

the Beatles! (album) 35, 87, 97; "Michelle" (song) 32, 92, 99; *I* (album) 91; "Penny Lane" (song) 90; "Please Mr. Postman" (song) 87; "Please Please Me" (song) 32; "P.S. I Love You" (song) 32–37, 91; *Ram* (album) 88; *Revolver* (album) 92; *Rubber Soul* (album) 88, 99; *Sgt. Pepper's Lonely Hearts Club Band* (album) 88, 90, 92, 99, 127; "She Loves You (Yeah, Yeah, Yeah)" (song) 126; Shea Stadium concert (1965) 35–36, 98; "Strawberry Fields Forever" (song) 90; "Till There Was You" (song) 87; "We Can Work It Out" (song) 36; White Sox Park concert, Chicago, Illinois (1965) 94; *Yellow Submarine* (album) 92; "Yesterday" (song) 91–92; "You've Got to Hide Your Love Away" (song) 91; *see also* The Beatles; Harrison, George; Lennon, John; Starr, Ringo
McCorkle, Jill 3, 77–81, 225
McEnroe, John 137
McNair, Carol Denise 20, 22–23; *see also* 16th Street Baptist Church Bombing, Birmingham, Alabama (1963)
McNichol, Kristy 185
"Me and Bobby McGee" (song) 127; *see also* Joplin, Janis
Meet the Beatles! (album) 35, 87, 97; *see also* The Beatles
Melanie (singer) 182; "Brand New Key" (song) 182
"Mercedes Benz" (song) 127, 130; *see also* Joplin, Janis
Mercury, Freddie 20
Mertz family (fictitious characters) 78; *see also I Love Lucy* (TV program)
The Merv Griffin Show 20; *see also* Griffin, Merv
"Michael, Row the Boat Ashore" (song) 46
"Michelle" (song) 32, 92, 99; *see also* The Beatles; Harrison, George; Lennon, John; McCartney, Paul; Starr, Ringo
The Mickey Mouse Club (TV program) 83
Midler, Bette (singer) 47, 131
A Midsummer Night's Dream (play) 209
The Mike Douglas Show 20; *see also* Douglas, Mike
Mill, Andy: marriage to Chris Evert 138
Millennium Falcon (fictitious spaceship) 155, 159; *see also Star Wars* (film and film series)
Miller, Dennis 31
Mingus, Charles 116
Miracle Legion (musical group) 204
Miss America, first African-

American (1987) 193, 195; *see also* Williams, Vanessa
"Mr. Tambourine Man" (song) 127; *see also* Dylan, Bob
Mitchell, Joni 39, 47, 99, 111–118, 176; *Blue* (album) 113; "Boho Dance" (song) 115–116; "Both Sides Now" (song) 117; "California" (song); "A Case of You" (song) 118; "The Circle Game" (song) 117; *Clouds* (album) 112; daughter 117; "The Dawn Treader" (song) 112; "Edith and the Kingpin" (song) 115; "For Free" (song) 118; *The Hissing of Summer Lawns* (album) 114; "The Jungle Line" (song) 115; *Ladies of the Canyon* (album) 111–113; "The Last Time I Saw Richard" (song) 113–114; "Little Green" (song) 117; Mingus, Charles, collaboration 116; "Sisotowbell Lane" (song) 112, 116; *Song to a Seagull* (album) 111–112; stroke 111
The Mod Squad (TV program) 150–154; Barnes, Julie (fictitious character) 150–154; Cochran, Pete (fictitious character) 150–154; Hayes, Lincoln "Linc" (fictitious character) 150–154; *see also* Lipton, Peggy
Monahan, D. Leo 133
The Monkees 3, 26, 38–44, 45, 48, 98, 219; "Daydream Believer" (song) 3, 42, 44; "Valleri" (song) 42; *see also* Dolenz, Mickey; Jones, Davy; Nesmith, Michael; Tork, Peter
Monkey (dance) 16
Monster (album) 207; *see also* R.E.M. (musical group); Stipe, Michael
Montgomery Bus Boycott, Montgomery, Alabama (1955–1956) 16
Moon, Keith 119
"Moonshadow" (song) 120–121; *see also* Stevens, Cat
Moonwalk (dance) 186, 220; *see also* Jackson, Michael
Moore, Mary Tyler 77–81, 150–152; Petrie, Laura (fictitious character), 77–81; Richards, Mary (fictitious character) 150–152; *see also The Dick Van Dyke Show; The Mary Tyler Moore Show;* Van Dyke, Dick
Moreno, Rita 84–85; Anita (fictitious character) 84–85; *see also West Side Story* (film)
Morgan v. Virginia (1946) 16
Morrison, Jim (rock star) 61–64
mothers and daughters 90–92, 139–144, 174–178
Motown 98
Mottola, Tommy 220
Mourning Becomes Electra (play) 85; *see also* O'Neill, Eugene
"Mrs. Brown, You've Got a Lovely

Daughter" (song) 24, 26, 31; *see also* Herman's Hermits; Noone, Peter
MTV Networks 38, 41
multiple sclerosis 58–59
multiracial families *see* racially mixed families
Murray, Arthur 20; *see also The Arthur Murray Party* (TV program)
The Music Man (musical comedy) 87; "Till There Was You" (song) 87
"My Guy" (song) 87; *see also* Wells, Mary
My Side of the Mountain (book) 160
My Three Sons (TV program) 79; Douglas, Chip (fictitious character) 79; Douglas, Ernie (fictitious character) 79; Douglas, Robbie (fictitious character) 79

Nancy (fictitious character from *Oliver Twist* and *Oliver!*) 60–64
Naruto shippūden (Japanese TV program) 214–218; Hokage (fictitious character) 214–218; Sabaku no Gaara (fictitious character) 214–218; Spider Man (fictitious character) 214–218
Nash, Gela: marriage to John Taylor of Duran Duran 171; *see also* Taylor, John
Nash, Graham 113
Native Son (book) 40
Navratilova, Martina 137–138
Nelson, Ricky: "Lonesome Town" 97
Nesmith, Michael 44; *see also* The Monkees
Neverland Ranch 163; *see also* Jackson, Michael
"The New Girl at School" 50; *see also* Sherman, Bobby
Newman, Lesléa 122–125, 225
Newman, Paul 10–15; Academy Award 14; *The Adventures of a Young Man* (film) 12; cancer 15; *Cat on a Hot Tin Roof* (film) 12; *The Color of Money* (film) 14; *Cool Hand Luke* (film) 14; death 15; *Exodus* (film) 12; *From the Terrace* (film) 12; *Hud* (film) 12; *The Hustler* (film) 12; *The Long, Hot Summer* (film) 10–12, 15; marriage to Joanne Woodward, 10–12, 15; *Paris Blues* (film) 12; *Sweet Bird of Youth* (film) 12; *The Verdict* (film) 14; *The Young Philadelphians* (film) 12
"Nightswimming" (song) 206; *see also* R.E.M. (musical group); Stipe, Michael
Nine Inch Nails (musical group) 206
1984 (book) 146–148
ninja 214–218
Nirvana (musical group) 206

Nobles, Gene 5, 9
Noone, Peter 1, 2–4, 24–31, 79; "I'm Henry the Eighth, I Am" (song) 24–25; "Jezebel" (song) 27; "Mrs. Brown, You've Got a Lovely Daughter" (song) 24, 26, 31; *On the Road* (album) 25; *Pirates of Penzance* (operetta) 24; "Rattler" (song) 27; *There's a Kind of Hush All Over the World* (album) 27; "There's a Kind of Hush All Over the World" (song) 24–25, 29–30; *see also* Herman's Hermits
Nouri, Michael 183; *see also Flashdance* (film)

Oates, Joyce Carol 137
Off the Wall (album) 187–188
The O'Jays (musical group) 221
Oliver! (Broadway musical and film) 43, 60–64; *see also* Artful Dodger (fictitious character); Reed, Oliver; Sikes, Bill (fictitious character)
Oliver Twist (book) 60–64
Olympics (Winter, 1988) 193–195
On the Road (album) 25; *see also* Noone, Peter
1 (album) 91; *see also* The Beatles
"One of Us Must Know" (song) 108; *see also* Dylan, Bob
O'Neil, Eugene: *Mourning Becomes Electra* 85
"Only Sixteen" (song) 18; *see also* Cooke, Sam
Ono, Yoko 44, 88; *Double Fantasy* (album) 88; marriage to John Lennon, 44, 88; *see also* The Beatles; Lennon, John
Organa, Leia (fictitious character) (also known as Princess Leia) 155–156; *see also Star Wars* (film and film series)
The Orlons (musical group): "Wah-Watusi" (song) 97
Orr, Bobby 3, 133–134
Orr on Ice (book) 134
Osho (also known as Rajneesh) 94
Our Lady of Fatima *see* Fatima, Our Lady of
OutKast (musical group) 222
Owens, Alexandra "Alex" (fictitious character) 183–185; *see also* Beals, Jennifer; *Flashdance* (film)

Page, Patti: "Tennessee Waltz" (song) 19
Palahniuk, Chuck: *Fight Club* (book) 200
Palmer Panthers (hockey team) 135
Paper Gods (album) 172; *see also* Duran Duran, Taylor, John
Paradis, Vanessa: relationship with Johnny Depp 168
Paris Blues (film) 12; *see also* Newman, Paul

Parks, Rosa 16
Parton, Dolly 116; *Trio* (album) 116
"The Patsy" (television play) 20
Paul Revere and the Raiders 26, 45–49; "Him or Me—What's It Gonna Be?" (song) 45; "Hungry" (song) 45; "(I'm Not Your) Steppin' Stone" (song) 48; "Just Like Me" (song) 48; "Kicks" (song) 45; Pink Puzz (pseudonym) 47; *see also* Lindsay, Mark; Revere, Paul
"Peace Train" (song) 121; *see also* Stevens, Cat
Pearl (album) 128; *see also* Joplin, Janis
"Penny Lane" (song) 90; *see also* The Beatles
Penthouse (magazine) 195
People (magazine) 15
Pepé Le Pew (cartoon character) 168
Percy, Walker: *Lost in the Cosmos* (book) 203
Perkins-Valdez, Dolen 192–197, 225
Perry Mason (TV program) 56–59; "The Case of the Ugly Duckling" 56; *see also* Burr, Raymond
Persian Gulf War (1991) 39, 201
Peter Pan syndrome 156, 164
Peter, Paul and Mary 97–98; "I Dig Rock and Roll Music" 98; *see also* Travers, Mary
Petrie, Laura (fictitious character) 77–81; *see also The Dick Van Dyke Show*; Moore, Mary Tyler
Petrie, Richie (fictitious character) 77–81; *see also The Dick Van Dyke Show*
Petrie, Rob (fictitious character) 77–81; *see also The Dick Van Dyke Show*; Van Dyke, Dick
Phillips, Michelle 88; *see also* The Mamas & the Papas
"Piece of My Heart" (song) 128–129, 130; *see also* Joplin, Janis
Pietrzyk, Leslie 154–159, 225
Pink Floyd 39
Pink Puzz (pseudonym for Paul Revere and the Raiders) 47
Pirates of Penzance (operetta) 24
Pirates of the Caribbean (film and film series) 168; Sparrow, Jack (fictitious character) 168; *see also* Depp, Johnny
Pitney, Gene 72, 75
Pittsburgh Penguins (hockey team) 134–135
The Pixies (musical group) 196–201; *Bossanova* (album) 198–200; *Come On Pilgrim* (album) 200; "Dig for Fire" (song) 198–199; *Fight Club* (film) 198, 200; "Hang On to Your Ego" (song) 200; *Live in Hull* (album) 200; *Surfer Rosa* (album) 200; *Trompe le Monde* (album) 200;

"Where Is My Mind?" (song) 198, 200; *see also* Black, Frank; Deal, Kim
Plasic, Richie (fictitious character) 184; *see also Flashdance* (film)
"Please Mr. Postman" (song) 87; *see also* The Beatles
"Please Please Me" (song) 32; *see also* The Beatles
pogroms—Russia 148–149
Ponderosa Ranch (fictional location) 78; *see also Bonanza* (TV program)
Pony (dance) 16, 18
Poppins, Mary (fictitious character) 80–81; *see also Mary Poppins* (film)
Porgy and Bess (opera) 128
Presley, Elvis 2–3, 5–9, 20, 24, 27, 29, 43–44, 79, 97, 126, 189; Charlotte (North Carolina) Coliseum concert 7–8; death 8–9, 24, 43; "Don't Be Cruel" (song) 6, 9; *Ed Sullivan Show* appearance 5–7; *The Elvis Presley Album of Juke Box Favorites* (sheet music) 8; "Heartbreak Hotel" (song) 9; "Hound Dog" (song) 6, 126; *Love Me Tender* (film) 6; "Love Me Tender" (song) 5–6, 9, 97; marriage to Priscilla Beaulieu Presley 29; "Ready Teddy" (song) 6; "Take My Hand, Precious Lord" (song) 9
Presley, Lisa Marie 163–164; marriage to Michael Jackson 163–164
Presley, Priscilla Beaulieu 29; *see also* Presley, Elvis
Pretty Woman (film) 166
Prince (singer) 77
Princess Leia (fictitious character) *see* Organa, Leia (fictitious character)
"P.S. I Love You" (song) 32–37, 91; *see also* The Beatles
puberty 10–11, 16–23, 139–144; *see also* adolescence
Pyle, Gomer (fictitious character) 79; *see also Gomer Pyle, U.S.M.C.*
Pyle, Goober (fictitious character) 79; *see also The Andy Griffith Show*
"PYT: Pretty Young Thing" (song) 161; *see also* Jackson, Michael

Queen (musical group) 48; "Under Pressure" 48
The Quick and the Dead (film) 62; *see also* Crowe, Russell

Race relations 5–9, 16–23, 99, 153, 160–164
Racially mixed families 219–222
"Radio Free Europe" (song and music video) 202–203; *see also* R.E.M.; Stipe, Michael

"Ragtime Cowboy Joe" (song) 6
Rajneesh *see* Osho
Ram (album) 88; *see also* McCartney, Paul
Ramone, Joey: death 43
Ramsey, Tootie (fictitious character) 193–194; *see also The Facts of Life* (TV program); Fields, Kim
Random Access Memories (album) 88–89; *see also* Daft Punk
"Rattler" (song) 27; *see also* Herman's Hermits; Noone, Peter
"Ready Teddy" 6; *see also* Presley, Elvis
Reagan, Ronald 51, 203
Reckoning (album) 203; *see also* R.E.M. (musical group); Stipe, Michael
Red Hot Chili Peppers (musical group) 206, 222
Redding, Otis: death 16, 20
Reed, Oliver 60–64
refugees: Cuba 148–149; Russia 148–149
relocation 160–164
R.E.M. (musical group) 40, 202–207; *Automatic for the People* (album) 206; "Begin the Begin" (song) 205; *Chronic Town* (album) 202; *Document* (album) 205; "Everybody Hurts" (song) 206; *Fables of the Reconstruction* (album) 203–204; "Fall on Me" (song) 205; *Green* (album) 206; "Just a Touch" (song) 205; *Late Night with David Letterman* appearance 202–203; *Lifes Rich Pageant* (album) 204; "Losing My Religion" (song) 206; *Monster* (album) 207; *Murmur* (album) 202–203; "Nightswimming" (song) 206; *Out of Time* (album) 206; "Radio Free Europe" (song and music video) 202–203; *Reckoning* (album) 202 "West of the Fields" (song) 202; *see also* Buck, Pete; Stipe, Michael
Remick, Lee 10–12
Revere, Paul (pop star) 45–48; death 48; "Him or Me—What's It Gonna Be?" (song) 45; "Hungry" (song) 45; "(I'm Not Your) Steppin' Stone" (song) 48; "Just Like Me" (song) 48; "Kicks" (song) 45; Pink Puzz (pseudonym for Paul Revere and the Raiders); *see also* Paul Revere and the Raiders
Revolver (album) 92; *see also* The Beatles
Rhodes, Nick 170; *see also* Duran Duran
rhythm and blues music 16–23
Ricardo family (fictitious characters) 78; *see also I Love Lucy* (TV program)
Richards, Keith 168; *see also* The Rolling Stones

Richards, Mary (fictitious character) 150–152; *see also The Mary Tyler Moore Show;* Moore, Mary Tyler
Ricks, Sandy (fictitious character) 79; *see also Flipper* (TV program)
Ride, Sally 183
"Rio" (song and music video) 171; *see also* Duran Duran; Taylor, John
Rivers, Johnny 24
Robertson, Carole 20, 22–23; *see also* 16th Street Baptist Church Bombing, Birmingham, Alabama (1963)
Robot (dance) 220
Rochester, Edward (fictitious character) 57
Rogers, Amy 45–49, 225
Rogers, Morgan Callan 119–121, 225
Rogers, Sally (fictitious character) 77–78; *see also The Dick Van Dyke Show*
role models, African-American 192–197
Rolling Stone (magazine) 2, 119
The Rolling Stones (musical group) 26, 41, 127, 168; *see also* Richards, Keith
Romper Stomper (film) 62; *see also* Crowe, Russell
Ronstadt, Linda: *Trio* (album) 116
Ross, Diana 3, 88, 128, 139–144; Chambers, Tracy (fictitious character) 142–144; *Diana* (album) 143; *Diana Ross Presents the Jackson 5* (album) 140; Gale, Dorothy (fictitious character) 221; Holliday, Billie 143; *Lady Sings the Blues* (film) 143; *Love Child* (album) 144; *Mahogany* (film) 142–144; *The Wiz* (film)
Roth, Philip 51
Rowe, Debbie: marriage to Michael Jackson 163–164
Royal Crown Hair Dressing 5, 9
Rubber Soul (album) 88, 99; *see also* The Beatles
Russell, Kurt 79
Rutherford, Lumpy (fictitious character) 79; *see also Leave It to Beaver* (TV program)
Ryan, Hank Phillippi 102–106, 225
Ryder, Winona 167; Boggs, Kim (fictitious character) 167; relationship and breakup with Johnny Depp; *see also Edward Scissorhands* (film)

Sabaku no Gaara (fictitious character) 214–218
St. John's Wood (London, England) 36
Sanderson, Derek 133
The Sandpipers (musical group) 104; "Guantanamera" (song) 104
Sanford, Mark: affair 164

Santana, Carlos (musician) 94
Sartre, Jean-Paul 114
Satchidananda, Swami 94
The Scarecrow of Romney Marsh (TV program) 86
Schafer, Natalie 150; Howell, "Lovey" Wentworth (fictitious character) 150; *see also Gilligan's Island* (TV program)
Schwarzenegger, Arnold 166; *see also Terminator* (film)
Scissorhands, Edward (fictional character) 167; *see also* Depp, Johnny; *Edward Scissorhands* (film)
Searle, Elizabeth 2–4, 50–55, 226
Seeger, Pete 68
segregation 151
Selma (film) 20; *see also* Duvernay, Ava
Sergeant Pepper's Lonely Hearts Club Band see Sgt. Pepper's Lonely Hearts Club Band
Seven and the Ragged Tiger (album) 170; *see also* Duran Duran
Seventeen (magazine) 193
Sex Pistols 48; "(I'm Not Your) Steppin' Stone" (song) 48
Sexton, Anne 94
Sgt. Pepper's Lonely Hearts Club Band (album) 88, 90, 92, 99, 127; *see also* The Beatles
"Shake" (song) 19; *see also* Cooke, Sam
Shalamar (musical group) 193; *see also* Watley, Jodi
Shankar, Ravi 94, 127
Shapiro, B.A. 32–36, 226
Shapiro, Susan 3, 107–110, 226
Sharpton, Al 220
Shattered Love (book) 76; *see also* Chamberlain, Richard
"Sh-Boom" (song) 5; *see also* The Chords (musical group); The Crew-Cuts (musical group)
"She Loves You (Yeah, Yeah, Yeah)" (song) 126; *see also* The Beatles; Harrison, George; Lennon, John; McCartney, Paul; Starr, Ringo
Shea, Tommy 135
Sherman, Bobby 1, 45, 48, 50–55, 61, 79; cereal-box records 50–51; "Easy Come, Easy Go" (song) 50; emergency medical services career 54–55; "Hey, Mister Sun" (song) 50; "La La La (If I Had You)" (song) 50; "The New Girl at School" (song) 50
"She's Out of My Life" (song) 188; *see also* Jackson, Michael
Shindig! (TV program) 88
Shore, Eddie 133
Sienkiewicz, Linda K. 60–64, 226
Sikes, Bill (fictitious character) 60–64; *see also Oliver!* (film); *Oliver Twist* (book)
Simon, Carly 120

Simon, Paul 39, 102–106; Clowes Memorial Hall concert, Indianapolis, Indiana (1967) 104; "Homeward Bound" (song) 104, 106; "I Am a Rock" (song) 103; marriage and divorce 105; *Sounds of Silence* (album) 103; writing process 105–106; *see also* Garfunkel, Art; Simon & Garfunkel

Simon & Garfunkel 39, 102–106; Clowes Memorial Hall concert, Indianapolis, Indiana (1967) 104; "Homeward Bound" (song) 104, 106; "I Am a Rock" (song) 103; *Sounds of Silence* (album) 103; *see also* Garfunkel, Art; Simon, Paul

Simpson, O.J. 39
The Simpsons (TV program) 51
Sinatra, Frank 3, 104
single mothers 174–178
"Sisotowbell Lane" (song) 112, 116; *see also* Mitchell, Joni
Sister Bertrille (fictitious character) *see* Bertrille, Sister
sisters 65–70
16 Magazine 26, 46
16th Street Baptist Church Bombing, Birmingham, Alabama (1963) 16, 20, 22–23; *see also* Collins, Addie Mae; McNair, Carol Denise; Robertson, Carole; Wesley, Cynthia
Skywalker, Luke (fictitious character) 155–156; *see also Star Wars* (film and film series)
Sloop (dance) 16, 18
Slop (dance) 16
Slow Drag (dance) 16, 18
Smith, Bessie 128
Smith, Patti 203; *Easter* (album) 203; *Wave* (album) 203
The Smiths (musical group) 198; *Strangeways, Here We Come* (album) 198
"Smooth Criminal" (song) 190
social action 65–70
social justice 65–70
Socialism 65–70
Solo, Han (fictitious character) 154–159; Ford, Harrison 154–159; *see also Star Wars* (film and film series)
Solo, Napoleon (fictitious character) 78–79, 145–149; *see also The Man from U.N.C.L.E.*
Son Volt (musical group) 207
Song to a Seagull (album) 111–112; *see also* Mitchell, Joni
Sonny & Cher 122–124; *Look at Me* (album) 124; *see also* Bono, Sonny; Cher
Sorrell, Maurice "Buddy" (fictitious character) 77–78; *see also The Dick Van Dyke Show*
Soucy, Michelle 38–44, 226
Soul Stirrers (musical group) 22
Soul Train (TV program) 140, 220

The Sound of Music (film) 183
Sounds of Silence (album) 103; *see also* Simon & Garfunkel
Spade, Sam (fictitious character) 52; *see also* Bogart, Humphrey
Sparrow, Jack (fictitious character) 168; *see also* Depp, Johnny; *Pirates of the Caribbean* (film and film series)
Spelling, Aaron 153
spies 145–149
Spin and Marty (TV program) 83; Evans, Spin (fictitious character) 83; Markham, Martin "Marty" (fictitious character) 83
The Spinners (musical group) 221
"Splish Splash" (song) 126
spousal abuse 168–169
Springfield Daily News 135
Springfield [Mass.] Indians (hockey team) 133
Star Trek: interracial kissing 153
Star Wars (film and film series) 154–159; *The Empire Strikes Back* (film) 154–159; *Millennium Falcon* (fictitious spaceship) 155, 159; Organa, Leia (fictitious character) (also known as Princess Leia) 155–156; Skywalker, Luke (fictitious character) 155; Solo, Han (fictitious character) 154–159; Vader, Darth (fictitious character) 155; Yoda (fictitious character) 156; *see also* Ford, Harrison; Hamill, Mark; Lucas, George
Stardust, Ziggy *see* Bowie, David
Starr, Ringo 33, 36, 86–87, 90, 93, 97–101, 119; *Abbey Road* (album) 88, 100; "All My Loving" (song) 36–37, 87; arrival in US (1964) 16, 22; "Ask Me Why" (song) 32; *Backbeat* (film) 91; *The Beatles* (album) (also known as The White Album) 88, 90, 92, 94, 100; "Do You Want to Know a Secret" (song) 34; *Ed Sullivan Show* appearance (1964) 22, 34–35, 86–87, 126; "Eight Days a Week" (song) 90–91; "Eleanor Rigby" (song) 99; "Getting Better" (song) 88; "Happiness Is a Warm Gun" (song) 88; *A Hard Day's Night* (film) 35, 87, 93; *Help!* (album) 88, 91; "Hey Jude" (song) 90; "I Me Mine" (song) 96; "I Saw Her Standing There" (song) 97; "I Want to Hold Your Hand" (song) 87, 91, 94, 97; "I Will" (song) 90, 92; "I'm Looking Through You" (song) 36–37; International Amphitheatre concert, Chicago, Illinois (1964) 93–94; *Introducing... The Beatles* (album) 32–37; "Love Me Do" (song) 91; "Lucy in the Sky with Diamonds" (song) 99; *Magical Mystery Tour* (album) 88; *Meet the Beatles!* (album) 35, 87, 97;

"Michelle" (song) 32, 92, 99; *1* (album) 91; "Penny Lane" (song) 90; "Please Mr. Postman" (song) 87; "Please Please Me" (song) 32; "P.S. I Love You" (song) 32–37, 91; *Revolver* (album) 92; *Rolling Stone* "100 Greatest Drummers of All Time" list 119; *Rubber Soul* (album) 88, 99; *Sgt. Pepper's Lonely Hearts Club Band* (album) 88, 90, 92, 99, 127; "She Loves You (Yeah, Yeah, Yeah)" (song) 126; Shea Stadium concert (1965) 35–36, 98; "Strawberry Fields Forever" (song) 90; "Till There Was You" (song) 87; "We Can Work It Out" (song) 36; White Sox Park concert, Chicago, Illinois (1965) 94; *Yellow Submarine* (album) 92; "Yesterday" (song) 91–92; "You've Got to Hide Your Love Away" (song) 91; *see also* The Beatles; Harrison, George; Lennon, John; McCartney, Paul
Stephens, Samantha (fictitious character) 151–152; *see also Bewitched* (TV program)
"Steppin' Stone" (song) *see* "(I'm Not Your) Steppin' Stone"
The Steve Allen Show 20; *see also* Allen, Steve
Stevens, Cat 119–121; conversion to Islam 121; detention at Bangor International Airport, Maine 121; "How Can I Tell You?" (song) 120; "Moonshadow" (song) 120–121; "Peace Train" (song) 121; relationship with Carly Simon 120
Stipe, John Michael *see* Stipe, Michael
Stipe, Michael 202–207; *Automatic for the People* (album) 206–207; "Begin the Begin" (song) 205; *Chronic Town* (album) 202; *Document* (album) 205; "Everybody Hurts" (song) 206; *Fables of the Reconstruction* (album) 203–204; "Fall on Me" (song) 205; gender identity 203–207; *Green* (album) 206; "Just a Touch" (song) 205; *Late Night with David Letterman* appearance 202–203; *Lifes Rich Pageant* (album) 204–205; "Losing My Religion" (song) 206; *Murmur* (album) 202–203; "Nightswimming" (song) 206; *Out of Time* (album) 206; "Radio Free Europe" (song and music video) 202–203; *Reckoning* (album) 203; "West of the Fields" (song) 202; *see also* R.E.M. (musical group)
Straight, Susan 219–222, 226
Strangeways, Here We Come (album) 198; *see also* The Smiths (musical group)

"Strawberry Fields Forever" (song) 90; *see also* The Beatles

Strempek Shea, Suzanne 3, 133–135, 226

"String of Pearls" (song) 57

The Stylistics (musical group) 221

Sugarfoot (TV program) 83–85; Brewster, Tom "Sugarfoot" (fictitious character) 83–85

suicidal behavior 68–69, 167

"Sukiyaki" (song) 87

Sullivan, Ed 5–7, 20, 22, 27, 34–35, 86–87, 126; *see also* The Ed Sullivan Show

Sullivan, Mary 208–212, 226

"Summertime" (song) 128, 130; *see also* Joplin, Janis

"Sunrise, Sunset" (song) 109

The Supremes 88, 139, 144; *see also* Ross, Diana

Surfer Rosa (album) 200; *see also* The Pixies (musical group)

Sutcliffe, Stuart: death 91; *see also* The Beatles

Swan, Nancy 10–15, 226

Sweet Baby James (album) 47; *see also* Taylor, James

Sweet Bird of Youth (film) 12; *see also* Newman, Paul

Swim (dance) 16

Les Sylphides (ballet) 178; *see also* Baryshnikov, Mikhail

System of a Down (musical group) 222

Szabo, Jeanie (fictitious character) 184; *see also* Flashdance (film)

"Take My Hand, Precious Lord" (song) 9; *see also* Presley, Elvis

Taliban 211

"Talking Dust Bowl Blues" (song) 70; *see also* Guthrie, Woody

Taylor, Andy (fictitious character) 78; *see also* The Andy Griffith Show; Griffith, Andy

Taylor, Darlene R. 139–144, 226

Taylor, James 8, 39, 47, 113; "Handy Man" (song) 8; *Sweet Baby James* (album) 47

Taylor, John 3, 170–173; marriage to Amanda de Cadenet 171; marriage to Gela Nash 171; Mohegan Sun concert, Uncasville, Conn. (1997) 172; *Paper Gods* (album) 172; "Rio" (song and music video) 171; *Seven and the Ragged Tiger* (album) 171; Worcester Centrum concert, 1984 170–172; Xfinity Center concert, Mansfield, Mass. (2016) 173; *see also* Duran Duran

Taylor, Opie (fictitious character) 78; *see also* The Andy Griffith Show

Teen Datebook (magazine) 4

teenage marriage 120–121

teenage pregnancy 107–110

The Temptations 177

"Tennessee Waltz" 19; *see also* Page, Patti

tennis 136–138

Terminator (film) 166; *see also* Schwarzenegger, Arnold

That Girl (TV program) 150–152; Marie, Ann (fictitious character) 150–152

"That's Where It's At" (song) 19; *see also* Cooke, Sam

There's a Kind of Hush All Over the World (album) 27; *see also* Herman's Hermits; Noone, Peter

"There's a Kind of Hush All Over the World" (song) 24–25, 29–30; *see also* Herman's Hermits; Noone, Peter

"This Land Is Your Land" (song) 46, 66, 68; *see also* Guthrie, Woody

Thomas, Bigger (fictitious character) 40

Thomas, Debi 193–195; Olympics (Winter, 1988) 195

Thompson, Hunter S. 167; *Fear and Loathing in Las Vegas* (book and film) 167; friendship with Johnny Depp 167; funeral 167; *The Great Shark Hunt* (book) 167; suicide 167

The Thorn Birds (TV program) 76; *see also* Chamberlain, Richard

Thriller (album) 161, 163, 186–190; *see also* Jackson, Michael

T.H.R.U.S.H. (Technological Hierarchy for the Removal of Undesirables and the Subjugation of Humanity) 145–149; *see also* The Man from U.N.C.L.E. (TV program)

"Tie Me Kangaroo Down, Sport" (song) 87

Tiger Beat (magazine) 3, 26, 45–46, 170

"Till There Was You" (song) 87; *see also* The Beatles

Timberlake, Justin 222

Time (magazine) 93–94

Titanic (film) 208–212; Bukater, Rose DeWitt (fictitious character) 208–212; Dawson, Jack (fictitious character) 208–212; Heart of the Ocean (fictitious jewel); *see also* DiCaprio, Leonardo

Titanic (steamship) 208–212

To Have and Have Not (film) 52; *see also* Bogart, Humphrey

To the Lighthouse 131; *see also* Woolf, Virginia

"Tom Joad" (song) 66; *see also* Guthrie, Woody

Tony (fictitious character) 85; *see also West Side Story* (film)

Tork, Peter 44; *see also* The Monkees

"Touch the Hem of His Garment" (song) 21; *see also* Cooke, Sam

Transcendental Meditation 94

Travers, Mary 97, 128; *see also* Peter, Paul, and Mary

Trio (album) 116; *see also* Harris, Emmylou; Parton, Dolly; Ronstadt, Linda

Trompe le Monde (album) 200; *see also* The Pixies (musical group)

"Try (Just a Little Bit Harder)" (song) 130; *see also* Joplin, Janis

21 Jump Street (film) 166

Twiggy 22

Twist (dance) 16, 18

"The Twist" (song) 97, 126; *see also* Checker, Chubby

Two-Step (dance) 18

Tyner, McCoy 150

U.N.C.L.E. (United Network Command for Law and Enforcement 145–149; *see also* The Man from U.N.C.L.E. (TV program)

"Undecided" 6

"Under Pressure" 48; *see also* Bowie, David; Queen

unrequited love 178–182

Urban Cowboy (film) 154

Vader, Darth (fictitious character) 155; *see also* Star Wars (film and film series)

Valentino, Rudolph 3

"Valleri" (song) 42; *see also* Jones, Davy; The Monkees

Van Dyke, Dick 3, 77–81; Bert (fictitious character) 80–81; *The Dick Van Dyke Show* 77–81; *Mary Poppins* (film) 80–81; Petrie, Rob (fictitious character) 77–81;

Vee, Bobby 4, 24

The Verdict (film) 14

Veruschka (model) 94

Vietnam War 47, 99, 127; protests 99, 127

Virgin Mary *see* Mary, Blessed Virgin, Saint

"Visions of Johanna" (song) 110; *see also* Dylan, Bob

Vogue (magazine) 94, 126

The Voyage of the Dawn Treader (book) 112

"The Wah-Watusi" (song) 97; *see also* The Orlons (musical group)

"Wake Up Little Susie" (song) 126

Wallace, Michele: myth of the black superwoman 196

Warner, Jack 51

Warner Brothers 51

Warwick, Dionne 128, 195

Watergate Affair (1972–1974) 151

Waters, John: *Cry-Baby* (film) 166

Watley, Jodi 193; *see also* Shalamar (musical group)

Watts, Stephanie Powell 174–177, 226

Watusi (dance) 16

Wave (album) 203; *see also* Smith, Patti

WBTV television station, Charlotte, North Carolina 5
"We Can Work It Out" (song) 36; *see also* The Beatles
"Weekend in New England" (song) 175; *see also* Manilow, Barry
Welles, Orson 10–12
Wells, Mary: "My Guy" (song) 87
Wesley, Cynthia 20, 22–23; *see also* 16th Street Baptist Church Bombing, Birmingham, Alabama (1963)
West Side Story (film) 84–85; Anita (fictitious character) 84–85; Bernardo (fictitious character) 84–85; Sharks (fictitious gang) 84–85; Tony (fictitious character) 85; *see also* Chakiris, George; Moreno, Rita
Westerns 82–85
"When You're Smiling" (song) 81
"Where Is My Mind?" (song) 198, 200; *see also Fight Club* (film); The Pixies (musical group)
"Where the Boys Are" (song) 97; *see also* Francis, Connie
White Album *see The Beatles* (album)
White Oak Dance Project, Minneapolis, Minnesota 181
Whitwam, Barry 29; *see also* Herman's Hermits
The Who 26, 39, 119
Wicked Witch of the West (fictitious character) 82

Wilco (musical group) 207
Wilder, Gene 43
Williams, Billy Dee 143
Williams, Clarence, III 150–154; Hayes, Lincoln "Linc" (fictitious character) 150–154; *see also The Mod Squad* (TV program)
Williams, Vanessa: first African-American Miss America (1987) 193, 195
Willy Wonka and the Chocolate Factory (film) 43
Wilson, Tamra 2–4, 24–31, 227
Wilson, Tym 24–31
The Wiz (film) 221
The Wizard of Oz (film) 183, 221
Wonderful Town (play) 54; *see also* Bacall, Lauren
The Wonderful World of Disney (TV program) 86
Wonka, Willy 43
Woodring, Susan 160–165, 227
Woodward, Joanne 10–12, 15; *see also* Newman, Paul
Woolf, Virginia 131; *To the Lighthouse* 131
World Trade Center Bombing, New York, N.Y. (1993) 39
Wright, Richard *see Native Son* (book)
A Wrinkle in Time (book) 160
Wynn, Ed 80; *see also Mary Poppins* (film)

Yastrzemski, Carl 136

Yellow Submarine (album) 92; *see also* The Beatles
"Yesterday" (song) 91–92; *see also* The Beatles
Yoda (fictitious character) 156; *see also Star Wars* (film and film series)
Yogi Bear (fictitious character) 77
"You Send Me" (song) 17; *see also* Cooke, Sam
Young, Neil 119; "Cinnamon Girl" (song) 119; "Cowgirl in the Sand" (song) 119; "Down by the River" (song) 119; *Everybody Knows This Is Nowhere* (album) 119
The Young Philadelphians (film) 12; *see also* Newman, Paul
Your Hit Parade (TV program) 7
"You're a Big Girl Now" (song) 109; *see also* Dylan, Bob
"You're Gonna Make Me Lonesome When You Go" (song) 109; *see also* Dylan, Bob
"You've Got to Hide Your Love Away" (song) 91; *see also* The Beatles

Zappa, Frank 39, 47
Ziggy Stardust and the Spiders from Mars (film) 213; *see also* Bowie, David